THE APPLICATION OF GPSS V TO DISCRETE SYSTEM SIMULATION

GEOFFREY GORDON
INTERNATIONAL BUSINESS MACHINES CORPORATION

PRENTICE-HALL, INC.
ENGLEWOOD CLIFFS, NEW JERSEY

Library of Congress Cataloging in Publication Data

Gordon, Geoffrey.
  The application of GPSS V to discrete system simulation.

  Bibliography
  1. Digital computer simulation. 2. GPSS (Computer program language) I. Title.
  T57.62.G67   003   74-23807
  ISBN 0-13-039057-7

© 1975 by Prentice-Hall, Inc., Englewood Cliffs, N.J.

All rights reserved. No part of this book
may be reproduced in any form or by any means
without permission in writing from the publisher.

10 9 8 7 6 5 4 3 2 1

Printed in the United States of America

PRENTICE-HALL INTERNATIONAL, INC., *London*
PRENTICE-HALL OF AUSTRALIA, PTY. LTD., *Sydney*
PRENTICE-HALL OF CANADA, LTD., *Toronto*
PRENTICE-HALL OF INDIA PRIVATE LIMITED, *New Delhi*
PRENTICE-HALL OF JAPAN, INC., *Tokyo*

162663

CONTENTS

PREFACE   ix

1
MODELING AND SIMULATION   1

    1-1 Introduction   1
    1-2 Systems   2
    1-3 Models   4
    1-4 Simulation Technique   7
    1-5 Comparison of Simulation and Analytic Methods   8
    1-6 Simultation Studies   9
    1-7 Continuous System Simulation   10
    1-8 Discrete System Simulation   13
    1-9 Progress of Simulation Study   14

2
DISCRETE SIMULATION PROGRAMMING TECHNIQUES   18

    2-1 Simple Machine Shop   18
    2-2 Representation of the System   19
    2-3 System Image   19
    2-4 Execution of Simulation   22
    2-5 Concurrent Events   23
    2-6 Statistical Outputs   24
    2-7 List Processing   24
    2-8 Transaction Chains   26
    2-9 Simulation Languages   27

3
GPSS CONCEPTS   29

    3-1 Block Diagrams   29
    3-2 Transactions   30
    3-3 Representation of Time   31
    3-4 Permanent Entities   31

3-5	Data Elements	32
3-6	Simple Machine Shop in GPSS	32
3-7	Input Statement Format	35
3-8	Comments Statements	36
3-9	Execution of GPSS Problems	36
3-10	Coding of Simple Machine Shop Example	37
3-11	Program Output	40
3-12	SIMULATE Statements	44
3-13	START Statements	45
3-14	Multiple Runs of a Model	45
3-15	RESET Statements	46
3-16	CLEAR Statements	47
3-17	JOB Statements	50
3-18	END Statements	50
3-19	Controlling Runs When There Are Several Users	50
3-20	Note Regarding Listings	51
3-21	Error Outputs	51
3-22	Output Editor	56

4 CREATING AND MOVING TRANSACTIONS 61

4-1	Action Times	61
4-2	GENERATE Blocks	63
4-3	TERMINATE Blocks	66
4-4	ADVANCE Blocks	66
4-5	TRANSFER Blocks	67
4-6	Unconditional Mode of TRANSFER Block	67
4-7	Fractional Mode of TRANSFER Block	68
4-8	Traffic System Example	69
4-9	Analysis of Block Counts	74
4-10	Standard Numerical Attributes	77
4-11	System SNAs	78
4-12	Block SNAs	78
4-13	Timing Considerations	78
4-14	Time Scale	79

5 FACILITIES AND STORAGES 83

5-1	Facilities	83
5-2	SEIZE Blocks	85
5-3	RELEASE Blocks	85
5-4	Factory Model 1: Using Facilities	86
5-5	Storages	87
5-6	STORAGE Control Statements	88
5-7	ENTER Blocks	89
5-8	LEAVE Blocks	89
5-9	Factory Model 2: Using Storages	89
5-10	Conditional Mode of TRANSFER Block	91
5-11	Factory Model 3: Using Conditional Transfer Mode	91
5-12	Factory Model 4: Storages as Counters	93
5-13	PICK and ALL Modes of TRANSFER Block	96
5-14	Comparison of Facilities and Storages	97
5-15	Equipment Availability	98
5-16	FUNAVAIL Blocks	99

5-17	Conditions Under Which FUNAVAIL Options Will Not Be Honored	102
5-18	FAVAIL Blocks	102
5-19	SUNAVAIL Blocks	103
5-20	SAVAIL Blocks	103
5-21	Facility and Storage Output Statistics	103
5-22	Facility and Storage SNAs	106
5-23	Utilization as Design Factor	106

6 PRIORITY 112

6-1	Order of Priority	112
6-2	Simultaneous Events	113
6-3	PRIORITY Blocks	116
6-4	Machine Operating With Priority	116
6-5	Effects of Priority	118
6-6	BUFFER Blocks	121
6-7	Example of BUFFER Block	122
6-8	Priority Used for Scan Control	124

7 PREEMPTING FACILITIES 129

7-1	PREEMPT Blocks in Interrupt Mode	130
7-2	RETURN Blocks	130
7-3	Machine Operating With Interruptions	131
7-4	PREEMPT Blocks in Priority Mode	132
7-5	Machine Operating With Priority Preemptions	134
7-6	Preempted Transaction Not at ADVANCE Block	140
7-7	Simulating Disk Units	141

8 GATHERING STATISTICS 146

8-1	Queues	147
8-2	QUEUE Blocks	147
8-3	DEPART Blocks	147
8-4	Queue Statistics	148
8-5	Queue Example	148
8-6	Transit Time Measurements	150
8-7	MARK Blocks	150
8-8	TABULATE Blocks	151
8-9	TABLE Control Statements	152
8-10	Weighted Tabulations	153
8-11	QTABLE Control Statements	154
8-12	Example of Statistics Gathering	155
8-13	Response Times and Grade of Service	160
8-14	Difference and Interarrival Modes of Tabulation	162
8-15	Rate Mode of Tabulation	163
8-16	Example of Tabulation Modes	164
8-17	SNAs Associated With Statistics	166

9 FUNCTIONS 169

9-1	Generating Nonuniformly Distributed Random Numbers	170
9-2	Exponential Distribution	176

9-3   Normal Distribution   178
9-4   Definition of Functions   182
9-5   Continuous and Discrete Functions   183
9-6   List Functions   183
9-7   Specifying Functions   185
9-8   Evaluating Functions   186
9-9   Shopping Example   188
9-10 Function Mode of TRANSFER Block   191

10
PARAMETERS AND SAVEVALUES   195

10-1   Parameters   196
10-2   Savevalues   198
10-3   Matrix Savevalues   198
10-4   MATRIX Control Statements   199
10-5   INITIAL Control Statements   199
10-6   ASSIGN Blocks   200
10-7   SAVEVALUE Blocks   201
10-8   MSAVEVALUE Blocks   202
10-9   Use of Parameters as Operands   203
10-10 Communication System   203
10-11 Parameter Mode of TRANSFER Blocks   207
10-12 Subroutine Mode of TRANSFER Blocks   208
10-13 LOOP Blocks   209
10-14 INDEX Blocks   209
10-15 Controlling Loops   209
10-16 Transaction and Savevalue SNAs   210

11
STANDARD NUMERICAL ATTRIBUTES   215

11-1   SNA Notation   215
11-2   Principal SNAs   216
11-3   Indirect Addressing   218
11-4   Uses of SNAs   220
11-5   SNAs as Block Operands   220
11-6   SNAs in Indirect Addressing   223
11-7   Push-Down Lists   225
11-8   SNAs as Function Arguments   226
11-9   SNAs in Attribute Valued Functions   229
11-10 Ragged Tables   229
11-11 Stochastic Processes   231
11-12 SNAs as Table Arguments   234
11-13 Variable Statements   236
11-14 Data Packing   237
11-15 Floating-Point Variable Statements   240

12
TESTING SYSTEM CONDITIONS   244

12-1   Logic Switches   245
12-2   LOGIC Blocks   246
12-3   GATE Blocks   246
12-4   Shipping Example   248
12-5   TEST Blocks   249

12-6 Single and Multiple Releases With GATE and TEST Blocks 252
12-7 Simultaneous Mode of TRANSFER Block 254
12-8 Boolean Variable Statements 256
12-9 COUNT Blocks 258
12-10 SELECT Blocks 258
12-11 Gasoline Filling Station Example 259
12-12 Simulating Time Constraints 260

13
SYNCHRONIZATION OF EVENTS 267

13-1 Assembly Sets 267
13-2 SPLIT Blocks 269
13-3 MATCH Blocks 270
13-4 Simulation of Wait Operation of Control Programs 272
13-5 GATHER Blocks 272
13-6 ASSEMBLE Blocks 274
13-7 Furniture Factory Example 274
13-8 GATE Block in Match Mode 278

14
MANAGEMENT OF SETS 281

14-1 User Chains 282
14-2 LINK Blocks—Without Use of Field C 283
14-3 UNLINK Blocks 284
14-4 Simulating Scheduling Rules With User Chains 285
14-5 LINK Blocks—Using Field C 290
14-6 Limiting Waiting Time on Queues 292
14-7 Groups 294
14-8 JOIN Blocks 295
14-9 REMOVE Blocks 295
14-10 EXAMINE Blocks 297
14-11 SCAN Blocks 298
14-12 ALTER Blocks 299
14-13 Allocation of Manpower Example 300
14-14 Group and Chain SNAs 307

15
MODEL CONTROLS 310

15-1 TRACE and UNTRACE Blocks 311
15-2 PRINT Blocks 312
15-3 CHANGE Blocks 314
15-4 EXECUTE Blocks 315
15-5 WRITE Blocks 316
15-6 JOBTAPE Control Statements 318
15-7 REWIND Control Statements 319
15-8 SAVE Control Statements 320
15-9 READ Control Statements 321
15-10 UPDATE Feature 323

16
MODIFYING THE GPSS PROGRAM 324

16-1 HELP Blocks 324

  16-2 *Allocation of Storage Space* *326*
  16-3 REALLOCATE *Control Statements* *328*
  16-4 AUXILIARY *Control Statements* *329*
  16-5 LOAD *Statements* *331*

Appendix 1
RANDOM NUMBER GENERATORS 333

  A1-1 *Random Numbers* *333*
  A1-2 *Continuous Uniformly Distributed Random Numbers* *334*
  A1-3 *GPSS Random Number Generators* *334*

Appendix 2
GPSS ASSEMBLY PROGRAM 337

  A2-1 *Symbols* *338*
  A2-2 *Relative Addressing* *338*
  A2-3 *Symbolic Entities* *340*
  A2-4 EQU *and* SYN *Statements* *340*
  A2-5 *Entity Functions* *340*
  A2-6 *Symbolic SNA References* *342*
  A2-7 *Macros* *343*
  A2-8 *Absolute Statements* *346*
  A2-9 *Redefinition of Statements* *347*
  A2-10 *Listing Control Statements* *348*

Appendix 3
BLOCK STATEMENT FORMATS 349

Appendix 4
CONTROL STATEMENT FORMATS 358

Appendix 5
STANDARD NUMERICAL ATTRIBUTES 362

Appendix 6
GPSS SCANNING ALGORITHM 368

  A6-1 *GPSS Transaction Chains* *368*
  A6-2 *Delay Chains* *369*
  A6-3 *Simultaneous Events* *370*
  A6-4 *GPSS Scan of Events* *371*
  A6-5 *Time-Consuming Blocking Conditions* *373*
  A6-6 *Possible Violations of Simultaneity Rule* *374*

Appendix 7
COMPARISON OF GPSS V AND GPSS/360 375

BIBLIOGRAPHY 378

 General Bibliographies *378*
 General Textbooks *379*
 Simulation Languages *380*
 Applications *383*
 Statistical Considerations *385*

INDEX 387

PREFACE

This book aims to demonstrate the application of discrete system simulation, using as a medium the General Purpose Simulation System, or GPSS. This incorporates a block diagram language which provides an excellent teaching tool since it offers a natural and familiar way of describing systems without the encumberance of coding details. At the same time, it introduces the reader to a well-established and very popular simulation language that has been applied in many different areas.

The book has been organized for a one semester course. The first two chapters discuss the general principles of simulation and the programming techniques used in discrete system simulation. On the assumption that the course will be supplemented with working experience of running simulation programs, Chap. 3 brings together the procedures and details involved in coding and running GPSS problems, and the book contains over 100 problems which can be coded and run. The following 11 chapters describe a series of models of generally increasing complexity. While the presentation is organized around the GPSS language, each chapter is concerned with an aspect of system simulation that needs to be understood whatever language is used. The last two chapters describe features of the GPSS program that are concerned with controlling system simulation studies rather than with techniques of modeling. Separate appendices describe the GPSS V random number generators, the assembly program, the event scanning algorithm, and bring together all the coding details. There is also a comparison between GPSS V and GPSS/360.

The specific language used is the IBM version of GPSS V. The description is complete to the point that the book provides an alternative to the User's Manual, issued with the program, except that certain detailed tables giving information about the internal organization of GPSS V, which might be needed when using the HELP block, and complete format details for the Output Editor, have not been duplicated. While the presentation is heavily oriented to GPSS and may, in places, go beyond the level of detail needed for a course in system simulation, a student is very likely to progress to research work or a career involving simulation studies. Learning the application of system simulation through the medium of an active language will provide valuable continuity.

Many people have contributed to the widespread use of GPSS. However, I would particularly like to acknowledge the contributions of Mssrs. John F. Bult and Robert L. Gould who have been deeply involved in the development and production of several versions of GPSS and, in particular, GPSS V. I would also like to thank Mr. Karamet A. Syed for his generous help in the preparation of the worked examples for the text.

1
MODELING AND SIMULATION

1-1
Introduction

Simulation is a technique of solving problems. In the broadest sense, it is a form of imitation in which a problem that needs solving is represented by a model which, in effect, replaces the problem by a second problem that is easier to solve. In this sense of the word, there are many different types of simulation: scale models in wind tunnels and training devices for pilots are examples of simulations, as are simulations based on an analogy between such physical systems as mechanical and electrical, or electrical and hydraulic.

Most simulation studies, however, are based on computations carried out by computers. The widespread use of digital computers for this purpose has led to the development of many programming languages that simplify the task of preparing simulations. This book describes one particular simulation program called the General Purpose Simulation System V, or GPSS V. This is a program product supplied by IBM in versions suitable for use with the IBM OS/360 Operating System or with the IBM DOS/360 Disk Operating System (41–43).† As the name implies, there have been earlier versions of the language. One of these, GPSS/360, is compatible with GPSS V in the

---

† Numbers in parentheses refer to items in the Bibliography at the end of the book.

sense that GPSS/360 programs will run under GPSS V; in general, however, GPSS V programs will not run under GPSS/360. Appendix 7 compares these two versions of GPSS.

Although several versions of GPSS language have been written for non-IBM machines, the IBM programs are written in assembly language and cannot be assembled for other manufacturers' machines. In this book we shall be concerned only with the IBM version of GPSS V. For brevity, the term GPSS will be used to mean specifically the GPSS V version of the language, except where a direct comparison with earlier versions is being made. Before describing the language, however, we shall give a general description of the principles on which simulation is based. For other general descriptions, see (6–24).

Soon after computers became available, engineers and scientists began to recognize the value of digital computers for simulation and started using them for this purpose. In fact, the development of many products of modern technology, such as missiles, spacecraft, nuclear reactors, and computers themselves, has been significantly aided by the use of digital computer simulation. The development of simulation programming languages combined with the increasing availability of computers has resulted in the spread of simulation beyond scientific and engineering applications to problems in business, economics, sociology, ecology, politics, and many other fields. See (59–95) for information regarding such applications.

1-2
Systems

The type of problems best solved with simulation are those involving systems. Missiles, for example, are components of a weapon system, and the evaluation of their effectiveness must take into account not only the missile performance but also the characteristics of the launching device, the target acquisition methods, the logistic support, as well as variations in operating conditions and target tactics. Simulation is a technique that makes it possible to understand the effects of such interactions among the elements of a system.

If we look at a system, we see various objects of interest, each having its own characteristics, and interactions that cause changes in the system. We use the term *entity* to mean an object of interest in a system and refer to the characteristics of an entity as its *attributes*. The interactions will be called *activities*. Table 1-1 gives some examples of how these terms might be applied in several different systems.

Consider an aircraft that is flying under the control of an autopilot. The entities might be the autopilot, the aerilons, and the airframe, which have such attributes as error signal, angle of setting, and heading. The activi-

Table 1-1 Examples of Systems

System	Entities	Attributes	Activities
Aircraft	Autopilot	Error	Signaling
	Aerilons	Angle	Forcing
	Airframe	Heading	Turning
Factory	Workpieces	Number	Ordering
	Machines	Capacity	Machining
	Employees	Skill	Scheduling
Business	Products	Price	Manufacturing
	Customers	Demand	Selling
	Markets	Size	Advertising
Political	Parties	Size	Fund raising
	Issues	Acceptance	Campaigning
	Social groups	Income	Migrating

ties could be the actions of producing a guidance signal, applying force, and turning the aircraft. Consider next a factory. The entities might be the workpieces, the machines, and the employees. Typical attributes might be the number of workpieces, the machine capacities, and the employees' skill levels. The activities might be the placing of orders, the machining of workpieces, and the scheduling of the employees. A business system study might use such elements as products, customers, and markets as entities; typical attributes might be price, demand, and size; manufacturing, selling, and advertising might be typical activities. The entities involved in a study of a political system could be the political parties, campaign issues, and social groups, which could be given such attributes as size of the parties, acceptance of the issues, and the income of the social groups. The system activities could include fund raising, campaigning, and migration of the social groups.

Even in this abbreviated list, the broad range of systems that can be reduced to a common descriptive format is apparent. Sometimes the system elements are concrete, distinctive factors, such as the machines in the factory system. At other times the entities are somewhat difficult to identify, such as a social group in a political system; in addition, the attributes and activities, such as the acceptance of an issue or the effects of campaigning on the acceptance, are hard to reduce to specific quantities and relationships. Nevertheless, the abstraction involved in describing systems in this manner provides a means of viewing problems in such a way that they can be simulated.

1-3

Models

Simulation replaces a system to be studied by some other representation called a *model*. When digital computers are used for simulation, the model takes the form of a set of equations or numbers. For simulation purposes, a distinction is drawn between continuous and discrete models, because the methods of constructing the models and consequently the methods of carrying out a simulation are different in nature.

A *continuous model* is described by algebraic and differential equations in which variables represent the attributes of the entities, and functions represent the activities. The effect of the activities is to produce smooth changes in the values of the attributes. Figure 1-1, for example, is the output of a continuous model representing an aircraft under autopilot control. It shows how the rudder angle and aircraft heading respond continuously to a signal to turn the aircraft to a new heading. Continuous models are frequently solved by using analog computers.

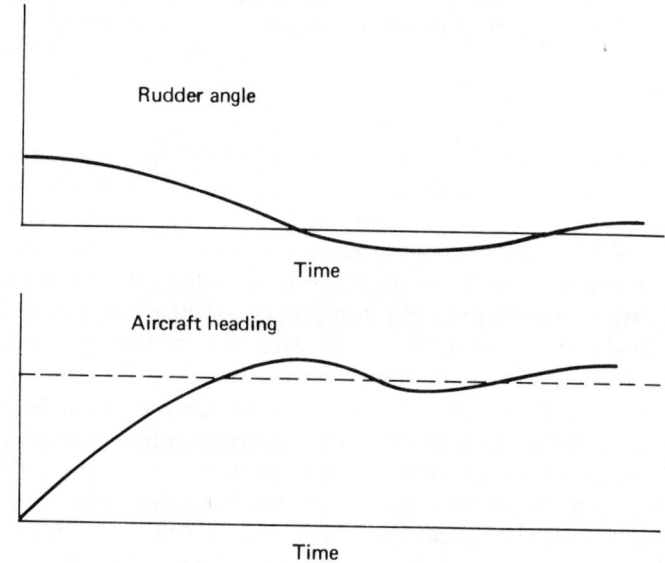

Figure 1-1. Motion of aircraft under autopilot control.

A *discrete model* takes the form, principally, of a set of numbers that count the entities and indicate their status. Logical rules, or probability statements, control the times at which changes occur. The output of a discrete model will show sudden changes. For example, Fig. 1-2 is the output of a discrete model that represents the performance of a machine in a factory. New parts arrive at discrete points in time while the machine alternates between periods of being busy and free. As each part arrives or

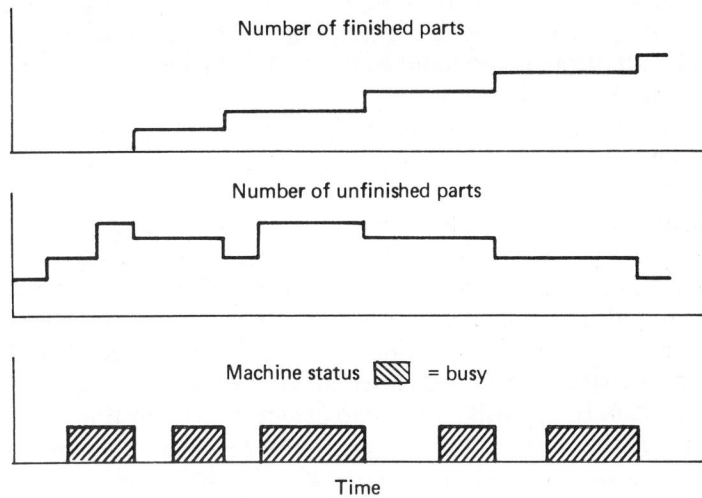

Figure 1-2. Output of a machine.

is finished, the results are reflected in a discrete, sudden change in the number of unfinished and finished parts.

It may sometimes be possible to express a discrete model as a formal set of mathematical equations and then to solve the equations. For example, if the probability distributions of the arrival times of the parts and the machining times can be given, queuing theory can be applied. However, when applying simulation to discrete models, it is not usual to express the model in such a formal manner. Instead, an essentially procedural description of the model is presented to programs that can construct the appropriate counters and state indicators, and then execute the changes caused by the succession of events in the system.

For the purposes of simulation, the distinction between continuous and discrete behavior is made between models rather than systems. Although systems are either continuous or discrete in nature, an analyst may not always choose to represent them by the corresponding type of model. For example, if the purpose of studying an aircraft is to track its path over a scheduled journey, there would be no point in following the details of *how* it turns. A discrete model that provides instantaneous changes of direction and moves the aircraft position in jumps from point to point of the course is sufficient. Similarly, if the number of parts in the factory is large, there may be no point in following the history of each part. Instead, the numbers of unfinished and finished parts could be represented by continuous, nonintegral variables, and the machines could be described by the rate at which they convert unfinished to finished parts.

The decision as to which type of model to use depends upon the nature and purpose of the study. The analyst must consider the level of detail and accuracy he needs in the output, as well as the nature of the system itself. Most continuous systems will be studied with continuous models. In such engineering fields as mechanics, electricity, chemistry, hydraulics, aeronautics, studies are generally made of systems that are essentially continuous in nature. In all these disciplines well-established procedures exist for the application of mathematics to the description of processes that lead to differential equations and, consequently, continuous models. A substantial proportion of all continuous simulation is related to system design problems in these fields.

Differential equations relate to rates of change, which, in turn, can be equated to growth rates. Consequently, continuous models are also useful in the study of economics and business systems. Generally, such studies will be concerned with long-range or strategic planning problems where the short-term random fluctuations in conditions can be discounted and only the longer-range trends need be considered. In a similar manner, in the consideration of trends, growth rates, and decay rates, continuous models are often used to simulate problems in the biological, political, and social sciences.

Continuous models are even applied at the more detailed operational level of businesses and industries where the effects of discrete changes—such as the arrival of orders or the existence of finite delays—cannot be altogether ignored. By averaging the arrival rates of the orders and replacing finite delays by decay rates, it is still possible to construct continuous models of what are essentially discrete systems. This approach has been called "industrial dynamics," (70) since it draws an analogy between industrial systems and engineering systems. Applied to, say, an inventory control problem, such a model might not be accurate enough to predict the precise levels of inventory, but it could provide insight in evaluating the effect of delays on the responsiveness and general stability of the system.

Although it may be possible to smooth the fluctuations of an essentially discrete system to the point where a continuous model can be applied, there are many systems that must be represented by discrete models if any degree of realism is to be maintained. The activities of the system may be dependent on the exact state of the system to the point where there can be no smoothing or averaging—for example, in modeling digital computer systems or switching systems. Or, there may be too few states to permit averaging. Studies in reliability or logistics are often in this category. Problems concerned with such stochastic measures as response times, waiting times, queue lengths, or the probability of certain events, such as being out-of-stock, usually need discrete models that reflect the individual events occurring in the system. This is not to say that all problems involving stochastic events must use discrete models. Randomness is often introduced in continuous models as a way of testing the sensitivity of solutions to the particular parameters of the system.

Sometimes systems that are essentially continuous will be simulated with discrete models. For example, in an economic model concerned with interacting growth rates, it may be sufficiently accurate to reduce the model to difference equations in which solutions are found for uniform steps in time, such as a year. During the intervals, the variables are all assumed to hold constant values. Reduction of the problem to discrete steps thus allows discrete simulation programs to be applied to the problem.

1-4
Simulation Technique

Usually the purpose of constructing a mathematical model is to solve the equations and to derive an analytic solution that can be used to predict the behavior of the system. Although such analytic solutions use mathematical models, they are not examples of the simulation method of solving problems. The element that distinguishes them from simulations is that mathematical techniques are used to produce answers in a direct manner. If an engineer can solve the equations of motion of an aircraft, he does not have to use the equations to plot the motion of the aircraft, as has been done in Fig. 1-1, and then observe whether the motion is oscillatory. Instead, he is able to derive the relationship between the variables for which the mathematical theory *tells* him the motion is oscillatory. Having derived that relationship he has, in effect, a statement of all the possible combinations of circumstances that can cause oscillation.

In contrast, simulation would not solve the equations of motion directly. Instead, the simulation technique is to compute the response step by step. Using simulation, the engineer would indeed plot the motion of the aircraft and see whether the output contains oscillations. In effect, the simulation user is in the position of an experimenter working with the actual system. He is operating only a model of the system, but he makes observations and measurements much as he would if he were experimenting with the real system.

Digital simulation is thus a numerical computation method. On the other hand, not all numerical computation can be called simulation. Many analytic solutions occur as complex expressions that need to be evaluated numerically. Sometimes the analytic solution is expressed as the roots of an equation, and these must be found numerically. The distinctive feature of the numerical computation used in simulation is that the outcome of each step of the calculation can be interpreted as the state of the system at some point in time. We can therefore define *system simulation* as the technique of solving problems by the observation of the performance, over time, of a dynamic model of the system.

In some problems the time element is not significant, but a step-by-step calculation representing the successive stages of development in a system is appropriate. For example, one can evaluate the outcome of a sequential decision process, in which a number of successive choices must be made with given probabilities assigned to each choice, step by step to find the probability of reaching each particular final outcome. Problems of this nature are often solved by simulation programs, in which use is made of the intrinsic step-by-step processing built into the program. In such simulations, time is not explicitly involved. In effect, the model in use is assumed to change at uniform intervals of time and, since only the results of the final step are of interest, there is no purpose in giving a specific value to the interval; it is therefore set to zero.

1-5
Comparison of Simulation and Analytic Methods

Compared with the analytic solution of problems, the main drawback of simulation is apparent: it gives specific solutions rather than general solutions. In the study of aircraft motion, for example, an analytic solution gives all the conditions that can cause oscillation. Each execution of a simulation tells only whether a particular set of conditions did or did not cause oscillation. To try to find all such conditions requires that the simulation be repeated under many different conditions. The mathematical solution is obviously preferable, particularly when the solution being sought is some maximizing condition. A single mathematical solution might give such a condition, whereas many simulation runs may be needed to find a maximum, and yet still leave undecided the question of whether it is a local or global maximum.

The range of problems that can be solved mathematically is limited, however. Mathematical techniques require that the model be expressed in some particular format—for example, that it be in the form of linear algebraic equations or continuous linear differential equations. The system must be approximated or abstracted in order to derive a model that fits the format of a mathematical technique. All too often, the process amounts to making the problem fit the solution rather than the other way round.

In approaching a system study, it is essential to consider first what mathematical techniques might be applied to derive analytic solutions. It is a matter of judgment to decide whether the degree of abstraction required to apply analytic methods is too severe. To make that judgment it is necessary to consider carefully what questions need to be answered in the system study, and to what degree of accuracy the answers need to be known.

When the decision is made to simulate in order to use a more realistic model, it is still important to limit the amount of detail in the model to the minimum level necessary. The step-by-step nature of the simulation technique means that the amount of computation increases very rapidly as the amount of detail increases. Coupled with the need to make many runs to explore the range of conditions, the extra realism of simulation models can result in a very extensive amount of computing.

In many ways, the ideal way of using simulation is as an extension of mathematical solutions that might have been obtained at the cost of too much simplification. There are many simple limitations on a system, such as physical stops, finite time delays, or nonlinear forces, which render what would otherwise be a soluble mathematical model insoluble. Simulation easily removes these limitations, and it can then provide a powerful extension of known mathematical solutions.

Even when a model with a known solution is considered adequate, there are still times when a simulation will provide a quicker or more convenient way of deriving results. Many analytic results occur in the form of complex series or integrals that still require extensive evaluation. It is often more convenient to use simulation to obtain results directly from a model with specific values rather than to perform the numerical evaluation of the analytic solution.

1-6
Simulation Studies

In simulation studies, the nature of the problem to be studied and the purpose involved in understanding its solution must be considered; there are various possibilities. Many simulation studies are concerned with *system analysis*, which is designed to understand an existing system with a view, perhaps, to changing a policy or procedure in order to modify the system performance. Typical of such studies are analyses of business systems, traffic systems, and the organization of work.

In other studies the principal concern is with *system design*. The problem is to define a system, or a major reorganization of an existing system, by choosing among alternative system components or organizations. The design of computer systems for particular applications is typical. Other engineering problems, such as the design of switching systems or the development of an industrial control system, present system design problems.

Another general category of problem relates to *system postulation*, where the need is to produce a reasonable explanation of the structure of a system. Problems of this nature occur in such areas as medicine, biology, and sociology, where, unlike system analyses, it is not possible or practical to examine the individual system components independently. Instead, an attempt is made to gain insight into the nature of the system structure by testing whether various hypotheses lead to models that explain the known overall system response.

Whatever the nature of the problem, the technique of simulation remains essentially experimental. The response of a model to a given set of conditions must be measured and any conclusions or predictions drawn about the system must be based on these observations. Simulation by itself cannot answer qualitative questions, such as: "What is the best system?" or "What is the optimum performance?" Instead it answers quantitive questions with numbers that denote such factors as queue sizes, response times, loadings on equipment, the probability of certain outcomes, or the time taken to perform some function.

It is important, therefore, to establish the objectives of a simulation study clearly and to express them in terms of specific measures that can be reasonably derived from a model. Since the model is, in effect, a substitute for the system, it is clearly important to establish the validity of the model so as to be confident that the results to be obtained from the model are relevant and representative of the system. This is a difficult task, the outcome of which relies a great deal on the judgment of people familiar with the system. A danger at this point is that a model may become too elaborately detailed because the modeler does not circumscribe the significant factors. It has already been pointed out that computation time tends to increase very rapidly with model complexity. Too much complexity also tends to cloud the interpretation of the results by providing too much output data. In subsequent chapters, an attempt will be made to point out ways in which certain aspects of systems can be simplified or approximated to remove unnecessary detail.

1-7

Continuous System Simulation

Although the principal subject of this book is discrete system simulation, it may be of interest to look briefly at *continuous system simulation* so that the numerical computation techniques of the two types of simulation can be contrasted. Continuous system simulation is, of course, the application of simulation to continuous models. To illustrate the method of constructing models and applying simulation, consider the following example.

A builder observes that the rate at which he can sell houses depends directly upon the number of families who do not yet have a house. As the number of people without houses diminishes, the rate at which he sells houses drops. Let y_0 be the potential number of house-owning families, and y be the number of families with houses. The situation is represented in Fig. 1-3; the horizontal line at y_0 is the total potential market for houses. The curve for y indicates how the number of houses sold increases with time. The slope of the curve (i.e., the rate at which y increases) decreases as $y_0 - y$ gets less. This reflects the slowdown of sales as the market becomes saturated. Mathematically, the trend can be expressed by the equation

$$\dot{y} = K_1(y_0 - y), \quad y = 0 \text{ at } t = 0$$

Consider now a manufacturer of central air conditioners designed for houses. His rate of sales depends upon the number of houses built. (For

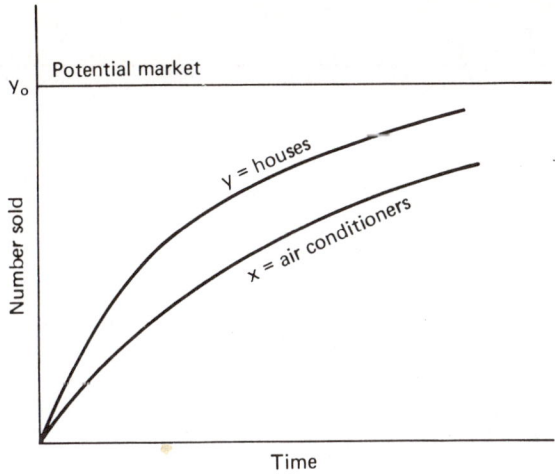

Figure 1-3. Sale of houses and air conditioners.

simplicity, it is assumed that all houses will install an air conditioner.) As with house sales, the rate of sales diminishes as the unfilled market diminishes.

Let x be the number of installed air conditioners. Then the unfilled market is the difference between the number of houses and the number of installed air conditioners. The sales trend may be expressed mathematically by the equation

$$\dot{x} = K_2(y - x), \quad x = 0 \text{ at } t = 0$$

The change of x with time is also illustrated in Fig. 1-3. The two equations constitute a model of the growth of air conditioner sales. Because of its simplicity, it is in fact possible to solve the model analytically. However, it quickly becomes insoluble if it is expanded to become more representative of actual marketing conditions. The market limit, for example, may not be stable. It could grow with population growth or fluctuate with economic conditions. The coefficients that determine the rates of growth could be influenced by the amount of money spent on advertising, and there could be competitive influences, such as mobile homes or apartment housing. These influences could also depend upon the population growth or prevailing economic conditions, and so further complicate the model.

The simple model, however, will serve to illustrate the general methods applied in continuous simulation. The simulation technique is to compute the output step by step. Suppose that the computation is made at uniform intervals of time and that the calculation has already progressed to the time t_i, when the two variables of the problem have the values y_i and x_i. Figure 1-4 shows the next step in the calculation.

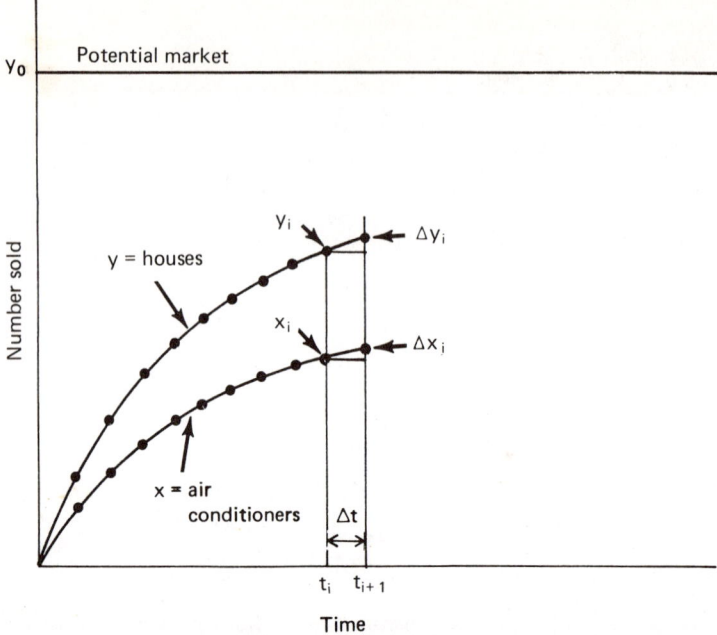

Figure 1-4. Calculations for house and air conditioner sales model.

The calculation steps forward an interval Δt to $t_{i+1} = t_i + \Delta t$. The rates of sales are assumed to be constant over the interval. The rates can be interpreted as the amount of change per unit time. That is,

$$\text{rate of change of } y = \frac{\Delta y_i}{\Delta t_i}$$

$$\text{rate of change of } x = \frac{\Delta x_i}{\Delta t_i}$$

From the equations of the model, these may be written

$$\Delta y_i = K_1(y_0 - y_i)\,\Delta t$$

$$\Delta x_i = K_2(y_i - x_i)\,\Delta t$$

Since y_i and x_i are known, it is a simple matter to get the values of y and x at time t_{i+1}. However, it will be noticed that the equation for Δy_i must be solved first to get the value of y_i needed in the equation for x_i. In preparation for the solution of a continuous system model, therefore, there must be a careful sorting of the equations to establish a workable order.

Repetition of the calculation using the new values of y and x produces the output at the end of the next interval. As illustrated in Fig. 1-4, the calculation is equivalent to calculating the slope at each point and projecting a short straight line at that slope. The simulation output is a series of such line segments, approximating the continuous curve that represents the true output of the model.

The method described is a very simple way of integrating differential equations numerically, but it is not a very accurate method, unless small steps are used, compared with the rate at which the variables change. There are other much more accurate, and often more efficient, ways of integrating numerically which do not rely simply upon the last-known value of the variables. Rather, they use several previous values to predict the rate at which the variables are changing. (Special methods are used to supply initial values to start the process.) In addition, the computation interval is often adjusted in size to match the rate at which the variables are changing.

There are many programming systems available that incorporate continuous system simulation languages. They usually include a number of computational methods for the user's selection.

1-8

Discrete System Simulation

Discrete system models were characterized in Sec. 1-3 as models in which discontinuous changes of states occur. The term *event* is used to mean such a change occurring at a specific point in time. An event may change the value of an entity attribute, it may create or destroy an entity, or it may start or stop an activity.

Since the technique of simulation consists of following the changes in a system model, the task of simulating discrete systems requires a program that can construct the sequence of events. Records must be kept of all the activities in progress and the entities involved, and the records must be periodically updated to reflect the sequence of events. To do so, records must be kept of all event times, and calculations must compute future event times as the simulation proceeds.

The passage of time is recorded as a number called *clock time*, or simply the *clock*. The clock is initially set to zero and, as the simulation proceeds, it is updated to reflect the passage of time. It is possible to update the clock in uniform steps, as was done in the continuous simulation example. In that case, the program must determine if an event is due to occur at the new time. Usually, however, the program keeps records of future events in chronological order, and the clock time is updated to the time of the next most imminent event.

As an example, consider a machine shop where parts arrive to be processed. Each part can be one of a number of types, chosen at random. The pattern of arrivals can be described by measuring the interval between successive arrivals. That number may also vary randomly. The time to machine a part could also be a random variable. In Sec. 9-1 we will show how such random variables are created in a digital computer. It is apparent that with random timings, the arrivals and departures of parts do not necessarily alternate. Furthermore, if there is more than one machine operating, so that several parts can be machined simultaneously, it does not necessarily follow that parts finish in the order in which they start, because the machining times vary. If a waiting line forms, the event of a part finishing implies the starting of another part, so that one event is conditional upon another.

A discrete system simulation must keep records of all these types of events, organize them chronologically, and be aware of the conditional dependencies. The simulation must follow the effects of the successive events, producing, in effect, results such as those in Fig. 1-2, which illustrated the way the number of arriving and departing parts varies over time. The results are usually summarized in terms of the distributions and means of waiting times and queue lengths. In Chap. 2 we will demonstrate, by a worked example, the way to control a discrete system simulation.

1-9

Progress of Simulation Study

It is apparent from the general discussion of the preceding sections that simulation is a very general method of studying problems. No formal procedure can be given for showing how a simulation study will proceed. There is not even a simple way of deciding whether to simulate or not, or, if simulation is used, whether to use a continuous or discrete model. However, some of the steps involved in the progress of a simulation study are illustrated by the flowchart of Fig. 1-5. The flowchart is illustrative: it is not intended to suggest a formal procedure.

An initial step is to describe the problem to be solved in as concise a manner as possible so that there is a clear statement of what questions are being asked and what measurements need to be taken in order to answer those questions. Based on this problem definition, a model must be defined. It is at this point that it becomes apparent whether the model can be kept in a form that allows analytic techniques to be used.

It should be understood that there is not, in fact, a single model for any given system. In the course of a study *many* different models are likely to be constructed as understanding of the system behavior increases. A possible course, which is to be recommended if it does not entail too much extra effort, is to explore first a model that can be solved analytically, even though it is clear that the simplifications required to produce the model are too drastic. The results will help guide the simulation study.

When it is decided to simulate, the experimental nature of the simulation technique makes it essential to plan the study by deciding upon the major parameters to be varied, the number of cases to be conducted, and the order in which runs are to be made [see (102, 103, 105)]. This procedure will help gauge the magnitude of the simulation effort and may cause a

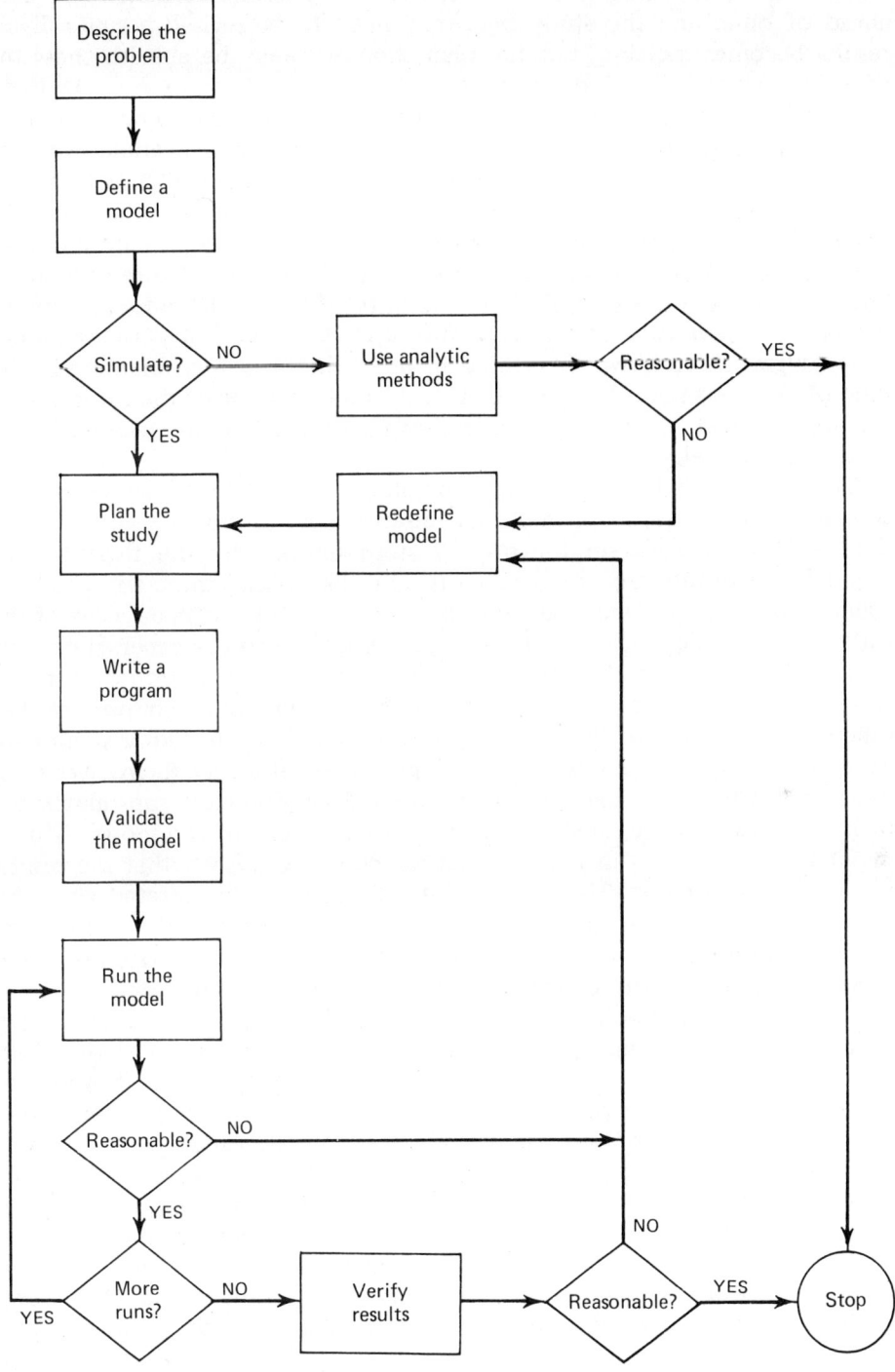

Figure 1-5. The process of simulating.

reappraisal of the model. Of course, it is not possible to plan every step ahead of time, and the study plan may need to be revised periodically as results become available; but the plan should always be able to show the direction in which the study is going.

Given that the simulation is to be on a digital computer, a program must be written. Actually this step is likely to be carried out in parallel with the study planning, once the model structure has been decided. As will be discussed in Sec. 2-9, many simulation languages can help in writing the program. Figure 1-5 does not show the choice between using a continuous or discrete model: that choice was discussed in Sec. 1-3. The figure does show, however, the step of establishing the validity of the model before beginning the major set of runs [see (22)]. This is an important step that requires good judgment. It is worth bearing in mind the need for validation at the time of deciding upon the model. It could be that some of the earlier, oversimplified models may provide guidelines for establishing the reasonableness of the final model.

The study will then move into the stage of executing a series of runs according to the study plan. As has already been intimated, the study is not likely to proceed in the orderly steps implied by the flowchart of Fig. 1-5. As results are obtained, it is quite likely that there will be many changes in the model and the study plan. Frequently, the main value of the early runs in a simulation study is to gain insight into the general behavior of the system, rather than to extract data. In the construction of a model certain parameters of the system are clearly going to be important and others unimportant—to the point where they can be neglected or simplified. There will also be parameters whose importance, either by themselves or in interaction with other parameters, is not so clear. The early runs may make their significance clear, and so lead to a reassessment of the model. This is implied by the blocks in Fig. 1-5 that ask the question whether the results are reasonable or not. This should not, however, be interpreted as an incentive to include numerous parameters in the model on the assumption that the unimportant ones can be quickly eliminated. As was emphasized in Sec. 1-6 it is essential to keep the model as simple as possible.

A major factor that needs to be considered in the presence of random variables is the problem of statistically verifying the results. The flowchart of Fig. 1-5 shows this step as following the runs, but, in fact, it must also be considered on each planned run. Once random variables enter a model, almost all measures of interest will also be random variables. The results of a single run will give just one sample of the measured variable. It is thus essential to repeat the run with a different set of random numbers so that more than one sample is available; it is then possible to judge the variability of the results. The number of repetitions needed depends upon the nature of the system and the importance to be attached to the results (100–105).

Sometimes it is useful to repeat runs such that parts of the model have different random numbers while the rest use exactly the same random numbers on each run. By comparing the results obtained under these conditions with the case where all parts of the system have different random numbers, it is then possible to analyze the cause of the variance in the results. For these reasons, GPSS, in common with most other discrete simulation programming systems, provides several independent random number generators and can arrange for any of them to produce a different sequence of random numbers by changing a seed value. (See Appendix 1 for an explanation of random number generators.)

The problem of verifying simulation results is complex. A section of the Bibliography lists a number of papers that discuss the problem [see also (10)]. A major factor that presents difficulties is the presence of autocorrelation. In measuring the mean time spent on a queue, for example, it is apparent that the time one entity waits depends on the time spent by every other entity that precedes it in the queue. Measuring the waiting time of successive members of the queue will not therefore give independent measurements. It is a statistically valid procedure to estimate the mean waiting time by taking the average of all measurements but it is not valid to estimate a variance by the usual procedure of computing the average squared deviation about the mean. The presence of autocorrelation will affect the measurements. To get a true estimate of the variance, and thereby establish confidence limits for the mean value, it is advisable to use spectral analysis techniques. For descriptions of these techniques and examples of their application see (97-99, 106, and 107).

2

DISCRETE SIMULATION PROGRAMMING TECHNIQUES

In Chap. 1 we considered the example of a simple machine shop to illustrate the nature of a discrete system model. In this chapter the same example will be used to demonstrate how to perform a discrete system simulation. A detailed step-by-step calculation will be carried out. This will be followed by a discussion of some of the programming techniques used in writing simulation programs and the problems that arise in maintaining the correct order in handling events, mainly as a result of simultaneous events.

2-1

Simple Machine Shop

Assume that parts arrive at a machine shop with interarrival times that are exponentially distributed† with a mean value of 20 minutes. The parts are of five types and they are randomly distributed among the types with known probabilities. The time required to machine parts (regardless of type) is normally distributed with a mean of 60 minutes and a standard deviation of 20 minutes.

†The exponential distribution used here for the interarrival time is described in Sec. 9-2. The normal distribution, which will be used for the machining time, is described in Sec. 9-3.

There are three machines all equally able to machine any part. If a machine is available at the time a part arrives, machining begins immediately. If all machines are busy upon arrival, the part will wait for service. Waiting parts are serviced with a first-in, first-out (FIFO) rule; that is, parts are serviced in the order in which they arrive. On completion of machining, the parts will be dispatched to a destination, depending upon their type. The progress of the parts will not be followed after dispatch from the shop. However, a count of the number of parts dispatched to each destination will be kept.

2-2

Representation of the System

Clearly, there are two types of entities in the system, parts and machines. A stream of entities will represent the parts that enter and leave the system. There is no point in representing the different types as different entities; rather, the type is an attribute of the parts. Each part will also have two other attributes, the length of time required for its machining and its arrival time. The latter attribute is usually derived from the interarrival time, as explained in Sec. 1-8. It is more convenient here to carry the actual time of arrival and omit the step that computes the arrival time by accumulating the interarrival times.

Unlike the parts, which are only in the system temporarily, the machines are permanently in the system. However, there is no need to make a separate entity of each machine, since they can be used interchangeably on any part. It is simpler to consider the group of machines as a single entity having as attributes the number of parts that can be machined simultaneously, and a count of the number of parts currently being machined.

The activities that cause changes in the system are the generation of parts, waiting, machining, and departing. An event occurs when a part is involved in any of the following actions:
- (a) Arrives in the system
- (b) Joins the waiting line
- (c) Leaves the waiting line
- (d) Begins machining
- (e) Ends machining
- (f) Leaves the system

2-3

System Image

A set of numbers is needed to reflect the state of the system at any time. This set of numbers can conveniently be called the *system image*, since it describes the state of the system. The simulation will proceed by the programmer first deciding from the system image when the next event is due to occur and what type of event it is, then testing whether it can be executed, and finally, executing those changes in the image implied by the event.

The image must have a number that represents clock time, and this number will be advanced with the succession of events in the system. For each part record, there will be four numbers to represent the following items:

(a) Part type
(b) Machine time
(c) Arrival time
(d) Next event time

The first three items are attributes of the parts that form part of the simulation input data. Each is a random variable.† The next event time will sometimes be known; but, when the execution of one event is conditional upon another, as occurs when a part has to wait for service, the value will have to be calculated as the simulation proceeds. Note that it is not customary to precalculate all the random variables that form part of the input. Instead, each random variate would be calculated at the time it is needed, so an actual simulation program will be continually switching between the examination and manipulation of the system image and the subroutines that calculate the random variates.

The next event times are an essential element of the simulation. By scanning these times, it is possible to determine what is the next event, or, more precisely, the next potential event. By knowing the activity that the event is associated with, it is possible to know what the next step is, and thus to test whether the event can be executed. If so, the image is changed accordingly. If not, the event becomes delayed. Upon executing an event, it is necessary to see whether a delayed event has been released. (This check may in fact also need to be made when the event is *not* executed. There are times when a delayed event can act as a trigger for the commencement of some other activity—for example, an increase in the number of available machines if the waiting line exceeds certain limits.)

The organization that will be used for the system image is illustrated in Fig. 2-1. There are four frames in the figure, representing successive states of the system. The frames are to be read from left to right, top line first. The frame in the top left corner is the initial state. The description of the system image will be made in terms of that particular frame.

The top line represents the part that is due to enter the system next. As shown here, it is a type 2 part; it will require 75 minutes of machining; and it is due to arrive at time 1002. This, of course, is also its next event time. As indicated, it is necessary to keep a record of only one future arrival.

---

†The way the random variates are calculated is described in Secs. 9-1, 9-2, and 9-3.

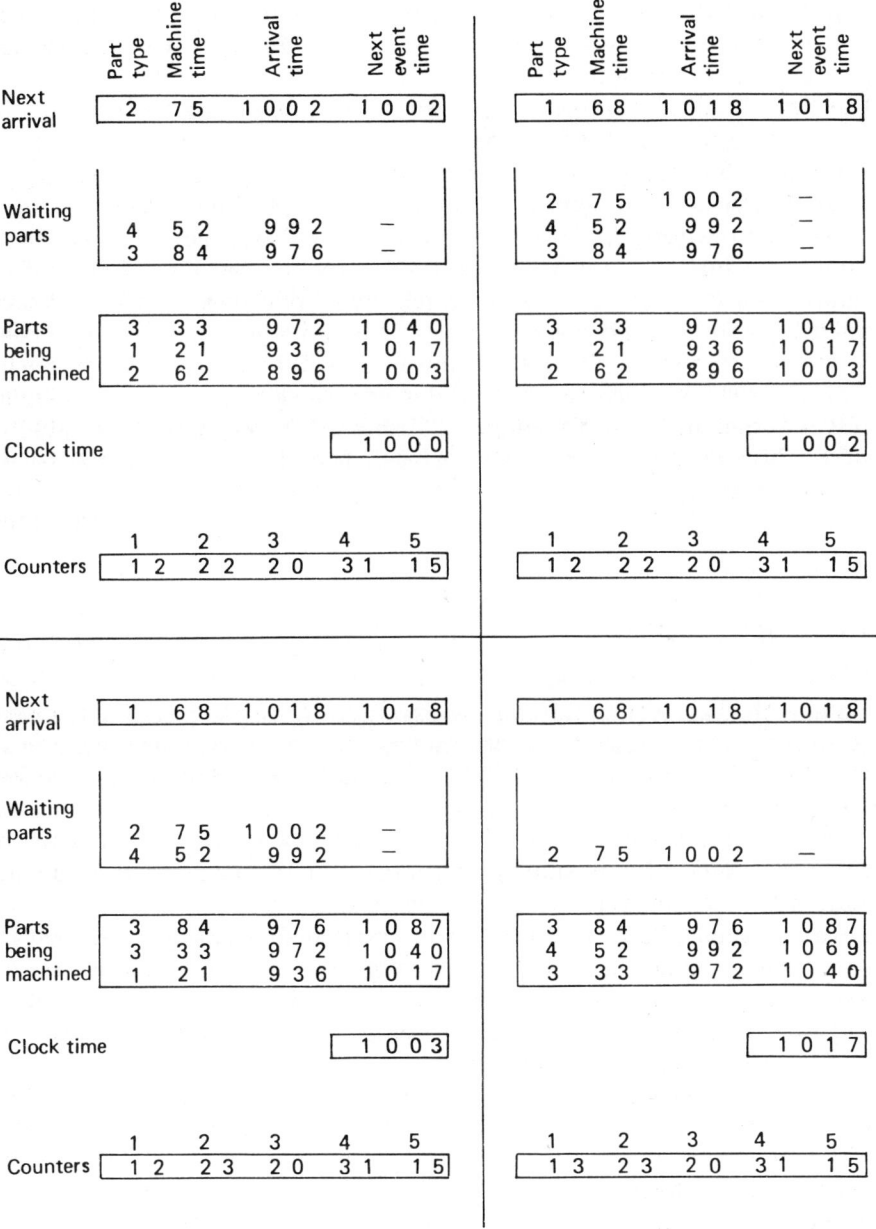

Figure 2-1. System image of simple machine shop.

When the event representing that arrival is executed, the following arrival will immediately be computed and recorded as a future event.

Below the next arrival listing is an open-ended list of parts that have arrived and are now waiting for service. Currently there are two waiting parts. As indicated, they are listed in order of arrival. Because the waiting parts are delayed, it is not possible to predict a next event time for them. It will be necessary to see whether there is a waiting part when a machine finishes and offer service to the first part in the waiting line.

The next level of numbers in the image represents the parts being machined, limited in this case to three. In a computer program there would be two counters, one for the maximum number of parts that can be processed simultaneously, and one counting the number of machines currently busy. To avoid complicating the figure, these counters have been omitted. Once machining begins, the time to finish machining can be derived by adding the machining time to the time at which machining starts. Three parts are assumed to be occupying the machines at this time and the parts have been listed in the order in which they will finish. As will be seen, this is not necessarily the order in which machining started. Finally, a number represents the clock time, here set to an initial value of 1000, and there are five counters showing how many parts of each type have been completed so far in the simulation.

2-4

Execution of Simulation

Assume that all events that can be executed up to time 1000 have been processed. It is now time to begin one more cycle of the simulation algorithm. The first step is to find the next potential event in the system, which can be done by scanning all the next event times of the parts. Because of the ordering of the parts being machined, it is, in fact, only necessary to compare the time of the next arrival with the first listed time in the machine section. With the numbers shown in frame 1, the next event is the arrival of a part at time 1002, so the clock is updated to this time. The arriving part finds all machines busy and must join the waiting line. The successor to the part that just arrived must be generated and inserted as the next future arrival, due at time 1018. The second frame of Fig. 2-1 shows the state of the system when these actions have been completed.

Another cycle can now begin. The next event is the completion of machining a part at time 1003. The clock is updated to 1003 and the finished part is removed from the system, after incrementing by 1 the counter for that part type. A check of the delayed events shows that there is a waiting part; machining is thus started on the first part in the waiting line, and its next event time, derived from the machining time of 84, is calculated as 1087. The records in the waiting line and the machine segment are all moved down one line. In this case the new part for machining has the largest finish time and it joins the end of the machine list. The third frame of Fig. 2-1 shows the state of the system at the end of this event.

There is then another completion, at 1017, which, as before, leads to a counter being incremented and service being offered to the first part in the waiting line. In this case, however, the machining time is short enough for the new part to finish ahead of one whose machining started earlier, so, instead of being the last listed part, the new part becomes the second in the list. This is shown in frame 4.

As mentioned before, it is not customary to calculate attributes ahead of time, but only to compute them as necessary. In the present case, this means that the machine time would probably not be calculated until the part leaves the waiting line to be processed. It is also unnecessary for all the attribute values to coexist. In this example, in fact, the interarrival time has already been discarded. The arrival time could also be discarded after the part arrives, unless it is needed to gather information about how long the part stays in the system.

2-5
Concurrent Events

An activity such as machining schedules an isolated future event that corresponds to the end of machining a part. In certain other circumstances, one change implies other changes occurring at the same time. For example, the end of machining, when there is a waiting line, implies dispatching the finished part, removing a part from the waiting line, and beginning machining on that part—all these changes occurring at the same time.

It is a matter of interpretation as to whether interrelated changes of this nature should be regarded as a single complex event or as a set of simultaneous elemental events. In GPSS, the latter is assumed; the example would be executed as three separate events. However, when there is a set of concurrent events occurring to the same entity and it is implicit that they occur together, they are executed immediately without intervention by events affecting other entities that happen to occur at the same time. Thus, in GPSS, the part removed from the waiting line would immediately be placed on a machine and would not find that the program gave the machine to some other waiting part between the events of being removed from the waiting line and starting machining. Similarly, if a part arrived in the system at a time when there was no waiting line and a machine was available, the GPSS program would execute a concurrent series of four events concerned with entering the system, joining the waiting line, leaving the waiting line, and getting the machine. These events would be executed consecutively before executing events occurring at the same time to other parts, such as entering the next arrival.

2-6
Statistical Outputs

What has been described in Sec. 2-4 is the logic of a simulation algorithm. The purpose of the simulation, of course, is to learn something about the system performance. In this case only the counts of the number of completed parts by type has been kept, and, because the model is so simple, the expected values of these counts are known; they simply reflect the original probability distribution that was used to determine the part type. Depending upon the purpose of the simulation study, other statistics would be gathered. Simulation language programs include routines for collecting certain typical statistics. Among the commonly used types of statistics are the following:

(a) *Counts* giving the number of entities of a given type, or the number of times some event occurred
(b) *Utilization* of an item of equipment, in terms of the fraction of time it is in use
(c) *Occupancy* of a multiunit item of equipment, in terms of the average number of units in use
(d) *Distributions* of random variates, such as processing times and response times, together with their means and standard deviations

Counts are easy to maintain. The example given earlier counted the number of parts processed, which is a cumulative number. Other counts, such as the number of parts waiting for service, will fluctuate. When this happens, it is often useful to also determine a maximum value by seeing whether any increment raises the count beyond its previous highest value.

The methods used to derive utilization and occupancy are described in Sec. 5-21; the measurement of distributions is discussed in Sec. 8-8. These sections describe the specific methods used in GPSS, but they are typical of the methods used in system simulation programs.

2-7
List Processing

When using the machine shop example to explain the simulation process, we found it convenient to describe the records as though they were located in one of three places, corresponding to whether they represented parts that were arriving, waiting, or being processed. The progress of the simulation was described in terms of moving the records from one place to the next, possibly with some re-sorting. A computer program that used this approach would be very inefficient because of the large amount of data movement involved in the processing. Instead, the majority of simulation programs would make use of *list processing*, a programming technique that allows records to be regrouped or reordered without physically moving them in storage. The technique is illustrated in Fig. 2-2. Each record consists of a number of contiguous words (or bytes), some of which are reserved for constructing a list of the records. Each record contains, in a standard position, the address of the next record in the list. This is called a *pointer*. A special word, called a *header*, which is located in a known location, contains a pointer to the first record in the list. The last record in the list has an end-of-list symbol in place of its pointer. If the list happens to be empty, the end-of-list symbol appears in the header.

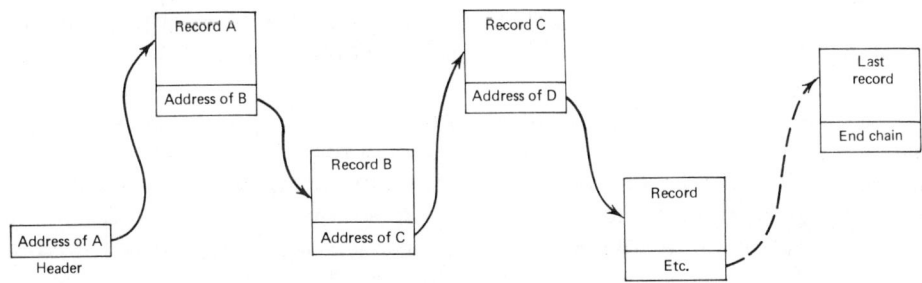

Figure 2-2. List processing.

The set of pointers beginning from the header places the records in a specific order and allows a program to search the records by following the chain of pointers. These lists are, in fact, usually called *chains*. There will sometimes be another special word, called the *trailer*, that points to the last record on the chain so that a record can be added to the end of the chain quickly. There may, in fact, be another set of pointers starting from the trailer and tracing through the chain from end to beginning so that a program can move along the chain in either direction. It is also possible for a record to be on more than one chain, simply by reserving pointer space for each possible chain.

Removing or adding a record or reorganizing the order of a chain now becomes a matter of manipulating pointers. To remove C from a chain of the records A, B, C, D, ..., the pointer of B is redirected to D. If the record is being discarded, its storage space would probably be returned to another chain from which it can be reassigned later. To put the record Z between B and C, the pointer of B is directed to Z and the pointer of Z set to indicate C. Reordering a chain consists of a series of removals and insertions.

As can be seen, list processing does not require that records be physically moved. It therefore provides an efficient way of logically transferring records from one category to another by moving them on and off chains, and it can easily manage lists that are constantly changing size—two properties that are very desirable in simulation programming.

2-8
Transaction Chains

To return to the example of the machine shop, the records were logically located in three categories: arriving, waiting, and being machined. List processing could implement this organization by using three lists, but it is apparent that this is an organization specific to the particular model being used. A more useful organization is to divide the records into those that have future event times and those that are delayed. The logical location of the record in the system would then be carried in the record. Most simulation programs, and in particular GPSS, use these two basic types of chain. There may also be other chains, as will be explained later. Since the main purpose of this book is to describe GPSS, the specific terminology of GPSS will now be used.

In GPSS, the records are called *transactions*. The locations where they may be logically placed are called *blocks*. What has been called an event time is called a *block departure time*. The simulation progresses by logically moving transactions from block to block, an action that corresponds to the execution of an event. When a transaction has a block departure time that is ahead of the current clock, so that it represents a future event, it is placed on the *future events chain*. When the transaction is delayed, or blocked in its progress, it is placed on the *current events chain*. If the machine shop example were programmed in GPSS, each part would be represented by a transaction. Those transactions that represent parts being machined and the part due to arrive next would be on the future events chain. Those transactions that represent waiting parts would be on the current events chain.

The GPSS simulation algorithm proceeds by advancing the clock to the next future event time and executing that event together with any other events on the current events chain that become unblocked. The current events chain, therefore, is constantly being scanned. To improve efficiency, GPSS allows certain types of blocked transactions to be removed from the current events chain and placed on either a match chain, an interrupt chain, or one of many possible user-defined chains. The transactions are returned to the current events chain when the blocking condition is known to have been removed. In general, blocked transactions left on the current events chain could be released by the movement of any number of other transactions, whereas transactions moved to the match, interrupt, or a user chain will usually be unblocked only by the movement of one known transaction which can be made to initiate the transfer back to the current events chain by entering a particular block type.

A complete description of the GPSS scanning method is given in Appendix 6. Familiarity with the details of this method becomes necessary only when one is modeling systems where operations can be interrupted or where the order of execution is controlled by assigning levels of priority; under these conditions, it is important to know the exact order in which simultaneous events will be processed. An initial reading of Appendix 6 will be helpful, but the reader will probably find it easier to return to the appendix after gaining some experience with GPSS.

2-9
Simulation Languages

It can be seen from the worked example and the discussion of discrete programming techniques that the writing of a complete simulation program can be a formidable task. The growth of simulation applications, however, has led to the development of many simulation programming systems that considerably simplify the task. In general, these programming systems incorporate a language with which to describe a model. Based on this description, the programming system is able to construct a system image, execute a simulation algorithm, gather statistics, and produce output reports. The extent to which any or all of these functions is made automatic depends on the particular programming system.

The earliest simulation languages were devoted to continuous systems, largely because a considerable body of experience using analog computers to simulate continuous systems existed before the appearance of modern digital computers.

Many languages, both for continuous and discrete systems, are *special purpose*, meaning that they have been designed for specific types of system; the language can then be very closely adapted to that type of system. In general, the programming systems using these languages will perform all the simulation programming functions, leaving the user only to specify the model.

Other languages are designed to be *general purpose* so that they can be applied to many different types of system. One section of the Bibliography provides a selected list of references to many discrete system simulation languages. Of those listed, the following are considered to be general purpose (listed in the order in which they appear in the Bibliography): CSL (Control and Simulation Language) (25, 27); SIMULA (29); SIMSCRIPT (31, 45-47, 51); GPSS (32-35, 37, 39, 41-43, 56); SIMON (40); SIMPL/I (44); SOL (49); AS (53); GASP (54); and DYNAMO (55).

The extent varies to which these general-purpose languages make the diverse tasks of constructing a simulation program automatic. Although all these languages have a wide application, it is generally considered that raising the level to which they make the simulation process more automatic introduces some rigidity and, consequently, some inefficiency. However, the presence of automatic features can considerably shorten the time necessary to conduct a simulation study. Reviews that compare some of these languages and discuss the issues involved in their design and selection will be found in (26, 48, 52, 57, 58). The GPSS language, in particular the GPSS V language discussed in this book, is generally considered to be among the more formal languages, which provides automatic functions to a high degree, thus making it one of the easier languages to apply.

3
GPSS CONCEPTS

The purpose of this chapter is to introduce many of the elements of the GPSS language and to demonstrate how GPSS is used by modeling and coding the machine shop example used in the previous chapter. The discussion will be brief since it is intended as an introduction. We will describe the elements and the concepts in full in later chapters.

3-1
Block Diagrams

The system to be simulated in GPSS must be described as a block diagram, where the blocks are drawn from a set of specific *block types*. Each block type has a name, which is usually descriptive of the block action, and it is represented in the block diagram by a particular symbol.

Block types are designed to represent individual actions that are characteristic of systems. Therefore, they are used in representing the system activities. In general, there will not be just one block for each system activity. An appropriate group of blocks must be selected and interconnected to represent each system activity. The groups are then joined to indicate the sequence of activities that can be executed by the system. Where there is a choice of activities, some of the block types specify the decision rule for making a choice. Altogether there are 48 block types, each of which may be used repeatedly. The total number of blocks that can be used in a block diagram depends upon the version of the program being used. The normal limit is 1000 blocks.† The number can, in fact, be reassigned by exchanging space reserved for other elements of the GPSS program (see Sec. 16-3).

Most block types have only one exit that joins the block to its successor. There is, however, no limit on how many blocks can lead into a given block, except that the GENERATE block cannot be entered from any other block, since it represents a point of origin. The TERMINATE block is the only block that has no exit, since it represents a terminal point.

3-2
Transactions

The block diagram, in effect, represents the structure of the system, since it describes the activities and indicates how they are interconnected. Moving through the system are entities that depend upon the nature of the system. For example, a communication system is concerned with the movement of messages, a traffic system with the movement of vehicles, and so on. These temporary entities that move through the system are represented in GPSS by transactions. The sequence of events that occurs in the system is simulated by the movement of transactions from block to block.

Each transaction is represented in the program by a group of computer words. Some words are used by the program to identify the transaction and control its movement. Others, called *parameters*, are available to the user for recording data. As a rule, transactions represent temporary entities that enter and leave the system during the course of the simulation. The parameters usually represent the attributes of the temporary entities. Sometimes, however, a transaction remains in the block diagram throughout the simulation, possibly cycling through a closed loop of blocks with the parameters being used to count the number of cycles. The transaction may then represent a permanent entity involved in several activities, or it may be a transaction introduced to control some cyclic activity.

There can be many transactions in the block diagram simultaneously. At all times, each transaction is located at some block. Generally, blocks can contain any number of transactions simultaneously. Constraints in the system, however, may place a limit on the number in a particular block. There

---

† As issued, the GPSS V program has a user option allowing one of three sizes to be selected according to the amount of core space that is available. The largest size is for option C, which uses 178 K bytes of core. Throughout the book the term "normal limits" gives the number of GPSS entities available under option C. Table 16-1 gives details of the normal allocation of space for the three versions. In addition to the option, the user can reallocate space to rebalance the numbers of entities. Reallocation is described in Sec. 16-3.

is an upper limit on the number of transactions in the block diagram at any one time. The normal limit is 1200 simultaneous transactions. There is no limit, however, to the total number of transactions that may be created and moved through the block diagram during the course of the simulation.

3-3
Representation of Time

As mentioned previously, time is represented by a number called clock time, or simply, the clock. It is an integral number, with the unit of time being chosen by the user. The time unit is not specifically stated; it is implied by expressing all times in the same unit.

One block type, called ADVANCE, is concerned with the expenditure of time. Whenever a transaction enters an ADVANCE block, the program computes an *action time* from specifications given at the block. The action time can be a constant, including zero, or it may be a random variable. In addition, it can be made to depend upon the particular transaction or upon the prevailing conditions in the system. The action time is added to the current clock time to produce a block departure time. The transaction remains in the ADVANCE block until the clock reaches the block departure time. At that point, the program will attempt to move the transaction to the next block.

The only other block type that involves time is the GENERATE block, which creates transactions. There, the action time controls the interval between successive transaction creations.

3-4
Permanent Entities

The permanent entities of a system include such factors as items of equipment or manpower which remain throughout the simulation. Three elements of GPSS, facilities, storages, and logic switches, are used to represent permanent entities. There can be many instances of each element.

A *facility* is a permanent entity that can be used by only one transaction at a time, although it is possible to interrupt its use. For example, a facility might be used to represent an inspector in a factory who normally inspects jobs, represented by transactions, one at a time. He may occassionally be interrupted by being called away to answer the telephone.

A *storage* is used to represent any permanent entity that has a capacity and can be engaged, or occupied, by more than one transaction simultaneously—a warehouse storing goods, for example, or, in the case of the simple machine shop example, the group of three machines.

A *logic switch* is a two-state element that is either set (on), or reset (off). It is similar to a facility, which can be either busy or free. A logic switch can be used to represent a permanent entity when the only information needed is whether the entity is available or not. More commonly, however, it is used to represent some condition prevailing in the system, such as whether a work shift has started or not.

3-5

Data Elements

Provision must be made for both the entry and collection of data. The program contains elements called *savevalues*, which can be used for either purpose. They can be initialized to enter data, and they can be used during the simulation as temporary storages or for the collection of output data. It is also possible to use *functions*, which are actually tables of numbers relating an input to an output. They can be used simply as tables of data, or the program can approximate a function by assuming that straight line segments join the defined points.

The program also makes available the current value of many items of data that describe the system being simulated—for example, the current number of transactions in a storage or the length of a queue. These items of data associated with the model are called *standard numerical attributes*, or *SNA*s. Computations can be carried out using *variable statements*, or, more simply, *variables*, which are mathematical statements that combine SNAs.

3-6

Simple Machine Shop in GPSS

Figure 3-1 shows a GPSS block diagram that represents the model of the simple machine shop described in Sec. 2-1. The names of the block types have been included in the figure, although this would not usually be done by a person familiar with GPSS. A brief description will now be given of how the model operates. Fuller descriptions of all the block types will be given in later chapters.

At the top of the figure is a GENERATE block, which creates transactions that represent the parts to be machined. The time unit being used is 1 minute. The arrivals are randomly distributed and the mean interarrival time is to be initialized from a location called ARR. The notation FN$EXP denotes the inverted exponential distribution function, which is used to create random arrivals in a manner to be explained in Sec. 9-2. The transactions pass to an ASSIGN block, which places in parameter number 1 a

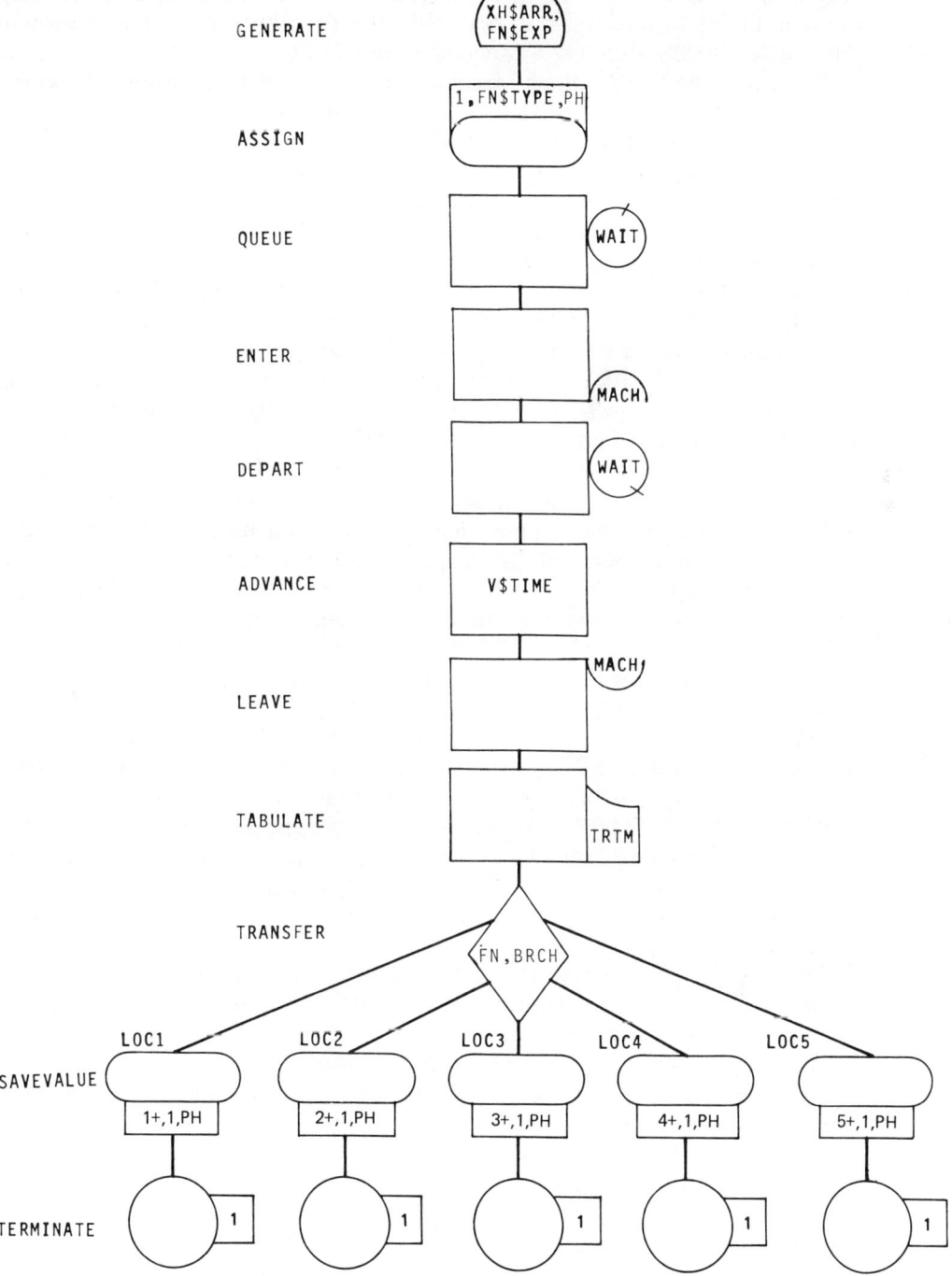

Figure 3-1. Simple machine shop example in GPSS.

part number selected randomly from 1 to 5. The method of generating these numbers is explained in Sec. 9-1; the distribution used is shown in Table 9-1. This is entered as a function called TYPE.

From the ASSIGN block, transactions go to a QUEUE block, where they join a queue called WAIT. They then attempt to go into an ENTER block associated with a storage called MACH, which allows them to take up one unit of space in the storage, representing the group of machines. The storage capacity is limited to three (by a control statement that is not shown); so, if the storage is full, the transactions will have to wait for a part to finish processing before they can move into the ENTER block. The program automatically detects the change of conditions and effects the transfer when the space becomes available.

As soon as the transactions have moved into the ENTER block, they continue into the DEPART block to be removed from the queue of waiting parts. The program will automatically collect statistics about the queue. The transactions then move into an ADVANCE block representing the machining, and they will stay there for a length of time calculated from a function called NORM, which is used to generate random numbers from a standard normal distribution (see Sec. 9-3). The machining time is normally distributed with a mean of 60 minutes and a standard deviation of 20 minutes. The calculation needed to convert from the standard normal distribution is carried out with a variable statement (not shown in the figure), called TIME, and denoted by V$TIME.

If there is no waiting when a part arrives at the ENTER block, a transaction will pass straight through the first five blocks into the ADVANCE block. This is an example of a set of concurrent events, described in Sec. 2-5, and it illustrates a GPSS rule that a transaction is always moved through as many blocks as possible, once it starts moving.

While in the ADVANCE block, transactions represent future events. Because of the capacity limit set by the ENTER block, there cannot be more than three transactions simultaneously in the ADVANCE block. When the machining is over, the transactions leave the ADVANCE block and go to the LEAVE block, where they give up the storage space they took at the ENTER block. The next block is a TABULATE block, which tabulates, in a table called TRTM, the time it took the transactions to reach that point, from the time they entered the system.

The next block is a TRANSFER block, which sends the transactions to one of five locations according to the part type, as recorded in parameter number 1. The locations, called LOC1, LOC2, and so on, are listed in a function called BRCH. At their respective locations, after the transfer, the transactions enter a SAVEVALUE block to count the number of finished parts by type. These counts will be printed as part of the final output report. Finally, the transactions are removed from the simulation by going to a TERMINATE block.

3-7
Input Statement Format

Input statements defining blocks consist of three major fields, as follows:

(a) Location
(b) Operation
(c) Operands

Statements other than block definitions generally follow the same structure but contain control information or data. The significance of the fields for those statements will be given as they are defined.

GPSS coding can be carried out in one of two formats—fixed or free. The fixed format is normally used for card input, where a tabulation operation to shift fields is easy to do while keypunching. The free form is better suited to input from a terminal, where it is desirable to minimize the number of characters being transmitted.

In the fixed format, each field must begin in a particular column. The location field is from columns 2 to 6, inclusive. When it is necessary, or desirable, to identify a block, the name or number assigned to the block is placed in this field. If the blocks follow each other sequentially, it is not usually necessary for the user to assign names or numbers; the program will number the blocks automatically.

If names are used, they must consist of from three to five characters selected from the alphabetic characters A to Z and the digits 0 to 9. *The first three characters must be alphabetic*, and there cannot be any blanks. It is permissible to use numbers in the location field, but the user must make sure that they are compatible with any numbers already assigned automatically by the program. Usually numbers will be used only in small models, or when additions or alterations are being made to a previously assembled model. An example is shown in Sec. 7-5.

Column 7 is always blank in a block statement. The field from columns 8 through 18 is the operation field. It contains the name of the block type, which must begin in column 8. Some block types have a control code in the operation field, following the block name, after a blank space—for example, TEST E.

Beginning in column 19 are a series of operands, consisting of the fields A, B, C, and so on, appearing in alphabetic order. The fields must be separated by a comma, and there cannot be any blanks. A blank field is indicated by two successive commas, or an initial comma if field A is blank. All blank fields are set to zero. In addition, all fields beyond the last defined field are set to zero, so it is not necessary to use commas to indicate trailing blank fields.

The first blank encountered in the operands field will terminate the field. The remaining columns, through column 71, can be used to contain remarks that will be printed in the output listing but not affect the model in any way. Columns 72 through 80 are not used, nor are they listed.

When using the free format method of entering input, the location field begins in column 1; but none of the other fields has a fixed starting position. Instead, a single blank has the effect of tabulating from one field to the next. More than one blank can, in fact, be used between fields, but if operands are to be used, they must begin before column 21. For those blocks that have a control character in the operation field, such as TEST E, the program recognizes that this blank does not mean a tabulation. If a block does not have any operands, any remarks must begin beyond column 20.

Free form coding gives a ragged printed appearance since no fields are lined up. It is therefore more difficult to read. However, when used with terminals as input to on-line computing systems, it minimizes the number of characters to be transmitted between the computer and terminal. As a rule, on-line coding is executed very soon after being entered, and the output of an assembly returns a fixed format printout of the input.

An example of the free form of the input is given in Appendix 2 as Fig. A2-1. It should be compared with the listing to be given shortly in Fig. 3-2.

3-8

Comments Statements

If column 1 of an input statement contains an asterisk (*), the entire statement is interpreted as a comment that will be printed in the program listing. The statement does not otherwise affect the program. (Column 7 of a comments statement does not have to be blank.) It is illegal to have a completely blank statement. If a space is wanted in the listing, a statement with * in column 1 (but otherwise blank) is used. An asterisk is an illegal character for a symbolic name, so in the free form mode, the program recognizes the difference between a comment and a name starting in column 1.

3-9

Execution of GPSS Problems

The initial phase of the GPSS programming system consists of an assembly program that reads and prepares the input for execution. A successful assembly results in the assembly phase being replaced by an execution phase, unless the execution phase is specifically suppressed. At the end of a run the execution phase, in turn, is replaced by a report generation phase.

A principal task of the assembly phase is to check that all block and control statements are correctly completed, in the sense that they contain legitimate entries. An incomplete statement results in an error message being written beneath the statement in the output listing, and the suppression of the execution phase. All statements are read, however, to find as many errors as possible on each use of the program. All symbolic references are also examined by the assembly program and, as far as possible, resolved. Any unresolved references will also cause an error message and suppress the execution.

Any reference to a location can be made with a symbolic name. As well as appearing in the location fields of blocks, symbolic names for locations may appear in some operand fields.

In addition, all GPSS entities, with the exception of transactions and their attributes, priority, mark time, or parameters, can take symbolic names. Upon encountering a symbolic name in an operand field that should contain an entity number, the program assigns the number of a free entity of the appropriate type. Each type of entity has its own sequence of names and numbers.

All symbols follow the rules given in the previous section. One reason for these rules is that the standard numerical attributes of the program are denoted by one or two character names. Using three initial characters for the symbolic names avoids confusion. The SNAs can also take symbolic names, and, when this is done, the letters defining the type of SNA and their symbolic name must be separated by the special symbol $; thus a facility, which has the symbol F, may be denoted by F$NAME. The symbolic name NAME will then be replaced by a number upon assembly.

A full description of the assembly program is given in Appendix 2. Other capabilities described there include the following:

(a) The use of macro statements which allow the user to define frequently used segments of code (up to 10 parameters can be specified at the time the macro is called)
(b) Creation of master data sets to hold input decks, and the capability to update them by adding, deleting, or changing statements
(c) Combining and controlling mixtures of assembled and unassembled input statements

3-10

Coding of Simple Machine Shop Example

Whichever format is used for the input, the first phase of the output received from the execution of the GPSS program is a listing of the input in the fixed format. Figure 3-2† shows the first section of the output for the simple machine shop model shown in Fig. 3-1. It will be used to describe the coding briefly. Subsequent chapters will describe all coding details of the statements as the blocks they represent are defined.

Shown in Fig. 3-2 is a complete listing of all the input statements, under an initial heading that explains the contents of the fields. As the statements are listed, the locations (or block numbers) are sequentially assigned to block definition statements, and the assignments are listed to the left of the block statement. On the right, every statement, including the comments, is given a sequential statement number. Both these sets of numbers are placed there by the program: they are not entered by the user.

The listing shown in Fig. 3-2 contains comments and blank lines to make the listing easier to read. They are all indicated by an initial * in column 1. The first problem statement is a SIMULATE control statement, calling for a simulation to be attempted. Without this statement, only an assembly of the input will be performed. Following the SIMULATE statement are the definitions of the four functions used by the model. A complete description of how functions are defined will be given in Chap. 9, but, as can be seen, each requires a FUNCTION control statement, followed by a series of function data statements. The function name appears in the location field of the FUNCTION control statement. The A operand indicates the SNA that is to provide the input to the function, and the B operand denotes the type of function and the number of points used in its definition. The first three functions all use a uniformly distributed random number between 0 and 1 as input. The last uses halfword parameter 1 of the transactions.

Following the functions are the statements defining the blocks. Their roles have been described in Sec. 3-6. The remarks they carry also indicate their purpose. In the GENERATE block, the A field carries the mean value of the time between successive arrivals. The program has been arranged so that the mean is taken from a halfword savevalue called ARR, where it can easily be initialized at the beginning of the run.

Following the block definition statements are some control statements. A VARIABLE statement defines the calculation needed to derive the ADVANCE block time from the standard normal function called NORM, and a STORAGE statement gives the capacity of the storage called MACH, representing the machines, as three. Following that is another control statement, TABLE, which defines the number and size of the table intervals to be used with the TABULATE block. The A operand indicates the quantity to be tabulated; in this case, the symbol M1 means the transit time from point of entry into the system up to the TABULATE block. The INITIAL statement gives the value for initializing the halfword savevalue ARR. The last four control statements control the running of the problem. The first START statement runs the problem until 10 transactions have been proc-

---

†To simplify reproduction this, and many of the subsequent listings, have been slightly modified in order to reduce their width.

```
BLOCK                                                                STATEMENT
NUMBER  *LOC    OPERATION   A,B,C,D,E,F,G,H,I        COMMENTS         NUMBER
                SIMULATE                                                1
        *                                                               2
        EXP     FUNCTION    RN1,C24             INVERTED EXPONENTIAL FUNCTION   3
        0,0/.1,.104/.2,.222/.3,.355/.4,.509/.5,.69                      4
        .6,.915/.7,1.2/.75,1.38/.8,1.6/.84,1.83/.88,2.12                5
        .9,2.3/.92,2.52/.94,2.81/.95,2.99/.96,3.2/.97,3.5               6
        .98,3.9/.99,4.6/.995,5.3/.998,6.2/.999,7/.9997,8                7
        *                                                               8
        TYPE    FUNCTION    RN1,D5              DISTRIBUTION OF PART TYPES      9
        .1,1/.35,2/.57,3/.85,4/1.0,5                                   10
        *                                                              11
        NORM    FUNCTION    RN1,C25             INVERTED STANDARD NORMAL FUNCTION  12
        0,-5/.00003,-4/.00135,-3/.00621,-2.5/.02275,-2/.06681,-1.5     13
        .11507,-1.2/.15866,-1/.21186,-.8/.27425,-.6/.34458,-.4/.42074,-.2  14
        .5,0/.57926,.2/.65542,.4/.72575,.6/.78814,.8/.84134,1/.88493,1.2  15
        .93319,1.5/.97725,2/.99379,2.5/.99865,3/.99997,4/1,5           16
        *                                                              17
        BRCH    FUNCTION    PH1,L5              SEPARATES PARTS        18
        1,LOC1/2,LOC2/3,LOC3/4,LOC4/5,LOC5                             19
        *                                                              20
        *       SIMULATION OF SIMPLE MACHINE SHOP                      21
        *                                                              22
 1              GENERATE    XH$ARR,FN$EXP       CREATE PARTS           23
 2              ASSIGN      1,FN$TYPE,PH        PICK TYPE              24
 3              QUEUE       WAIT                JOIN QUEUE             25
 4              ENTER       MACH                GET MACHINE            26
 5              DEPART      WAIT                LEAVE QUEUE            27
 6              ADVANCE     V$TIME              MACHINE PART           28
 7              LEAVE       MACH                GIVE UP MACHINE        29
 8              TABULATE    TRTM                TABULATE TIME IN SYSTEM 30
 9              TRANSFER    FN,BRCH             BRANCH BY TYPE         31
        *                                                              32
10      LOC1    SAVEVALUE   1+,1,XH             ADD 1 TO COUNT OF TYPE 1 PARTS  33
11              TERMINATE   1                   DESTROY TRANSACTION    34
        *                                                              35
12      LOC2    SAVEVALUE   2+,1,XH                                    36
13              TERMINATE   1                                          37
        *                                                              38
14      LOC3    SAVEVALUE   3+,1,XH                                    39
15              TERMINATE   1                                          40
        *                                                              41
16      LOC4    SAVEVALUE   4+,1,XH                                    42
17              TERMINATE   1                                          43
        *                                                              44
18      LOC5    SAVEVALUE   5+,1,XH                                    45
19              TERMINATE   1                                          46
        *                                                              47
        TIME    VARIABLE    20*FN$NORM+60       COMPUTES MACHINE TIME  48
        STORAGE             S$MACH,3            NUMBER OF MACHINES     49
        TRTM    TABLE       M1,0,20,12          TABLE FOR TRANSIT TIME 50
                INITIAL     XH$ARR,25           SET MEAN ARRIVAL TIME  51
        *                                                              52
                START       10,NP               INITIALIZE WITH 10 PARTS  53
                RESET                           WIPE OUT STATISTICS    54
                START       500                 RUN FOR 500 PARTS      55
                END                                                    56
```

Figure 3-2. Coding of simple machine shop example.

essed, in order to load the system. The RESET statement wipes out the statistics gathered during that period. The last START statement signals the main run of the program, in which 500 more parts are processed and statistics are gathered. Finally there is an END statement showing that all runs are finished.

Note that the blocks are broken into segments. One segment stretches from the initial GENERATE block to the TRANSFER block. There are then five short segments, one for each part. Only those locations that must be specified in order that segments be correctly linked have been given, although it would do no harm to name other blocks. As the program reads the input, it will assign block numbers, beginning at 1 for the first block and continuing to 19 for the last. So long as the sequence within the segments is maintained and the segments are linked by symbolic names, the order in which the individual segments are presented does not matter.

3-11

Program Output

Following the initial listing of the input, the program prints the set of cross-references shown in Fig. 3-3. For each type of entity for which a symbolic assignment was made, a table lists the symbol and the number assigned to the symbol. The numbers of the statements that make reference to the symbol are also given.

If the assembly is successful, the cross-reference table is followed by a second listing of the input, this time in assembled form. This second listing is shown in Fig. 3-4. All symbols are replaced by numbers. Remarks are also removed from the block statements. The function data are listed in a manner entirely different from the entry data. The x, y values are spaced in 6 columns with not more than three pairs to a line. This format is called the *assembly format*. Statements in this format can be accepted without having to be reassembled, and they can be mixed with statements in the other input formats, under control of the assembly program. Both the original listing and the assembly listing can be suppressed by the use of assembly control statements called LIST and UNLIST. The cross-reference table can also be suppressed with another assembly control statement called NOXREF. (See Appendix 2 for a description of the assembly program.)

In all later listings of program outputs that occur in this book, the assembly listing and the cross-reference tables will be omitted to save space. All models are small enough for the cross-references to be made easily by inspection. What will be shown is the listing of the input that appears as the first part of the output. The statement numbers inserted on the right by the program will not be given. However, the block locations on the left, also inserted by the program, will be given. It is important to note that these are not inserted by the user.

SYMBOL	CROSS-REFERENCE BLOCKS NUMBER	REFERENCES		
LOC1	10	19		
LOC2	12	19		
LOC3	14	19		
LOC4	16	19		
LOC5	18	19		
SYMBOL	CROSS-REFERENCE STORAGES NUMBER	REFERENCES		
MACH	1	26	29	49
SYMBOL	CROSS-REFERENCE QUEUES NUMBER	REFERENCES		
WAIT	1	25	27	
SYMBOL	CROSS-REFERENCE TABLES NUMBER	REFERENCES		
TRTM	1	30	50	
SYMBOL	CROSS-REFERENCE VARIABLES NUMBER	REFERENCES		
TIME	1	28	48	
SYMBOL	CROSS-REFERENCE FUNCTIONS NUMBER	REFERENCES		
BRCH	4	18	31	
EXP	1	3	23	
NORM	3	12	48	
TYPE	2	9	24	
SYMBOL	CROSS-REFERENCE HALFWORD SAVEVALUES NUMBER	REFERENCES		
ARR	6	23	51	

Figure 3-3. Cross-reference table.

The listings will omit the SIMULATE or END statements because these are needed only once, no matter how many different problems are run. All the problems in the book were run in one large group and did not need individual SIMULATE and END statements.

After the assembly listing, there comes the output of the run, which is normally a standard output report. (Other forms of output are discussed in Sec. 3-22.) Figure 3-5 shows the output for the simple machine shop example. First, there is a line showing the clock time at which the run stopped. There were, in fact, two runs—the first being a short run to load the system. The output of that run was suppressed by the NP in field A of the first START statement. The output shown in Fig. 3-5 is the result of the second run. The time marked "relative" is the time since the restart. The time marked "absolute" is the time since the beginning of the first run.

```
        SIMULATE
*
   1    FUNCTION    RN1,C24
 0       0          .1         .104      .2         .222
 .3      .355       .4         .509      .5         .69
 .6      .915       .7         1.2       .75        1.38
 .8      1.6        .84        1.83      .88        2.12
 .9      2.3        .92        2.52      .94        2.81
 .95     2.99       .96        3.2       .97        3.5
 .98     3.9        .99        4.6       .995       5.3
 .998    6.2        .999       7         .9997      8
*
   2    FUNCTION    RN1,D5
 .1      1          .35        2         .57        3
 .85     4          1.0        5
*
   3    FUNCTION    RN1,C25
 0       -5         .00003     -4        .00135     -3
 .00621  -2.5       .02275     -2        .06681     -1.5
 .11507  -1.2       .15866     -1        .21186     -.8
 .27425  -.6        .34458     -.4       .42074     -.2
 .5      0          .57926     .2        .65542     .4
 .72575  .6         .78814     .8        .84134     1
 .88493  1.2        .93319     1.5       .97725     2
 .99379  2.5        .99865     3         .99997     4
 1       5
*
   4    FUNCTION    PH1,L5
 1       10         2          12        3          14
 4       16         5          18
*
*        SIMULATION OF SIMPLE MACHINE SHOP
*
   1    GENERATE    XH6,FN1
   2    ASSIGN      1,FN2,PH
   3    QUEUE       1
   4    ENTER       1
   5    DEPART      1
   6    ADVANCE     V1
   7    LEAVE       1
   8    TABULATE    1
   9    TRANSFER    FN,4
*
  10    SAVEVALUE   1+,1,XH
  11    TERMINATE   1
*
  12    SAVEVALUE   2+,1,XH
  13    TERMINATE   1
*
  14    SAVEVALUE   3+,1,XH
  15    TERMINATE   1
*
  16    SAVEVALUE   4+,1,XH
  17    TERMINATE   1
*
  18    SAVEVALUE   5+,1,XH
  19    TERMINATE   1
*
   1    VARIABLE    20*FN3+60
        STORAGE     S1,3
   1    TABLE       M1,0,20,12
        INITIAL     XH6,25
*
        START       10,NP
        RESET
        START       500
```

Figure 3-4. Assembly listing.

```
RELATIVE CLOCK          12547   ABSOLUTE CLOCK          12919
BLOCK COUNTS
BLOCK CURRENT TOTAL     BLOCK CURRENT TOTAL     BLOCK CURRENT TOTAL
  1      0    500         11      0      55
  2      0    500         12      0     129
  3      0    500         13      0     129
  4      0    500         14      0     123
  5      0    500         15      0     123
  6      2    500         16      0     124
  7      0    500         17      0     124
  8      0    500         18      0      69
  9      0    500         19      0      69
 10      0     55
```

```
*******************************************
*                                         *
*              STORAGES                   *
*                                         *
*******************************************
```

```
                                       AVER  UTIL DURING
STORAGE  CAPACITY  AVERAGE   ENTRIES  AVERAGE   TOTL AVAL UNAVL  CURRENT  PCNT   CONTENT
                  CONTENT            TIME/UNIT  TIME TIME TIME   STATUS  AVAIL   CURR MAX
MACH        3      2.405       502    60.121    .801 .801 .000     A     100.0    2    3
```

```
*******************************************
*                                         *
*               QUEUES                    *
*                                         *
*******************************************
```

```
QUEUE  MAXIMUM  AVERAGE   TOTAL    ZERO   PERCENT  AVERAGE   $AVERAGE   TABLE    CURRENT
       CONTENT  CONTENT  ENTRIES ENTRIES  ZEROS   TIME/TRAN  TIME/TRAN  NUMBER   CONTENT
WAIT      5      .782      500     201     40.1    19.643    32.849
$AVERAGE TIME/TRANS = AVERAGE TIME/TRANS EXCLUDING ZERO ENTRIES
```

```
*******************************************
*                                         *
*               TABLES                    *
*                                         *
*******************************************
```

```
TABLE   TRTM
ENTRIES IN TABLE   MEAN ARGUMENT   STANDARD DEVIATION    SUM OF ARGUMENTS
          500         79.863            26.437              39932.000      NON-WEIGHTED

        UPPER    OBSERVED    PER CENT   CUMULATIVE   CUMULATIVE   MULTIPLE   DEVIATION
        LIMIT    FREQUENCY   OF TOTAL   PERCENTAGE   REMAINDER    OF MEAN    FROM MEAN
           0        0          .00          .0         100.0       -.000      -3.020
          20        6         1.19         1.1          98.7        .250      -2.264
          40       27         5.39         6.5          93.3        .500      -1.507
          60      149        29.79        36.3          63.6        .751       -.751
          80      114        22.79        59.1          40.8       1.001        .005
         100       95        18.99        78.1          21.8       1.252        .761
         120       64        12.79        90.9           9.0       1.502       1.518
         140       35         6.99        97.9           2.0       1.752       2.274
         160        8         1.59        99.5            .4       2.003       3.031
         180        2          .39       100.0            .0       2.253       3.787
REMAINING FREQUENCIES ARE ALL ZERO
```

```
*******************************************
*                                         *
*          HALFWORD SAVEVALUES            *
*                                         *
*******************************************
```

```
NUMBER CONTENT   NUMBER CONTENT   NUMBER CONTENT   NUMBER CONTENT   NUMBER CONTENT
   1      56       2      133       3      123       4      127       5       71
  ARR     25
```

Figure 3-5. Output for simple machine shop example.

Following the times is a set of block counts. For each block two figures are listed. One, headed "current," is the number of transactions in the block at the end of the run. The other, headed "total," is the count of how many transactions entered the block, including those still there at the end of the program. In this case, at the end of the run, there were two parts being processed at block number 6, and there were no parts waiting for service in block 3. The total counts at the TERMINATE blocks show how many parts were processed by type. Of the 500 parts processed, the number of parts by type, compared with what would be expected, is as follows:

Type	Actual	Expected
1	55	50
2	129	125
3	123	110
4	124	140
5	69	75

Following the block counts is a line of statistics for the storage. The headings explain what the fields contain. A definition of the listed quantities will be given later in Sec. 5-21. A similar line of statistics for the queue follows, showing that the average queue length (including the times the queue was empty) was 0.782. The statistics gathered by the TABULATE block are then given, the data being expressed in several ways. The definition of these statistics will be given in Sec. 8-8. As can be seen, the mean time to complete processing, after arrival in the system, was 79.863 minutes. Finally, there is a printout of all the nonzero savevalues. The counts in the first five savevalues give the total numbers of parts by type that were processed in both runs. Savevalue number 6 has the initialization value for the mean interarrival time.

3-12

SIMULATE Statements

To arrange for the execution of a problem, a control statement that has the word SIMULATE in the operation field must be included in the input. It can appear anywhere in the input, except that it must follow any use of the REALLOCATE, AUXILIARY, or UPDATE features, described in Chap. 16. It is advisable, however, to make it the first statement so that its presence is obvious. Without this statement, the problem is assembled and no execution is initiated. If there are multiple runs (see Sec. 3-13), there need be only one SIMULATE statement.

The A field can be used to specify a computer run time limit. Should the limit expire while the program is in the assembly or output phase, the program will go to the end of the phase. If the limit expires during the simulation run, there are several options that can be given in field B. The run can be saved, or a time extension can be given. Since these options involve operator interaction, they are explained in the GPSS V *Operator's Manual* (42, 43).

3-13
START Statements

A MARK statement serves two necessary functions. It marks the end of the input for a problem, and it provides the information needed to control the length of the run. There can be multiple runs of the same model, so there may be more than one START statement per model.

The length of the simulation run is controlled by a termination count. Each transaction can increment the counter when it reaches a TERMINATE block. The block may have a number in field A to indicate the amount by which the count is to be incremented. Usually, if there is a count, it is for an increment of 1, but sometimes some transactions may carry more weight than others, and the TERMINATE block they reach has a higher count. Many TERMINATE blocks will have no count because terminations at that point are not considered significant. There must, however, be at least one TERMINATE block with a nonzero count. The START statement carries, in field A, the count to be reached or exceeded for the first time, in order to finish the run.

The B field can be used to suppress the program output at the end of a run by containing the letters NP: the field is otherwise left blank. In addition to the output at the end of a run, it is possible to get intermediate printouts, called *snaps*. If a number, n, is placed in the C field of the START statement, the program will print an output, in exactly the same form as the output at the end of a run, when the terminate count first reaches or exceeds n. The program then continues with the simulation. Another snap will be produced at a count of $2n$, $3n$, and so on, until the program is ended by the count in field A. The B field cannot suppress snaps.

If the D field of a START statement contains a nonzero character, say 1, then the printouts, both at the end of a run and for snaps, will include a printout of the transaction chains, which normally is printed only at the time of an error dump.

3-14
Multiple Runs of a Model

As has been seen in the simple machine shop example, there can be multiple runs of a model. A START statement marks the end of a problem input.

Upon encountering the statement, the program immediately runs the problem. When it has completed running the problem, the program does not assume that the current job is terminated. The model will be maintained exactly as it existed at the end of the run. After printing the output of the run, the program looks at the input following the START statement. It will only destroy the model of the completed run when it finds a JOB or END statement. If it should find another START statement, the program will restart the simulation, so that, within one job, it is possible to have multiple runs of a model. Furthermore, it is possible for input statements between START statements to modify the model between runs.

If one START statement immediately follows another, the run simply continues from the point at which it was left. The only effect will have been that the program paused to produce a printout. As a rule, there are input statements between successive START statements which modify the model. In particular, there may be one of two control statements, CLEAR or RESET, that control the conditions under which the model is rerun.

3-15

RESET Statements

The purpose of a second run of the same model may be to eliminate the initial part of a simulation run. If the system is initially empty, the early part of the simulation is not typical of normal operation. To eliminate the bias caused by this initial, empty state, a first, relatively short run may be planned to load the system, followed by a second, longer run in which to examine the system. The statistics required are from the second run only and the printout from the first run will not usually be of interest.

A control statement with the word RESET in the operation field will wipe out the statistics gathered up to the time the statement is read. It does not, however, disturb the transactions that exist in the model. The relative clock is also set to zero. The input shown in Fig. 3-2 concluded with the following sequence of statements:

```
START        10,NP
RESET
START        500
END
```

The problem was first run for 10 terminations. The characters NP in field B suppressed the output of the first run. The RESET statement cleared the statistics, reset the relative clock, but left in the model those transactions that happened to be in the block diagram at the time the run ended. The second START statement then ran the model for an additional 500 terminations, without suppressing the output.

Note that the RESET statement does not reset the random number generators (see Appendix 1). It does not change savevalue or matrix contents, nor does it reset any logic switches.

The statistics that relate to certain other entities can be left untouched by the RESET statement. Symbols representing the entities that are to be omitted are placed in the operands field, each separated by a comma. For completeness, the entity types and their symbols are listed here: the meanings of the statistics will be explained later.

Chain attributes	CHj
Facility attributes	Fj
Queue attributes	Qj
Storage attributes	Sj
Tables	TBj

The letter j stands for the number of the entity to be left untouched. It is also possible to specify a range of consecutive numbers, for example, the notation F1-F7 will leave the statistics of facilities 1 through 7 untouched. Note that there are no blanks. As an example, the following statement will leave the statistics for storage 2, facilities 1 through 7, and table 15 unchanged by a RESET statement:

> RESET   S2,F1-F7,TB15

3-16

CLEAR Statements

Another reason for rerunning a model is to examine a system with some attribute varied over a range of values. The simulation is to be repeated with some values changed. The values will most likely be defined by the INITIAL and STORAGE control statements. The new values can be introduced by statements between the START statements. As the program reads the new statements, it overrides the values that were previously set.

Under these circumstances, the simulation should be reinitialized so that the second run is identical, except for the planned changes. This is achieved by including, anywhere between the START statements, a control statement with the word CLEAR in the operations field. Upon encountering the statement, the program will clear all statistics gathered in the model, remove all transactions that remain in the model, and reset to zero both the relative and absolute clock times. However, the CLEAR statement does not reset the random number generators. Consider the following sequence of statements:

> START   1000
> CLEAR
> START   1000

They will cause two runs that are the same, except that the random number generators in the second run will not have been reset. If there are any random processes in the model, the second run will differ statistically from the first because it will have the last generated number of the first run as the initial number for the second run in each generator. A different set of random numbers will therefore be produced. This technique is used to get two or more statistically independent examples of the model output.

The CLEAR and RESET statements will often have to be used in conjunction with each other to get proper statistics. For example, suppose that the machine shop example is to be run with different mean interarrival times to see how the mean time to process parts depends upon the system load. A series of runs is then needed with the savevalue ARR initialized to different values. It is not good enough to simply reset the statistics and start a new run with a different value in ARR, because a queue of waiting parts can have built up. The size of that queue is characteristic of the system load under which it was created. Under the new load conditions, another size of queue will develop, and it could take some time for the new equilibrium to develop, especially when the load is heavy.

It is safer to clear the system and reinitialize by the same procedure on each run. Following the first run, a series of runs need to be made with a set of control statements, as follows:

```
          CLEAR
          INITIAL      XH$ARR,20
          START        10,NP
          RESET
          START        500
```

Each such set of statements sets the value of the mean interarrival time for one run.

Figure 3-6 shows two sets of results for the mean transit time against system loading, acquired by running the simple machine shop example with different mean interarrival times. The shorter the mean time, the higher the load on the system. The results are, in fact, plotted as a function of the utilization of the system, defined as the mean service time divided by three times the mean interarrival time. This concept of utilization is explained more fully in Sec. 5-23.

To arrive at the curve marked "CLEAR and RESET" in Fig. 3-6, the method just described was used. For the curve marked "RESET only," the CLEAR statements were not used, but the conditions were otherwise exactly the same. As can be seen, there is a significant difference when the system is heavily loaded and the utilization high. The runs were made with the mean interarrival time increasing from one run to the next, so that the loading was being dropped between runs. The values from the "RESET only" curves are too high because a large residual queue is being left at the

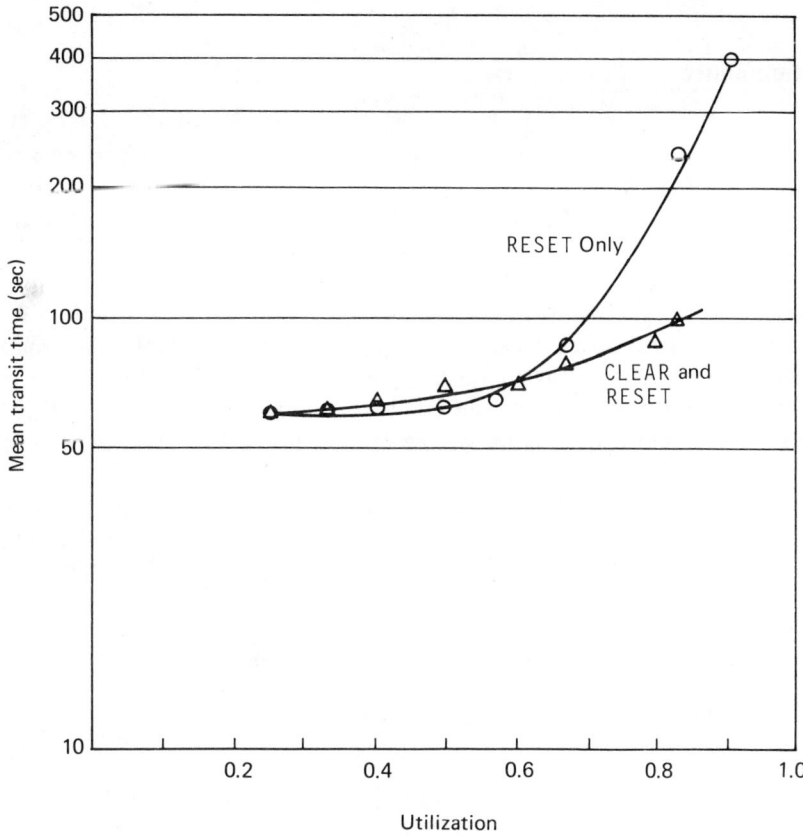

Figure 3-6. Two different results from measuring transit time.

end of each run and there has not been enough time for the queue to disappear.

Since the savevalues and matrices, to be described later, are often used as a means of entering initialization data, provision is made for making the CLEAR statement omit certain savevalues and matrices so that they are not cleared. The entities to be omitted are listed in the operands field in exactly the same way as a RESET statement is used to omit certain entities. The symbols for savevalues and matrices are, respectively, Xxj and Mxj, where x is a letter denoting the type and j a number (or name) identifying the specific item. A range can also be specified, using the same notation as in a RESET statement.

When a CLEAR statement is read, the transactions located at GENERATE blocks are destroyed. New transactions are created as though the program were reloaded. In addition, any count in field D, which can control the number of transactions generated, is reinitialized. The CLEAR statement will also reset all logic switches.

3-17

JOB Statements

There can be any number of independent problems, referred to as jobs, executed at one loading of the program. The jobs are placed in sequence, separated by JOB control statements. These statements have the word JOB in the operation field. The rest of the statement can be used for remarks. No JOB statement is required in front of the first, and possibly only, job.

Given an input with multiple jobs, the program will pass all jobs through the assembly phase before attempting any executions. It will then read the assembled input up to and including the first JOB statement and, if the assembly was good, it will execute the problem, provided a SIMULATE statement was encountered somewhere in the input. It then proceeds to the next job, and so on.

Each JOB statement wipes out all traces of the previous job and re-initializes the GPSS program. In particular, it resets the random number generators to the values they had when the program was first loaded.

3-18

END Statements

The last statement of the input must be an END statement that has the word END in the operation field. The statement signals the end of all GPSS problems and causes control to revert to the computer operating system. Even if there is only one job, it is still necessary to use an END statement.

3-19

Controlling Runs When There Are Several Users

If the execution of the GPSS program is to be for a single job, whether it has multiple runs or not, the input must include a SIMULATE statement and must end with an END statement. A JOB statement should not be used. If more than one job is involved, at least one SIMULATE statement must appear, and a single END statement must be placed at the end of the input. (Multiple SIMULATE statements will be accepted.) The first job should not be preceded by a JOB statement, but all subsequent jobs should be immediately preceded by a JOB statement.

Whenever GPSS jobs are being submitted independently to a computer center by more than one user, it is advisable to establish the convention that all users precede their input by an initial JOB statement, even if it is only one job, and that nobody uses a SIMULATE or END statement. One individual is then made responsible for collecting all inputs, adding an initial SIMULATE statement and a final END statement, and converting the JOB statement of the first job into a comments statement.

Note that the program passes all jobs in the input stream through the assembly phase before attempting the execution of any of them. A SIMULATE statement anywhere in the input stream will signal the simulation mode. It is not possible, therefore, to mix simulation jobs with jobs that are to be assembled only.

3-20

Note Regarding Listings

Many examples of GPSS coding are shown throughout this book. The figures used are based on the listings produced as part of the program output when the input is in fixed format. Figure 3-2 is an example of how that output appears in its entirety. In all other listings shown in the book, the statement numbers appearing on the right are omitted. The location numbers, on the left, however, will be left in, although they are not part of the input but are placed there by the assembly program. The reason for retaining the numbers is that the assembled form of the listing and the cross-reference tables, of which Figs. 3-3 and 3-4 are examples, are being omitted. The numbers are needed, therefore, to provide a cross-reference to the block counts. If these examples are copied, the location numbers should not be included.

In addition, the listings in the text do not include any SIMULATE, JOB, or END statements. The user must decide for himself which of these statements are necessary, according to the rules given in the previous section.

3-21

Error Outputs

There are three types of error messages. Assembly errors are detected during assembly and cause the simulation to be canceled. Execution errors can occur during the running of the simulation, causing the run to be terminated. There are also warning messages that do not stop the run.

In the case of an assembly error, an error message appears in the input listing, immediately beneath the statement that is in error, briefly describing the error. An error number, or numbers, is given, and the *User's Manual* (41) lists the errors, by number. All input statements are examined, even when errors have been detected, so that as much checking as possible will be done with each loading. At the end of the input listing there will be a comment that the simulation was deleted because of the errors.

Figure 3-7 is an example of an unacceptable assembly. The first error, number 4, indicates that a location, LOC2, is undefined. The second, number 117, arises because a storage has been omitted in the ENTER block. The last, number 55, is the result of an incorrect format for the specification of a savevalue.

```
            EXP    FUNCTION    RN1,C24              INVERTED EXPONENTIAL FUNCTION
        0,0/.1,.104/.2,.222/.3,.355/.4,.509/.5,.69
        .6,.915/.7,1.2/.75,1.38/.8,1.6/.84,1.83/.88,2.12
        .9,2.3/.92,2.52/.94,2.81/.95,2.99/.96,3.2/.97,3.5
        .98,3.9/.99,4.6/.995,5.3/.998,6.2/.999,7/.9997,8
            *
            TYPE   FUNCTION    RN1,D5               DISTRIBUTION OF PART TYPES
        .1,1/.35,2/.57,3/.85,4/1.0,5
            *
            NORM   FUNCTION    RN1,C25              INVERTED STANDARD NORMAL FUNCTION
        0,-5/.00003,-4/.00135,-3/.00621,-2.5/.02275,-2/.06681,-1.5
        .11507,-1.2/.15866,-1/.21186,-.8/.27425,-.6/.34653,-.4/.42074,-.2
        .5,0/.57926,.2/.65542,.4/.72575,.6/.78814,.8/.84134,1/.88493,1.2
        .93319,1.5/.97725,2/.99379,2.5/.99865,3/.99997,4/1,5
            *
            BRCH   FUNCTION    PH1,L5               SEPARATES PARTS
        1,LOC1/2,LOC2/3,LOC3/4,LOC4/5,LOC5
ERROR       4 SYMBOL IN ABOVE STATEMENT CANNOT BE RESOLVED
            *
            *      SIMULATION OF SIMPLE MACHINE SHOP
            *
 1                 GENERATE    XH$ARR,FN$EXP        CREATE PARTS
 2                 ASSIGN      1,FN$TYPE,PH         PICK TYPE
 3                 QUEUE       WAIT                 JOIN QUEUE
 4                 ENTER
ERROR       117 OPERAND OMITTED WHICH MUST BE SPECIFIED
 5                 DEPART      WAIT                 LEAVE QUEUE
 6                 ADVANCE     V$TIME               MACHINE PART
 7                 LEAVE       MACH                 GIVE UP MACHINE
 8                 TABULATE    TRTM                 TABULATE TIME IN SYSTEM
 9                 TRANSFER    FN,BRCH              BRANCH BY TYPE
10          LOC1   SAVEVALUE   1+,1,XH              ADD 1 TO COUNT OF TYPE 1 PARTS
11                 TERMINATE   1                    DESTROY TRANSACTION
            *
12                 SAVEVALUE   2+,1,XH
13                 TERMINATE   1
            *
14          LOC3   SAVEVALUE   3+,1,HX
ERROR       55 C OPERAND OF SAVEVALUE BLOCK IS ILLEGAL
15                 TERMINATE   1
            *
16          LOC4   SAVEVALUE   4+,1,XH
17                 TERMINATE   1
            *
18          LOC5   SAVEVALUE   5+,1,XH
19                 TERMINATE   1
            *
            TIME   VARIABLE    20*FN$NORM+60        COMPUTES MACHINE TIME
                   STORAGE     S$MACH,3             NUMBER OF MACHINES
            TRTM   TABLE       M1,0,20,12           TABLE FOR TRANSIT TIME
                   INITIAL     XH$ARR,25            SET MEAN ARRIVAL TIME
            *
                   START       10,NP                INITIALIZE WITH 10 PARTS
                   RESET                            WIPE OUT STATISTICS
                   START       500                  RUN FOR 500 PARTS
```

Figure 3-7. Assembly error listing.

A major error during the execution of a run also prints a message with an error stop number. Again, the *User's Manual* lists the error by number. The program will print the standard output with the statistics updated to the time at which the error occurred. It also prints a listing of all the transactions that were in the system at the time the error occurred, separated into the different chains on which the transactions appear.

Figure 3-8 shows the error dump that occurs in the simple machine shop example when the storage at the LEAVE block has been given the wrong name. The first transaction that tries to enter the LEAVE block will be attempting to return space that was never taken and so cause error stop number 425.

First, the program prints an error message that identifies the transaction movement, or attempted movement, that caused the error, together with the clock time at which the error occurred. The normal block counts are given, followed by a print of all the transactions in the system as they appear on the chains. In this case only the future events and current events chains are in use.

The format for each transaction is the same, irrespective of the chain it is on. The output first shows a number for the transaction, which is an internal number, not available to the user. It is not a unique number, in the sense that, when a transaction leaves the system, its number may be reused. Two columns show where the transaction was located and where it was trying to move to. The time of the next move is shown under the heading "ADV BLK DEPART" for transactions on the future events chain. For other transactions, this time is the last time at which the transaction left an ADVANCE block. After giving the priority, which is zero for all transactions in this model, a column is shown with the *mark time*. This is initially the time at which the transaction entered the system. It may be reset by the MARK block, described in Sec. 8-7. The reference to an assembly set in the next column will not be understood until the SPLIT block is described in Sec. 13-2. Briefly, each transaction is a member of an assembly set containing at least itself. The SPLIT block increases the membership by creating copies of transactions. The members of a set are chained together through their transaction numbers. In this case, since they are all one-member sets, the number shown under the heading "ASSEM SET" is the transaction's own number.

There are then a series of flags that are reported as being set by putting an X in the appropriate column. The trace flag is set when a transaction enters a TRACE block and is reset when the transaction enters an UNTRACE block (see Sec. 15-1). While set, any movement of the transaction causes an output message to be printed. The delay flag is used in conjunction with the SIM mode of the TRANSFER block, which is explained in Sec. 12-7. The chain indicator shows which chain holds the transaction, with the following meanings:

ERROR   425 ATTEMPT TO LEAVE A STORAGE BY MORE THAN CURRENT CONTENTS

```
            *******************************************
            *                                         *
            *            ERROR DIAGNOSTICS            *
            *                                         *
            *******************************************
```

TRANS   1 FROM   6 TO   7 CLOCK   81 TERMINATIONS TO GO   10
BLOCK COUNTS
BLOCK CURRENT TOTAL   BLOCK CURRENT TOTAL   BLOCK CURRENT TOTAL
  1   0   3   11   0   0
  2   0   3   12   0   0
  3   0   3   13   0   0
  4   0   3   14   0   0
  5   0   3   15   0   0
  6   2   3   16   0   0
  7   0   0   17   0   0
  8   0   0   18   0   0
  9   0   0   19   0   0
 10   0   0

```
            *******************************************
            *                                         *
            *          CURRENT EVENTS CHAIN           *
            *                                         *
            *******************************************
```

*TRANS   CUR   NEXT   ADV BLK PRIORITY   MARK   ASSEM   SEL   TRACE   DELAY   CHAIN   PREEMPT
         BLOCK   BLOCK   DEPART   TIME   SET   CNT/FLA
   1   6   7   81   0   1   1   C

         HALFWORD PARAMETERS
           1   2   3   4   5   6   7   8   9   10
 1-10   2   0   0   0   0   0   0   0   0   0
 11-12   0   0

```
            *******************************************
            *                                         *
            *          FUTURE EVENTS CHAIN            *
            *                                         *
            *******************************************
```

*TRANS   CUR   NEXT   ADV BLK PRIORITY   MARK   ASSEM   SEL   TRACE   DELAY   CHAIN   PREEMPT
         BLOCK   BLOCK   DEPART   TIME   SET   CNT/FLA
   2   6   7   83   0   23   2   F

         HALFWORD PARAMETERS
           1   2   3   4   5   6   7   8   9   10
 1-10   2   0   0   0   0   0   0   0   0   0
 11-12   0   0
*TRANS   CUR   NEXT   ADV BLK PRIORITY   MARK   ASSEM   SEL   TRACE   DELAY   CHAIN   PREEMPT
         BLOCK   BLOCK   DEPART   TIME   SET   CNT/FLA
   4   1   99   0   -3   4   F

         HALFWORD PARAMETERS
           1   2   3   4   5   6   7   8   9   10
 1-10   0   0   0   0   0   0   0   0   0   0
 11-12   0   0
*TRANS   CUR   NEXT   ADV BLK PRIORITY   MARK   ASSEM   SEL   TRACE   DELAY   CHAIN   PREEMPT
         BLOCK   BLOCK   DEPART   TIME   SET   CNT/FLA
   3   6   7   123   0   43   3   F

         HALFWORD PARAMETERS
           1   2   3   4   5   6   7   8   9   10
 1-10   5   0   0   0   0   0   0   0   0   0
 11-12   0   0

Figure 3-8. Execution error listing.

C Current events   F Future events
U User chain   M Match
I   Interrupt   D Delay

As explained in Appendix 6, the transaction must be on one of the five chains other than a delay chain. Being on a delay chain implies being on the current events chain, in an inactive state.

If a transaction is on the current events chain but is not on a delay chain, it implies that either it has just joined the chain and has not yet been scanned or that it is delayed by one of the conditions mentioned in Sec. A6-5 of Appendix 6, for which the program is unable to make the transaction inactive. In the former case, the advance block depart time will be equal to the clock time. In the latter case, the column headed "SEL," for select, contains a B or A when the blocking occurs at a TRANSFER block with a BOTH or ALL selection mode. The column is otherwise blank.

Finally, two columns are used for transactions that have been preempted, that is, that have been interrupted in their use of a facility and are due to have the use returned to them. The column marked "COUNT" counts the number of preemptions in effect. The last column, headed "FLA," is used if the transaction was interrupted when it was not at an ADVANCE block. In that case the transaction is not suspended but can continue to move until it does enter an ADVANCE block, at which time it will be placed on the interrupt chain (see Sec. 7-6).

The values of the transactions' parameters are then listed in groups of ten. In this example, the transactions all have two halfword parameters, which was a selection made in the F field of the GENERATE block.

Transaction number 4, on the future events chain, is the next transaction to enter the system through the GENERATE block. Its current location is left blank and its next location is set to the number of the GENERATE block. The block statistics will not show its presence. Its mark time is also set negative, as a further indication that the transaction is unusual.

Section 8-15 describes a rate mode of gathering statistics, in which the program needs to keep measuring a uniform time interval. If this feature is being used, there will be a transaction in the system whose sole purpose is to measure the time interval. It will be transaction number 0, it will not have a block location, and the interval size is placed in the mark time field.

Following the error output, there is a listing of the rest of the standard output. This part of the output has not been reproduced in Fig. 3-8.

Note that the error listing given in Fig. 3-8 occurred during the first run of the simple machine shop example, which was for 10 terminations, and was scheduled to have the output suppressed by the NP in field A of the START card. In spite of this fact, the program still prints a full output report, including the standard output.

There are some error warning messages that occur under conditions that are not serious enough to stop the simulation. Some statistics, however, may be incorrect as a result of the condition. Most of these warnings, in fact, are

Sec. 3-21 / Error Outputs

concerned with fields of information overflowing their maximum limits. The messages are collected together and printed after the input listing, immediately preceding the statistical output. If there is a multiple occurrence of a warning condition, a message is created only on the first occurrence. Figure 3-9 is an example. In this case the warning is caused by the fact that a large number has been added to a halfword savevalue and caused an overflow.

```
WARNING - EXECUTION ERROR NUMBER 851.    BLOCK NUMBER    10, CLOCK    372.    SIMULATION
                                                                                CONTINUES

        RESET
        START       500

RELATIVE CLOCK         12547   ABSOLUTE CLOCK        12919
BLOCK COUNTS
BLOCK CURRENT TOTAL    BLOCK CURRENT TOTAL    BLOCK CURRENT TOTAL    BLOCK CURRENT TOTAL
  1      0     500     11      0      55
  2      0     500     12      0     129
  3      0     500     13      0     129
  4      0     500     14      0     123
  5      0     500     15      0     123
  6      2     500     16      0     124
  7      0     500     17      0     124
  8      0     500     18      0      69
  9      0     500     19      0      69
 10      0      55
```

Figure 3-9. Warning message.

3-22

Output Editor

The output described in Sec. 3-11 is the standard output produced without any specific request from the user. It is also possible to create an output report more suited to the particular requirements of the user, including the possibility of printing graphs. An output editor module produces written reports to the user's specifications, and a graphic output module, working in conjunction with the output editor module, produces the graphs.

A control statement with the word REPORT in the operation field is placed immediately after the last START statement of a job. Once an edited output is called for in this way, the normal output is suppressed, unless the user specifically calls for it, in its entirety, by including an output control statement with the word OUTPUT in the operation field. Also, normal output will replace the edited output in the event of an error condition. The edited output occurs for all runs within a job and will also appear on "snapped" outputs.

Figure 3-10 shows an example of the statements that follow the REPORT statement to produce an edited output. In this case, the example is for the output of the simple machine shop discussed in this chapter. Figure 3-11 shows the graphic portion of the output report that is produced when the

```
         REPORT
      10 TEXT         SIMPLE MACHINE SHOP EXAMPLE
         SPACE        4
         TEXT         NUMBER OF PARTS   #Q1,4/XXX#
         SPACE        2
   STO   TITLE        ,MACHINE GROUP STATISTICS
   STO   INCLUDE      S$MACH/1,2,3,5
         SPACE        2
   IISV  TITLE        ,NUMBER OF PARTS SENT TO
      10 FORMAT       1-5/XH1,XH2
         GRAPH        TP,TRTM
         ORIGIN       50,10
         X            ,4,4,20,1,9
         Y            0,5,8,5
      22 STATEMENT    6,36,DISTRIBUTION OF TIME
      13 STATEMENT    23,8,PER CENT
      13 STATEMENT    25,2,OF
      13 STATEMENT    27,5,PARTS
      29 STATEMENT    54,20,TRANSIT TIME (SECS.)
         ENDGRAPH
```

Figure 3-10. Output editor statements.

output report statements of Fig. 3-10 are used with exactly the same run that produced the normal output report shown in Fig. 3-5. The capabilities of the output editor will be described in terms of this example. A full description of the output editor appears in Chap. 23 of the *User's Manual* (41); included are many detailed tables (not repeated here) which describe all the GPSS data items that can form part of the output and the symbols by which they are denoted in the output editor.

The simplest form of editing consists of writing lines of text with a TEXT statement. The text begins in the column given in the location field. It can be a simple comment, like the first TEXT statement of Fig. 3-10 or it can include items of data selected from almost any field of the normal output report. Normal comments statements are also acceptable. The TEXT statements and the comments statements, as used in the output report, will allow the text to be extended to a second statement, up to a total of 132 print positions, by putting a nonblank character in column 72 to signify the continuation. To improve the appearance of the output, a SPACE statement will skip the number of lines shown in field A, and an EJECT statement will advance to a new page.

The normal blocks of output data for each type of entity can be edited. The simplest form of editing is to put a title over the statistics by using a TITLE statement. The location field selects the entity type, and field A can give the number, or name, of a single member of that entity group which is to be printed. If the A field is blank, all members are printed, unless the INCLUDE statement, described next, selects otherwise. Field B has the title to be printed. As with a TEXT statement, the text can be continued in a second statement, except that the limit is for 124 positions.

The INCLUDE statement selects only those members and those columns of statistics that the user wants. The location field indicates the type of entity, and the A field gives a single entity number or a range of numbers. The fields following the A field identify the columns of the output statistics

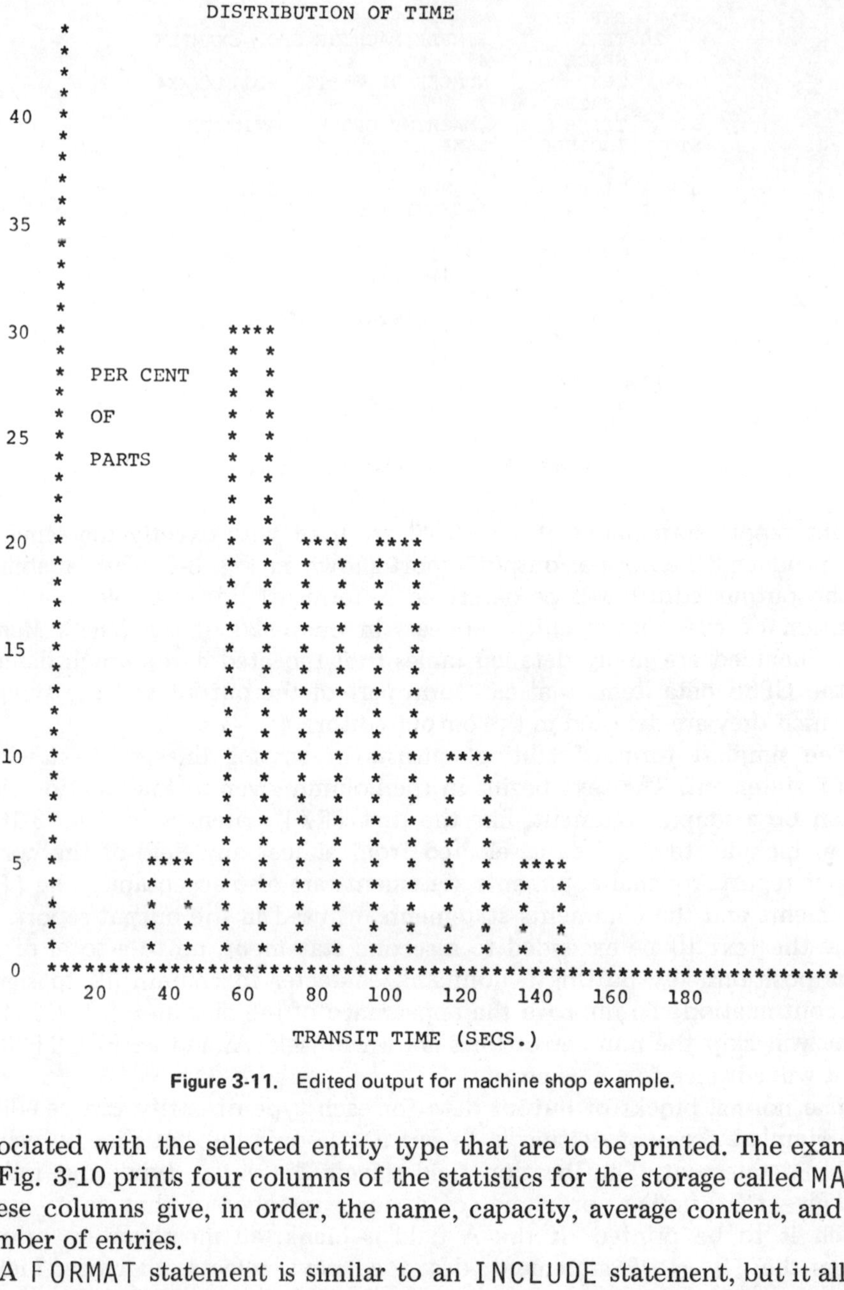

Figure 3-11. Edited output for machine shop example.

associated with the selected entity type that are to be printed. The example in Fig. 3-10 prints four columns of the statistics for the storage called MACH. These columns give, in order, the name, capacity, average content, and the number of entries.

A FORMAT statement is similar to an INCLUDE statement, but it allows statistics for different types of entities to be combined in a table. A range of entity numbers is given in field A, and the following fields list the columns of statistics to be printed. In the example of Fig. 3-10, the request is for the number and contents of halfword savevalues numbers 1 through 5. If there had been a separate queue for each type of part, the average number in each queue could have been added by putting Q3 in field D, and so on.

The location field specifies the position of the first print column.

A request for a graph is made with the following six types of statements:

        GRAPH
        ORIGIN
        X
        Y
        STATEMENT
        ENDGRAPH

The GRAPH statement identifies, in field A, the type of statistic to be printed. Fields B and C normally give the upper and lower limits of the numbers of that type of entity to be printed. For example, GRAPH FR,1,10 will plot the utilization for facilities 1 through 10. Each utilization would appear as a bar spaced along a horizontal axis. In the case of plotting data from the GPSS tables, the B field gives the table number, or name, and the C field is left blank. The D field can then specify the character to be used in the printing of the graph. The default value is an asterisk. The example of Figs. 3-10 and 3-11 plots the "percent of total" field of the table, called TRTM.

The graph must be regarded as appearing in a matrix of 60 rows and 132 columns, where the 60 rows are the lines of a normal printer output page, and the 132 columns are the print positions. The rows, or lines, however, are counted from the *top* of the page. The columns are read in the normal left to right order. The ORIGIN statement specifies the origin by giving its X and Y location in this matrix as the A and B fields, respectively. For example, ORIGIN   55,10 puts the origin 55 lines from the top of the page (5 lines from the bottom), and at the tenth column from the left-hand side of the page.

The X statement has two forms. The one shown in Fig. 3-10 is for use with table statistics. The A field is then blank. The B field specifies the width of the bar for each plotted item, including the end points, and the C field is the spacing between bars. The D field is the upper limit of the lowest frequency class to be plotted. If desired, a number of consecutive frequency classes can be merged. The number to be merged into one output bar is given in field E, which defaults to 1 if left blank. The F field is the number of increments to be plotted. The numeric values of the plotted frequency classes are printed along the x-axis, unless they are suppressed by a NO in field G.

For entities other than tables, the A field can contain the word SYM, in which case the symbolic names of the entities being plotted will appear along the x-axis. A blank will result in their only being numbered. Fields D, E, and F are not used. The other fields, B, C, and G, have the same meaning as for use with tables.

The Y statement controls the vertical scale. Field A specifies the lower limit for the y-axis label. Field B specifies the size of the increments to be used, and the C field is the number of increments. Field D specifies how many lines are to be given to each increment. The Y statement of Fig. 3-10, for example, labels the y-axis origin with 0, and marks a scale in steps of 5 for 8 increments, to an upper limit of 40. Each increment is assigned 5 lines.

Any number of STATEMENT statements may be included to insert text on the graph. The location field specifies the line. Fields A and B give the starting column and number of characters, respectively; field C has the text. A continuation statement can be used by putting a nonblank character in column 72. The STATEMENT statements must be in order of increasing row number. The set of statements relating to one graph are ended with an ENDGRAPH statement; many different graphs can be specified. Each definition must follow the format just described, and in each case the individual types of statements within the definition must follow the order given.

4
CREATING AND MOVING TRANSACTIONS

In this chapter we discuss four block types that are concerned with creating, moving, and destroying transactions, where movement refers either to advancing time or to selecting a path to be followed by the transaction. The GENERATE and TERMINATE blocks are the principal blocks used to create and destroy transactions. The ADVANCE block moves transactions through time, and the TRANSFER block is the principal block for selecting a path.

Figure 4-1 shows the block diagram symbols for these four block types. Letters in the symbols correspond to the operand fields. The dotted line for the flag of the GENERATE block symbol indicates that this flag is usually omitted if fields C to I of the block are not used, which is frequently the case. In this, and other block diagram symbols, flags are often placed on the left-hand side for convenience in drawing the block diagrams.

4-1
Action Times

The GENERATE and ADVANCE blocks are the only ones that specifically invoke the expenditure of time, although a transaction can be delayed anywhere in the block diagram and be forced to wait for a change of system conditions. Each appearance of a transaction in a GENERATE or ADVANCE

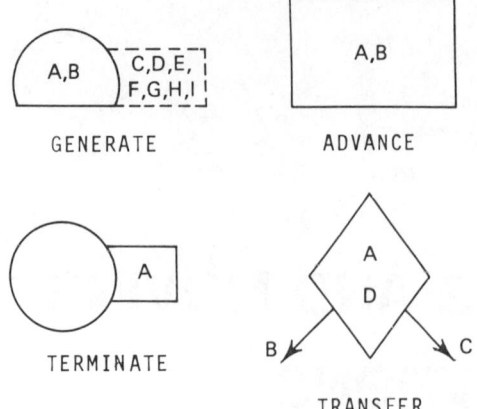

Figure 4-1. Block types 1.

block results in the calculation of an action time to determine how long the transaction will stay at the block before attempting to leave. For an ADVANCE block the calculation is made at the time the transaction enters the block. In the case of the GENERATE block, no transaction already in the block diagram is allowed to enter the block. An error stop will occur if such an attempt is made. Instead, the GENERATE block creates a series of transactions and enters them into the block diagram. The action time is used to compute the interval between successive arrivals.

The action time in both the ADVANCE and GENERATE blocks is determined by fields A and B. Field A gives the mean value. Field B, called either a *spread* or a *modifier*, produces a random variation about the mean. If field B is a constant, less than or equal to the mean, it is called a spread, and the action time is computed to be any integer in the range of the mean plus or minus the spread, with equal probability being given to each number in the range. For example, the values A = 5, B = 3 will produce one of the numbers 2, 3, 4, 5, 6, 7, or 8, each number having a probability of $\frac{1}{7}$. If the spread is 0 or field B blank, the action time is a constant equal to the mean. The mean may also be 0, making the action time identically zero.

The uniform distribution of time produced by using a mean and spread is sometimes an appropriate representation of a random action time. However, the principal purpose of representing a random time this way is to provide a quick way of computing an action time when it is known to be random but no information is immediately available about the distribution. The construction and testing of the logic of a model can proceed while data are being gathered. Frequently, early tests with the simplified model will indicate what data are likely to be of critical importance and to what degree of accuracy they should be collected. We will frequently use the notation A ± B to indicate an action time calculated from a mean and spread; thus, the notation 5 ± 3 describes the numerical example just calculated.

It is possible to introduce functions in field B of an ADVANCE or GENERATE block. The field is then said to be a *modifier*. The functions are, in fact, tables of values, approximating functions by a series of straight line segments. The action time is calculated by evaluating the function and *multiplying* the result by the mean in field A. If field A is left blank, the value 1 is assumed, so that the function value becomes the action time. It is often useful, however, to use the same function with different means in different parts of the block diagram, particularly when using the exponential distribution.

The input to a function can be a uniformly distributed random number, in which case any desired probability distribution can be approximated, using the technique to be described in Sec. 9-1. The function input may also depend upon some system attribute, so that the function introduces a relationship between the action time and the state of the system. Functions will be fully described in Chap. 9.

Function values are kept in floating-point form so they can be nonintegral values. When they are used to compute action times, the multiplication by the mean is carried out in floating-point form. Since all action times must be integral, the result is *truncated* to an integer. Truncation means that the fractional part is dropped, as opposed to being rounded to the nearest integer. For example, if the result of multiplying the function value by the mean is 79.98, the value given to the action time will be 79.

4-2

GENERATE Blocks

GENERATE blocks create transactions and enter them into the block diagram. They therefore simulate the arrival of entities into the system. There can be many GENERATE blocks in a diagram, and they operate independently of each other.

An initial transaction is created for each GENERATE block as the model is loaded. As a result, only certain SNAs may be used at a GENERATE block (see Sec. 11-5). In addition, if a GENERATE block refers to a function, the function must have been defined ahead of the GENERATE block. The action time for the initial transaction usually becomes the time that transaction is to leave the GENERATE block that created it. However, if the time for the first transaction should be zero, it is arbitrarily set to 1 in order to get the clock moving. Any subsequent calculation of a zero time is not altered; it merely represents the generation of two transactions simultaneously.

When the first transaction leaves, a second action time is calculated. The result is added to the current clock time at the time of creation (i.e., the time of the previous departure), and the second transaction attempts to leave at that time. The creation process continues this way.

The time between arrivals, therefore, is normally controlled by the A and B fields of the GENERATE block. However, there can be only one transaction at a time in a GENERATE block. Should a transaction be unable to leave at its appointed departure time, the creation of its successor, and the calculation of its departure time, is delayed until the blocked transaction leaves. If the GENERATE block is to represent an exogenous source, which supplies transactions without regard to conditions within the system, it is important to ensure that it leads to a block that cannot cause blocking. An ADVANCE block with zero time is sometimes placed at the exit of a GENERATE block to ensure that this condition occurs. An example will be given in Sec. 5-4. However, most block types will accept any transaction at any time, and it is not usually necessary to introduce such a buffer block.

It is permissible for the mean and modifier of the GENERATE block to be both zero, in which case the block will attempt to generate a continuous stream of transactions at the same clock time. It is then essential to have some block at the exit of the GENERATE block which deliberately causes a blocking condition in order to control the flow. By imposing and removing the blocking condition (for example, by turning a logic switch on and off), it is then possible to enter batches of transactions into the system.

In addition to the fact that an initially computed first action time of 0 is automatically offset to 1, it is possible to offset the arrival of the first transaction deliberately. If field C is not blank, its content is interpreted as an offset time at which the first transaction is due to leave. It overrides the computation of the action time for the first transaction; thereafter, the normal process is used.

Field D can be used to control the number of transactions created at a GENERATE block. If it is left blank, there is no limit and the block will continue to create transactions as long as the simulation runs. If it contains a positive integer value, the GENERATE block will play no further part in the simulation run after it has created that number of transactions. A CLEAR control statement, used to prepare a second run of a model (see Sec. 3-16) will restore the count to its initial value, whether it was expended or not. It also re-creates the initial transactions at all GENERATE blocks.

Transactions can have priority. If field E is blank, the priority of the newly created transactions is 0, which is the lowest level; otherwise the priority takes the level indicated in field E, up to level 127, which is the highest. A mark time, which is used to measure how long the transaction has been in the system, is initially set to the time the transaction is due to leave the GENERATE block (i.e., to enter the system) irrespective of whether the transaction actually manages to leave at that time. The use of the mark time is explained in Chap. 8.

Transactions also carry a number of parameters which are words of data representing attributes of the transactions. All parameter values are initially set to zero. They can exist in four different forms. The four types, with the labels used to indicate them, are as follows:

(a) Fullword   PF
(b) Halfword   PH
(c) Byte size   PB
(d) Floating-point   PL

Fullword, halfword, and byte-sized parameters take positive or negative integral values. The range of values are $\pm 2^{31} - 1$ for fullword size; $\pm 2^{15} - 1$ for halfword size; and $\pm 2^7 - 1$ for byte-size. The magnitudes of the three numbers are, respectively, 2,147,483,647; 32,767; and 127. Floating-point parameters are nonintegral numbers in the range $\pm 2^{24} - 1$ (1,677,215), without loss of precision, and beyond that range with varying degrees of lost precision.

Fields F through I of the GENERATE block are used to select the number of each type of parameter for the transactions generated at that block. Individual specifications can be made at each block. Up to 255 of each type of parameter can be specified, to give a possible maximum of 1020 parameters. The desired number for each type, followed immediately by the label for the type, is placed in one of the fields F through I. The order is irrelevant but the fields must be filled from F on, with no blanks. If no reference is made to one or more of the types, no parameters of that type will be created, except that if all fields are left blank, the program will, by default, create transactions with 12 halfword parameters. If no parameters at all are wanted, field F should be used to indicate zero for any one type, for example, by using 0PF.

The following are some examples of GENERATE block specifications using the parameter fields:

```
GENERATE    5,4,100,1000,15,10PF,10PH,10PB,10PL
GENERATE    5,4,,,,0PF
GENERATE    5,4,,,,10PH,6PB
GENERATE    5,4,,,,6PB,10PH
GENERATE    5,4
```

All these examples will produce transactions with interarrival times of 5 ± 4, since fields A and B are all 5 and 4, respectively. The first example uses all the fields of the GENERATE block. In addition to specifying the action time in fields A and B, it specifies that the first transaction will appear at time 100 (field C), that there will be a limit of 1000 on the number of transactions created (field D), and that the priority of the transactions will be 15 (field E). Fields F through I specify that there will be 10 of each type of parameter. In contrast, the second example gives the simplest form of transaction. It has no parameters of any type, it has zero priority, and the creation begins from time zero, as occurs in the subsequent examples. The third and fourth examples both create transactions with 10 halfword parameters and 6 byte-sized parameters; demonstrating that the order of specification is irrelevant. The last example, by default, creates transactions with 12 halfword parameters.

Most of the examples used in this book will follow the last example and use transactions with 12 halfword parameters. Unless more parameters are needed, or the other formats are needed, it is customary to use these default values. Sometimes, with large models, it is important to save space, and the parameters may then be kept to their minimum number. The size of the transactions does not affect the execution time of the program.

The next transaction to arrive at an active GENERATE block is always present within the program. However, since its arrival time is usually ahead of the current clock time, special arrangements are made for certain statistics. Until its time of arrival, a transaction is not considered to be at any block, and it will be listed this way in any system printout. In addition, the block count at a GENERATE block will not register the presence of a transaction until its arrival. Usually a transaction is created at a GENERATE block and immediately leaves. The total count is incremented by 1 and the current count stays zero. If the current count shows a count of 1, it means a transaction has been created at the block and is unable to leave. The current count cannot be more than 1 because of the rule that not more than one transaction can be in a given GENERATE block at one time.

4-3
TERMINATE Blocks

A transaction is destroyed and removed from the simulation as soon as it enters a TERMINATE block. A *termination counter* is maintained by the program to count terminations and so control the length of the simulation run. If field A of the TERMINATE block is blank, the termination counter is not incremented. Such blocks are used to represent points of departure that are not of prime interest to the user. If field A contains a positive integer, frequently 1, that value is added to the counter. There must be at least one such block in the diagram. When the termination counter equals or first exceeds the value supplied by the A field of the START statement controlling the run, the run will be terminated. The termination count also controls the printing of snaps (see Sec. 3-13).

If it is required that the simulation run finish at a specific clock time, the usual way to achieve this is to include a GENERATE block that creates a single transaction at that time and sends it immediately to a TERMINATE block with field A set to 1. No other TERMINATE block in the model uses field A and the START statement has 1 in field A. The creation of that one transaction will then stop the simulation at the desired time.

4-4
ADVANCE Blocks

ADVANCE blocks are used to represent the expenditure of time. An action time is computed from fields A and B for each transaction entering the block. The transaction remains at the block for that length of time before attempting to leave. If it is unable to leave at that time, it will remain at the block until conditions allow it to leave. Its presence at the block will not interfere with other transactions that enter the block. This rule that transactions can stay blocked without interfering with other transactions passing through the block is valid for all block types, except the GENERATE block, where the blocking of one transaction holds up all successors.

An ADVANCE block never refuses entry to a transaction, and there can be many transactions at the block simultaneously. Even in the absence of blocking, which might hold back some transactions, the transactions do not necessarily leave in the order in which they arrive because the action time of a later transaction can be shorter than a preceding transaction, leading to an earlier departure.

4-5
TRANSFER Blocks

The TRANSFER block is designed to allow a transaction to select among alternative paths. There are nine selection rules for deciding upon the choice. Field A contains a *selection factor* to determine the rule. Table 4-1 lists the rules and shows the selection factor to be used for each choice. At this point only two of the rules will be described. The table indicates where the description of the others will be given.

Table 4-1   Transfer Modes

Mode	Selection factor	Described in Sec.
Unconditional	blank	4-6
Fractional	.xxx	4-7
Conditional	BOTH	5-10
Pick	PICK	5-13
All	ALL	5-13
Function	FN	9-10
Parameter	Px	10-11
Subroutine	SBR	10-12
Simultaneous	SIM	12-7

4-6
Unconditional Mode of TRANSFER Block

Transactions normally move from one block to the block with the next highest number. There are, however, many occasions when this sequential order needs to be altered. Transactions moving along different segments of blocks may need to be merged into a common stream. Frequently, sections of coding are written at different times or by different people, and they need to be linked together.

To allow for these circumstances, one selection mode, called the *unconditional mode*, transfers all transactions that enter the block to the location given in field B. To use this mode, field A is left blank, so the operations field begins with a comma to indicate the blank A field, followed by the transfer location. For example, the following block sends all transactions to the location called EXIT:

        TRANSFER   ,EXIT

4-7

Fractional Mode of TRANSFER Block

Another frequent requirement is to divide transactions randomly between two paths. A certain fraction is sent one way, the remainder the other way—the choice for an individual transaction being made randomly. The selection factor for this mode is a decimal fraction of up to three digits, with the decimal point included. The choice is between the locations given in fields B and C, which will often be called exits 1 and 2, respectively. If S is the value in field A, a fraction S of the transactions goes to the location given in field C (exit 2), and the remaining fraction $1 - S$, goes to the location given in field B (exit 1). (This choice of order in the definition is intended to be consistent with the fact that, if S is zero, the A field is zero, which indicates the unconditional mode; all transactions then go to the location in field B, and none goes to the location in field C.) As an example, the following block sends one eighth of the transactions to location BBB, and the other seven eighths to AAA:

        TRANSFER   .125,AAA,BBB

It will frequently occur that the next sequential block is one of the choices. If the B field is left blank, the program will assume that the next sequential block is intended for exit 1. For example, the following block sends one eighth of the transactions to location BBB, and the other seven eighths to the ADVANCE block that follows the TRANSFER block:

        TRANSFER   .125,,BBB
        ADVANCE

If it happens that it is more convenient for the section labeled BBB to follow the TRANSFER block immediately and have the section AAA as the remote section, the selection factor value can be redefined. For example, the following arrangement will still send seven eighths of the transactions to AAA, but the segment labeled AAA is not the segment following the TRANSFER block:

```
TRANSFER    .875,,AAA
ADVANCE
```

If the block to which the transaction is to go cannot be entered, the blocked transaction remains at the TRANSFER block until it can go. The choice is not recomputed.

When drawing block diagrams, we usually assume that the exit to the left is exit 1. It is not always convenient to draw the diagram that way, in which case the exits must be marked with a 1 or 2.

4-8
Traffic System Example

To illustrate the use of the four block types that have been described, a series of models will be given. They represent the flow of traffic through a network of streets. For simplicity, the streets are considered to be one-way. Each vehicle will be represented by a transaction, and a time unit of 1 second is chosen.

Suppose, first, that we wish to represent the flow of traffic down a single street. Figure 4-2 shows a block diagram for the model. A GENERATE block creates transactions with the mean and spread determining the interarrival times. Suppose that a vehicle arrives on the average every 10 seconds and that the variation in interarrival time can be represented by a spread of 8 seconds. Then the GENERATE block has field A set to 10 and field B set to 8. The transactions pass to an ADVANCE block where the action time represents the time to pass down the street. The time used here is a mean of 20 seconds and a spread of 5 seconds. In this simple model, there is no further interest in the movement of the vehicles, so the transactions go to a

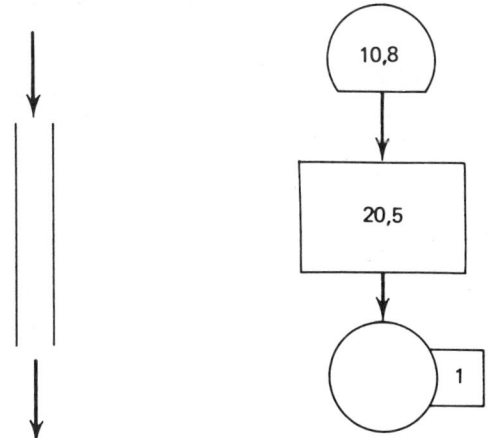

Figure 4-2. Traffic system 1.

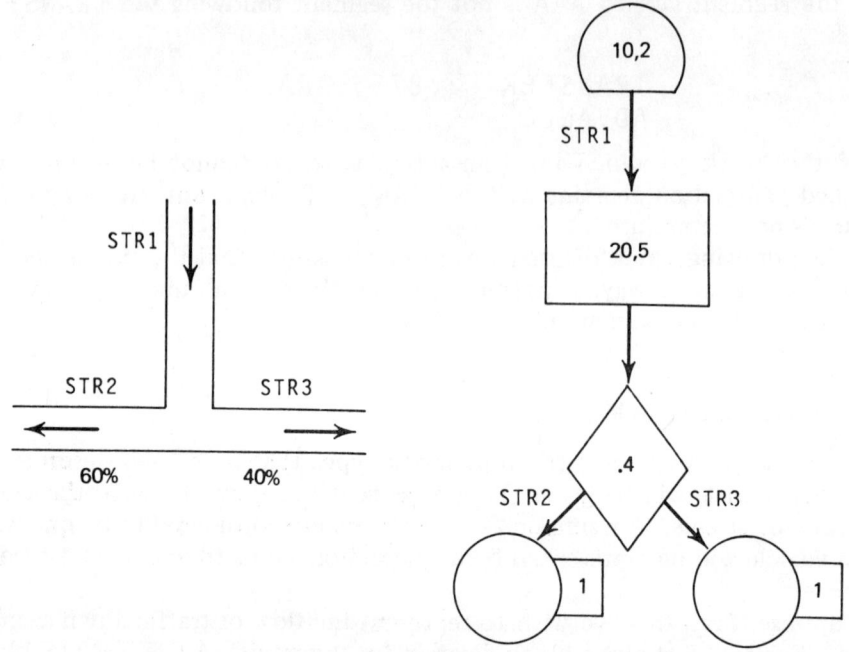

Figure 4-3. Traffic system 2.

TERMINATE block. Field A of the block is set to 1, so the termination counter will be incremented by one for each termination.

Next, suppose that the street leads to a T-junction at which each vehicle must turn left or right, and suppose that 40 percent turn left. The system and its model are shown in Fig. 4-3. A TRANSFER block, using a fractional mode, has been added, and there are now two TERMINATE blocks. The model simulates the traffic turning at the TRANSFER block into one of two streets, but it does not follow the movement of the traffic along these streets. The

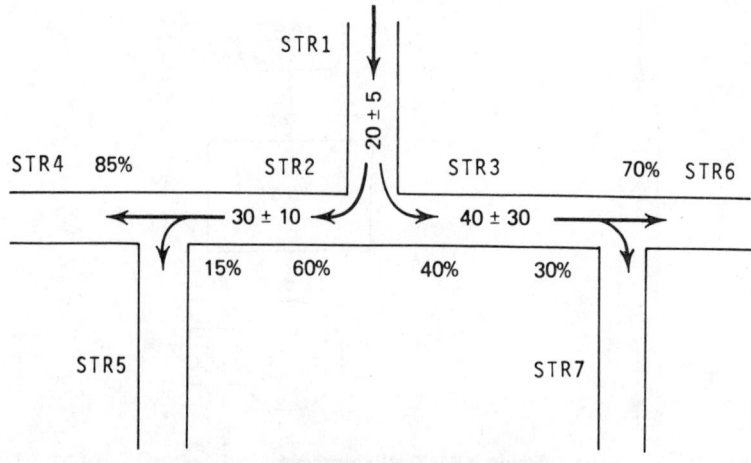

Figure 4-4. Traffic system 3.

two TERMINATE blocks are labeled STR2 and STR3, while the ADVANCE block, representing the original street, has been labeled STR1. The selection factor at the TRANSFER block is set to .4, so that 40 percent of the traffic goes to exit 2, which is the TERMINATE block labeled STR3, and 60 percent go to the TERMINATE block labeled STR2.

The model can be extended to simulate the movement of the traffic down streets 2 and 3, and on to further branch points. Figure 4-4 illustrates a network of seven streets, which have been labeled STR1, STR2, and so on. The times taken to move down the streets are marked in the figure; so also are the percentages of traffic that turn in each direction at the junctions. As before, traffic is generated at an interarrival time of 10 ± 8. Figure 4-5

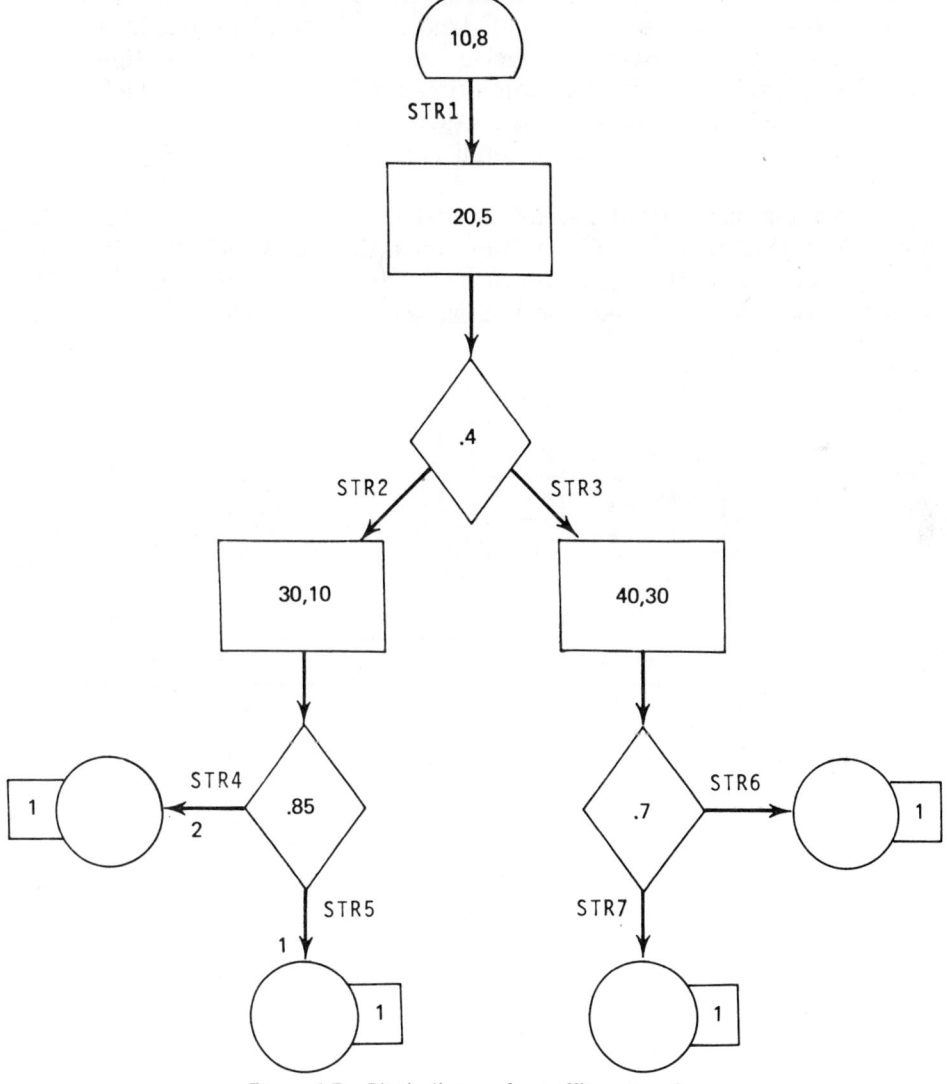

Figure 4-5. Block diagram for traffic system 3.

71

shows a block diagram for this system.

Suppose now that street 5 joins street 7 and leads into street 8. Also suppose that there is a factory on street 1 which closes 1000 seconds after the simulation starts, and lets a total of 85 cars into the street, at the rate of one every 10 ± 5 seconds. Figure 4-6 illustrates the system, and Fig. 4-7 shows a block diagram. Traffic leaves the system by entering streets 4, 6, or 8, so these streets are represented by TERMINATE blocks. The other streets are represented by ADVANCE blocks. Only the TERMINATE block for street 8 has a 1 in field A—the rest are blank—so the simulation run length will be controlled by the number of vehicles leaving by way of street 8. The previous models counted the traffic at all exits.

A second GENERATE block has been added to represent the factory. It has an offset time of 1000 in field C, and a limit of 85 in field D. The first transaction, representing a car leaving the factory, does so at time 1000; the other 84 will leave with separation time intervals of 10 ± 5. A TRANSFER block in an unconditional mode is needed to merge the factory traffic with the traffic of street 1. Another unconditional TRANSFER block joins streets 7 and 8.

The coding and output for this model are shown in Fig. 4-8. The only output for this simple model is the clock time at which the simulation finished and the block counts. Since there was only one run and no RESET control statement was used, the relative and absolute clocks times are the same (see Sec. 3-15).

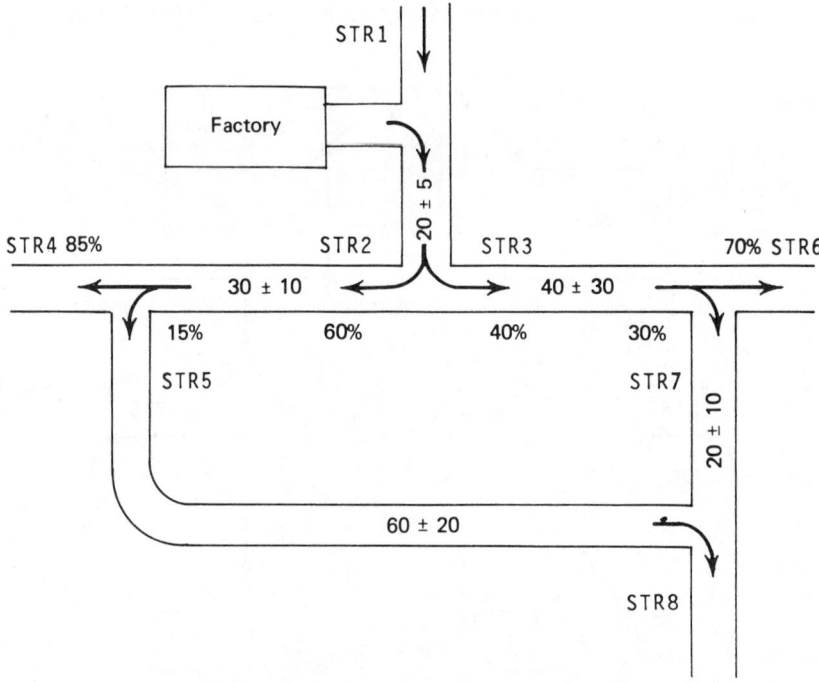

Figure 4-6. Traffic system 4.

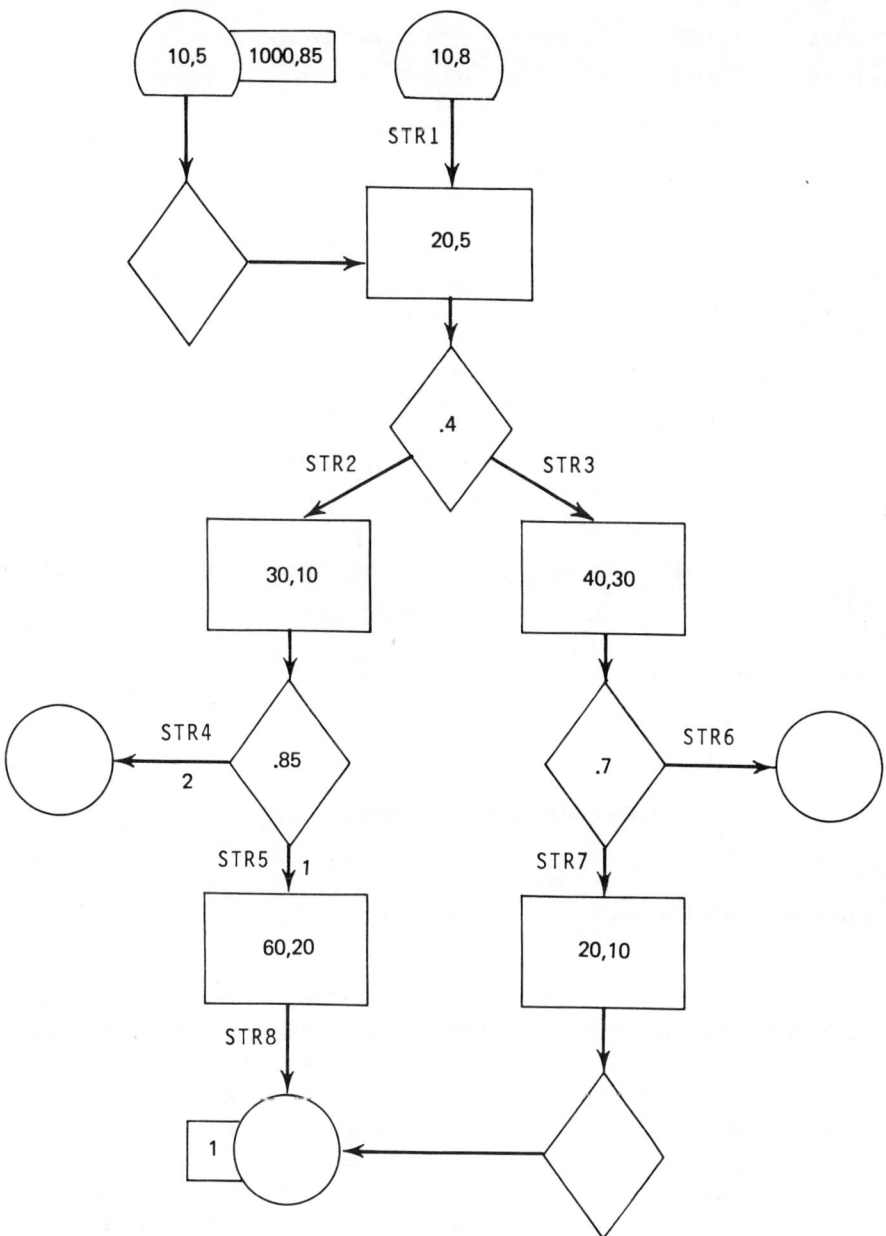

Figure 4-7. Block diagram for traffic system 4.

```
            *         MODEL OF TRAFFIC SYSTEM - 4
            *
 1                    GENERATE     10,8            CREATE STREET TRAFFIC
 2          STR1      ADVANCE      20,5            STREET NO 1
 3                    TRANSFER     .4,,STR3
 4                    ADVANCE      30,10           STREET NO 2
 5                    TRANSFER     .85,,STR4
 6                    ADVANCE      60,20           STREET NO 5
 7          STR8      TERMINATE    1               EXIT BY STREET NO 8
            *
 8          STR3      ADVANCE      40,30           STREET NO 3
 9                    TRANSFER     .7,,STR6
10                    ADVANCE      20,10           STREET NO 7
11                    TRANSFER     ,STR8
            *
12          STR4      TERMINATE                    STREET NO 4
13          STR6      TERMINATE                    STREET NO 6
            *
            *         FACTORY TRAFFIC
14                    GENERATE     10,5,1000,85    CREATE 85 CARS AT 1000
15                    TRANSFER     ,STR1
            *
                      START        1000            RUN FOR 1000 TERMINATIONS AT STR8


RELATIVE CLOCK          44561   ABSOLUTE CLOCK        44561
BLOCK COUNTS
BLOCK  CURRENT  TOTAL   BLOCK  CURRENT  TOTAL   BLOCK  CURRENT  TOTAL   BLOCK  CURRENT  TOTAL
  1       0     4447     11       0     574
  2       4     4532     12       0     2253
  3       0     4528     13       0     1271
  4       1     2682     14       0     85
  5       0     2681     15       0     85
  6       2      428
  7       0     1000
  8       1     1846
  9       0     1845
 10       0      574
```

Figure 4-8. Output for traffic system 4.

4-9
Analysis of Block Counts

Analysis of the block count figures shows where the transactions went and provides valuable information in checking the validity of the model. Figure 4-9 reproduces the block diagram of Fig. 4-7, without including the coding details in the blocks. Instead, each block shows, at the top, the number assigned to the block, derived from the output of Fig. 4-8. The block counts from the output have been transferred to the figure. In the center of each block is the total number of transactions that entered the block, and at the bottom is the current count, that is, the number present at the end of the run.

The current count will show if transactions have accumulated at any point in the diagram. A large current count could indicate a block diagram error that is preventing transactions from flowing as planned, or it could point out a bad feature of the system design that is causing congestion. In the present case, the current counts indicate that, at the end of the run, there was one

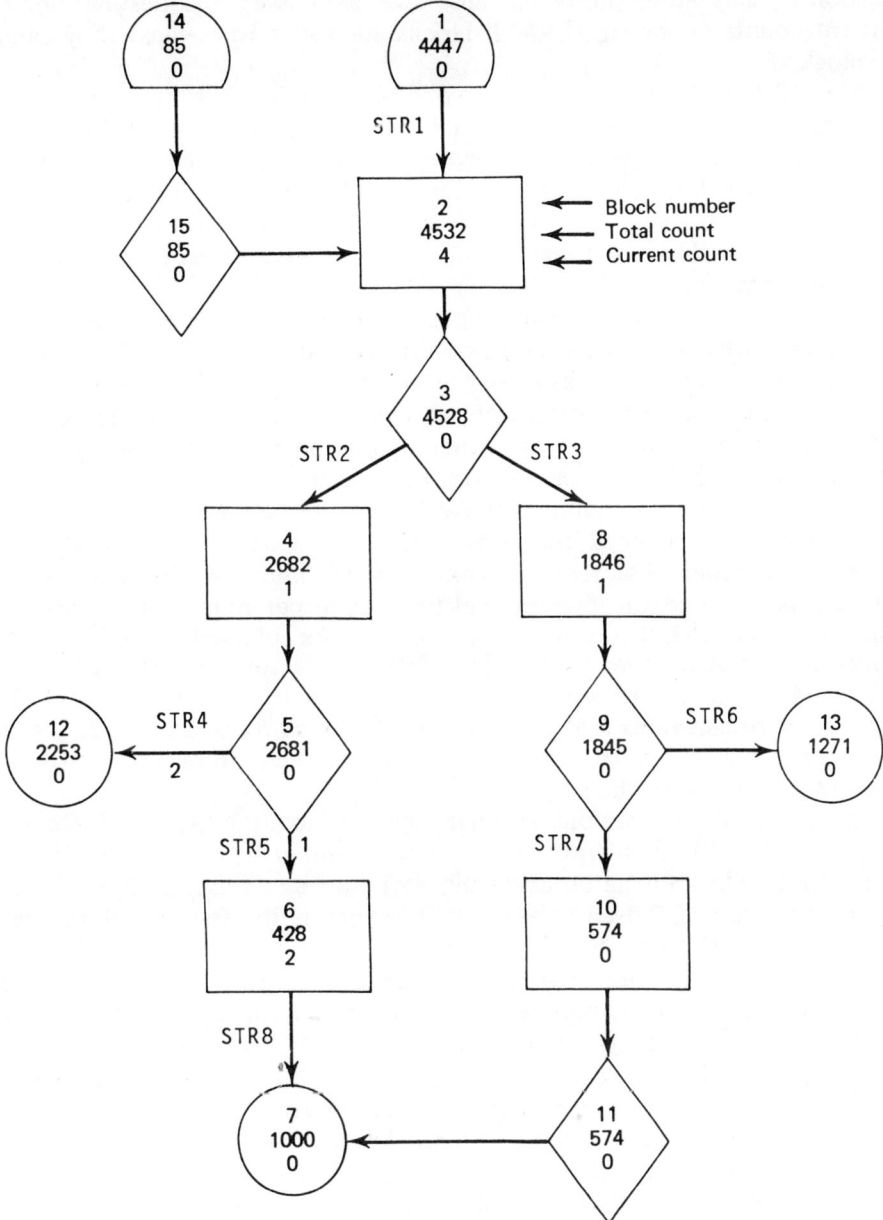

Figure 4-9. Block counts in traffic system 4.

vehicle in each of streets 2 and 3, there were two vehicles in street 5, and 4 in street 1. The other streets were empty. The current counts at the TERMINATE blocks are all zero, as they always will be because transactions are removed as soon as they enter the block. The current counts at the TRANSFER blocks are also zero because nothing can block the exits, and transactions will leave

Sec. 4-9 / Analysis of Block Counts

as soon as they enter the blocks and have been assigned a destination. The current counts at the GENERATE blocks are also zero because they cannot be blocked.

The ADVANCE block is the only one that requires a transaction to spend some time at the block. There, the current count could reflect either transactions that are not yet due to leave the block or transactions that cannot leave. At all other block types, a nonzero block count means that transactions are unable to leave. The user should check all these nonzero counts to see whether they are consistent with system conditions or whether they represent errors in model building.

A common type of programming error is to allow a transaction to leave the system without resetting some potential blocking condition—for example, not releasing a facility it has seized or not returning storage it has occupied. As a result, transactions accumulate at some point. Often the accumulation gets so large that the program limit on the number of simultaneous transactions is reached, and a program error stop occurs.

The total transaction count indicates what direction the transactions took. They should be checked for consistency. For example, the total at the GENERATE block that represents the factory, block 14, shows 85 vehicles left the factory; so the factory had finished dispatching vehicles when the simulation finished. The other GENERATE block, block 1, shows that 4447 vehicles came into street 1, other than from the factory. The sum of the two counts, 4532, is the total count at block 2, which represents street 1. The number of transactions that entered block 3, which follows block 2, is 4528, which is consistent with the fact that four vehicles were left in street 1, block 2, at the end of the run.

The flow of transactions through the fractional TRANSFER blocks is summarized in Table 4-2, which shows the number of transactions that entered the blocks and the numbers that left by way of exit 2. The table also shows the value of S used at each block, which is the fraction of the transactions expected to go to exit 2. The actual fractions that went that way have been calculated and entered in the table. It can be seen that there is reasonably good agreement between the actual values and the expected values.

Checks of this nature should always be made because a common programming error is to reverse the exit 1 and exit 2 fields of the TRANSFER block. Because of the stochastic nature of the fractional mode, the actual fraction of transactions that go to exit 2 is unlikely to be exactly the expected value, but it should be reasonably close. Wide differences are cause for suspicion. Any block with a total count of zero should also be checked. It could be a block in a rarely used part of the system, but, particularly when there is a string of such blocks, it could mean that some model error is preventing transactions from reaching that part of the model.

The CLEAR and RESET control statements that were described in Secs. 3-15 and 3-16 affect the block counts. The CLEAR statement wipes out all counts and all transactions. The RESET statement wipes out only the total

Table 4-2 Checking the Flow of Transactions Through TRANSFER Blocks

Block number	Exit 2	Expected	Total count	Exit 2 count	Actual
3	8	0.4	4528	1846	0.41
5	12	0.85	2681	2253	0.80
9	13	0.7	1845	1271	0.79

counts and leaves transactions. This can cause an apparent anomaly in the run following the RESET statement. Transactions remaining in the block diagram will contribute to the total counts of blocks they enter but, because the total counts were wiped out, they do not appear in the total count of the block they occupied at the time the second run started. The total counts in that run, therefore, may not balance.

4-10
Standard Numerical Attributes

It was mentioned in Sec. 3-5 that the program makes available certain items of data about the system so the user can collect data or control conditions in the system, based on these values. Collectively, these items of data are called *standard numerical attributes*, abbreviated SNAs. Most of them are positive or negative integers. Some of them are Boolean variables, which only take one of the two values 0 or 1. For example, the state of a facility as being busy or not busy is represented by an SNA that is Boolean.

A fuller discussion of SNAs will be given in Chap. 11. However, as the various entities of GPSS are described, the SNAs associated with them will be defined. Appendix 5 gives a complete listing of SNAs.

All SNAs are denoted by one or two letters, and a number or name. If a name is used, it is separated by a $ sign. For example, function number 1 is denoted by FN1. If it is named ABC, it is denoted by FN$ABC. In defining and describing SNAs, we shall use a notation of the form SNAj, where j stands for the number or name of the SNA. A few SNAs are unique and do not have to carry numbers. However, they usually carry the number 1, to conform to the general rule of an SNA being denoted by one or two characters followed by a number. The rule that a symbolic name starts with three alphabetic characters makes it easy for the assembly program to distinguish between an SNA and a symbol. Sometimes, if the user erroneously breaks this rule, the assembler becomes confused and issues an error message relating to an SNA, when the true error is an incorrect symbol.

4-11
System SNAs

Most SNAs are associated with a specific type of GPSS entity, but four are of such a general nature they are said to belong to the system as a whole. The following are the system SNAs:

- C1   The current value of the relative clock time, that is, since the beginning of the run, or since the last RESET or CLEAR statement.
- AC1   The absolute clock time, that is, the time since the beginning of the run, or the last CLEAR statement.
- TG1   The amount by which the termination counter remains to be incremented to end the run.
- RNn   ($1 \leq n \leq 8$). A uniformly distributed random integer between 0 and 999, inclusive, except when it is specified as the input to a function, when its value lies between 0 and 0.999999. In both cases all values in the range are equally likely to occur. The number n selects from one of eight generators. (See Appendix 1.)

4-12
Block SNAs

There are only two SNAs associated with the blocks:

- Nj   The number of transactions that entered block j
- Wj   The number of transactions currently at block j

4-13
Timing Considerations

Using GPSS, there is an initial, usually small, overhead in computing time caused by the reading of input and the assembly phase. When the model is large enough for this time to become significant, the model will usually be well defined. The READ/SAVE feature, described in Secs. 15-8 and 15-9, can then be used to allow a binary version of the assembled model to be saved and reloaded quickly. The assembly program also allows previously assembled input statements to be mixed with unassembled statements to minimize assembly time (see Appendix 2).

There is also an expenditure of time in the final report stage. The execution time needed to produce the report is usually relatively unimportant. With large models, however, the standard output can involve a lot of printing. If the listings are not wanted, or only new parts are wanted, the LIST/UNLIST and NOXREF control statements, used in the assembly phase, can suppress the printing. The report generator, described in Sec. 3-22, can also be used to reduce the output to the essential details.

The principal factor accounting for time is the execution of the simulation model. There is, of course, no direct connection between the time taken to execute a simulation model and the time the actual system takes to perform the simulated function. Depending upon the level of detail, the ratio of simulated to real time varies over a wide range. A simulation of an electronic circuit, which operates in microseconds, might be many thousands of times longer than the actual action time, while a simulation of an economic system, using a time scale of a year, might cover several decades of real time in a minute or two.

The main factor determining execution time in a GPSS model is the number of transactions transferred from one block to another. The transfer time depends upon the types of blocks and the conditions prevailing in the system, but as a first rough measure, the number of transaction transfers will be proportional to the length of the run. This figure, of course, is not the same as the number of blocks. A large model may have sections that are seldom used, while other models may have small sections that are heavily used.

Extensive use of SNAs in providing block arguments, described in Chap. 11, and the use of variable statements tend to slow down execution because of the interpretive nature of GPSS. Large numbers of simultaneously delayed transactions also slow the program by lengthening the scan time. Avoiding these conditions, and using the user chains (described in Chap. 14) to get long-delayed transactions off the current events chain, will help speed up the execution.

4-14

Time Scale

The time scale of the simulation model is selected by the user, who specifies all times in terms of a common unit. By itself, the time scale does not affect the running time of a model. If all times were rescaled—for example, if they were all multiplied by ten, and no further detail were introduced—

the execution would involve exactly the same number of transaction transfers, and the running time would be the same. The critical factor is the amount of detail included in the model since this will control the number of events that must be simulated for a given equivalent real time in the actual system.

Naturally, the shortest significant activity should determine the time scale, but a lot of attention should be paid to the question of what is significant. A useful check is to calculate the approximate range of time intervals involved in all the activities being simulated. The smaller this range, the better. No firm rule can be given on how small the range should be, but, if the range between the shortest to the longest activity is less than 100 to 1, the simulation will be reasonably fast. As this range grows, the simulation will be expending a greater proportion of its time in detail, and the execution time relative to the real time will become excessive.

For example, suppose that a model is to simulate a computer system with messages being keyed in from terminals. The model is to represent the reception of messages, the processing of a reply, and transmission of the reply. Messages might appear at an individual terminal every 100 seconds. If the simulation model were to attempt simulating the execution of individual instructions in the computer, it would be necessary to use a time scale of the order of 1 microsecond. A message from one terminal would then occur on the average every 100,000,000 time units: clearly a model with so much detail will be extremely slow.

It would be essential to raise the level of detail so that the smallest activity being considered is the execution of a major computer subroutine, which can be measured in seconds, or tenths of seconds. If at first it is not possible to get this information, it may be necessary to consider simulating two models: one to operate at the microsecond level, which can assess the time taken to process messages, and the other at the tenth-of-seconds level, considering the traffic flow in and out of the computer. The first model would need to aggregate all the input into a common stream presenting the total load on the computer. The response time, as seen from a particular terminal, would be lost. However, the second model, which has aggregated the computer response into a set of service times by message type, can afford to model the transmission network in some detail, while treating the computer as a service device. The two separate models are not equivalent to an integrated model; but they can form a reasonable approximation that requires substantially less time to execute than would be needed for the full model.

Exercises

4-1 People arrive at a newsstand at the rate of one every 10 ± 5 seconds. Most people buy only one paper but 20 percent buy two papers. It takes 5 ± 3 seconds to buy one paper and 7 ± 3 seconds to buy two papers. Simulate the sale of 100 papers, starting from the time the newsstand opens.

4-2 A series of moving stairways carry customers in an upward direction between four floors of a department store. People arrive at the foot of the stairs, on the first floor, at the rate of one every second. Some people walk on the stairs. As a result, the time to transfer between any two floors is found to be 20 ± 10 seconds. The destinations of the customers are as follows: second floor, 50 percent; third floor, 25 percent; and fourth floor, 25 percent. Simulate the arrival of 100 people on the top floor, starting from the time the store opens.

4-3 People arrive at an exhibition at the rate of one every 3 ± 2 minutes. The exhibition is arranged in three rooms. Everybody goes to rooms A and C but 20 percent of them miss room B. Simulate the system, assuming that each room takes 40 ± 5 minutes. Arrange for 500 people to pass through the exhibition.

4-4 Twenty people simultaneously take a test that requires 5 ± 2 minutes. Their chance of success is such that 20 percent pass on each trial. Those that fail wait 10 minutes before taking the test again. They keep retrying until they finally pass. Arrange to pass all the people, and measure how long it takes.

4-5 Cars bring spectators to a sports event at the rate of one car every 20 ± 10 seconds. The percentages of cars with a given number of passengers are as follows: 1 passenger, 10 percent; 2 passengers, 30 percent; 3 passengers, 45 percent; and 4 passengers, 15 percent. Find how long it takes for 1000 people to arrive.

4-6 People arrive at a cafeteria at the rate of one every 15 ± 5 seconds. There are two counters, A and B, and people want items from them in the following proportions: A only, 30 percent; A and then B, 60 percent; and B only, 10 percent. Simulate completion of service to 100 people.

4-7 The delivery of some product is being limited by the availability of suitable containers. New containers are being made at the rate of one every 20 ± 5 minutes. They are filled and dispatched as soon as they are ready. Delivery takes 40 ± 10 minutes. About one in every 50 containers is damaged beyond repair during delivery. The rest are returned, taking 40 ± 10 minutes, and are immediately reused for another delivery. Beginning from time zero, find how many containers will be in the process of delivery after 8 hours.

4-8 A subway station has two entrances. Passengers arrive at entrance 1 at the rate of one every 10 ± 5 seconds, and they move along a corridor that takes 15 ± 5 seconds to walk. At entrance 2, passengers arrive at the rate of one every 5 ± 2 seconds and they walk along a corridor that takes 20 ± 8 seconds. The two streams of passengers merge to pass along a third corridor for 5 ± 3 seconds. At the end of that corridor, 60 percent of the passengers turn for the northbound platform, the rest turn for the southbound platform. Simulate the arrival of the first 100 passengers on the southbound platform, starting from an empty system.

4-9 Parts that are manufactured at the rate of one every 50 ± 10 seconds go through an inspection that takes 30 ± 10 seconds. The inspection passes 85 percent of the parts. Of the remainder, 5 percent are scrapped, and the rest are sent for reworking. Reworking takes 100 ± 30 seconds, after which the parts are again sent for inspection with the same probability of rejection. Simulate the acceptance of 100 parts. How many parts have been reworked by that time?

4-10 A north-to-south, two-way highway, crosses another two-way highway going east to west. A junction is made by a traffic circle in which all traffic moves to the right. The time to traverse each quarter circle is 10 ± 5 seconds. Assume that traffic arrives at the rate of one vehicle every 5 ± 2 seconds at each entrance to the circle. Assume also that approximately 25 percent of the traffic approaching each exit from the circle will turn off there. (Some cars may do more than one full circle, and it is possible that cars will go back the way they came.) Simulate the passage of 1000 vehicles through the circle.

5

FACILITIES AND STORAGES

This chapter introduces two GPSS entities, facilities and storages, which are designed primarily to represent permanent entities of a system. There can be many facilities and storages in a model. The normal limit for each type of entity is 300.

Four block types, SEIZE, RELEASE, PREEMPT, and RETURN, are concerned with the use of facilities. Two others, ENTER and LEAVE, are concerned with the use of storages. Four block types, FAVAIL, FUNAVAIL, SAVAIL, and SUNAVAIL, can be used to make facilities and storages available or unavailable, as occurs, for example, when the equipment they represent breaks down and is subsequently repaired.

Discussion of the PREEMPT and RETURN blocks will be deferred until after Chap. 6, which discusses priority, because their action is affected by priority levels. Figure 5-1 shows the block diagram symbols for the eight blocks to be discussed in this chapter.

5-1
Facilities

A facility in GPSS represents a system entity that can be used by only one transaction at a time. Facilities are therefore used to model permanent

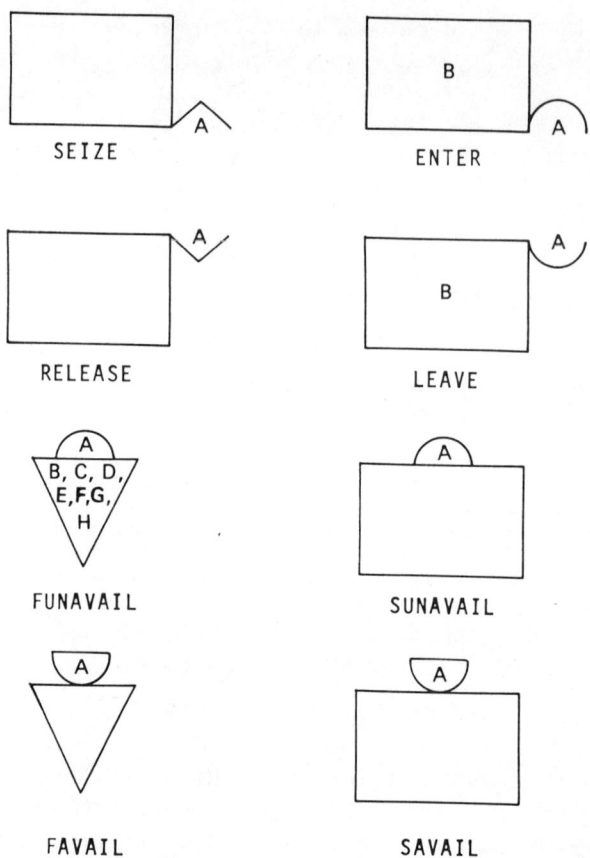

Figure 5-1. Block types 2.

entities time-shared between temporary entities represented by transactions. Typically, a facility represents a machine or person. However, the time-shared characteristic of a facility will often lead to the use of a facility for control purposes, rather than as the representation of a system entity. For example, if some part of a system can be used by only one temporary entity at a time, entry to the corresponding section of the block diagram may be made dependent upon having control of a facility.

The SEIZE and RELEASE blocks are used to allow a transaction to gain and relinquish control of a facility. Normally, a transaction that has seized a facility remains in control until it releases the facility. However, it is possible for control to be interrupted by other transactions with the use of the PREEMPT and RETURN blocks, to be discussed in Chap. 7. To perform these functions, the program keeps records of which transactions have control of the facilities. As a result, only the transaction that has seized a facility can release it.

The fact that only one transaction at a time can control a facility does not mean that each facility can be used in only one part of a system; there can be many blocks referring to the same facility. The use of a facility in one part, however, will prevent its being used simultaneously in any other part.

5-2

SEIZE Blocks

A transaction entering a SEIZE block takes control of the facility named in field A. Only one transaction at a time may have control of a given facility. A transaction that attempts to enter a SEIZE block for which the facility is already engaged will be blocked. There is no limit, however, on how many facilities may simultaneously be seized by a given transaction.

If a transaction that has seized a facility attempts to seize the facility again, it will be blocked. The transaction will become permanently blocked if no alternative is offered.

If a transaction enters a SPLIT block (described in Sec. 13-2) subsequent to seizing a facility, the original transaction maintains control of the facility. The copies produced by the SPLIT block are not associated with the facility.

5-3

RELEASE Blocks

A transaction entering a RELEASE block gives up control of the facility named in field A. To do so, it must have previously seized the facility; if it has not, there will be an error stop. If the transaction has seized more than one facility, only the one named in field A is released. The release occurs as soon as the transaction enters the block. Should the transaction have to stay in the RELEASE block, its presence has no influence on the facility.

The fact that a transaction that seized a facility has to release it does not imply that SEIZE and RELEASE blocks must be assigned in pairs. After seizing a facility, a transaction may branch in many directions. It is not necessary that it always be brought to a common RELEASE block; there can be a separate RELEASE block in each branch. Similarly, a facility could be seized at several different points and released at one or more common points. These principles also apply to the way that storages are used.

Care should be taken, however, to see that a seized facility is eventually released. The program does not check whether a transaction being destroyed is in control of a facility at that time. A common programming error in GPSS is to allow a facility to become permanently seized in this manner, with the result that some part of the system becomes permanently blocked. Similar remarks apply to the control of storage space with ENTER and LEAVE blocks.

5-4
Factory Model 1: Using Facilities

We give now a simple example of using facilities. Suppose that in a factory there is an assembly line sending parts to a machine that can operate on only one part at a time. The machine will therefore be represented by a facility. Suppose that the assembly line delivers parts at the rate of one part every 50 seconds and that the machining operation takes 40 ± 35 seconds.

A block diagram that represents the system is shown in Fig. 5-2. Using a time unit of 1 second, a GENERATE block with a mean of 50 creates transactions that represent the parts supplied by the assembly line. The transactions move to an ADVANCE block with zero time, which will be explained shortly. They pass to a SEIZE block to take over a facility, called MACH, that represents the machine, and then go immediately to another ADVANCE block. Only one transaction at a time can be in this ADVANCE block, which determines the machining time. At the end of the action time, the transaction moves to a RELEASE block to give up the facility, and, since there is no further interest in its movement, it then goes to a TERMINATE block.

The mean machining time is less than the interarrival time of parts; therefore, the machine is able to keep up with the work to be done. However, because of the variation in machining time, it is possible for one part to arrive before the previous one has finished being machined. If the previous part has finished, a transaction leaving the GENERATE block will immediately pass through the ADVANCE block with zero time, seize the facility, and enter the second ADVANCE block. If, however, the previous part is still being machined when a second part leaves the GENERATE block, the second part will not be able to enter the SEIZE block. Instead, it will wait in the ADVANCE block with zero time until the facility is released, at which time it will immediately seize the facility.

It will be recalled that one of the properties of the GENERATE block is that it temporarily stops creating new transactions if the last transaction it created is unable to leave the GENERATE block (see Sec. 4-2). The zero-time ADVANCE block has been inserted here to ensure that transactions can leave the GENERATE block; the model thus represents a system in which the assembly line continues to supply parts, regardless of whether they are machined in time. Without this block, the model would represent a system in which failure to machine a part in time for the next arrival would hold up the assembly line.

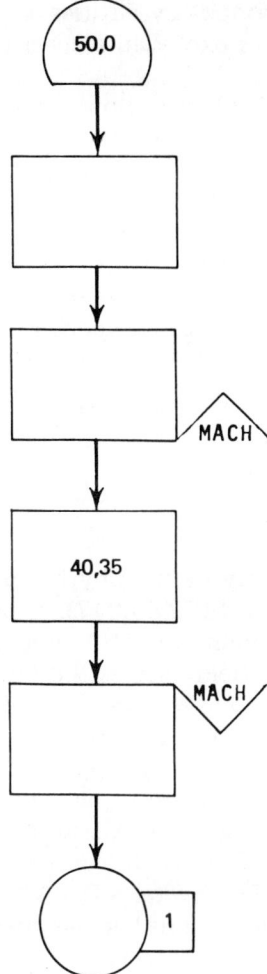

Figure 5-2. Factory model 1.

5-5
Storages

Storages represent system entities that can be occupied or engaged simultaneously by many transactions. An upper limit on the capacity of each storage is assigned by the program user. As the name implies, a storage can be used to represent any entity, such as a warehouse or a truck, that has a capacity for holding a specific number of items. It is also used to represent a multiserver entity, such as a machine designed to process a number of workpieces simultaneously or a group of people assigned to perform a task. Sometimes a storage will be used as a counting device that will collect together a given number of temporary entities or give a warning that the number of temporary entities has exceeded a specific limit. An example is given in Sec. 5-12.

The ENTER and LEAVE blocks allow a transaction to occupy and give up space in a storage. In contrast to the way facilities are treated, the program does not maintain records of which particular transactions have entered a storage; it merely maintains a count of the number of storage units occupied at any time. It is not essential, therefore, that the transaction that enters a storage ultimately leave the storage, although that is usually the case. The actions of incrementing and decrementing the number of occupied units are independent operations that can be performed by different transactions. The example to be given in Sec. 5-12 will illustrate this point.

5-6

STORAGE Control Statements

Each storage has a capacity defined by the program user. It must be less than or equal to $2^{31} - 1$ (2,147,483,647). If not specifically defined, it is assumed to have this maximum value. A control statement with the word STORAGE in the operation field defines the capacity. A number of storage capacities can be defined in one statement. Beginning in column 19, a notation of the form Sn,N is used. This sets the capacity of storage number n to N. Following a slash (/), a second capacity can be defined. If a series of consecutively numbered storages are to have the same capacity, the following notation may be used: $Sa-Sb,N$. All storages numbered $a, a + 1, \ldots,$ b will be set to a capacity of N. There can be no blanks and the statement cannot go beyond column 71. Several STORAGE statements can be used but no one storage definition can be split between two statements.

As an example consider the following:

   STORAGE S10,200/S2-5,500/S1,1000.

This will set storage 10 to 200, storages 2, 3, 4, and 5 to 500, and storage 1 to 1000. Note that the storages do not have to be given in numerical order.

If the storages are to be referred to by name, the name, preceded by a dollar sign, ($), replaces n. Thus a storage called MAIN can be set to a capacity of 100 with the storage statement

   STORAGE S$MAIN,100.

The storage contents, however, may not be given symbolically.

If the capacity of a storage is defined more than once, the later definition overrides previous definitions. This is frequently done between simulation runs (see Sec. 3-16). When the capacity is redefined, an error stop will occur if the new capacity is less than the current content of the storage.

Storage definition statements may appear anywhere in a problem definition, ahead of the START statement. It is customary, however, to collect them at the end of the problem definition, just ahead of the START statement.

5-7

ENTER Blocks

A transaction entering an ENTER block occupies space in the storage named in field A. If field B is blank, one unit of space is occupied. Any amount, up to the storage capacity, can be occupied by putting the desired amount in field B.

If the required amount of space is not available, a transaction will be refused entry to an ENTER block. Another transaction, with a lesser requirement that can be met, may be processed ahead of such a blocked transaction, even though it may have requested the space at a later time. Field B may contain a zero, in which case the transaction will always enter without changing the storage content. A transaction may be entered in any number of storages simultaneously.

5-8

LEAVE Blocks

A transaction entering a LEAVE block will return space to the storage given in field A. If field B is blank, one unit of space is returned. Any amount, up to the storage capacity, can be returned by putting the desired amount in field B. If the transaction attempts to return more units than are currently occupied, an error stop will occur. The transaction that leaves a storage does not need to have previously entered the storage. If it did, it does not have to return the same number of units that it occupied.

5-9

Factory Model 2: Using Storages

Consider again the factory model that was discussed in Sec. 5-4. That model assumed a single machine that was represented by a facility. Suppose that the work station on the assembly line has three machines but that, for the purpose of the study, it is not necessary to follow the detailed performance of each. It is only necessary to reflect the effects of the capacity on the system performance. If we assume the same arrival rate, three machines would be justified if the machining time were approximately three times as long. We will therefore take the machining time to be 120 ± 105. The system can then be modeled as shown in Fig. 5-3.

ENTER and LEAVE blocks, using a storage called MACHS, replace the SEIZE and RELEASE blocks, respectively. When the model is coded, a storage definition statement is needed to set the capacity of MACHS to 3. The model operates in the same way as the model of Fig. 5-2, except that there can now be up to three transactions simultaneously in the ADVANCE block that represents the machining.

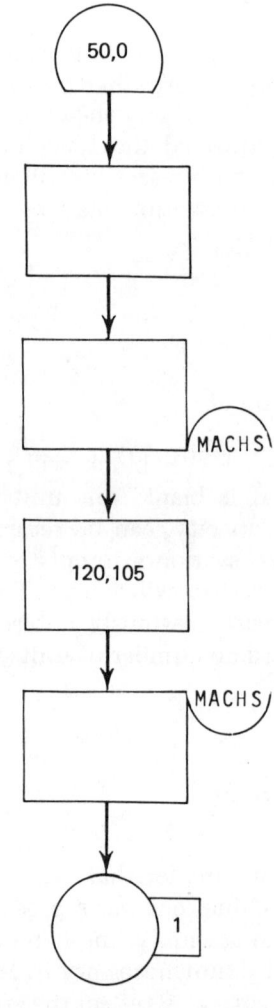

Figure 5-3. Factory model 2.

5-10

Conditional Mode of TRANSFER Block

In Secs. 4-6 and 4-7 two modes of the TRANSFER block were described, the unconditional and the fractional modes. We now discuss a third mode, the *conditional mode*, which is used when the progress of a transaction is blocked—for example, when it is unable to get control of a facility or enter a storage. The conditional mode is indicated by setting the selection factor of the TRANSFER block to the word BOTH and specifying locations in fields B and C.

If a transaction that enters a TRANSFER block in a conditional mode can leave by way of exit 1 (field B), it will do so. If it cannot, it will attempt to leave by way of exit 2 (field C). Should both exits be blocked, the transaction waits for the first to become free, giving preference to exit 1 if they become free simultaneously. The conditional mode therefore allows a transaction to take some alternative action if system conditions are not satisfactory for its first choice of action. As in the case of a fractional mode, if exit 1 is the next sequential block, field B can be left blank.

As will be explained in Appendix 6, the transactions kept blocked at a TRANSFER block in a conditional mode involve extra processing that slows down the program. This condition should be avoided, or the time that a transaction spends blocked this way should be kept to a minimum.

5-11

Factory Model 3: Using Conditional Transfer Mode

We illustrate the use of the conditional mode of transfer with an expanded version of the factory model. Suppose that the assembly line consists of a turntable that carries work past three work stations. A part can be machined at any of the stations. Parts are placed on the table, and they take 120 seconds to reach the first station. If that station can accept the part, it will do so. If it is busy, however, the part is carried to the second station, where it arrives after 120 seconds. Again the part is accepted if possible, otherwise it passes to a third station after another 120 seconds. Should that station be busy, the table carries the part back to the first station for another pass. We will assume that not more than six parts can be placed on the table at any one time and that, should the limit be reached, new parts will be rejected.

A block diagram of the system is shown in Fig. 5-4. A GENERATE block enters a new part every 50 seconds. The parts go to a TRANSFER block with a conditional mode that tests whether a storage called TABLE has any spare space. The capacity of TABLE is set to be 6. If there is no space, the part is rejected by being sent to a TERMINATE block called REJ. If the part

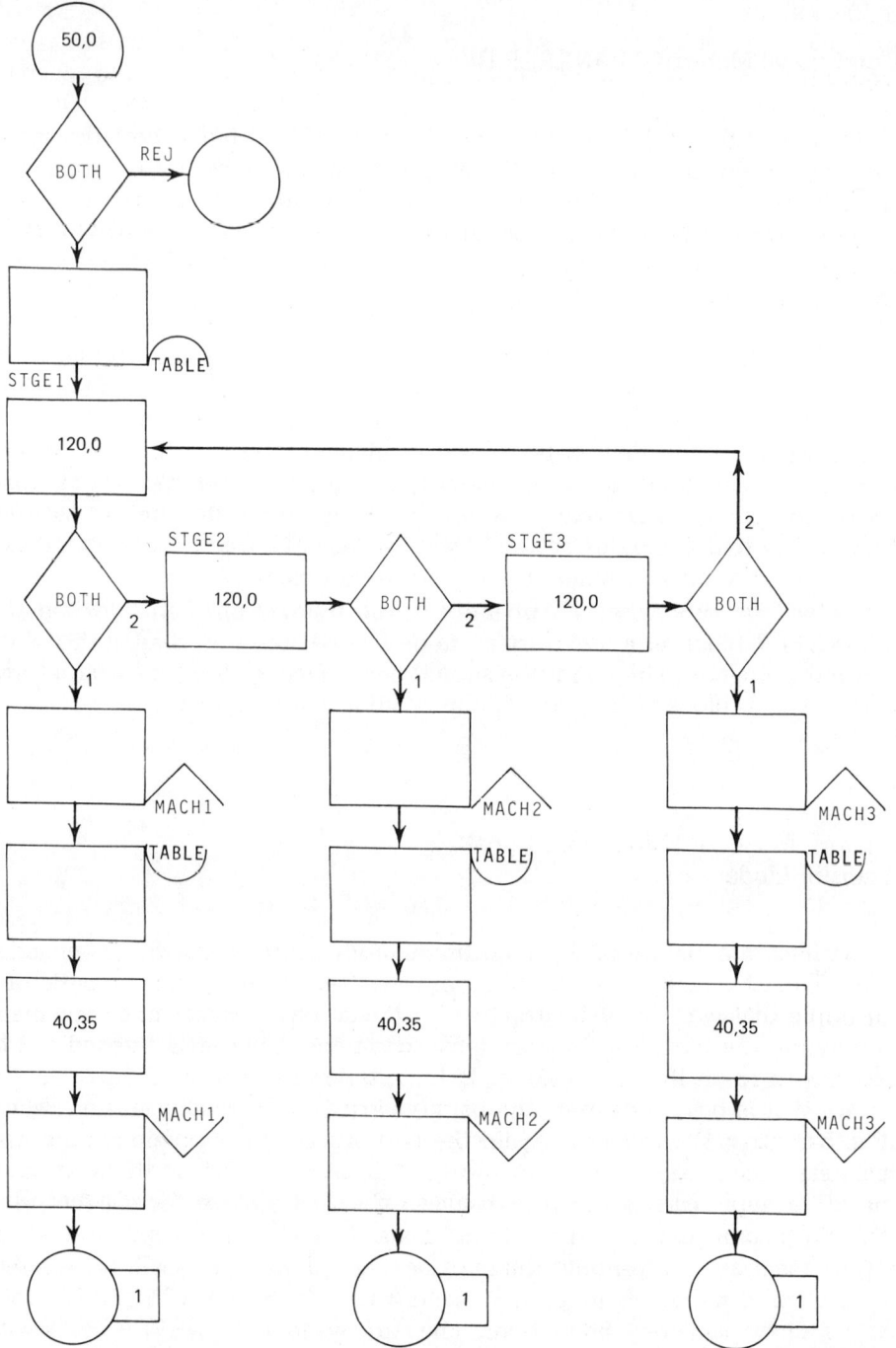

Figure 5-4. Factory model 3.

finds room on the table, it goes to an ADVANCE block called STGE1 with a mean of 120 to represent the time to reach the first work station. There, another conditional mode TRANSFER block checks whether the machine, represented by a facility MACH1, is busy. If not, the transaction seizes the facility and leaves the storage TABLE to represent the fact that the part is removed from the table. The part is then machined, as it was in the first model, with a machining time of 40 ± 35 seconds.

Parts that are not taken by the first work station take 120 seconds to move to the next station, where the same logic is applied. A similar section of the model represents the third stage, and, if the part is not taken by the third stage, it returns to the ADVANCE block STGE1 to be recycled.

The coding and output for the factory system model 3 is shown in Fig. 5-5. Note how the capacity of the storage called TABLE has been defined. Note, also, that the order in which the SEIZE and LEAVE blocks are placed in the machine operation segments is important. Although these actions are executed at the same instant, if the LEAVE block comes first, the part will be removed from the storage without the TRANSFER block testing the availability of the facilities.

The model has been arranged to count the total number of finished parts. An initialization run of 10 parts is made, followed by a RESET statement and a main run of 1000 parts. The output that would have arisen from the initialization has been suppressed by the NP in field B of the first START statement. The output shown relates to the period between the 10th and 1010th terminations.

5-12

Factory Model 4: Storages as Counters

We now illustrate the use of storages as counters that will trigger an action when the number of temporary entities reaches a given limit. In the course of doing so, we also demonstrate the fact that incrementing and decrementing storage contents are independent operations that can be carried out by different transactions.

We return to the simple factory model of a single work station given in Fig. 5-2. Suppose that, following the machining operation, the parts go to a packing machine that collects the finished parts and dispatches them in boxes of 20. Figure 5-6 shows a block diagram of the system. A storage called BOXES has been defined to have a capacity of 19. Following the release of the facility representing the machine, transactions enter a conditional mode TRANSFER block. Nineteen transactions will be able to go by exit 1 to enter the storage. They then leave the system at a TERMINATE block. The 20th transaction will find the storage full and, consequently, will be diverted to the LEAVE block. The B field of this block is set to 19 so that

```
            *       FACTORY MODEL-3
                *
 1                  GENERATE     50                CREATE PARTS
 2                  TRANSFER     BOTH,,REJ         CHECK IF THERE IS SPACE
 3                  ENTER        TABLE             PUT ON TABLE
 4         STGE1    ADVANCE      120               MOVE TO FIRST STATION
 5                  TRANSFER     BOTH,,STGE2       CHECK IF IT IS FREE
 6                  SEIZE        MACH1             TAKE OVER MACHINE 1
 7                  LEAVE        TABLE             REMOVE FROM TABLE
 8                  ADVANCE      40,35             MACHINE PART
 9                  RELEASE      MACH1             RELEASE MACHINE 1
10                  TERMINATE    1                 FINISH WITH PART
                *
11         STGE2    ADVANCE      120               MOVE TO STATION 2
12                  TRANSFER     BOTH,,STGE3       CHECK IF IT IS FREE
13                  SEIZE        MACH2             TAKE OVER MACHINE 2
14                  LEAVE        TABLE             REMOVE FROM TABLE
15                  ADVANCE      40,35             MACHINE PART
16                  RELEASE      MACH2             RELEASE MACHINE
17                  TERMINATE    1                 FINISH WITH PART
                *
18         STGE3    ADVANCE      120               MOVE TO STATION 3
19                  TRANSFER     BOTH,,STGE1       CHECK IF IT IS FREE
20                  SEIZE        MACH3             TAKE OVER MACHINE 3
21                  LEAVE        TABLE             REMOVE FROM TABLE
22                  ADVANCE      40,35             MACHINE PART
23                  RELEASE      MACH3             RELEASE MACHINE
24                  TERMINATE    1                 FINISH WITH PART
                *
25         REJ      TERMINATE                      REJECT PARTS
                *
                    STORAGE      S$TABLE,6
                *
                    START        10,NP
                    RESET                          RESET STATISTICS
                    START        1000              RUN FOR 1000 MACHINED PARTS
RELATIVE CLOCK            49982   ABSOLUTE CLOCK         50709
BLOCK COUNTS
BLOCK CURRENT TOTAL       BLOCK CURRENT TOTAL    BLOCK CURRENT TOTAL    BLOCK CURRENT TOTAL
    1     0    1000         11     0    265        21     0    0
    2     0    1000         12     0    266        22     0    0
    3     0    1000         13     0    266        23     0    0
    4     3    1000         14     0    266        24     0    0
    5     0     999         15     0    266        25     0    0
    6     0     734         16     0    267
    7     0     734         17     0    267
    8     1     734         18     0     0
    9     0     733         19     0     0
   10     0     733         20     0     0
```

```
          ******************************************
          *                                        *
          *             FACILITIES                 *
          *                                        *
          ******************************************
                         AVERAGE UTIL DURING-
FACILITY    NUMBER   AVERAGE   TOTAL   AVAIL   UNAVAIL   CURRENT   PERCENT        TRANS    NUMBER
            ENTRIES  TIME/TRAN TIME    TIME    TIME      STATUS    AVAILABILITY   SEIZE    PREEMPT
MACH1        734     40.050    .588    .588    .000      A         100.0          2
MACH2        267     39.734    .212    .212    .000      A         100.0
          ******************************************
          *                                        *
          *              STORAGES                  *
          *                                        *
          ******************************************
                                          AVER UTIL DURING
STORAGE  CAPACITY  AVERAGE    ENTRIES  AVERAGE      TOTL AVAL UNAVL  CURRENT  PCNT    CONTENT
                   CONTENT             TIME/UNIT    TIME TIME TIME   STATUS   AVAIL   CURR MAX
TABLE       6      3.038      1003     151.411      .506 .506 .000   A        100.0    3   4
```

Figure 5-5. Coding and output for factory model 3.

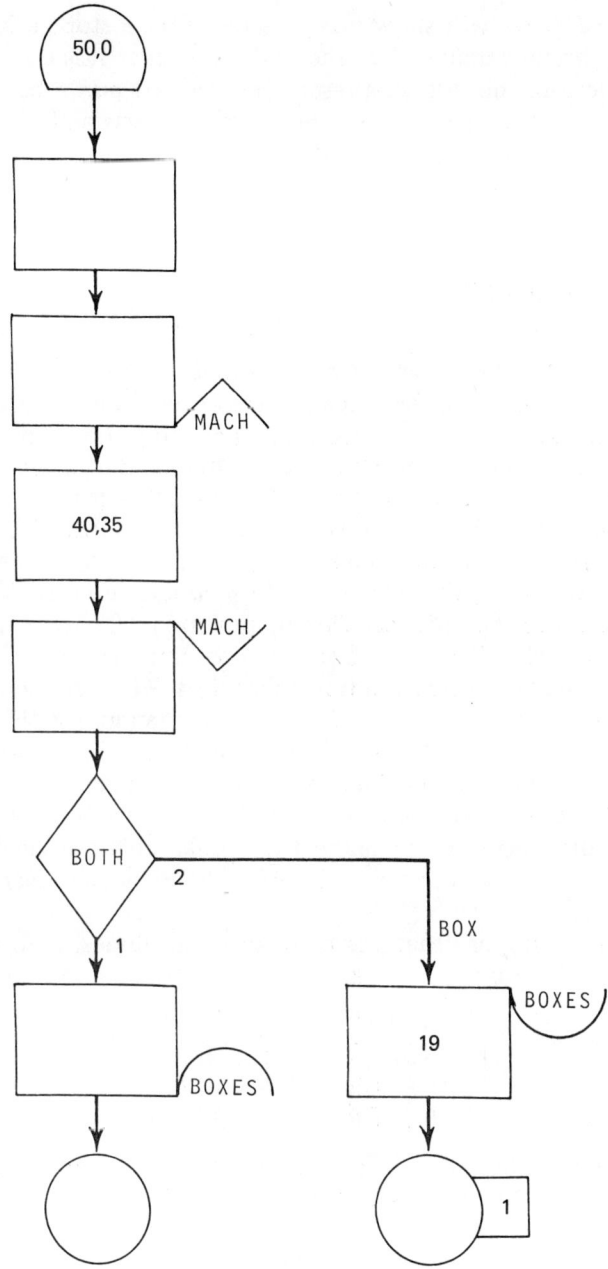

Figure 5-6. Factory model 4.

the transaction will reduce the storage content to zero. It then passes to a TERMINATE block whose total block count will show how many boxes have been completed.

Later (Sec. 12-3) we will show how the fact that a storage is full can be used to trigger the movement of a transaction, so that it is not necessary to have one transaction, the 20th, represent both a part and a box. Two independent streams of transactions, one representing parts and another boxes, can then be programmed.

5-13
PICK and ALL Modes of TRANSFER Block

The fractional and conditional transfer modes of the TRANSFER block make a choice between only two paths. Two other transfer modes, PICK and ALL, are analogous to the fractional and conditional mode, respectively, but the choice can be over many exits. There are, however, restrictions in the numbering of the blocks to which they lead. The function and parameter transfer modes (which will be described in Secs. 9-10 and 10-11) usually offer simpler ways of performing the same task, particularly if the number of choices is large. However, the PICK and ALL modes are sometimes useful.

The PICK transfer mode is specified by putting PICK in the A field, and locations in both fields B and C. The location number in field C must be greater than that in field B. The action taken in a PICK mode is to choose one of the locations $B, B + 1, B + 2, \ldots, C$, at random with equal probability. There are $C - B + 1$ possible exits and each has a probability of $1/(C - B + 1)$ of being selected. Once the selection is made, it is maintained, even if the exit proves to be blocked. Since the exits are consecutively numbered, it is usually necessary to make the blocks at those locations either TERMINATE blocks or unconditional TRANSFER blocks, except possibly the highest location.

As an example, suppose that there are three machines, each of which is equally likely to be assigned work. The following coding could be used:

```
            TRANSFER    PICK,AAA,BBB
    AAA     TRANSFER    ,MACH1
            TRANSFER    ,MACH2
    BBB     TRANSFER    ,MACH3
```

The three unconditional TRANSFER blocks need not immediately follow the TRANSFER block in a PICK mode but they must be consecutive to each other.

The ALL transfer mode makes a conditional transfer between a number of exits. It is coded by putting ALL in field A, locations in fields B and C, and a number in field D. The number in field D is an indexing factor, and the location in field C must be such that $C = B + nD$, where n is a positive integer. There are $n + 1$ possible exits numbered $B, B + D, B + 2D, \ldots,$ C. The exits will be tested in that order and a transaction leaves the TRANSFER block by the first exit found to be unblocked. This requires that the segments of coding to which transfers may be made (except the last) be of equal length. Should all exits be blocked, the transaction leaves by the first to become available. (SNAs may not be used with the ALL mode: see Sec. 11-5.)

The ALL mode, like the BOTH mode, can cause extra processing when a transaction remains blocked (see Appendix 6). Transactions should be held in this state for as little time as possible.

5-14
Comparison of Facilities and Storages

It is apparent that a storage of capacity 1 can function as a facility. It is also apparent that several facilities can be used in place of a storage of more than unit capacity. A logical difference is that only the transaction that seized a facility can release the facility, whereas a storage count can be independently increased and decreased by different transactions. An example of such independent actions was given in Sec. 5-12, but it is not a common characteristic of systems. In most models, the transactions that enter a storage will be the same ones that leave the storage. In addition to the logical difference, there is a practical difference. The program keeps a record of which transaction controls a facility. In the case of a storage, it does not record the transactions that have entered: it simply keeps a count of storage units in use. Processing facilities, therefore, involves more record-keeping, leading to the use of more execution time.

In constructing models, facilities should only be used where some unique system entity, such as a particular machine, is intended. Wherever there is a multiserver entity, it will be better to represent the entity by a storage. This is quite evident in those cases where the only point of interest about an entity is its capacity, for example, a warehouse. It is less evident in other cases, such as the second factory model, discussed in Sec. 5-9. At first sight, the fact that there are three machines suggests three facilities. However, from the point of view of modeling, the machines are completely interchangeable. They can be regarded as a group and be represented by a storage. Constructing the model in this way is simpler and more efficient. Representing the machines individually by facilities would need more blocks, and the individual statistics that the program produces would take more time to generate and would probably need to be reduced manually to produce the most significant statistic, the machine group utilization.

Where the service capacity is only 1, it is a matter of choice whether to use a facility or storage. The difference in record-keeping and efficiency at that level is minor, and it is then better to emphasize the unique nature of the entity by using a facility. However, if the service of an entity can be interrupted, either by a breakdown or by being preempted by a more important task, it is essential that a facility be used. Modeling these conditions will be discussed in Sec. 5-15 and in Chap. 7.

When grouping entities to form multiserver units, certain assumptions are being made. One is that the FIFO queuing discipline applies over the entire group, that is, that a common waiting line forms and service goes to the transaction at the head of the line, regardless of which server next becomes free. This may be true in the machine example, where the parts are fed to the machines by an assembly line. However, in the case of checkout counters in a supermarket, although the counters may be interchangeable, separate queues form. Some averaging occurs when customers select a counter but, having joined a queue, most customers will stay on that queue. The system, therefore, it not strictly a FIFO multiserver system. It is a matter of judgment whether the approximation involved in using a simple FIFO multiserver system is justified. In the context of studying the overall time to shop in a supermarket, the error introduced is minor. However, in a study of customer behavior it may be essential to represent the counters separately so that different queuing rules can be modeled.

Another assumption that we are making is that the entities grouped together are, in fact, interchangeable. Again, it is a matter of judgment to decide whether any known differences are big enough to warrant the extra detail of representing the units separately. In a supermarket, for example, it would obviously be essential to separate express checkout counters from normal counters, whereas, in the machine shop example, it is probably sufficiently accurate to use an average productivity rate rather than distinguish between the performances of individual machines or workers.

Later, in Chap. 12, we will discuss logic switches. These are simple two-state elements for which no usage statistics are kept. If a single-server entity is to be modeled and the usage statistics are not needed, it is simpler and more efficient to use a logic switch in preference to a facility. For example, in modeling sections of railway track, where each section can be used by only one train at a time, facilities could be used to represent the sections. However, logic switches being turned on and off would provide a simpler and faster way of representing the use of the sections. If there were only a few sections, the difference between using facilities and logic switches would be small, but, if there were many sections, the difference could be significant.

5-15

Equipment Availability

A frequent requirement is to simulate the fact that some system entity, represented by a facility or storage, is not available during certain periods of time. The cause may be an intermittent breakdown, or it may be a periodic withdrawal of service, such as periods between work shifts or the changing of the tide. Provision is made to control the availability of any facility or storage. Two block types, FUNAVAIL and SUNAVAIL, make facilities and storages, respectively, unavailable, and two others, FAVAIL and SAVAIL, restore them to the available state. All entities are initially available.

The transactions that enter these blocks to control availability are not usually representing any system entity. Instead, they are control transactions. However, they are treated just the same as transactions that do represent system entities.

The times at which failures occur are described in the same general manner as arrival times. Statistics are given for the distribution of time between failures. The mean time is called the mean time between failures (MTBF). It is found, in practice, that the distribution of the time between failures is often well represented by a particular distribution called the *Weibull distribution*. It is a distribution that depends upon at least two, and sometimes three, parameters. The reader is referred to textbooks on reliability theory for an explanation of how the parameters are defined and fitted to particular sets of data [see (18), pp. 376 ff].

5-16

FUNAVAIL Blocks

The block type FUNAVAIL is used to make one or more facilities unavailable and stop the gathering of statistics about the facility while it is unavailable. Unlike the other three blocks concerned with controlling availability, it is a relatively complicated block because it has many options that decide what to do with any transaction that has seized or preempted the facility at the time it becomes unavailable, as well as what to do with any transactions waiting to use the facility at that time.

As a simple example of how FUNAVAIL can be used, let us suppose that the facility used to represent a machine in Fig. 5-2 is subject to random breakdowns. The block diagram of Fig. 5-7 could be used. A string of five blocks has been added to the block diagram of Fig. 5-2, forming a separate section. Transactions created at the new GENERATE block enter a FUNAVAIL block to represent the occurrence of the breakdown. They then wait in an ADVANCE block to represent the time to make a repair, after which they restore the machine by entering a FAVAIL block. The transactions are then destroyed. The mean time between failures is 1000, with a distribution controlled by function number 1, and the mean breakdown time is 100 with a distribution controlled by function 2.

Field A of the FUNAVAIL block must be given. It identifies either a single facility or a range of consecutively numbered facilities to be made unavailable. When a range is specified, the lower and upper limits are given, in that order, separated by a hyphen with no intervening blanks. If a specified facility happens to be unused at the time of being made unavailable, all the

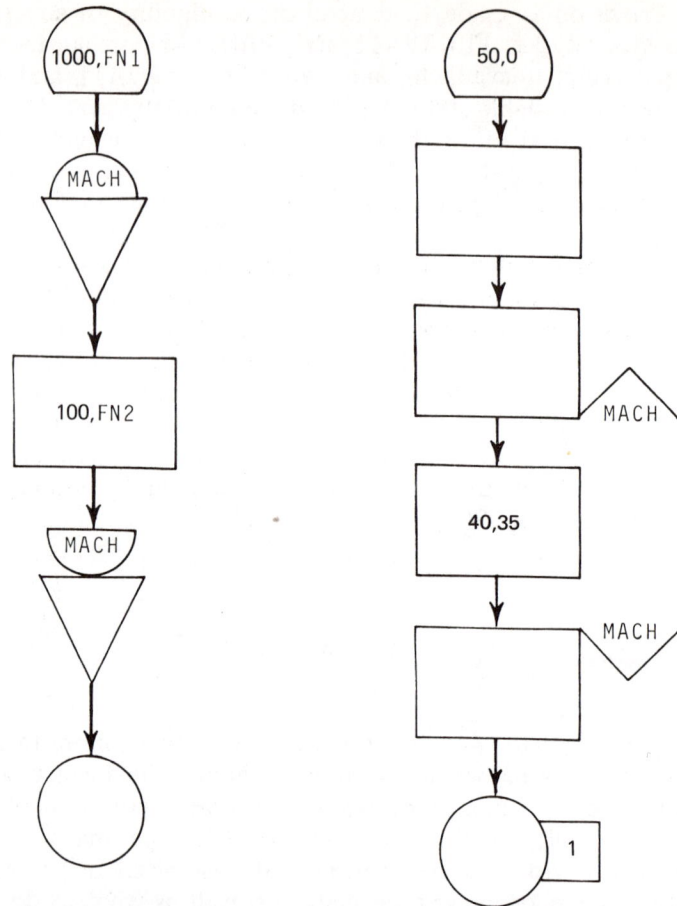

Figure 5-7. Modeling machine breakdowns.

options represented by the remaining fields are inoperative for that facility. If a specified facility is already unavailable, no further action is taken for that facility. Once a facility has been made unavailable, any transaction that attempts to seize or preempt the facility will be placed on a delay chain, to be made active again when the facility becomes available.

When only field A is used and the facility is in use, the transaction that was using the facility will be interrupted and remain delayed during the period of unavailability. The interrupted transaction will regain control when the unavailable period ends, unless a transaction attempted a preemption during the period, in which case the preemption will take precedence at the end of the period.

Fields B, C, and D are optional. They relate to the transaction that was in control of the facility at the time the facility became unavailable. Field B contains either CO or RE. The CO (for continue) allows the controlling transaction to continue using the facility in spite of the breakdown, but the facility is unavailable for subsequent transactions until availability is returned. This extra period of utilization is recorded in the facility statistics. An RE in field B (for remove) results in the transaction immediately losing control. A location must then be given in field C and the transaction that loses control is sent to that location.

A location can also be given in field C when the CO option is used in field B. In that case, the transaction remains in control but is also displaced to the location given in field C. It is then the user's responsibility to ensure that the transaction eventually releases or returns the facility.

Field D is optional and it can be used with either the RE or CO option in field B. The field identifies a parameter that will be used to store the length of time for which any interrupted transaction was due to control the facility at the time of unavailability. The parameter cannot be of the floating-point type.

Fields E and F are used as options for any transaction that was preempted at the time the facility was made unavailable. (Preemption is explained fully in Chap. 7. It allows a transaction to take over the use of a facility that has been seized.) The E field contains either CO or RE and the F field may contain a location. The F field is required with the RE option but is optional with the CO option. A CO option in field E is usual if a CO option was also given in field B. Just as a CO option in field B allows a transaction in control at the time of a breakdown to finish its use, so the CO option in field E allows a transaction that was preempted in the use of the facility to take over and complete its remaining use when the preempting transaction has finished, in spite of the breakdown. The RE option removes the preempted transaction from contention and sends it to the location named in field F.

The G and H fields are concerned with the disposition of any transactions that were delayed because they wanted to seize or preempt a facility. They operate in exactly the same way as the E and F fields treat preempted transactions. That is, field G has either CO or RE and field H must have a location if field G has RE.

There are many combinations of options for the FUNAVAIL block. The large number arises from the fact that there are three categories of transactions to be considered, the transaction currently using the facility, the transaction that has been preempted in its use, and the transactions waiting their turn to use the facility. The commonest use is with field A only being specified. This corresponds to the facility being interrupted and the action continuing with no change after the interruption. However, unlike the interruption caused by a PREEMPT block, the facility is considered out of use during the interruption. A second common case is to specify all CO options, which corresponds to the case where a service is to be withdrawn but all people currently waiting for service will be served: new arrivals will have to wait. A third common case is to exercise all RE options, which corresponds to removing the transactions now using, or waiting to use, the facility. They may be sent to another facility or destroyed. When the D field option is used, the transaction that was using the facility can be rescheduled for the remainder of its time, either at some other facility or at the same facility when it becomes available again.

5-17

Conditions Under Which FUNAVAIL Options Will Not Be Honored

In the normal course of events, a transaction that is interrupted by the unavailability of a facility is using the facility at some ADVANCE block, so that the transaction is on the future events chain. It is possible that it is just leaving an ADVANCE block, with the result that the transaction is on the current events chain but as yet has not been processed. Also, a transaction that was preempted will normally be on the interrupt chain, and transactions waiting for the facility will be on one of the delay chains associated with that facility. Under all these circumstances the CO and RE options of the FUNAVAIL block are effective because the program is able to locate the transactions involved by searching the chains. It is possible for transactions that logically should be eligible for the options to be on some delay chain not associated with the facility. These are abnormal conditions that should be avoided. They arise for one of several reasons:

(a) The transaction that should be in charge of the facility may have passed through a SEIZE or PREEMPT block but be unable to enter an ADVANCE block because of some other blocking condition.
(b) Similarly a transaction may have stopped using a facility by leaving an ADVANCE block and be unable to enter a RELEASE or RETURN block because of some intervening blocking condition.
(c) A preempted transaction may have been displaced to a block which it cannot enter and so finds itself on a delay chain not associated with the facility.
(d) A transaction may have been dispatched to seize or preempt a facility but has been blocked by some other condition.

Under these conditions the options cannot be exercised and the program proceeds as though they had not been used.

5-18

FAVAIL Blocks

A transaction entering an FAVAIL block will return the facility, or facilities, named in field A to the available state. A range of facility numbers can be given, in which case lower and upper limits of the range are given, separated by a hyphen. No other field of the block is used. If a facility is already available, no action is taken for that facility.

5-19

SUNAVAIL **Blocks**

A transaction entering a SUNAVAIL block will make a storage, or a number of storages, unavailable. Field A identifies a single storage or gives a range of storages by specifying the lower and upper limits, separated by a hyphen.

Unlike the FUNAVAIL block, there are no options available. Transactions currently occupying a storage at the time it becomes unavailable continue to use it and their usage is counted in the storage statistics. No new transaction, however, will be allowed to enter the storage.

5-20

SAVAIL **Blocks**

A transaction entering a SAVAIL block reverses the action of a transaction that entered a SUNAVAIL block by making a storage, or storages, available. The A field is used in the same way as in a SUNAVAIL block.

5-21

Facility and Storage Output Statistics

The program automatically gives a line of output for each facility and storage. The headings shown in Fig. 5-5 describe the data.

A computation is made of the utilization of each facility, calculated in the manner illustrated in Fig. 5-8(a). The facility is either free or busy at any time. Suppose that the facility is used N times and it becomes busy at the odd-numbered times t_1, t_3, t_5, etc., and it becomes free at the even-numbered times t_2, t_4, t_6, etc. Let T be the total time of the simulation run. Time is either the relative time since the last RESET statement or, if there has been no RESET, the time since the beginning of the run or the last CLEAR statement. The shaded areas of Fig. 5-8(a) represent the accumulated time integral I, where

$$I = \sum_n (t_{2n+2} - t_{2n+1}), \quad n = 0, 1, \ldots, N-1$$

If the facility is in use at the beginning of a run (as the result of using a RESET statement) t_1 is automatically set to 0, and if the facility is busy at the end of the run t_{2N} is set to T.

Figure 5-8(a) relates to a case where the facility is always available. Simultaneously, the program keeps similar statistics for the periods in which the facility is unavailable. (The facility may, nevertheless, be used in these periods because of the CO options of the FUNAVAIL block.) The total time the facility is unavailable is denoted by T' and the time integral of usage during unavailability is denoted by I'.

Based on these four quantities T, T', I, and I', together with a count, N, of the total number of times the facility was used, either at a SEIZE block or a PREEMPT block, the program prints the statistics shown in Fig. 5-5. The items are defined as follows:

(a) Number of entries N
(b) Average time/transaction I/N
(c) Average utilization during
    (i) Total time I/T
    (ii) Available time $(I - I')/(T - T')$
    (iii) Unavailable time I'/T'
(d) Percent availability $100(T - T')/T$

The column headed "current status" contains A if the facility was available at the time the run ended, and contains NA if it was not. The last two columns give the numbers of any transactions that were either seizing or preempting the facility at the time the run ended.

The occupancy of each storage is also computed, and the computation is illustrated in Fig. 5-8(b). Suppose that the storage content changes R times at the instants $t_1, t_2, t_3, \ldots, t_R$, and the contents after each change are $n_1, n_2, n_3, \ldots, n_R$ (including the possibility of zero). T is the total time defined as for the case of facility utilization. The accumulated time integral is again the shaded area; in this case, defined by

$$I = \sum_r n_r(t_{r+1} - t_r), \quad r = 1, 2, \ldots, R - 1$$

Again, a RESET statement will make $t_1 = 0$, and, if the storage is occupied at the end of the run, t_R will be set to T.

The program also keeps the total time a storage in unavailable, T', and also computes the accumulated time integral of usage during periods of unavailability, denoted by I'. These four numbers, T, I, T', and I', together with the total number of units that entered the storage, N, and the storage capacity, C, define the following items that appear in the output for each storage (see Fig. 5-5):

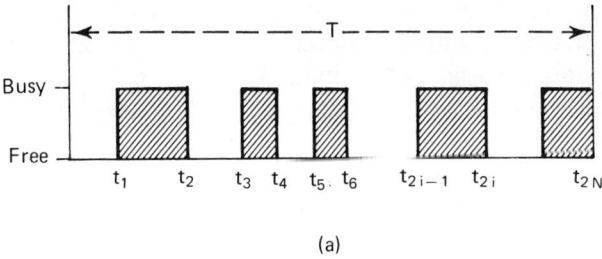

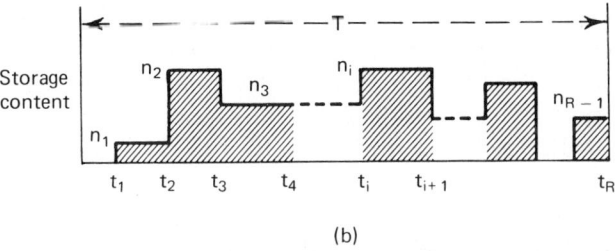

Figure 5-8. Facility and storage statistics: (a) facility utilization; (b) storage occupancy.

(a) Capacity C
(b) Average contents I/T
(c) Entries (number of units) N
(d) Average time/unit I/N
(e) Average utilization during
   (i) Total time I/TC
   (ii) Available time $(I - I')/(T - T')C$
   (iii) Unavailable time $I'/T'C$
(f) Percent availability $100(T - T')/T$

A column of output also shows whether the storage was available or not available at the end of the run, using A or NA respectively. The last two columns show the current content at the end of the run and the maximum content that occurred during the run.

For each RESET statement there are two runs that are contiguous in time. By using the above formulas, we can define the statistics for the combined runs, except for the average time per transaction of facilities and storages. If a facility is in use at the time of resetting, the fact that the facility was occupied will be counted in both runs so that, in combining the statistics, a single occurrence of engaging the facility will be counted twice. Similarly, if a storage is occupied at the time of resetting, the number of units occupying the storage at that time will be counted twice. The average time statistics, therefore, should only be used over a single run.

5-22

Facility and Storage SNAs

The principal SNA associated with a facility is its status, F_j, a variable that takes the value 1 when the facility is busy and 0 when it is free. For storages, the principal SNAs are the current content, S_j, and its complement, the remaining space, R_j. The other SNAs listed below are concerned with statistical measures. They are, in fact, the current values assumed by the statistics that appear in the standard output report, described and defined in Sec. 5-21. Utilization refers to utilization for the total time.

F_j	The status of facility j
FR_j	Utilization of facility j (in parts per thousand)
FC_j	Number of transactions that have used facility j
FT_j	Average utilization of facility j
S_j	Current content of storage j
R_j	Remaining space in storage j
SA_j	Average content of storage j (truncated to an integer)
SR_j	Utilization of storage j (in parts per thousand)
SM_j	Maximum content of storage j
SC_j	Number of units to have entered storage j
ST_j	Average time in storage j (truncated to an integer)

5-23

Utilization as Design Factor

The utilization statistics for facilities and storages are very significant measures of system performance since they reflect the extent to which the system entities are being used. A small utilization figure implies a light loading on the average, although there could have been short periods of heavy loading. A utilization of 1, or 100 per cent, implies that the entity is fully loaded, that is, that it was in use throughout the entire period of measurement.

The figures reported for utilization in the simulation output are for a particular run. They are affected by the conditions of the run. In particular, they are influenced by the initial conditions. If the system starts from an empty state, the reported figures will be biased to a lower value than should exist because of the time it takes to load the system up to its normal level. The RESET control statement, described in Sec. 3-15, is designed to remove this initial bias.

When random variables are involved, the statistics from one run are just one sample. A repeat with different random numbers will give another sample. A complete analysis of the system should include many such runs so that the variability of the system measures can be measured. The RESET statement helps to make such repeat runs.

An estimate of what utilization is to be expected can usually be made from the attributes of the system. In the terminology normally used in connection with queuing theory, a facility is a single-server entity, while a storage is a multiserver entity, with the number of servers equal to the storage capacity. The use made of a storage to represent a group of machines in the machine shop example of Chap. 3 illustrates this point. The principal attribute of a service unit is the mean service time, T_s, which is the mean time to serve each user, irrespective of the number than can be served simultaneously. The arrival of units for service is characterized by the mean interarrival time, T_a. Both these attributes can also be expressed in terms of rates, which give the number of units that can be served or that can arrive in a unit of time. The service rate is usually denoted by μ, and the arrival rate by λ. The rates and mean times are inversely related to each other, so that,

$$\mu = \frac{1}{T_s}$$

$$\lambda = \frac{1}{T_a}$$

Under steady-state conditions, where the initial bias due to starting has been removed or made negligible, the utilization to be expected can be expressed in terms of either the times or the rates. The utilization is denoted as ρ. In the case of a single server, it is defined as

$$\rho = \frac{T_s}{T_a} = \frac{\lambda}{\mu}$$

Since a multiserver entity can be simultaneously serving, say, N units, the loading for the same mean time is only one Nth of that for a single server entity, so that, in general,

$$\rho = \frac{T_s}{NT_a} = \frac{\lambda}{N\mu}$$

The significance of this measure is that most characteristics of a service system are functions of the expected utilization, ρ. However, the results depend upon the nature of the distributions for both the arrival times and the service time, and not just upon their means. For example, Fig. 5-9 shows

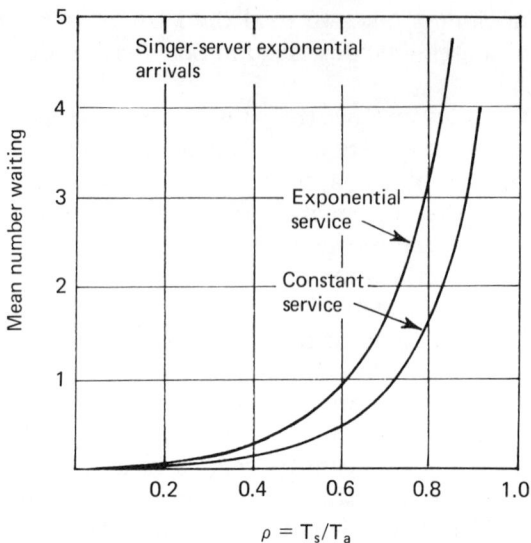

Figure 5-9. Expected number waiting in single-server system.

the expected number of units waiting to be served in a single-server system where the arrival time distribution is exponential and the service time distribution is either exponential or constant. Results for both systems can be plotted against ρ but different curves exist because of the different service time distributions. The fact that the results can be plotted against ρ means that different systems can be reduced to the same set of results, provided they match the distributions and system constraints under which the results were derived. Given one single-server system with, say, $T_s = 8$ and $T_a = 10$, the expected number waiting will be the same as another single-server system (with the same distributions) where $T_s = 16$ and $T_a = 20$, because they have the same value of ρ.

Other measures of a system can be similarly expressed as a function of utilization—for example, the mean waiting time or the probability of waiting more than a given amount of time. In Fig. 8-7 we will show the probability of waiting a given time for service to begin in a single-server system with exponentially distributed interarrival and service times. As will be seen, those results are plotted as a function of ρ.

Results for a multiserver system can also be expressed as a function of ρ, where ρ is defined as T_s/NT_a. Figure 5-10 shows the expected number of units waiting for service to begin in a multiserver system where both the interarrival and service times are exponentially distributed. For a given number of servers it is still possible to equate two systems with the same value of ρ, but two systems with the same ρ and different values of N are not equivalent. For example, doubling N and halving T_a keeps ρ unchanged, but, as can be seen from Fig. 5-10, the system with the greater number of servers has a smaller queue.

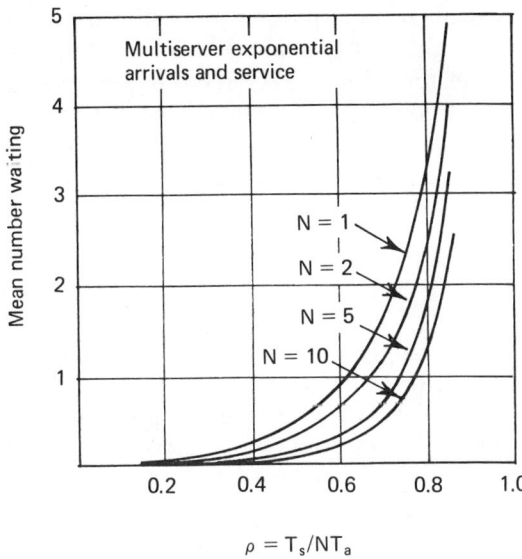

Figure 5-10. Expected number waiting in a multiserver system.

The results shown in Figs. 5-9 and 5-10 are theoretical. Nevertheless, they illustrate a point that is characteristic of all service systems. As the value of ρ increases, the system becomes more heavily loaded. Such measures as the number of units waiting for service to begin or the mean waiting time increase dramatically as ρ approaches the value 1. (When ρ exceeds 1, the system is overloaded and the queue lengths and waiting times continually increase.)

A good system design, therefore, is one that will keep the utilizations low and so minimize delays due to waiting for service. On the other hand, if ρ is too low, the system is being underutilized and is therefore costly. Most system design work is concerned with deciding on a balance between these opposing considerations.

In simple systems, it is relatively easy to check the value of ρ. For example, the factory model of Fig. 5-2, uses a facility with $T_a = 50$ and $T_s = 40$. Since this is a single-server system, the value of ρ is 0.8. The factory model of Fig. 5-3 used a storage of capacity 3 with $T_a = 50$ and $T_s = 120$. Since this is a system with three servers, the value of ρ also is 0.8. Estimating the value of ρ for the factory system of Fig. 5-4, however, is much more difficult because, once entered, the storage of that system can be left at different points, each associated with a different usage time, and the proportions of transactions that will leave at the different points is not known. This system is more typical of the type of system where simulation is needed to derive the utilization.

Knowing the general way in which system measures depend upon the utilization gives some insight into how the system must be changed to alter its performance. If a utilization is judged to be too high, so that the delays are becoming too high, the system can be improved by lowering the value of ρ, which means either reducing the service time, increasing the interarrival time, or increasing the number of servers. The formula for ρ shows the equivalency of different types of change. Correspondingly, if ρ is judged to be too low, it is possible to decide what changes will increase ρ.

Exercises

5-1 Workers come to a supply store at the rate of one every 5 ± 2 minutes. They have requisitions for supplies that take 8 ± 4 minutes to be processed by one of two clerks. The requisitions are then passed to a single storekeeper, who takes 4 ± 3 minutes to fill them, one at a time. Find how long it takes to fill 50 requisitions.

5-2 Extend Exercise 4-1 to include the fact that there is only one man selling newspapers.

5-3 Cars arrive at the rate of one every 5 ± 2 minutes at a parking lot that has a capacity for 100 cars. They stay for 30 ± 10 minutes. Program a model that, starting with an empty lot, will determine when the first car is turned away because the lot is full.

5-4 People arrive at the rate of one every 10 ± 5 minutes to use a single telephone. If the telephone is busy, 50 per cent of the people will come back after 5 minutes to try again. The rest give up trying. Assuming that a call takes 6 ± 3 minutes, count how many people will have given up by the time 1000 calls have been completed.

5-5 Consider again Exercise 4-3 of Chap. 4. Suppose that everybody must first check his coat with a single checker, who takes 2 ± 1 for each person. Also, the capacity of each room is limited to 10 people. If a room is full, people wait for space. Reprogram the exercise under these circumstances.

5-6 Trucks arrive at a dock at the rate of one every 30 ± 10 minutes. The dock can hold three trucks. If there is not room at the time of arrival, a truck will come back 20 ± 5 minutes later to try again. There is one work gang to unload all trucks, and they take 8 ± 4 minutes for each unloading. Simulate the unloading of 50 trucks.

5-7 Ships arrive in a harbor at the rate of one every $1 \pm \frac{1}{2}$ hours. There are six berths to accommodate them. They need the services of a crane to unload, and there are five cranes. After unloading, 10 per cent of the ships stay to refuel before leaving; the others leave immediately. The cranes are not needed for refueling. Assume that it takes $7\frac{1}{2} \pm 1$ hours to unload a ship, and $1 \pm \frac{1}{2}$ hours to refuel. Find how long it takes to clear 100 ships through the harbor.

5-8   Customers come to a barber shop at the rate of one every 5 ± 3 minutes. The shop cannot hold more than five customers at a time, counting people being served and waiting. If the shop is full, arriving people go elsewhere. There are three barbers and the customers are served in order of arrival. The customers like barber number 1 best and number 3 least. If there is a choice when their turn comes, the customers choose barbers in that order of preference, but they will not wait if there is any barber free. A haircut takes 10 ± 5 minutes. Simulate 100 haircuts.

5-9   A message is being received for transmission over a single channel every 5 ± 2 minutes. It takes 3 ± 1 minutes to complete transmission. The channel is taken out of service for 10 minutes every hour, on the hour. Any message being transmitted at the time is rescheduled. It will be restarted after any messages that happened to be waiting for transmission at the time service is removed, but ahead of any messages that arrive while service is out. Simulate for six hours of total time.

5-10   A doctor opens an office at 2 p.m. Patients arrive at the rate of one every 8 ± 2 minutes beginning at 2 p.m. The office can hold up to 10 patients, including the patient being examined. If the office is full, patients are turned away. The patients are examined, one at a time, for 10 ± 5 minutes. The office is closed at 5 p.m. but the doctor will see patients still waiting at that time. What time will the doctor finish work, and how many patients will have been examined?

6
PRIORITY

Provision must be made for the assigning of priorities to transactions. In this chapter we discuss two block types, PRIORITY and BUFFER, that are concerned with the control of priorities. Symbols for these blocks are shown in Fig. 6-1.

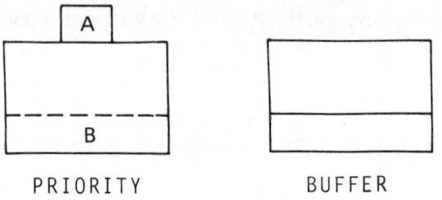

Figure 6-1. Block types 3.

6-1
Order of Priority

Priority is concerned with the order in which waiting transactions are sequenced. The program keeps such transactions in order of priority. Transactions having the same priority are listed in a first-in, first-out (FIFO) order.

That is, the transactions are kept in the order of their waiting times, the transaction that waits the longest being first. Unless stated otherwise, it will always be assumed that any group of waiting transactions are moved or scanned in order of priority, and by FIFO within a priority level. Other queuing disciplines can be programmed by using the chain feature described in Chap. 14.

The principal use of priority is in modeling systems where transactions compete for facilities or storages. A higher priority allows one transaction to go ahead of a lower-priority transaction. However, a higher priority by itself does not allow one transaction to interrupt the use of facilities or storages by a lower-priority transaction. In the case of transactions using facilities, such interruptions can be programmed by using preemption, described in Chap. 7.

There are 128 levels of priority denoted by the numbers 0 through 127, with 0 being the lowest level. Each transaction is assigned a priority when it is created. The value is determined by field E of the GENERATE block that creates the transaction. If the field is left blank, the priority is zero. At any point in the block diagram, the priority can be reset up or down, to any other level by entering a PRIORITY block.

6-2
Simultaneous Events

Transactions that cause events to occur simultaneously must be processed by the program sequentially, during the same clock instant. If the simultaneous transactions have the same priority, the order chosen is, in effect, random. The program follows a precise algorithm so that, if the simulation run is repeated, exactly the same order will result. However, determination of the order may require retracing the movement of the transactions through several previous steps to determine which arrived first. It may be possible to do this, but, for all practical purposes, simultaneous events caused by transactions of the same priority should be regarded as randomly ordered.

The choice of order may be of no consequence in the system behavior: the potential randomness may be characteristic of the system. Some thought, however, should always be given to the question of simultaneous events when modeling a system. If simultaneous events in the system will always be resolved in a certain order, the program user should make sure the priorities reflect that order.

While an exact duplication of a simulation run will always produce exactly the same sequence of events, minor changes to a model, which logically make no difference, can change the order of processing simultaneous events. For example, processing differences can be caused by altering the order in which the model is assembled, so that location assignments are different. Figure 6-2 is a trivial but instructive example. Two GENERATE blocks are

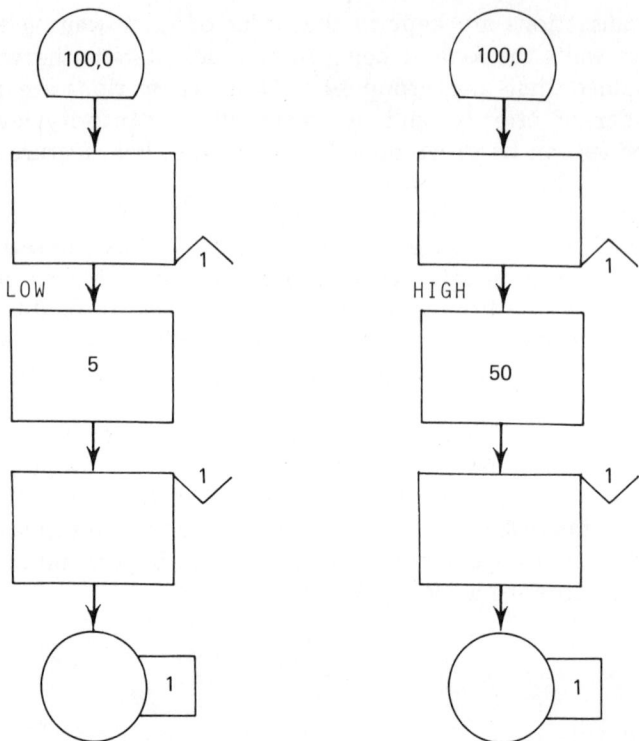

Figure 6-2. Processing simultaneous events.

producing transactions at 100-second intervals and sending the transactions to seize the same facility. One stream seizes it at the location LOW and uses it for 5 seconds, the other seizes it at HIGH and uses it for 50 seconds.

GPSS creates the initial transactions in the order in which it encounters GENERATE blocks in the input, and it files them in priority order and FIFO within priority class. In the present case, where both GENERATE blocks create transactions at the same time, the initial order will be maintained, since, as each transaction is processed, its successor is created and filed immediately.

The facility is seized at times 100, 200, 300, etc. If the transaction from the LOW segment goes first, the facility will be used for 5 seconds and then be immediately turned over to the simultaneously generated transaction from the HIGH segment, when it will be used for another 50 seconds. The times at which transactions release the facility and terminate, in that case, will be 105, 155, 205, etc. If the order is reversed, the times are 150, 155, 250, etc.

Shown in Fig. 6-3 are four ways the problem can be programmed. The two examples on the left have placed the LOW segment first, while the two on the right have put the HIGH segment first. In the upper two cases, all trans-

```
 1              GENERATE    100         1              GENERATE    100
 2              ADVANCE                 2              ADVANCE
 3              SEIZE       1           3              SEIZE       1
 4       LOW    ADVANCE     5           4       HIGH   ADVANCE     50
 5              RELEASE     1           5              RELEASE     1
 6              TERMINATE   1           6              TERMINATE   1
         *                                      *
 7              GENERATE    100         7              GENERATE    100
 8              ADVANCE                 8              ADVANCE
 9              SEIZE       1           9              SEIZE       1
10       HIGH   ADVANCE     50         10       LOW    ADVANCE     5
11              RELEASE     1          11              RELEASE     1
12              TERMINATE   1          12              TERMINATE   1
         *                                      *
                START       3                          START       3

     RELATIVE CLOCK         205             RELATIVE CLOCK         250
                 (a)                                    (b)


 1              GENERATE    100,,,,1     1              GENERATE    100
 2              ADVANCE                  2              ADVANCE
 3              SEIZE       1            3              SEIZE       1
 4       LOW    ADVANCE     5            4       HIGH   ADVANCE     50
 5              RELEASE     1            5              RELEASE     1
 6              TERMINATE   1            6              TERMINATE   1
         *                                       *
 7              GENERATE    100          7              GENERATE    100,,,,1
 8              ADVANCE                  8              ADVANCE
 9              SEIZE       1            9              SEIZE       1
10       HIGH   ADVANCE     50          10       LOW    ADVANCE     5
11              RELEASE     1          11              RELEASE     1
12              TERMINATE   1          12              TERMINATE   1
         *                                       *
                START       3                           START       3

     RELATIVE CLOCK         205              RELATIVE CLOCK         205
                 (c)                                     (d)
```

Figure 6-3. Effects of priority on simultaneous events.

actions have a priority of 0. In the lower two cases the transactions in the LOW segment have been given a priority of 1, by putting a 1 in field E of the GENERATE blocks. Under each case is shown the time at which the third transaction terminated.

When there is no priority, the time is 205 if the LOW segment is first, and 250 if the HIGH segment is first. When the LOW segment transactions have a higher priority, the time is 205, whichever order is used.

Using a different set of random numbers in a stochastic system can always be expected to produce differences. The changes in such statistical measures as a mean value may be slight, but they might result in radically different outcomes when some critical system element is processed differently.

6-3

PRIORITY Blocks

A transaction entering a PRIORITY block has its priority set up or down to the level indicated in field A. The new level of priority remains in effect until the transaction enters another PRIORITY block. The transaction becomes the last member of its new priority class. This is, in fact, the only action if the new priority happens to be the same as the transaction's current priority.

Because the change will usually move the logical position of the transaction within the current events scan, the program sets the status change flag in the scan routine. The program will then restart the scan when it has finished processing the transaction. (See Appendix 6.)

If the word BUFFER is placed in field B of the PRIORITY block, the program immediately implements a rescan as though the transaction had entered a BUFFER block after the change of priority. This may affect the way the program processes other transactions, as will be explained shortly in Sec. 6-6.

6-4

Machine Operating With Priority

To illustrate the effects of priority, consider again the example of a machine given previously in Fig. 5-2. A block diagram for a revised version of the system is shown in Fig. 6-4.

One GENERATE block creates transactions that represent normal jobs at the rate of one every 5 minutes. The priority of these normal jobs is zero, so the GENERATE block has field E left blank. Higher priority jobs are represented by transactions created at a second GENERATE block at the rate of one every 11 minutes. These transactions have their priority raised at a PRIORITY block in order to illustrate the use of this block type. The priority could equally well have been selected at the GENERATE block. A more extensive model would have simulated the prior history of the transactions, during which time the two types may not have needed different priorities. In that case a PRIORITY block would be needed to raise the priority.

Figure 6-5 gives the coding and results of a run for the problem, and Fig. 6-6 illustrates the sequence of events that occur in a run. For purposes of comparison, the top line of Fig. 6-6 shows how the facility would be occupied if only the normal sequence of jobs is processed. The successive normal jobs have been labeled 1, 2, 3, ... The next line shows the sequencing when jobs of the second stream, labeled A, B, C, . . . , are introduced, but they have the *same priority* as the normal jobs. Arrows show

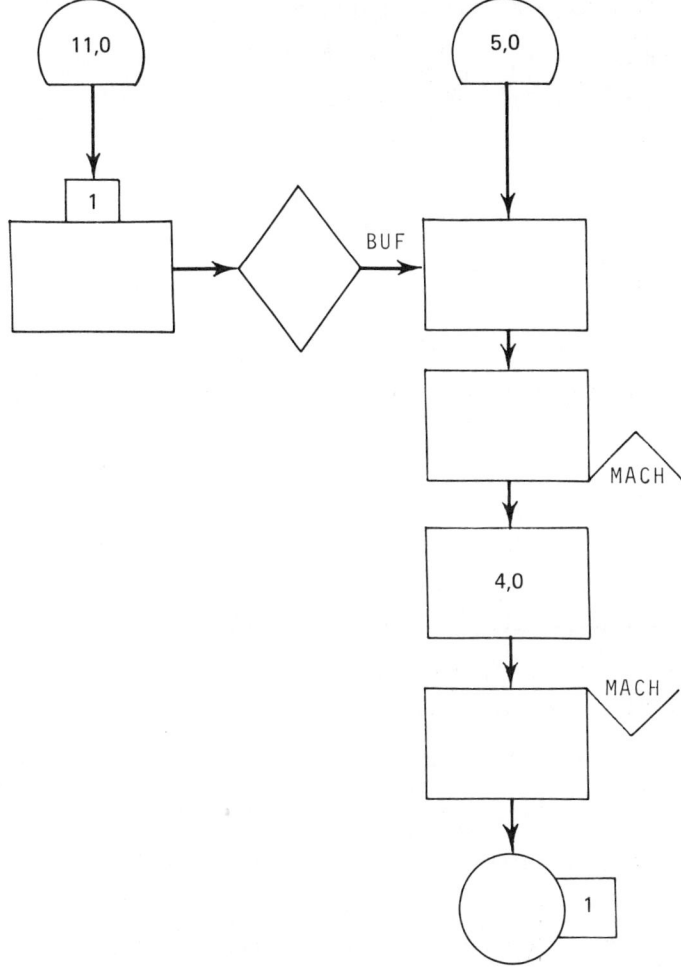

Figure 6-4. Machine operating with priority.

the arrival time of the jobs. With no difference in priority the sequence is FIFO, which in this case, is 1, 2, A, 3, 4, B, 5, 6, C, 7, 8, D, 9.

The third line shows the sequence when the rush jobs have a higher priority. When rush job A arrives, the facility is busy with job 2. The higher priority of job A does not entitle the rush job to interrupt job 2. It must wait for job 2 to finish. At that time there is no other waiting job, so job A starts at clock time 14, just as it would without higher priority. Job 3 is delayed by job A, and in turn it delays job 4. Rush job B arrives just as the facility becomes free and, because of its priority, it takes over, even though job 4 has been waiting. Similarly, job C is processed ahead of 6, and job D ahead of 8.

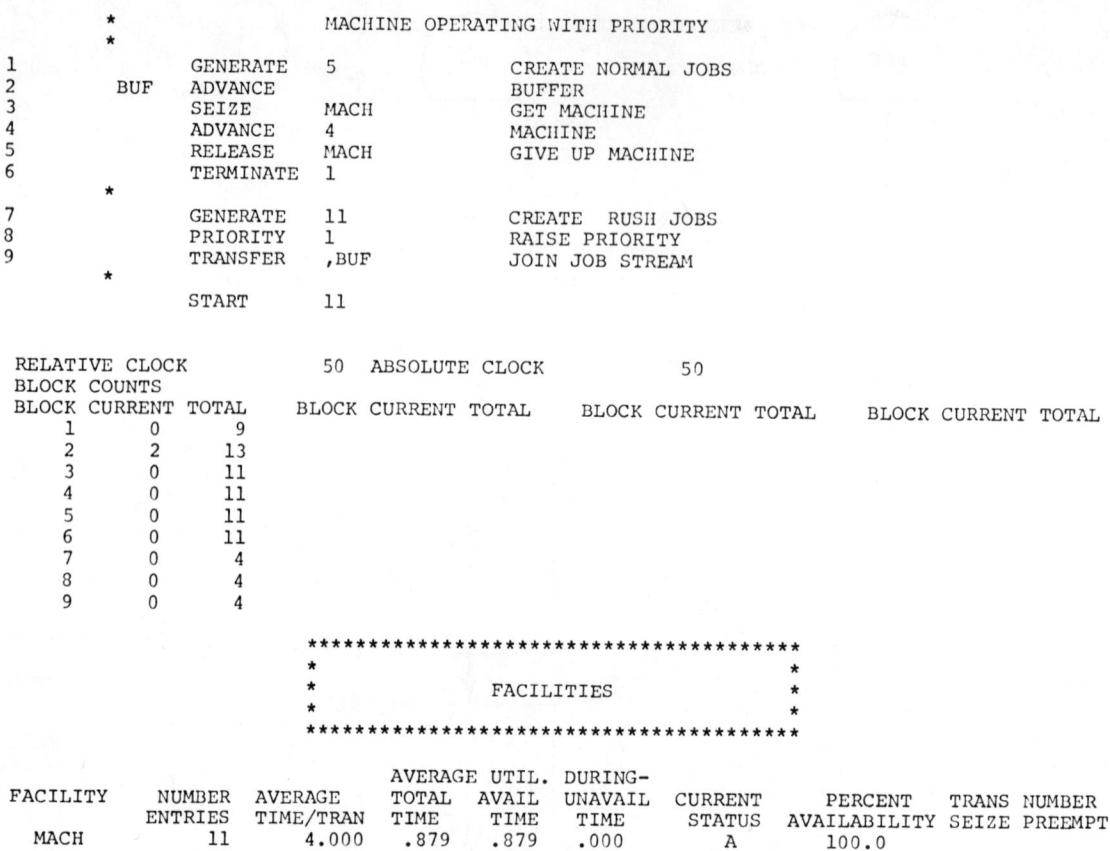

Figure 6-5. Coding and output for machine operating with priority.

6-5

Effects of Priority

When there is no congestion in a system, priority has no effect, but when queues form because there is contention for some system resource, such as a facility, priority selects the order of processing. Many statistical measures of the system may remain essentially unchanged because the same total amount of processing is involved. The mean waiting time and the mean queue length, measured for all transactions, without regard to priority, will remain the same. The reordering caused by priority may have the effect of taking a different sample; so, if random processes are involved, the output from two simulation runs may show slight differences in these measures, but they are essentially measuring the same quantity.

The individual measures for different-priority classes, are different, however. High-priority transactions will have a mean waiting time lower than

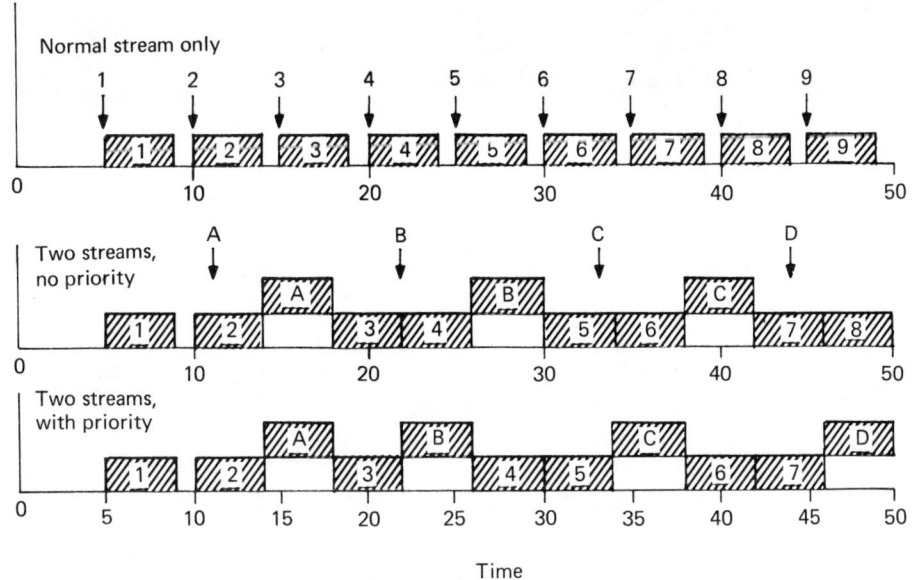

Figure 6-6. Sequencing of events with priority.

the overall average, which is gained at the expense of increasing the mean waiting time for the ordinary transactions. If the high-priority transactions form a small proportion of the total, their waiting time can be significantly decreased at the cost of a small increase for the others.

The improvement brought about by priority is illustrated in Fig. 6-7. Transactions being generated at the rate of one every 100 seconds are to be processed by a facility for an average of 95 seconds. They are divided into two groups, with 10 per cent being randomly selected to go to the location RUSH. Both groups use the same facility but the RUSH group has its priority raised to 1 at a PRIORITY block. To illustrate the differences, we anticipate some features of GPSS that will not be fully explained until Chap. 8. There are block types called QUEUE and DEPART, surrounding the SEIZE blocks, which will measure the queues forming at the two points at which the facility is being used. There are also two TABULATE blocks that will measure the total time the transactions spend in the system.

Table 6-1 compares the results when the RUSH transactions have priority with the case where they do not, that is, where the PRIORITY block is not used. The results are taken from runs of 1000 terminations, following an initialization of 10 terminations, and results are rounded to the nearest integer. Without priority there are only slight differences in the time spent on the queues and the total time spent in the system. The differences are the results of sampling. When there is priority, however, there are significant differences. The average time on the queue for the high-priority jobs is only 35 seconds, compared with 105, and the average total time is 133 against 201. It will be noticed that the average times for the ordinary transactions

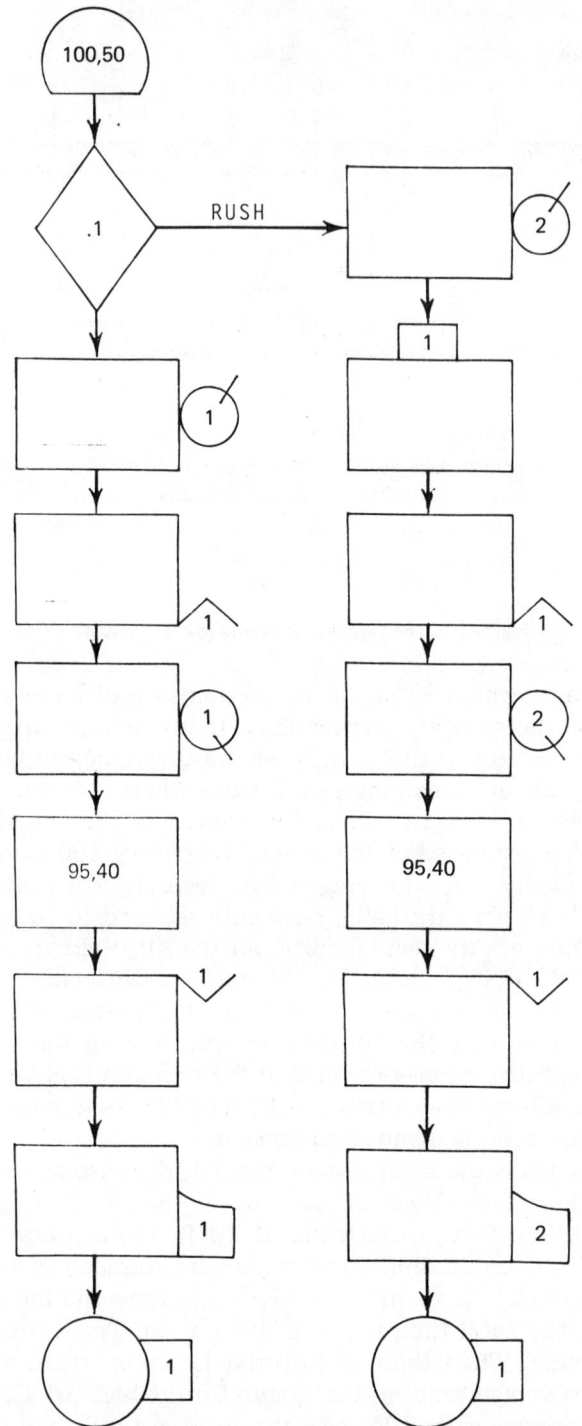

Figure 6-7. Effects of priority on mean waiting times.

Table 6-1 Effects of Priority on Processing Times

	No priority		With priority	
	Rush	Other	Rush	Other
Queue time	96	91	35	105
Total time	193	189	133	201

have been increased by the introduction of priority; the average queue time has gone from 91 to 105, and the average total time from 189 to 201. Another interesting comparison is that the facility utilization was 0.948 when there was no priority, and 0.949 when there was priority—showing that the introduction of priority has not changed the work load.

If there is no priority, there is no reason for splitting the transactions into two groups. However, this is another example of a situation in which two ways of programming the same system can produce slightly different results. If the results quoted in Table 6-1 for the case of no priority are compared with the case in which the transactions are not broken into two groups, slight sampling differences can arise. If the transactions are not divided, they are served in strict order of arrival. With the splitting into two groups, it is possible that one arrival may be directed to a group for which there is currently no waiting, while an earlier transaction could have been sent to the other group for which there currently is a wait. As a result, there is a difference is processing order. In this case, the difference will not be significant, but, if its origin is not understood, it could cause concern.

6-6
BUFFER Blocks

It will be recalled from Sec. 3-6 that, at each clock instant, the program moves a transaction as far as it can before turning its attention to other transactions. There are special occasions when this may violate the priority rules of the system. The transaction may cause a system change at one block and, by continuing to move at the same clock instant, it may take advantage of that change in another block. However, there could have been a higher-priority transaction waiting for the same system change. The normal processing rule would therefore result in the lower-priority transaction taking advantage of the change ahead of the higher-priority transaction. The BUFFER block is designed to prevent this.

A BUFFER block is coded by having only the word BUFFER in the operation field. When a transaction enters a BUFFER block, the program stops processing that transaction and immediately restarts scanning all waiting transactions, without changing the clock time. It recommences the scan from the highest-priority transaction. Eventually it will again reach the transaction in the BUFFER block and hence complete any additional movement which that transaction can make at the current clock time. However, if a higher-priority transaction is waiting for a change made by the transaction, it will be moved before the transaction leaves the BUFFER block. In effect a transaction pauses at a BUFFER block to give higher-priority transactions a chance to move. It is to be emphasized that the circumstances are rather unusual; the user does not normally have to concern himself with ensuring that the priorities are correctly recognized.

6-7

Example of BUFFER Block

An example of where a BUFFER block is needed is given in Fig. 6-8. Suppose that the system shown in Fig. 6-4 and discussed in Sec. 6-4 is extended in the following way. After the machining operation with facility 1 is finished, the parts should go to a second machine represented by facility 2. That machine operation takes 1 minute. However, machine 2 (but not machine 1) is also being used by a third stream of jobs that arrive every 12 minutes. If machine 2 is busy when a part finishes the first operation, that part stays on machine 1 for the second operation, unless there is a priority job waiting for machine 1. In that case the low-priority transaction gives up facility 1 and waits for machine 2 to become available.

When a transaction releases facility 1 after the first operation, it goes to a TRANSFER block with a conditional mode. If facility 2 is available, the transaction seizes it and moves to the ADVANCE block that represents use of facility number 2. If facility 2 is busy, the transaction goes to a BUFFER block and pauses there while the program rescans higher-priority transactions. Should there be one waiting for facility 1 at the ADVANCE block fed by the two GENERATE blocks, that transaction will seize the facility and move into the ADVANCE block with a 4-minute time. In the same instant the scan will return to the transaction at the BUFFER block and move it to another conditional TRANSFER block. If facility 1 is taken by a higher-priority transaction, the buffered transaction moves over to wait for facility 2; otherwise it takes over facility 1. Without the BUFFER block, the transaction would have taken over facility 1 as soon as it found facility 2 busy and would have violated the system's priority rule.

Special circumstances of the type just described often occur when a transaction changes priority. For this reason the PRIORITY block has a buffer option that, in effect, combines a BUFFER block with the PRIORITY block (see Sec. 6-3).

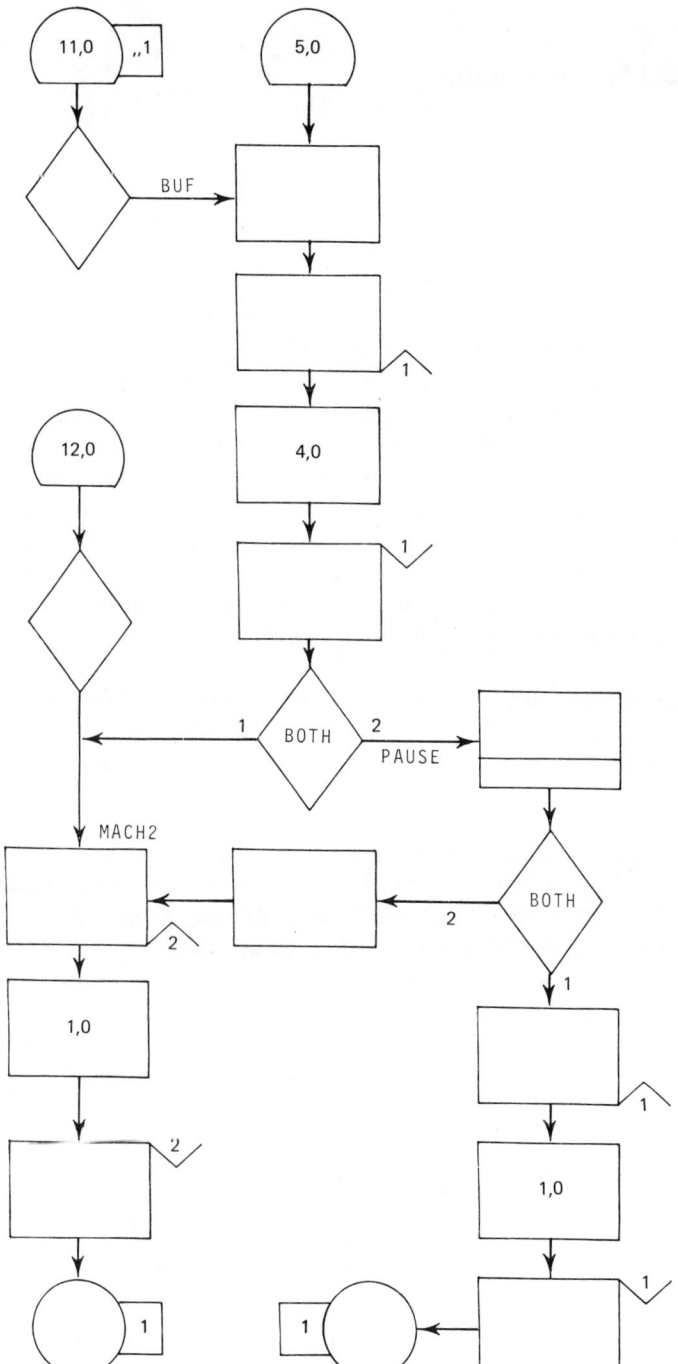

Figure 6-8. Use of the BUFFER block.

6-8
Priority Used for Scan Control

The use of priority in the previous example reflects a characteristic of the system that is being simulated; the parts have actually been assigned different priorities. Sometimes there are no such priorities in the system, but priorities are assigned in the simulation so that, with the aid of the BUFFER block, the order in which transactions move can be controlled. Events that are simultaneous in the system can then be executed in a specific order.

The chief occasion when such special attention may be needed is when transactions are inserted into the current events chain as the result of processing some transaction already on the current events chain. It will be recalled from Sec. 2-8 that transactions can be removed from the current events chain and, in effect, placed in suspense, by joining the match chain or one of the user chains. These features have yet to be explained; but whenever a transaction on these chains is reactivated, it returns to the current events chain by being inserted as the last transaction of its priority class. The reactivation is caused by some other transaction, currently being processed, that is performing one of the following acts:

(a) Satisfying a matching condition by entering a MATCH, ASSEMBLE, or GATHER block
(b) Unlinking a transaction from a user chain by entering an UNLINK block

A transaction can also be suspended by being removed to the interrupt chain. When the interruption is removed, however, the transaction is returned to the *future* events chain to expend the remainder of the time it was due to use a facility at the time of interruption.

When transactions are returned to the current events chain, some thought should be given to the relative priorities of the returned transaction and the transaction that caused the return, or any other transactions that are due to be processed at the time the reactivation occurs. (In the case of an ASSEMBLE block, the transaction that caused the reactivation will have been removed from the system.)

The reactivated transaction is placed on the current events chain as the last member of its priority class. It is made active and is marked as being about to enter the block at which it is reactivated. The program does not, however, immediately effect the entry into that block. Instead, it sets the status change flag in the scan routine (see Appendix 6) so that there will be a rescan at the current clock time. The reactivated transaction will therefore enter the block at the current clock time, but only after the program finishes processing the transaction that caused the reactivation and, possibly, some other transactions due to move at the same time, depending on the relative priorities of the transactions.

The order of processing may not be important, but, if it is, a rescan must be forced immediately by sending the transaction that causes the reactivation to a BUFFER block. If the reactivated transaction has a higher priority than the reactivating transaction, it will be processed first in the rescan. If it has a lower or equal priority, it will join the current events chain behind the reactivating transaction, and the rescan will not change the processing order. It is not possible to change the order by sending the reactivated transaction to a PRIORITY block because the program will not yet have made the move. To ensure that the reactivated transaction moves first, it must have a higher priority at the time of reactivation, or the method illustrated in Fig. 6-9 can be used. The figure illustrates the cases of MATCH and UNLINK blocks. Both block types will be described later. In the case of a MATCH block, there will be one transaction, logically located at the block called AAA, but actually on the match chain. When another related transaction enters the other MATCH block, called BBB, the transaction on the match chain is reactivated, and will be marked to go to block CCC. The reactivating transaction will continue to be processed, however, so it will enter the PRIORITY block, with a BUFFER option, that follows BBB. In the case of the UNLINK block, the reactivating transaction similarly moves into a PRIORITY block with a BUFFER option, while the reactivated transaction is marked as entering location CCC.

The BUFFER option will force a rescan immediately. If the priority of the reactivating transaction has been lowered below that of the reactivated transaction, the reactivated transaction will be processed first. If the transactions are of the same priority, it is enough to leave the priority unchanged or simply use a BUFFER block because the reactivating transaction will then be moved to the end of its priority class, which places it behind the reactivated transaction.

The same method can be used with a GATHER block, but it is not usually of any importance in that case. The GATHER block allows a number of transaction to be collected together at the GATHER block before all are allowed to proceed. The early arrivals are placed on the match chain, and the last arrival causes their reactivation. In the case of the ASSEMBLE block, a number of transaction are similarly brought together but only one is allowed to proceed. The remainder are destroyed. The first arrival is placed on the match chain, and the last arrival reactivates it before being itself destroyed.

One other case where a similar use of priority assignment with a BUFFER block might be needed occurs with a SPLIT block (to be described in Sec. 13-2). A transaction entering a SPLIT block causes copies of itself to be made. They always have the same priority as the original transaction, so they are entered in the current events chain behind the original transaction (but not necessarily immediately behind). The program does not turn on the status change flag because it is then certain that the scan will eventually reach the new transactions. If it is important that the copies be processed immediately, before continuing with the original, the method illustrated in

Fig. 6-9 should be used, without changing the priority of the original, so that the original is moved behind the copies before rescanning.

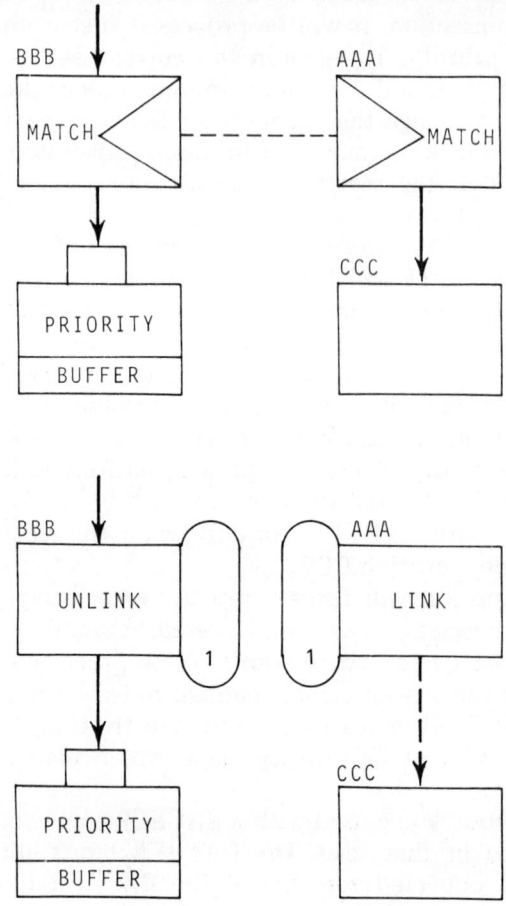

Figure 6-9. Changing the scanning order at MATCH and UNLINK blocks.

Exercises

6-1 People come to use a typewriter to type letters every 5 ± 3 minutes. When they finish, they take 1 minute to check the letter. They find an error in 20 per cent of the letters. They may then go ahead of anyone waiting in line and use the typewriter for 1 minute to correct the error. Assume that there are no additional errors after correction. Simulate completion of 100 letters.

6-2 People arrive to use a single telephone at the rate of one every 10 ± 5 minutes. A call takes 8 ± 3 minutes. If the telephone is busy at the time of arrival, half the people decide to wait, the other half go away for 5 minutes and then come back to wait until they do make their call. People who decide to wait in the first place go ahead of anybody who left. Simulate completion of 100 calls.

6-3 Boats sail upstream and pass through a lock. They then turn around and sail downstream to their starting point. The lock can only take one boat at a time, irrespective of direction. Assume that a boat starts every 5 minutes and that it takes 15 ± 5 to sail upstream. It takes 2 ± 1 minutes to go through the lock, 2 minutes to turn around, and 10 ± 3 minutes to sail downstream. Compare the times to complete 100 round trip journeys (1) when the lock services boats on a first-come, first-served basis, and (2) when downstream boats have priority.

6-4 Messages are created at the rate of one every 30 ± 10 seconds. They are sent over a communication channel, one at a time. Twenty per cent of them require a reply, which returns over the same channel after a delay of 60 ± 30 seconds. Assume the transmission time for the original message to be 25 ± 15 seconds and for the reply 15 ± 5 seconds. Assume also that both messages and replies can be stored for transmission, if necessary. Compare the time it takes to complete 100 replies (1) when the replies have priority and (2) when the messages have priority.

6-5 Two boats are being used to ferry troops across a river, one man at a time in each boat. One boat is primarily for officers, and it takes 5 minutes for a round trip. The other is used by other ranks and it takes 10 minutes for a round trip. However, if there are as many as three men waiting for the slower boat when a man arrives, the latter is sent to use the officer's boat; but he must wait for it to be completely free of waiting officers. Having being so assigned, he does not change boats. Occasionally, a staff officer appears, and he has top priority on the officer's boat. The rates of arrival, in minutes between arrivals, are as follows: other ranks, 10 ± 5; officers, 4 ± 2; and staff officers, 15 ± 10. Simulate the ferrying of 500 troops of all ranks.

6-6 An office has two copying machines. Secretaries from a general office arrive to use a machine at the rate of one every 5 ± 2 minutes. They choose a machine at random, whether it is busy or not, and they stay with their choice. A secretary from the president's office arrives at intervals of 15 ± 5 minutes. If a machine is free, it is used. If not, the secretary goes to the head of the line for machine number 1. Assuming that all jobs take 6 ± 3 minutes, simulate the completion of 100 jobs of all types.

6-7 Two lines of parts are being processed separately by two machines, A and B. The interarrival time on each line is 20 ± 10 minutes and processing takes 10 minutes. Once every 15 minutes, machine A is taken out of service for 5 minutes. Any job being processed at that time is transferred to line B, where it immediately takes the machine, if it is available, or it becomes the next in line to use it. Any parts waiting for machine A at the time it goes out of service are placed at the back of any line waiting for machine B. Arrivals for machine A while it is out of service will simply wait for machine A to become available again. Simulate the processing of 100 parts by machine A.

6-8 A 2-mile stretch of a single-rail track runs north and south. It is broken into two equal lengths and a siding placed at the junction. Southbound trains have priority. If a northbound train is on its first segment when a southbound train arrives, it must divert to the siding and wait for the southbound train to cover the full 2 miles before it can continue. Assume that all trains move at 30 mph, and ignore the time to divert onto the siding. Southbound trains arrive at the rate of one every 15 ± 5 minutes, and northbound trains arrive every 30 ± 10 minutes. Simulate the passage of 50 southbound trains.

6-9 A continuously running film takes 15 minutes to be seen completely. There are 10 seats for viewers, who arrive at the rate of one every 2 ± 2 minutes. If a seat is available, they immediately take it, otherwise they wait for a seat. Everybody would like to see the show a second time, so, when they have seen the show (i.e., 15 minutes after they get a seat), they will keep their seat for another full showing, unless there is somebody waiting, in which case they leave without seeing the show again. Simulate five hours of the showing.

6-10 An office has only one telephone. The office personnel use it on a first-come, first-served basis, except that the office manager always goes to the head of any queue. Some people from the general office want to make two calls when they get the telephone. So long as the manager is not waiting when they finish their first call, they make their second call. Otherwise they give way to the manager (who always makes only one call), but they immediately follow the manager for their second call. Assume that the general office personnel want to use the telephone every 6 ± 4 minutes, and that 25 per cent of them want to make a second call. The manager wants to make calls at intervals of 10 ± 5 minutes. All calls take 5 ± 2 minutes. Simulate the completion of 100 visits to the telephone.

7
PREEMPTING FACILITIES

A SEIZE block does not allow a transaction to take over a facility that is already in use, but the PREEMPT and RETURN blocks, to be described in this chapter, do allow a transaction to interrupt the use of a facility by another transaction. The block diagram symbols for the PREEMPT and RETURN blocks are shown in Fig. 7-1.

The PREEMPT block is one of the more complicated blocks of GPSS; its many options reflect such factors as whether an interrupting transaction can itself be interrupted, whether the interrupted transaction is allowed to resume use of the facility, and, if so, whether the resumption is immediate or must be in priority contention.

In its simplest mode of operation, called the *interrupt mode*, the PREEMPT block allows one transaction to interrupt another transaction, but the interrupting transaction cannot itself be interrupted. In addition, the interrupted

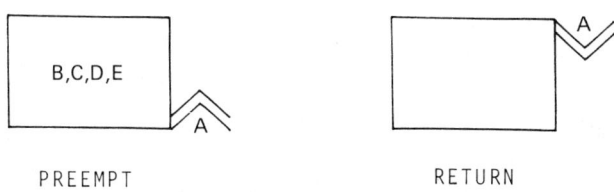

Figure 7-1. Block types 4.

transaction recovers control of the facility when the interrupting transaction gives up control of the facility. The reader may find it more convenient to concentrate on this simpler mode as it is described in Secs. 7-1 to 7-3, and return to the more complex mode after some experience with the program. The full details of the PREEMPT block, however, will be presented in this chapter.

In explaining the more complex mode we will use a model that modifies the block diagram between runs so that we can illustrate how this is done and, in particular, show how absolute locations of blocks are used.

7-1
PREEMPT Blocks in Interrupt Mode

A facility that has been seized by one transaction can be taken over by another transaction that enters a PREEMPT block, even if the transaction that seized the facility has a higher priority than the transaction that is preempting the facility. The facility to be preempted is given in the A field of the PREEMPT block, and, if the block is in the interrupt mode, which is indicated by leaving field B blank, no other fields are recognized.

If the facility happens to be free at the time a transaction enters a PREEMPT block, it will still be preempted, unless the facility has been made unavailable. When the facility is unavailable at the time a preemption is attempted, whether or not it is seized, the preemption will be deferred until the facility becomes available again.

In the interrupt mode, the transaction that preempts the facility cannot be further preempted. Any transaction that attempts such a second-level preemption will have to wait for the first preemption to be completed, even if the first preemption was made on a facility that was not seized at the time of preemption.

A transaction that had seized a facility and is then preempted is said to be interrupted. It is normally placed on the interrupt chain and returned to the future events chain when the interruption is removed. (Some exceptions will be discussed in Sec. 7-6.) When interrupted, the residue of time for which a transaction was due to use the facility is stored in the transaction and appears in any system printout under the heading "ADV BLOCK DEPART." A single transaction can be simultaneously interrupted on as many as 255 facilities. A preempt counter in the transaction keeps track of the number.

7-2
RETURN Blocks

A transaction entering a RETURN block releases control of the facility named in field A. The transaction must have preemptive control of the facility at the time of entering the block or there will be an error stop. If control of the facility was obtained by interrupting a transaction with a PREEMPT block in an interrupt mode, control will normally be passed back to the interrupted transaction. However, if there should be other transactions waiting to take over the facility at a PREEMPT block, control will pass to the highest priority of these.

If the transaction entering the RETURN block has control of more than one facility, it only returns control of the facility named in field A. Field A is the only field used for a RETURN block, whichever mode of preemption is involved.

A transaction that was interrupted is normally on the interrupt chain. When a return has been made, the transaction's preempt count is reduced by one, and, if all preemptions have been removed, the transaction is restored to the ADVANCE block at which it was using the facility, and placed on the future events chain. It will normally remain there for the residue of the time it was due to use the facility at the time of preemption. If the transaction is on the match chain or is blocked and therefore, on the current events chain at the time a preemption is removed, the preempt count is also reduced by one, and, if the result is zero, a flag that was set at the time of preemption—to indicate that the transaction is to go to the interrupt chain—is canceled.

7-3

Machine Operating With Interruptions

To illustrate the use of a PREEMPT block in an interrupt mode, we return to the machine operation discussed before in Sec. 6-4 and illustrated in Figs. 6-4 to 6-6. In that example, rush jobs that had priority could be machined ahead of lower-priority jobs that were waiting, but they could not interrupt the job in progress. It was possible to inject the rush job transactions into the stream of normal jobs because the program will automatically order the transactions by priority.

To allow the rush jobs to interrupt the job in progress, the model shown in Fig. 7-2 can be used. It is now necessary to use separate lines of blocks for the normal and the rush jobs. Using the same time values as before, the normal jobs are created every 5 time units and the rush jobs every 11 time units. The sequence of events that occurs is illustrated in Fig. 7-3. For comparison the top row of the figure shows what happens when there are no rush jobs. The normal jobs are labeled 1, 2, 3, . . . , and the rush jobs are labeled A, B, C, ... As shown in the second line of Fig. 7-3, rush jobs A, C, and D arrive when the machine is busy on normal jobs. They therefore interrupt jobs 2, 5, and 7. As shown, however, control of the facility passes back to these transactions when the preemption is over. Rush job B happens to arrive at an instant when the facility is being released by job 3. It does

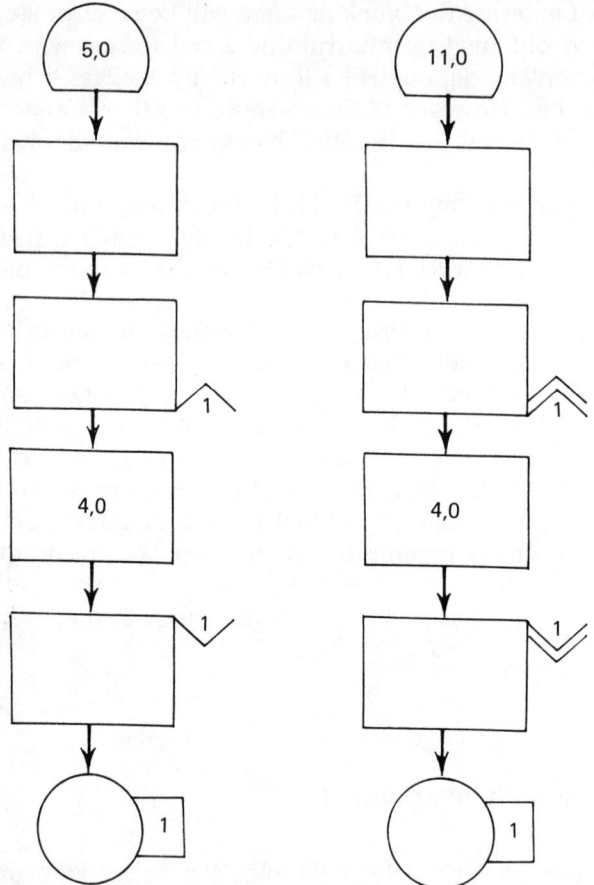

Figure 7-2. Interrupt mode of the PREEMPT block.

not have to interrupt any normal job, but it takes precedence over normal job 4. Coding and results for this example are shown in Fig. 7-4.

7-4

PREEMPT Blocks in Priority Mode

If a PREEMPT block carries the letters PR in field B, it operates in a priority mode and several options are open. A second transaction can preempt a transaction that is currently preempting a facility if the second has higher priority. If no other options are exercised through the use of fields C, D, or E, the lower-priority transaction that is preempted is treated in the same way as a transaction that originally seized the facility. That is, control

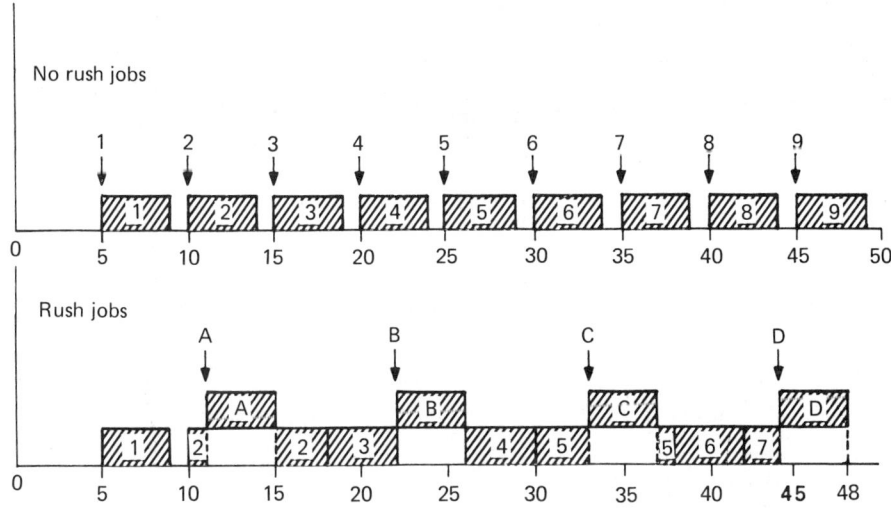

Figure 7-3. Sequence of events with interruption.

of the facility will be returned to the lower-priority transaction when the higher-priority transaction has finished using the facility. The process of multiple preemptions can be continued to many levels with transactions of increasing priorities. When a transaction does not have a higher priority than the transaction in control of the facility, it will wait until all higher-level transactions have finished. Note, however, this rule applies among transactions that are preempting the facility. A transaction that has gained control of a facility at a SEIZE block will be interrupted by a transaction entering a PREEMPT block, irrespective of priorities.

If, in addition to the letters PR in field B, field C carries a location, any transaction that is preempted, either one that originally seized the facility or a lower-priority preempting transaction, is displaced to that location. Displacement by itself does not remove the transaction from contention for the facility when the preemption is removed. If the displacement is also to mean that the transaction loses control of the facility altogether, the letters RE (for remove) must be placed in field E. If this is not done, care must be taken to see that the displaced transaction does eventually go to a RELEASE or RETURN block to give up the facility.

One additonal option that is available is to use field D to carry a parameter number. At the time of displacement, the program will then place in that parameter of the displaced transaction the time that remained for the transaction to use the facility at the instant of preemption.

Figure 7-5 is a flowchart that explains the options available at a PREEMPT block. It also shows the constraints that exist in the use of the fields. Field A must be given. Field B must be given for any of the higher fields to be effective. Similarly, field C must be given for fields D or E to be effective.

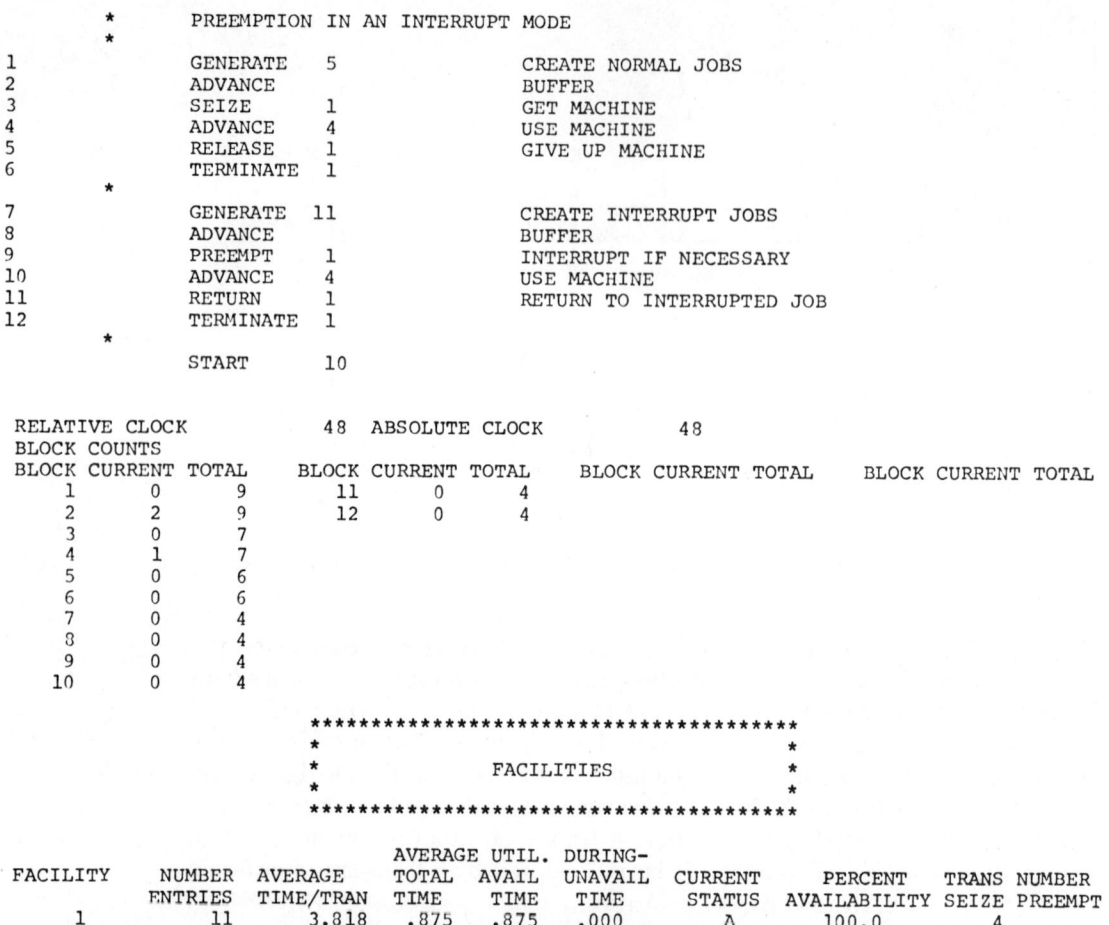

Figure 7-4. Coding and output for interruption example.

If a preempted transaction is not actually using the facility, that is, if it is not at an ADVANCE block with nonzero remaining time, none of the options is exercised (see Sec. 7-6).

7-5

Machine Operating With Priority Preemptions

To illustrate the use of preemption in a priority mode, we return to the machine operation example previously discussed in Sec. 7-3 and illustrated in Figs. 7-2 and 7-3. The model discussed there will be modified to allow multiple-level preemptions first without displacement and then with dis-

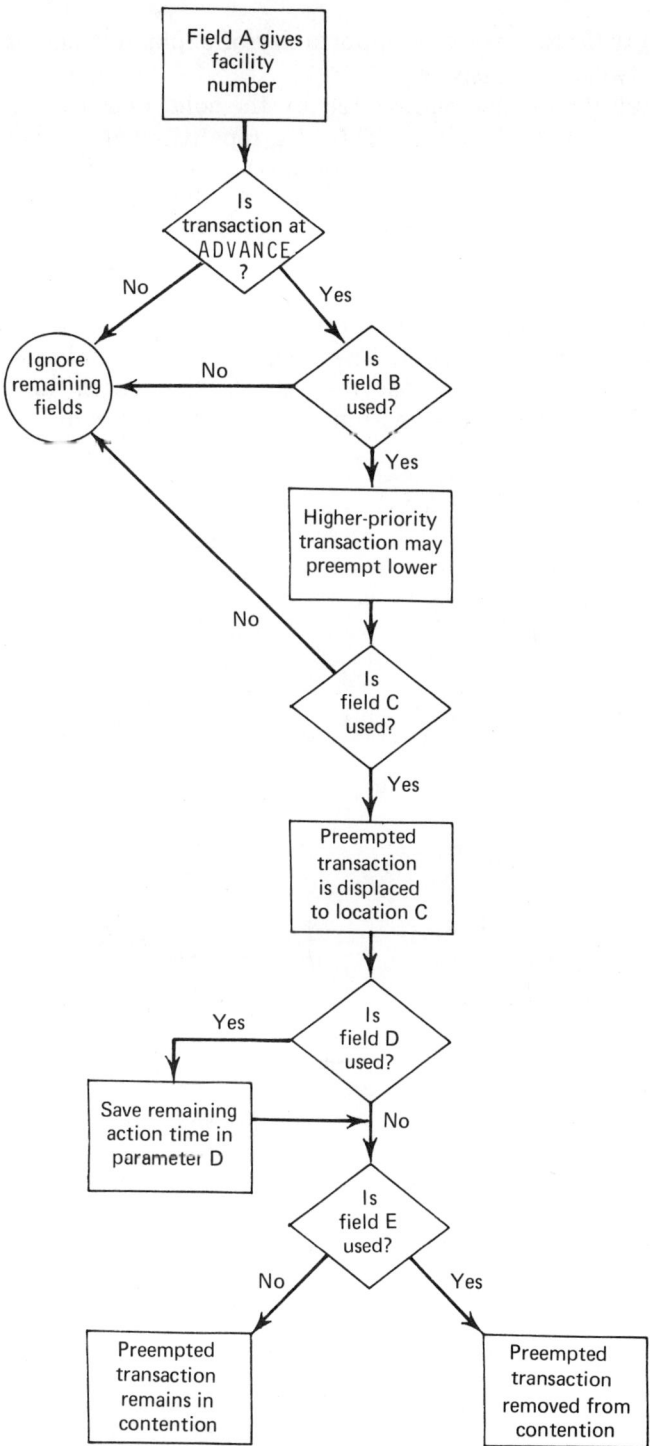

Figure 7-5. PREEMPT block options.

placement. We will also take this opportunity of explaining how models can be modified between successive runs.

Consider first the model represented by the solid lines of Fig. 7-6, that is, the columns marked I and I'. This is a repetition of the model using preemption in an interrupt mode that was given in Fig. 7-2 and coded in Fig. 7-4, except for the times used. We will first rerun that model and then modify the model twice in two other runs. The coding for all three runs, together with the outputs, is shown in Fig. 7-7. Figure 7-8 will be used to explain the sequence of events.

The first model, using only the interrupt mode, is the section of coding up to the first START statement. The PREEMPT block only uses field A. The top line of Fig. 7-8 shows the transactions that enter the PREEMPT block interrupting the transactions from the normal job stream.

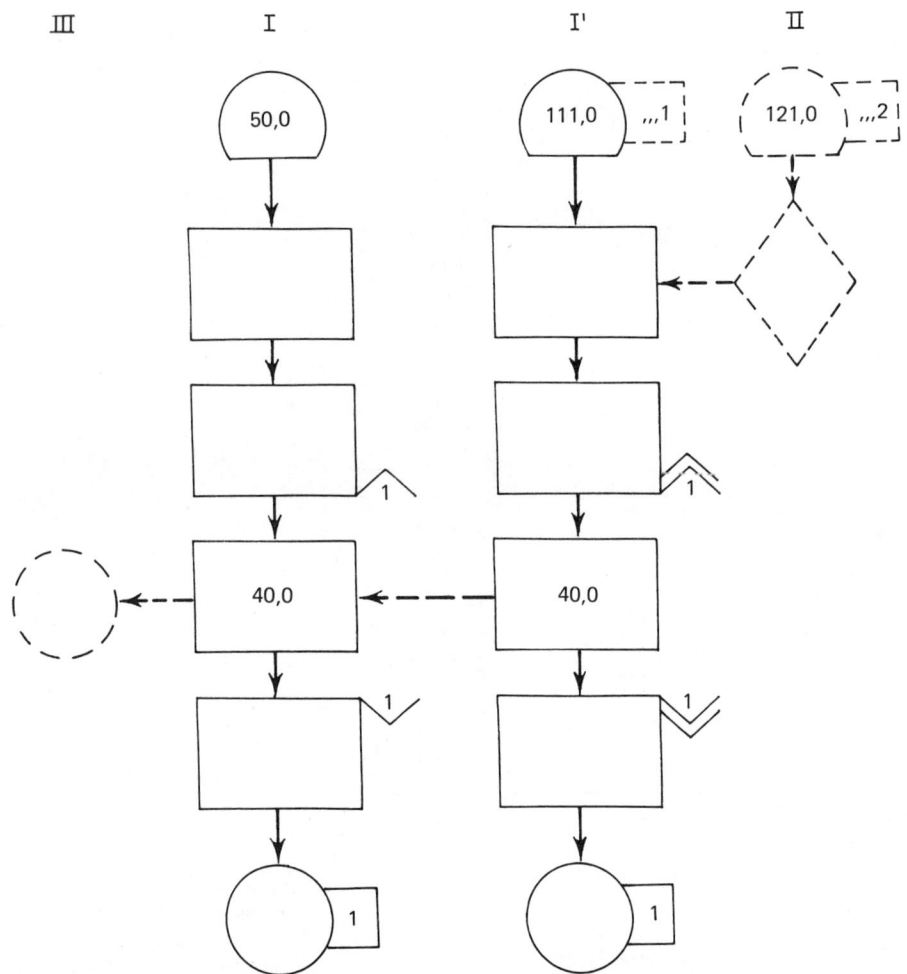

Figure 7-6. Preemption of facilities in priority mode.

```
         *        MACHINE OPERATION WITH PREEMPTION
         *
         *        EXAMPLE A-PREEMPTION IN AN INTERRUPT MODE
         *
 1                GENERATE    50              CREATE NORMAL JOBS
 2                ADVANCE                     BUFFER
 3                SEIZE       1               GET MACHINE
 4                ADVANCE     40              USE MACHINE
 5                RELEASE     1               GIVE UP MACHINE
 6                TERMINATE   1
         *
 7                GENERATE    111             CREATE INTERRUPT JOBS
 8                ADVANCE                     BUFFER
 9                PREEMPT     1               INTERRUPT IF NECESSARY
10                ADVANCE     40              USE MACHINE
11                RETURN      1               RETURN TO INTERRUPTED JOBS
12                TERMINATE   1
         *
                  START       7
         *
         *        EXAMPLE B- PREEMPTION WITH PRIORITY
         *
                  CLEAR
         *
                  ABS
 7                GENERATE    111,,,,1        RAISE PRIORITY OF INTERRUPT JOBS
 9                PREEMPT     1,PR            CHANGE PREEMPT TO PRIORITY MODE
13                GENERATE    121,,,,2        INTRODUCE HIGHER PRIORITY JOBS
14                TRANSFER    ,8
                  ENDABS
         *
                  START       7
         *        EXAMPLE C- PREEMPTION WITH DISPLACEMENT
         *
                  CLEAR
         *
                  ABS
 9                PREEMPT     1,PR,15,,RE     CHANGE PREEMPT TO DISPLACE
15                TERMINATE
                  ENDABS
         *
                  START       7
```

```
RELATIVE CLOCK          373    ABSOLUTE CLOCK        373
BLOCK COUNTS
BLOCK CURRENT TOTAL     BLOCK CURRENT TOTAL    BLOCK CURRENT TOTAL    BLOCK CURRENT TOTAL
   1      0      7        11      0      3
   2      2      7        12      0      3
   3      0      5
   4      1      5
   5      0      4
   6      0      4
   7      0      3
   8      0      3
   9      0      3
  10      0      3
```

```
                              ******************************************
                              *                                        *
                              *              FACILITIES                *
                              *                                        *
                              ******************************************

                         AVERAGE  UTIL. DURING-
          NUMBER  AVERAGE   TOTAL  AVAIL UNAVAIL  CURRENT  PERCENT       TRANS   NUMBER
FACILITY  ENTRIES TIME/TRAN TIME   TIME  TIME     STATUS   AVAILABILITY  SEIZE   PREEMPT
    1        8     39.125   .839   .839  .000        A       100.0         3
```

Figure 7-7. Coding and output for preemption in priority mode.

```
*          EXAMPLE B- PREEMPTION WITH PRIORITY
*
           CLEAR
 7         GENERATE    111,,,,1       RAISE PRIORITY OF INTERRUPT JOBS
 9         PREEMPT     1,PR           CHANGE PREEMPT TO PRIORITY MODE
13         GENERATE    121,,,,2       INTRODUCE HIGHER PRIORITY JOBS
14         TRANSFER    ,8
*
           START       7

RELATIVE CLOCK          403   ABSOLUTE CLOCK          403
BLOCK COUNTS
BLOCK CURRENT TOTAL     BLOCK CURRENT TOTAL     BLOCK CURRENT TOTAL     BLOCK CURRENT TOTAL
  1     0       8        11     0       5
  2     5       8        12     0       5
  3     0       3        13     0       3
  4     1       3        14     0       3
  5     0       2
  6     0       2
  7     0       3
  8     0       6
  9     0       6
 10     1       6
```

```
*********************************************
*                                           *
*                 FACILITIES                *
*                                           *
*********************************************
```

```
                          AVERAGE UTIL. DURING-
                          TOTAL  AVAIL  UNAVAIL  CURRENT  PERCENT        TRANS  NUMBER
FACILITY  NUMBER  AVERAGE
          ENTRIES TIME/TRAN TIME  TIME   TIME    STATUS   AVAILABILITY   SEIZE  PREEMPT
   1         9    38.111   .851   .851   .000       A         100.0        1
```

```
*          EXAMPLE C- PREEMPTION WITH DISPLACEMENT
*
           CLEAR
 9         PREEMPT     1,PR,15,,RE    CHANGE PREEMPT TO DISPLACE
15         TERMINATE
*
           START       7

RELATIVE CLOCK          443   ABSOLUTE CLOCK          443
BLOCK COUNTS
BLOCK CURRENT TOTAL     BLOCK CURRENT TOTAL     BLOCK CURRENT TOTAL     BLOCK CURRENT TOTAL
  1     0       8        11     0       3
  2     1       8        12     0       3
  3     0       7        13     0       3
  4     0       7        14     0       3
  5     0       4        15     0       6
  6     0       4
  7     0       3
  8     0       6
  9     0       6
 10     0       6
```

```
*********************************************
*                                           *
*                 FACILITIES                *
*                                           *
*********************************************
```

```
                          AVERAGE UTIL. DURING-
                          TOTAL  AVAIL  UNAVAIL  CURRENT  PERCENT        TRANS  NUMBER
FACILITY  NUMBER  AVERAGE
          ENTRIES TIME/TRAN TIME  TIME   TIME    STATUS   AVAILABILITY   SEIZE  PREEMPT
   1        13    29.461   .864   .864   .000       A         100.0
```

Figure 7-7. (continued).

Preemption without priority

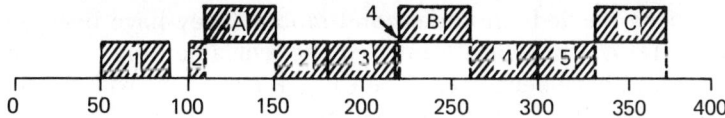

Preemption with priority

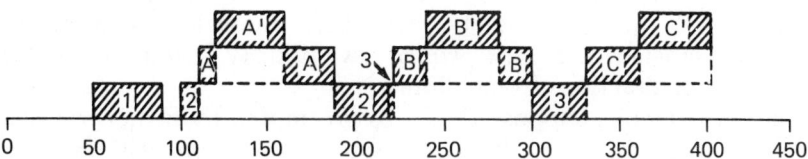

Preemption with priority and displacement

Figure 7-8. Sequence of events with preemption in priority mode.

For the second model, the rush-type transactions are given a priority of 1, and another stream of transactions with priority of 2 will be introduced. The model is extended by the addition of the GENERATE and TRANSFER blocks shown in column II of Fig. 7-6. Also, the PREEMPT block will be changed to a priority mode by entering PR in field B. No fields beyond B will be used, so the block allows transactions to interrupt lower-priority transactions but not to displace them.

Looking now at the coding in Fig. 7-7, we see that when the first model has finished, the program will read the CLEAR statement following the first START statement. This has the effect of removing all the transactions and statistics of the first run. The program then reads a set of four block statements enclosed between the assembly program statements ABS and ENDABS. This indicates that the statements are in absolute form so that all locations are given as numbers. (See Sec. A2-8 of Appendix 2, which describes the assembly program.) The first block statement rewrites the GENERATE block of column I' in Fig. 7-6. The priority of the transactions from this block now becomes 1. The next statement rewrites the PREEMPT block by adding

PR to field B. In both these statements, the location of the blocks being rewritten had to be known beforehand so that they could be put in the location fields. The last two statements add the new GENERATE and TRANSFER blocks needed for the second model. They have been assigned locations 13 and 14, which are known to be available; any other pair of free locations could have been used. The CLEAR statement will create a new transaction at the GENERATE block that has been left unchanged, and the loading of the new GENERATE blocks will have automatically created transactions at those blocks.

The sequence of events that occurs is shown in the second line of Fig. 7-8. The transactions coming from the highest priority GENERATE block are labeled A', B', ... As can be seen, these transactions can interrupt the transactions labeled A, B, . . . , which have priority 1, and they, in turn, can interrupt the transactions from column I.

As a last example, suppose that jobs preempted by higher-priority transactions are to be discarded. The preempted transactions will now be sent to a TERMINATE block, number 15, which is shown in Fig. 7-6 as column III. The PREEMPT block must be modified to add the location 15 in field C and the letters RE in field E.

The coding following the second START statement in Fig. 7-7 makes these changes and runs this third model. The events that result are shown as the last line of Fig. 7-8. In this case, as each preemption occurs, the preempted transaction goes to the TERMINATE block and leaves the system, irrespective of whether it got control of the facility at the SEIZE or PREEMPT block.

7 6

**Preempted Transaction
Not at ADVANCE Block**

Normally a transaction that is preempted is using the facility by being in an ADVANCE block. It is then on the future events chain, and the preemption results in its being transferred to the interrupt chain and a preempt count in the transaction being set to 1. If the transaction is already preempted (on some other facility), it will be on the interrupt chain. The preempt count is incremented by 1, and the transaction stays on the interrupt chain until the count is reduced to zero by transactions entering RETURN blocks.

The preempted transaction could be on the match chain or on a user chain. In that case a flag in the transaction is set to indicate to the program that the transaction is to be transferred to the interrupt chain when the matching condition is met or when it is unlinked. If the preemption is removed before that happens, the transfer is not made.

It is also possible that the preempted transaction is on the current events chain for one of the following reasons:

(a) It may have just left an ADVANCE block but the scan has not yet reached the transaction.
(b) It may have left an ADVANCE block but been unable to release the facility because some blocking condition has stopped it from entering a RELEASE or RETURN block.
(c) It may have seized the facility but been unable to enter an ADVANCE block because of some blocking condition.
(d) It may have been returned to the current events chain from a user chain or the match chain at some time earlier in the scan but is positioned so that the scan is yet to process the returned transaction.

In these cases the movement of the transaction is not immediately stopped by a preemption. The transaction can continue to move in the block diagram until it reaches an ADVANCE, MATCH, GATHER, or ASSEMBLE block, at which time it will be placed on the interrupt chain, or the match chain, with an indication that it is to be passed onto the interrupt chain. Should the preemption be removed before the transaction reaches one of these block types, the action will be canceled.

7-7
Simulating Disk Units

A computer must often react to events that occur in real time, meaning that it must be available to accept or dispatch data immediately upon the receipt of some signal not under its direct control. Arrangements are then made to interrupt the operations of the computer upon receipt of the signal and resume the interrupted operations when the data transfer is over. The preemption feature of GPSS provides the means for simulating such interruptions.

A typical example occurs when reading or writing data to or from a disk unit. The disk unit can handle only one data transfer at a time; it is therefore represented by a facility. Access to the disk unit is by way of a channel which also can handle only one data transfer at a time and which also must be represented by a facility. (There may be many disk units sharing one channel.)

Assuming that both the channel and the disk are available, the central processing unit (CPU), also represented by a facility, must be available to issue a command to the disk unit. The command is to start the input–output operation by signaling to the unit the track it is to locate. The disk unit will begin moving a reading head to that track. While it is doing so, the CPU and the channel are released for other tasks. When the head is located over the track, a further delay is involved while the beginning of the track record comes under the reading head. At that point the channel must be available. If it is not, a full revolution of the disk will be needed before another try can be made. When the channel is available, the CPU is interrupted by the channel so that it will accept the data.

Figure 7-9 shows how this action would be modeled. A SEIZE block first ensures that the channel is available. It is assumed that, elsewhere, a check has been made to ensure that the disk unit is available. The CPU facility is then used for a small interval of 2 time units to issue the start input-output command. For a medium-speed computer the time unit would probably be milliseconds. As shown here, the task will, if necessary, wait for the CPU to become available. In some systems, the CPU might be interrupted to get the transfer started as soon as possible. Both the channel and CPU facilities are released when the start input-output command has been given.

A delay is then introduced to represent the time taken by the arm to move to the required track. In this simple model the time is a uniform distribution with a mean of 25 and a spread of 10. A normal distribution would be more appropriate. Another delay follows to represent the time the beginning of the track will take to come under the head. Here it is appropriate to use a uniform distribution because, at the time the head reaches the correct track, the beginning of the track could be at any point around a 360° circumference, with equal probability of being at any point. The mean and spread are therefore both equal to half a revolution time, so that the selected time could be any value from zero to a maximum of one full revolution time, assumed here to be 18 time units.

When that delay is expended, the channel must be available for transmission of the data. A test at a conditional mode TRANSFER block checks the availability and, if the channel is busy, sends the transaction to an ADVANCE block to return for another try after one full revolution time. When the channel is available at the appropriate time, the CPU is interrupted for a time equal to the data transmission time. This will depend upon the message length and the channel speed, but it is shown here as a simple time of 5 units. The CPU is returned and the channel released to complete the operation.

Exercises

7-1   A clerk is checking invoices handed to him at the rate of one every 5 ± 2 minutes. It takes 3 ± 2 minutes to examine them. Thirty per cent are found to be in error, in which case he hands them to a second clerk, who takes 10 ± 3 minutes to make inquiries about the mistake. The second clerk must then interrupt the first clerk for 1 minute to complete processing of the document. Simulate the processing of 100 documents.

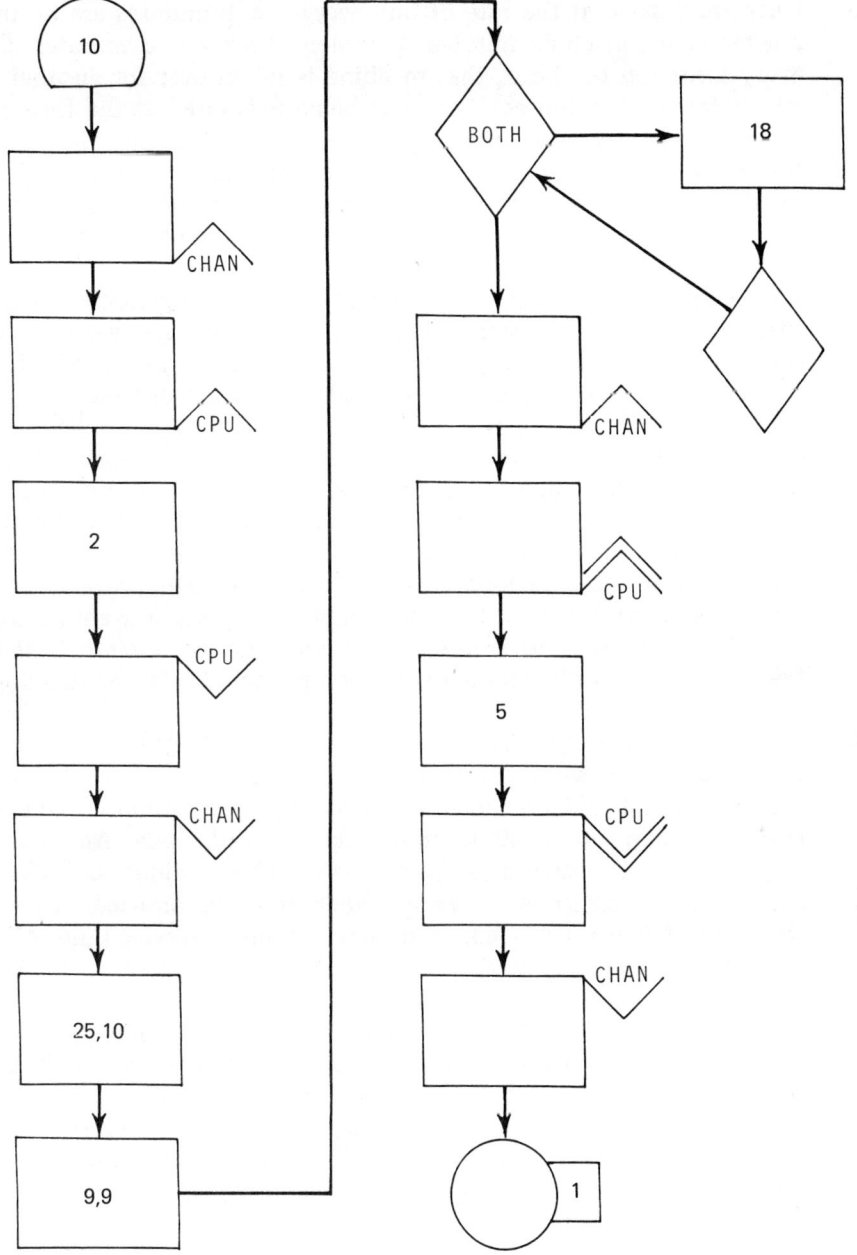

Figure 7-9. Simulating access to a disk unit.

7-2 In the barber shop example of Exercise 5-8, assume that barber number 1 also takes care of the till. He spends 1 minute to collect money immediately after each customer has finished. Simulate the problem under these circumstances.

Exercises

7-3   Parts that arrive at the rate of one every 5 ± 2 minutes are normally machined on machine number 1, which takes 4 ± 3 minutes. Once every hour, on the hour, that machine is taken over for another job, which takes 10 minutes. Any part being processed at the time must be restarted but need only be processed for the time it takes to finish the work. Any displaced part becomes the next normal job to use the machine. The utilization of the machine on both types of job is to be computed. Simulate the machining of 100 normal jobs.

7-4   Reprogram Exercise 6-1 on the assumption that a person who wants to type a correction interrupts anybody using the typewriter, except somebody who is making a correction. The person interrupted has to start again but does so ahead of anybody else who was waiting.

7-5   Students arrive at the rate of one every 5 ± 2 minutes to use a key punch. Their jobs take 4 ± 2 minutes. They can be interrupted by a professor, who arrives every 10 ± 3 minutes, or by the computer operator, who arrives every 12 ± 6 minutes. The computer operator can interrupt the professor, but not vice versa. The professor wants the key punch for 2 ± 1 minute, and the operator wants it for 1 minute. Anybody who is interrupted continues his job when he gets the key punch back. Simulate the completion of 100 student jobs.

7-6   Messages are being generated at the rate of one every 40 ± 20 seconds for transmission over a communications link, one at a time. The transmission takes 30 ± 10 seconds. At intervals of 5 ± 2 minutes, an urgent message, lasting 40 ± 20 seconds, takes over the line. Any message in progress at the time must be reprocessed for 1 minute before being submitted for transmission again. When it is resubmitted, it goes to the head of any waiting line. Simulate 1 hour of service time. All line utilization is to be counted.

7-7   Two laboratory workers want to use the same instrument, once every half hour. They schedule their work so that they alternate their use of the instrument every 15 minutes, with worker number 1 going first. The laboratory manager wants to use the instrument every 40 ± 20 minutes. If necessary, the manager will interrupt worker number 1; but will not interrupt worker number 2. Each use of the instrument takes 10 minutes. Simulate 100 uses.

7-8   Two machines are available for performing a certain job. Number 1 is faster, taking 6 ± 3 minutes. The other machine takes 8 ± 4 minutes. Workers arrive with jobs every 5 ± 2 minutes. They obviously prefer to use machine number 1, but they use machine number 2 if number 1 is busy. Every 15 ± 5 minutes a rush job arrives. If either machine is available, it is used, with preference being given to machine 1 if both are free. If both are busy, machine 1 is interrupted, and any part that was being processed must be restarted from the beginning as the next job on machine number 1. Simulate the completion of 100 normal jobs.

7-9 Reprogram the disk file simulation of Sec. 7-7 on the assumption that, following the location of the arm, the channel is immediately taken over, unless data are being read in from the file. When the channel is obtained, it is held until the data transfer is complete. The CPU is interrupted for 2 milliseconds before the system begins looking for the start of the track. The CPU is still interrupted when the data are to be read in. (With this arrangement, the system is always ready to accept data when the start of track appears under the head.)

7-10 Reprogram the simulation of disk files, discussed in Sec. 7-7, under the following conditions:
(a) Both the CPU and the channel are interrupted in order to issue the start input–output command.
(b) The CPU, but not the channel, can be further interrupted during the start input–output by the need to transmit data.

8
GATHERING STATISTICS

Some statistics, such as the block counts and the facility and storage statistics, are collected automatically. In addition, there are several block types specifically designed to gather statistics rather than represent system actions. Four such block types will be described in this chapter. They are the QUEUE, DEPART, MARK, and TABULATE blocks. The description of one other block type that can also be used for collecting statistics, the SAVEVALUE block, will be deferred to Chap. 10, where the system attributes with which it is associated will be described. The symbols for the blocks to be discussed are shown in Fig. 8-1.

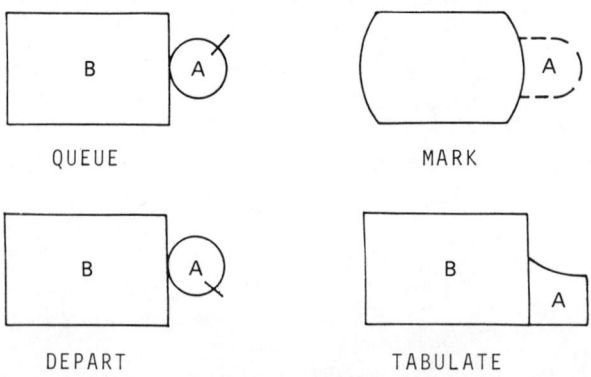

Figure 8-1. Block types 5.

8-1
Queues

Some of the more important statistics derived from a simulation are concerned with the queues that form in the system. The program automatically maintains its own queues of blocked transactions. However, it gathers statistics only for queues defined by the user. There can be many user-defined queues, normally up to 300. Transactions join a queue by entering a QUEUE block, and they leave by entering a DEPART block. Normal FIFO priority rules are observed for transactions in the queue. A transaction is not necessarily immobilized by being placed in a queue: it may still move in the block diagram. It can, in fact, be on up to five queues simultaneously. Usually, however, transactions join a queue because they are blocked by some system condition, and they do remain frozen in one block. It makes no difference to the statistics which block type the transaction stays in.

8-2
QUEUE Blocks

A transaction entering a QUEUE block joins the queue that is named in field A. If field B is blank, the queue length increases by one. If field B has a positive integer, the length increases by that amount. A transaction can be simultaneously entered in as many as five queues. An attempt to enter more than five will cause a warning message to be printed, without stopping the simulation. The current length and maximum length statistics for the queues beyond the fifth will be maintained, but the other statistics will not.

8-3
DEPART Blocks

A transaction entering a DEPART block leaves the queue named in field A. If field B is blank, the queue length decreases by one, otherwise it is reduced by the positive number in field B. If an attempt is made to reduce the queue length below zero, an error stop will occur. A transaction that enters and then leaves a queue does not have to increase and decrease the length by the same amount.

The transaction that is leaving a queue should have previously joined the same queue. If this is not so, a warning message will be printed, but the simulation continues. Only the maximum size statistic for that queue will be correct.

8-4

Queue Statistics

In addition to keeping the current queue length, the time at which the queue length last changed is also maintained internally. Using this time, the program is able to derive the average time transactions spent on the queue. The calculation is made in exactly the same way as that described in Sec. 5-21 for calculating storage statistics. The comments made there about the effects of CLEAR and RESET statements apply to queue statistics.

The program output records the total number of units that entered the queue. It also records how many units spent zero time on the queue, both as an absolute number, and as a percentage of all entries. Separate calculations are also made of the average contents and the average time per unit, excluding the units that spent zero time on the queue. Examples of the output will be given shortly.

Transactions that spend no time in the queue do not affect the averages. They may, however, affect the maximum contents. If no queue ever forms but at least one transaction moved into the queue for zero time, the average queue length will be zero, but the maximum queue length will be greater than zero. If the queue was never entered, both figures will be zero.

In addition to the average time spent on a queue, a distribution of the time spent on a queue can be obtained by using QTABLEs. The description of these tables will be deferred to Sec. 8-11, which follows the description of the tables used with a TABULATE block.

8-5

Queue Example

Figure 8-2 shows an example of how queues are used. Suppose that a facility represents a machine tool and that we wish to measure the queue of jobs in two ways. Statistics are needed for the line of jobs waiting for machining to start and for the queue for the machining to be finished. Two QUEUE blocks, referring to queues 1 and 2, are placed ahead of the SEIZE block at which the facility is to be used. Their order is irrelevant since both will accept a transaction at the same clock time. Queue 1 will be used to measure the line of jobs waiting for service to begin; so the DEPART block for queue 1 immediately follows the SEIZE block. The other queue is for completion of service, so its DEPART block follows the RELEASE block.

Transactions that find the facility busy will wait in the second QUEUE block, having been entered in both queues. If a transaction finds that the facility is not busy it will move immediately through the two QUEUE blocks, seize the facility, and then leave queue 1, thereby spending no time in that queue. Coding for the problem will be included in the example to be given

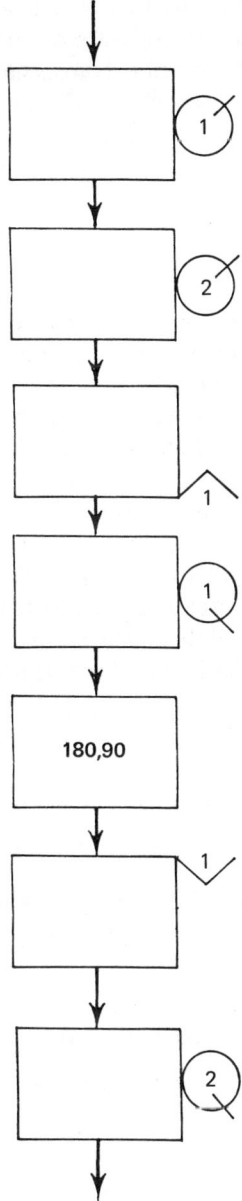

Figure 8-2. Example of queues.

later in Sec. 8-12.

An entity, such as a facility, might be used at several points in the block diagram, and queues could form at each of these points. The program will service all transactions waiting for that facility in priority order, regardless of their location, even if some of them have not been entered in a queue by a QUEUE block. By entering all transactions that wait for a multiply-used facility in the same queue, the program will give statistics for the combined total queue. If this is not wanted, separate queues can be used at each point. The program will continue to service transactions in priority order, but it will give separate statistics for each point of queuing.

8-6
Transit Time Measurements

Another important statistic that needs to be gathered is the time it takes transactions to move from one part of the system to another. A MARK block is used to indicate a point from which such a measurement is to be made. As noted previously, the time at which the measurement begins is called the mark time, and it is recorded in a transaction when the transaction enters the MARK block. The end of the measurement interval is indicated by a TABULATE block. The time the transaction takes to reach the TABULATE block from the MARK block is called the *transit time*. It is computed by subtracting the mark time from the time of arrival at the TABULATE block. Figure 8-3 illustrates the measurement of transit time.

The TABULATE block tabulates each transit time to produce a distribution. As will be seen later, this is only one of many types of statistics that a TABULATE block can measure.

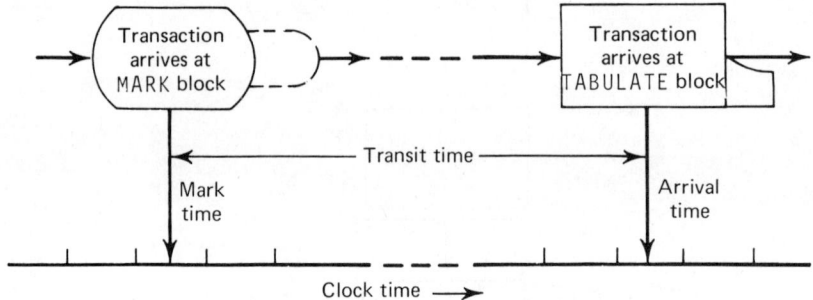

Figure 8-3. Transit time measurements.

8-7
MARK Blocks

As just noted, when a transaction enters a MARK block, a record—the mark time—is made of the clock time at which it entered. Every transaction has a special word, called the *mark time word*. If field A of the MARK block is blank, the mark time is placed in that word. As will be explained in more detail later, a transaction has a number of other words, called *parameters*, for recording data. If field A has the notation kPx, where x is a letter denoting the parameter type, and k is an integer giving a parameter number, the mark time is placed in that parameter, without disturbing the mark time word. A transaction can therefore be carrying several independent mark times, allowing the program to measure transit times for overlapping intervals. The parameter must be fullword or halfword. In the latter case, time is stored modulo 32,768. (See Sec. 11-2 for the symbolic naming of mark times.)

The mark time word is initially set to the time the transaction is created. Consequently, if a transit time is to be measured from the time of creation (but not the time of entry, because of possible blocking at the GENERATE block), a MARK block is not needed. If it is important to measure the transit time from time of entry and blocking can occur at the GENERATE block, a MARK block must immediately follow the GENERATE block.

8-8
TABULATE Blocks

When a transaction enters a TABULATE block, the program computes a statistic and tabulates the value. There can be many tables (normally up to 100), and field A identifies the table to be used. A control statement, which is described in the next section, defines the table. It also identifies the statistic to be tabulated. This can be any SNA except matrix savevalues or floating-point parameters and savevalues. For the time being, however, the only examples that will be discussed use the mark time.

A table is defined by a number of contiguous intervals. When a transaction enters a TABULATE block, the program takes the value of the statistic and decides in which interval the value lies. If field B of the TABULATE block is blank, the program adds one to a counter associated with that interval. If field B has a positive integer, the program will add that number to the counter. The table statistics are then said to be weighted. An example of this mode will be given in Sec. 8-10.

At the end of the simulation, the program automatically calculates the mean and standard deviation of the statistics. To do this, the program maintains a running total of the entries in the table and also their squares. If the statistics are not weighted and x_i, $i = 1, 2, \ldots, n$, represents the values that are tabulated, the mean, M, and standard deviation, S, are estimated as follows:

$$M = \frac{1}{n} \sum_{i=1}^{n} x_i$$

$$S = \left\{ \frac{1}{n-1} \sum_{i=1}^{n} (M - x_i)^2 \right\}^{1/2}$$

Although the tabulation is only made to the nearest interval, the calculation of the mean and standard deviation uses the actual values, even if they fall outside the defined range of the table.

The standard deviation should be used with some caution. If the data being measured are mutually independent, then S is the unbiased estimator for the standard deviation of the population from which the statistics are drawn. When the data are not independent, this is no longer true. The quantity S will then be affected by the correlation existing in the data. Usually this results in S being an underestimate of the true standard deviation. For further discussion of this point, see (97).

8-9

TABLE Control Statements

To tabulate a set of statistics, the user must define a table with a TABLE control statement. The definition of a table is illustrated in Fig. 8-4. There are N intervals, of which $N - 2$ are adjacent intervals of equal width, W, which begin from a lower limit, L. There are also an underflow interval and an overflow interval, the former covering all values less than the lower limit, and the latter covering all values beyond the highest defined table value.

The format for a TABLE statement is shown in Table 8-1. Field A identifies the SNA that is to be tabulated. Sections 8-14 and 8-15 will describe some special modes for operating tables, which are also indicated by using

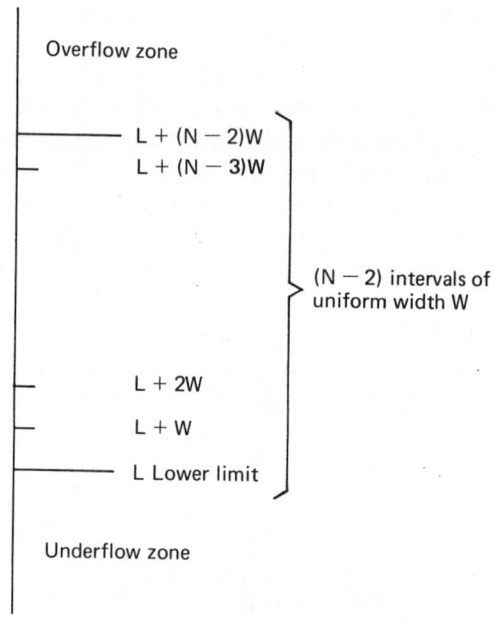

Figure 8-4. Definition of tables.

Table 8-1 Format for the TABLE Control Statement

Field	Content
Location	Table number (or name)
Operation	QTABLE
A*	Statistic to be tabulated
B	Lower limit, L
C	Interval size, W
D†	Number of intervals, N, including the underflow and overflow intervals
E	Arrival rate time interval (RT mode only)

*Followed by minus sign for difference mode.
†Precede by any alphabetic character for weighted statistics.

field A. The three numbers L, W, and N used to define the table appear as fields B, C, and D, respectively. Field E is used with the special mode to be described in Sec. 8-15. If weighted statistics are to be used, the number of intervals, N, is preceded by any alphabetic character.

8-10
Weighted Tabulations

With field B of a TABULATE block left blank (or set to 1), each transaction entering the block increments a table interval counter by 1. There are times when a transaction represents more than one item and weighted tabulations should be made. For example, suppose that the transaction represents a job lot where the number of parts in the job lot is placed in, say, halfword parameter number 5. The model may be representing a system that processes parts by the job lot, and the time to process a job lot can be measured by a transit time. It may be necessary to recognize the different lot sizes in order to tabulate the transit time by part. The weighted mode of tabulation would then be used as follows:

```
                    MARK
                    ...
                    TABULATE    TRTM,PH5
                    ...
         TRTM  TABLE         M1,100,100,A6
```

The notation PH5 denotes the halfword parameter number 5 of the transaction entering the TABULATE block. The program will now find the interval of the table called TRTM, which contains the transit time being tabulated, and adds the value of PH5 to that interval counter. It also adds PH5 to the total number of entries, PH5 times the transit time to the sum of the entries, and the latter quantity squared to the sum of the squares, so that the mean and standard deviation eventually calculated for the table are appropriately weighted.

To illustrate the difference between nonweighted and weighted tabulations, suppose that five transactions with the following statistics are tabulated in the table TRTM:

Transaction	Transit time	Lot size
1	250	5
2	320	8
3	30	2
4	150	4
5	220	6

The statistics appearing in the table would then be as follows:

	Nonweighted	Weighted
Number of entries	5	25
Mean	194.0	231.6
Standard deviation	110.1	84.9
100	1	2
200	1	4
300	2	11
400	1	8

8-11

QTABLE Control Statements

The average time that transactions spend on a queue is computed automatically and printed as part of the queue statistics. Frequently, the distribution of the time spent on the queue is also needed. This could be obtained by using a MARK block to note the time the transaction joined the queue, and using a TABULATE block to tabulate transit time when the transaction leaves the queue. However, a special control statement, QTABLE, will derive this statistic automatically, without the need for the two blocks. It is not possible to use weighted statistics with QTABLEs; so, if these are needed, the MARK and TABULATE blocks must be used.

The format for a QTABLE statement is shown in Table 8-2. The word QTABLE appears in the operation field and the table number appears in the location field. The queue number is in field A. The other fields are the same as for a normal table, except that field E has no relevance for a QTABLE and field D cannot indicate weighted statistics. The QTABLE and TABLE statements share the same set of table numbers.

Table 8-2 Format for the QTABLE Control Statement

Field	Content
Location	Table number (or name)
Operation	QTABLE
A	Queue to be tabulated
B	Lower limit, L
C	Interval size, W
D	Number of intervals, N, including the underflow and overflow intervals

8-12
Example of Statistics Gathering

We return to the queuing example discussed previously in Sec. 8-5 and illustrated in Fig. 8-2. The example is expanded in Fig. 8-5 to collect some transit time and queue time statistics. Transactions are generated with an interarrival time of 200 ± 100 seconds. Prior to reaching the facility, they are delayed by various time-consuming processes amounting to 50 ± 25 seconds, and, after processing by the facility, other delays amount to 50 ± 25 seconds. In addition to measuring the two queues previously discussed, the program is to gather the following statistics:

(a) The transit time from the time of arrival in the system to the point at which the facility begins processing the transactions

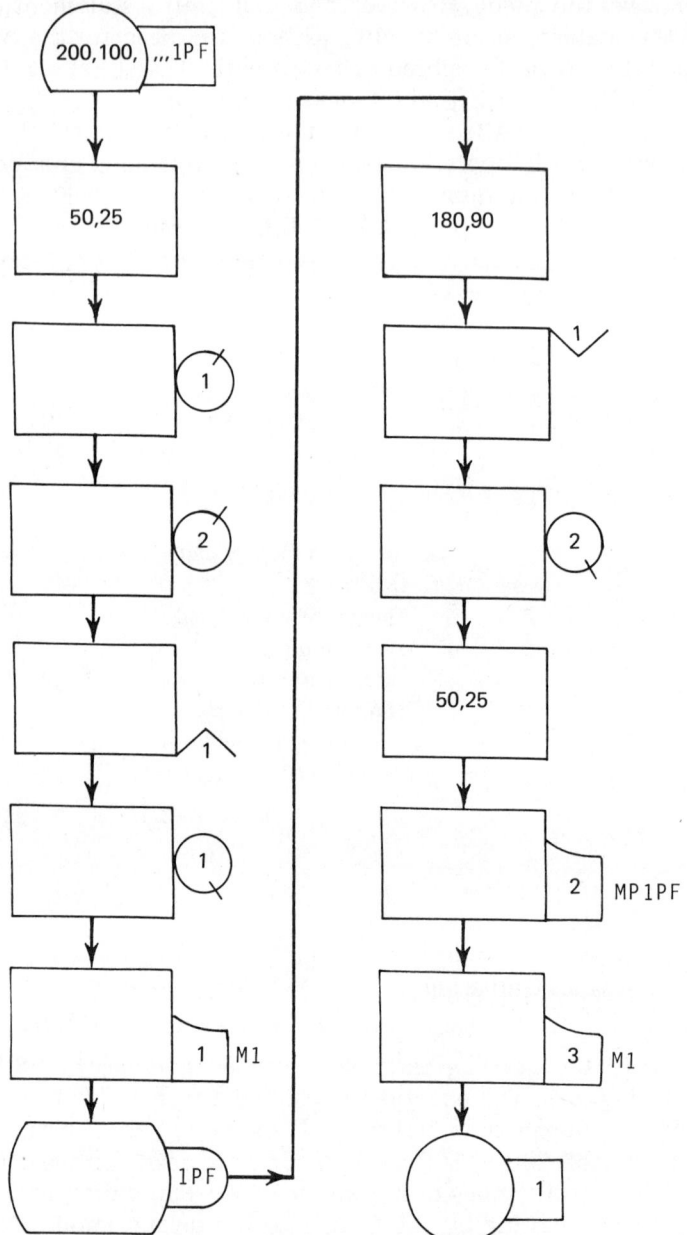

Figure 8-5. Example of statistics gathering.

(b) The transit time from the point at which the facility begins processing to the time the transactions leave the system
(c) The overall transit time from the time of arrival to the time of departure
(d) The distribution of time spent on queue 1

Transactions are generated and then passed through an ADVANCE block that represents the preprocessing time. The two QUEUE blocks previously discussed immediately precede the SEIZE block at which the transactions get control of the facility to begin their processing. Queue 1 is to measure the waiting line, so a DEPART block for queue 1 immediately follows the SEIZE block. One set of statistics to be measured is the transit time to this point, so a TABULATE block, using table 1, appears here. The transactions have not yet passed through a MARK block, so the mark time that is used is the arrival time of the transaction, placed in the mark time word at the time of creation and denoted by M1. A second set of statistics is the transit time from this point. A MARK block is therefore used next. Since the third set of statistics is to be the transit time through the entire system, the creation time will be left unaltered in the mark time word. Field A of the MARK block is set to 1PF so that the new mark time will be placed in fullword parameter number 1.

The transactions next pass to an ADVANCE block that represents the processing time of the facility. The facility is then released, and a second DEPART block takes the transactions out of queue 2, which measures the queue involved in completing the service. The transactions now go to an ADVANCE block that represents the processing that follows the facility operation. Finally, they go through two TABULATE blocks to a TERMINATE block. The first TABULATE block, using table 2, will measure the transit time since processing started, which is based on the mark time in parameter 1. The other TABULATE block uses table 3 to measure the total transit time, which is based on the mark time word, here being used for a second time. A QTABLE card, using table 4, will collect the statistics on the distribution of time spent in queue 1.

In this example, the precise order of several of the blocks is irrelevant. As noted before, the order of the two QUEUE blocks is irrelevant, so also is the order of the DEPART, TABULATE, and MARK blocks that follow the SEIZE block. The two final TABULATE blocks could also be interchanged. There are many similar occasions in the use of GPSS where a series of consecutive blocks accept transactions unconditionally and involve no time. Consequently, they represent actions that will be carried out at the same instant and the order in which they occur makes no difference.

Coding and the output from a run for the problem are given in Fig. 8-6.

```
         *        EXAMPLE OF STATISTICS GATHERING
         *
  1               GENERATE    200,100,,,,1PF
  2               ADVANCE     50,25            PRE-PROCESSING OPERATIONS
  3               QUEUE       1                ENTER WAITING LINE QUEUE
  4               QUEUE       2                ENTER QUEUE FOR JOB COMPLETION
  5               SEIZE       1                START MACHINING
  6               DEPART      1                LEAVE WAITING LINE QUEUE
  7               TABULATE    1                TABULATE TIME SINCE CREATION
  8               MARK        1PF              MARK TIME MACHINING BEGINS
  9               ADVANCE     180,90           MACHINE PART
 10               RELEASE     1                END MACHINING
 11               DEPART      2                LEAVE QUEUE FOR JOB COMPLETION
 12               ADVANCE     50,25            POST-PROCESSING OPERATIONS
 13               TABULATE    2                TABULATE TRANSIT TIME SINCE
         *                                     MACHINING BEGAN
 14               TABULATE    3                TABULATE TOTAL TIME IN THE SYSTEM
 15               TERMINATE   1
         *
      1           TABLE       M1,50,50,15      TABLE FOR TIME FOR START OF MACHINING
      2           TABLE       MP1PF,100,25,12  TABLE FOR MACHINING & POST-PROCESSING
      3           TABLE       M1,150,50,15     TABLE FOR TOTAL TRANSIT TIME
      4           QTABLE      1,0,50,10        TABLE FOR TIME ON QUEUE 1
         *
                  START       50,NP
                  RESET
                  START       1000
```

```
RELATIVE CLOCK        200413    ABSOLUTE CLOCK       211068
BLOCK COUNTS
BLOCK CURRENT TOTAL      BLOCK CURRENT TOTAL   BLOCK CURRENT TOTAL   BLOCK CURRENT TOTAL
  1      0    1000        11      0    1000
  2      1    1000        12      0    1000
  3      0     999        13      0    1000
  4      0     999        14      0    1000
  5      0     999        15      0    1000
  6      0     999
  7      0     999
  8      0     999
  9      0     999
 10      0    1000
```

```
            ******************************************
            *                                        *
            *              FACILITIES                *
            *                                        *
            ******************************************

                              AVERAGE UTIL. DURING-
FACILITY   NUMBER   AVERAGE   TOTAL  AVAIL  UNAVAIL  CURRENT   PERCENT       TRANS  NUMBER
           ENTRIES  TIME/TRAN TIME   TIME   TIME     STATUS    AVAILABILITY  SEIZE  PREEMPT
    1      1000     180.581   .901   .901   .000     A         100.0

            ******************************************
            *                                        *
            *                QUEUES                  *
            *                                        *
            ******************************************

QUEUE  MAXIMUM   AVERAGE   TOTAL    ZERO     PERCENT  AVERAGE   $AVERAGE   TABLE   CURRENT
       CONTENT   CONTENT   ENTRIES  ENTRIES  ZEROS    TIME/TRAN TIME/TRAN  NUMBER  CONTENT
  1       4       .571      999      300      30.0    114.557   163.723      4
  2       5      1.472     1000                .0     295.024   295.024
  $AVERAGE TIME/TRANS = AVERAGE TIME/TRANS EXCLUDING ZERO ENTRIES
```

Figure 8-6. Coding and output for statistics gathering example.

```
*******************************************
*                                         *
*                TABLES                   *
*                                         *
*******************************************
```

TABLE   1
ENTRIES IN TABLE   MEAN ARGUMENT   STANDARD DEVIATION   SUM OF ARGUMENTS
       999   164.517   132.187   164353.000   NON-WEIGHTED

UPPER LIMIT	OBSERVED FREQUENCY	PER CENT OF TOTAL	CUMULATIVE PERCENTAGE	CUMULATIVE REMAINDER	MULTIPLE OF MEAN	DEVIATION FROM MEAN
50	154	15.41	15.4	84.5	.303	-.866
100	297	29.72	45.1	54.8	.607	-.488
150	119	11.91	57.0	42.9	.911	-.109
200	113	11.31	68.3	31.6	1.215	.268
250	94	9.40	77.7	22.2	1.519	.646
300	66	6.60	84.3	15.6	1.823	1.024
350	51	5.10	89.4	10.5	2.127	1.403
400	40	4.00	93.4	6.5	2.431	1.781
450	29	2.90	96.3	3.6	2.735	2.159
500	11	1.10	97.4	2.5	3.039	2.537
550	9	.90	98.3	1.6	3.343	2.916
600	5	.50	98.8	1.1	3.647	3.294
650	5	.50	99.3	.6	3.950	3.672
700	2	.20	99.5	.4	4.254	4.050
OVERFLOW	4	.40	100.0	.0		

AVERAGE VALUE OF OVERFLOW   734.25

TABLE   2
ENTRIES IN TABLE   MEAN ARGUMENT   STANDARD DEVIATION   SUM OF ARGUMENTS
      1000   230.891   54.562   230892.000   NON-WEIGHTED

UPPER LIMIT	OBSERVED FREQUENCY	PER CENT OF TOTAL	CUMULATIVE PERCENTAGE	CUMULATIVE REMAINDER	MULTIPLE OF MEAN	DEVIATION FROM MEAN
100	0	.00	.0	100.0	.433	-2.398
125	7	.69	.6	99.2	.541	-1.940
150	60	5.99	6.6	93.2	.649	-1.482
175	126	12.59	19.2	80.7	.757	-1.024
200	137	13.69	32.9	67.0	.866	-.566
225	140	13.99	46.9	53.0	.974	-.107
250	136	13.59	60.5	39.4	1.082	.350
275	136	13.59	74.1	25.8	1.191	.808
300	143	14.29	88.4	11.5	1.299	1.266
325	87	8.69	97.1	2.8	1.407	1.724
350	28	2.79	100.0	.0	1.515	2.182

REMAINING FREQUENCIES ARE ALL ZERO

TABLE   3
ENTRIES IN TABLE   MEAN ARGUMENT   STANDARD DEVIATION   SUM OF ARGUMENTS
      1000   395.321   142.562   395322.000   NON-WEIGHTED

UPPER LIMIT	OBSERVED FREQUENCY	PER CENT OF TOTAL	CUMULATIVE PERCENTAGE	CUMULATIVE REMAINDER	MULTIPLE OF MEAN	DEVIATION FROM MEAN
150	1	.09	.0	99.8	.379	-1.720
200	30	2.99	3.0	96.8	.505	-1.370
250	94	9.39	12.4	87.5	.632	-1.019
300	160	15.99	28.4	71.5	.758	-.668
350	158	15.79	44.2	55.7	.885	-.317
400	169	16.89	61.1	38.8	1.011	.032
450	99	9.89	71.0	28.9	1.138	.383
500	77	7.69	78.7	21.2	1.264	.734
550	68	6.79	85.5	14.4	1.391	1.084
600	48	4.79	90.3	9.6	1.517	1.435
650	40	3.99	94.3	5.6	1.644	1.786
700	21	2.09	96.4	3.5	1.770	2.137
750	12	1.19	97.6	2.3	1.897	2.487
800	9	.89	98.5	1.4	2.023	2.838
OVERFLOW	14	1.39	100.0	.0		

AVERAGE VALUE OF OVERFLOW   892.42

Figure 8-6. (continued).

TABLE 4

ENTRIES IN TABLE	MEAN ARGUMENT	STANDARD DEVIATION	SUM OF ARGUMENTS	
999	114.557	132.500	114443.000	NON-WEIGHTED

UPPER LIMIT	OBSERVED FREQUENCY	PER CENT OF TOTAL	CUMULATIVE PERCENTAGE	CUMULATIVE REMAINDER	MULTIPLE OF MEAN	DEVIATION FROM MEAN
0	300	30.03	30.0	69.9	-.000	-.864
50	147	14.71	44.7	55.2	.436	-.487
100	123	12.31	57.0	42.9	.872	-.109
150	112	11.21	68.2	31.7	1.309	.267
200	102	10.21	78.4	21.5	1.745	.644
250	54	5.40	83.8	16.1	2.182	1.022
300	50	5.00	88.8	11.1	2.618	1.399
350	48	4.80	93.6	6.3	3.055	1.776
400	23	2.30	95.9	4.0	3.491	2.154
OVERFLOW	40	4.00	100.0	.0		

AVERAGE VALUE OF OVERFLOW   499.64

Figure 8-6. (continued).

8-13
Response Times and Grade of Service

The probability of waiting for a given length of time is often mentioned when specifying systems, especially communication systems and on-line computer systems, where the delay corresponds to a response time. Figure 8-7 is a typical example of the type of statistic being sought, in this case a set of theoretical results for the case of a single server with exponentially distributed interarrival time and service time. The curves give, on the vertical axis, the probability of the delay time being greater than the value shown on the horizontal axis. The time is given in units of the mean service time, T_s. Each curve is for a given value of loading, ρ, which, in this case of a single server, is defined as the ratio of the mean service time to mean interarrival time, T_s/T_a. For example, when $\rho = 0.6$, the probability of the delay being greater than 0—that is, the probability of any delay, however small—is 0.6. Similarly, the probability of t/T_s being greater than 2 is 0.28. If the system being studied has a mean service time of 10 seconds, the last statement says that 0.28 is the probability of the delay, t, being greater than 20 seconds.

These results might be stated in a different way by taking the complements of the probabilities. Thus, the two conditions just given are the same as saying that the probability of no delay is 0.4 (1 − 0.6) and that the probability of the delay being less than 20 seconds is 0.72 (1 − 0.28).

Frequently, a system design specification will call for delay statistics of this nature to meet certain criteria, often called the *grade of service* figures. For example, the request may be for the system to be designed so that the probability of there being no delay is at least 0.4, and the probability of the delay being greater than 20 seconds is not more than 0.1. It is usually impossible to meet more than one criterion exactly. The stated probabilities are taken as extreme values, and the final design will probably meet only one of the criteria exactly: all others will leave some spare allowance.

As an example of how these criteria are met, suppose that they are applied to the single-server system with exponentially distributed interarrival and service times, where the mean service time is 10 seconds. The curves of Fig. 8-7 then apply. The design is to find the maximum load the system can bear, subject to the two constraints on response time just given.

The first criterion, stated in complement form, says that the probability of the delay being greater than 0 (i.e., $t/T_s \geq 0$) shall be less than or equal to 0.6. From Fig. 8-7, this means that $\rho \leq 0.6$, or, from the definition of ρ with $T_s = 10$, the mean interarrival time must be greater than or equal to 16.7 seconds. A delay of 20 seconds with a mean service time of 10 seconds means that t/T_s is equal to 2. The second criterion says that this should correspond to a probability of not more than 0.1. It can be seen that the point for a t/T_s of 2 and a probability of 0.1 falls between the curves for $\rho = 0.2$ and 0.4. Interpolation between the curves gives the value of $\rho = 0.37$. With a mean service time of 10 seconds, this corresponds to a mean interarrival time of about 27 seconds.

The two criteria cannot be met simultaneously, and, in both cases, increasing the mean interarrival time improves the probabilities. The conclusion is that the mean interarrival time must be the larger of the two, which is 27 seconds. The second criterion is therefore the more stringent. The first criterion alone would allow the time to be almost halved, thereby doubling the system load. A result like this would require that the second criterion be closely examined.

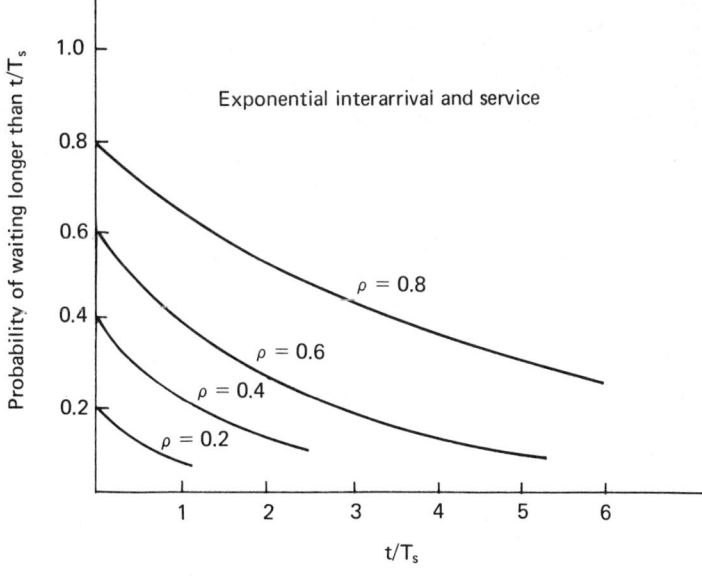

Figure 8-7. Probability of waiting for service to begin in a single-server system.

The type of curve on which this analysis has been based is, in fact, given by the standard table statistics of GPSS when the table has been established to measure transit time. Consider table 4 in Fig. 8-6, which is the result of measuring the delay in queue 1, when transactions are waiting for service at the facility in the model of Fig. 8-5. This system consists of a single server with uniformly distributed interarrival and service times. The mean interarrival time was 200 seconds, and the mean service time was 180 seconds, so the simulated case corresponds to a value of $\rho = 0.9$. The third, fourth, and fifth columns are expressed as percentages of all measured transactions. If these figures are divided by 100, they are estimates of the probabilities of the events they measure. The column headed "CUMULATIVE PERCENTAGE," divided by 100, is the probability of the delay being less than the time given in column 1, and the column headed "CUMULATIVE REMAINDER," divided by 100, is the complement—in other words, the probability of the delay being greater than the times of column 1.

The latter figures are plotted in Fig. 8-8, with the times of column 1, divided by the mean service time, 200, forming the horizontal scale. This puts Fig. 8-8 in the same form as the curve of Fig. 8-7. The single curve given in Fig. 8-8 corresponds to a ρ of 0.9. The simulation would have to be repeated with other values of the mean interarrival time to get a fuller set of design curves. Note that, because of the different distributions, Figs. 8-7 and 8-8 are not the same.

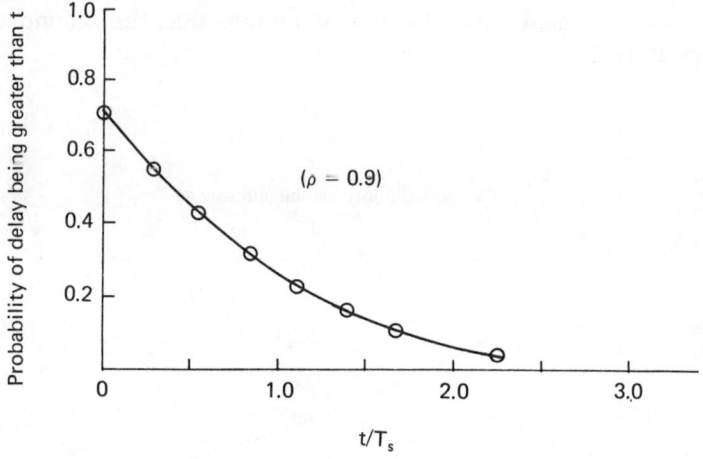

Figure 8-8. Probability of waiting for service to begin, derived from simulation.

8-14

Difference and Interarrival Modes of Tabulation

If desired, a TABULATE block can be made to operate in a difference mode by immediately following the SNA symbol in field A of the associated TABLE statement with a minus sign. Instead of tabulating the values of the SNA at the time a transaction enters the block, the program will then tabulate the difference in the SNA value since the last transaction arrived. The first transaction to arrive at the TABULATE block does not produce a record.

A frequently required form of difference statistic is the interarrival time of transactions at some point internal to the block diagram. By placing the symbol IA, without a minus sign, in field A of the TABLE statement, the program will automatically gather this information about transactions arriving at the TABULATE block. Again, the first arrival does not produce a record. The symbol IA is a special symbol: it does not represent an SNA.

8-15
Rate Mode of Tabulation

Another common requirement is to measure the rate at which transactions pass through a particular point. This requires counting the number of transactions that pass in successive, equal intervals of time, and tabulating the results. The rate mode of tabulation provides the means for gathering this statistic.

A TABULATE block is placed at the point of measurement, and the symbol RT is placed in the A field of the associated TABLE statement. The size of the time interval to be used in the measurement is placed in field E of the TABLE statement. An interval that is only partially completed at the end of the simulation is not counted. The letters RT do not represent an SNA.

The way in which the program computes rates in the RT mode is to create a "dummy" transaction for each rate mode TABULATE block, which is merged with the other transactions and scheduled to be processed at the end of each measurement interval. This transaction does not reside in the block diagram and does not interfere with any other transaction. The only time the user will be aware of its presence is when a transaction list is printed at the time of an error stop or at the special request of the user. The dummy transaction can be recognized by the fact that it is in assembly set 0 (see Sec. 13-1), and it has the measurement interval size in the mark time word.

The same process can be programmed by the user to sample any other statistic. For example, the following coding will create a single transaction that will periodically sample halfword savevalue number 6, in this case, every 100 time units, and tabulate the increment since the last sample:

```
         GENERATE   ,,,1
         ADVANCE    100
         TABULATE   SAMP
         TRANSFER   ,*-2
SAMP     TABLE      XH6-,10,10,10
```

8-16

Example of Tabulation Modes

To illustrate the use of the special modes of tabulation that have just been described, suppose that we wish to measure the pattern of the combined arrivals from five independent sources, each generating transactions every 1000 ± 500 seconds. Figure 8-9 represents the system.

There are five GENERATE blocks, representing the independent sources of supply, each feeding its transactions to two TABULATE blocks. Four of the GENERATE blocks need to use TRANSFER blocks to effect the merging. The first TABULATE block, using table 4, measures the interarrival time by using the interarrival mode. The second, using table 6, measures the rate of arrival with a measurement interval of 2000 seconds. Results of a run are shown in Fig. 8-10.

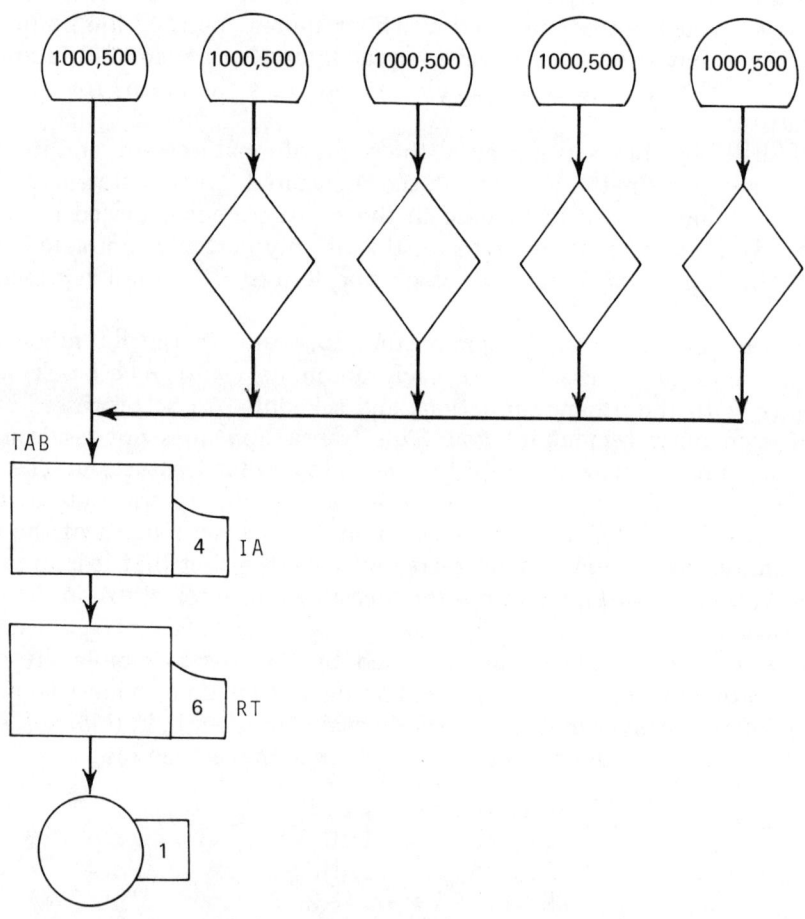

Figure 8-9. Use of special tabulation modes.

164

```
         *         USE OF VARIOUS TABULATION MODES
         *
1                  GENERATE     1000,500       SOURCE 1
2                  TRANSFER     ,TAB
3                  GENERATE     1000,500       SOURCE 2
4                  TRANSFER     ,TAB
5                  GENERATE     1000,500       SOURCE 3
6                  TRANSFER     ,TAB
7                  GENERATE     1000,500       SOURCE 4
8                  TRANSFER     ,TAB
9                  GENERATE     1000,500       SOURCE 5
10       TAB       TABULATE     4              TABULATE INTERARRIVAL TIME
11                 TABULATE     6              NO. OF ARRIVALS PER 2000 UNITS
12                 TERMINATE    1
         *
         4         TABLE        IA,0,50,15     TABLE FOR INTERARRIVAL TIMES
         6         TABLE        RT,5,1,20,2000 TABLE FOR RATE OF ARRIVAL
         *
                   START        50,NP
                   RESET
                   START        1000
```

RELATIVE CLOCK   200307   ABSOLUTE CLOCK   210417
BLOCK COUNTS
BLOCK CURRENT TOTAL   BLOCK CURRENT TOTAL   BLOCK CURRENT TOTAL   BLOCK CURRENT TOTAL
  1   0   205   11   0   1000
  2   0   205   12   0   1000
  3   0   195
  4   0   195
  5   0   197
  6   0   197
  7   0   206
  8   0   206
  9   0   197
 10   0   1000

```
*******************************************
*                                         *
*                  TABLES                 *
*                                         *
*******************************************
```

TABLE   4
ENTRIES IN TABLE   MEAN ARGUMENT   STANDARD DEVIATION   SUM OF ARGUMENTS
       1000   200.306   153.625   200307.000   NON-WEIGHTED

UPPER LIMIT	OBSERVED FREQUENCY	PER CENT OF TOTAL	CUMULATIVE PERCENTAGE	CUMULATIVE REMAINDER	MULTIPLE OF MEAN	DEVIATION FROM MEAN
0	0	.00	.0	100.0	-.000	-1.303
50	167	16.69	16.6	83.3	.249	-.978
100	161	16.09	32.7	67.2	.499	-.652
150	135	13.49	46.2	53.7	.748	-.327
200	112	11.19	57.4	42.5	.998	-.001
250	106	10.59	68.0	31.9	1.248	.323
300	82	8.19	76.2	23.7	1.497	.648
350	56	5.59	81.8	18.1	1.747	.974
400	57	5.69	87.5	12.4	1.996	1.299
450	34	3.39	90.9	9.0	2.246	1.625
500	37	3.69	94.6	5.3	2.496	1.950
550	27	2.69	97.3	2.6	2.745	2.276
600	16	1.59	98.9	1.0	2.995	2.601
650	4	.39	99.3	.6	3.245	2.927
OVERFLOW	6	.59	100.0	.0		

AVERAGE VALUE OF OVERFLOW   710.50

Figure 8-10. Rate and interarrival tabulation mode output.

```
TABLE     6
ENTRIES IN TABLE      MEAN ARGUMENT     STANDARD DEVIATION     SUM OF ARGUMENTS
        100              9.989                 1.226                999.000       NON-WEIGHTED

    UPPER      OBSERVED      PER CENT     CUMULATIVE     CUMULATIVE     MULTIPLE     DEVIATION
    LIMIT     FREQUENCY      OF TOTAL     PERCENTAGE     REMAINDER      OF MEAN      FROM MEAN
      5           0            .00            .0           100.0          .500        -4.063
      6           0            .00            .0           100.0          .600        -3.252
      7           2           1.99           1.9            98.0          .700        -2.437
      8           9           8.99          10.9            89.0          .800        -1.622
      9          24          23.99          34.9            65.0          .900         -.807
     10          29          28.99          63.9            36.0         1.001          .008
     11          26          25.99          89.9            10.0         1.101          .823
     12           9           8.99          98.9             1.0         1.201         1.638
     13           1            .99         100.0              .0         1.301         2.454
REMAINING FREQUENCIES ARE ALL ZERO
```

Figure 8-10. (continued).

8-17

SNAs Associated With Statistics

The mark time SNA is defined later in Sec. 10-16. The other SNAs associated with the statistical elements are as follows:

Qj	Current length of queue j
QAj	Average length of queue j
QMj	Maximum length of queue j
QCj	Total number of units to enter queue j
QZj	Number of entries spending zero time in queue j
QTj	Average time units spent in queue j (including zero times)
QXj	Average time units spent in queue j (excluding zero times)
TBj	Mean of table j
TCj	Total number of entries in table j
TDj	Standard deviation of table j

Exercises

8-1   Parts being turned out at the rate of one every 5 ± 3 minutes must go through two successive machining operations. The first uses a single machine and takes 4 ± 3 minutes. The second can use up to three machines simultaneously, and each part takes 12 ± 6 minutes. Measure the waiting line for the first operation to begin and also the waiting line to complete the first operation and begin the second. In addition, find the distribution of time to complete both operations and the distribution of time from the completion of the first operation to the finish of both operations. Initialize with 10 transactions and simulate for 500.

8-2 People arrive at a supermarket at the rate of one every 30 ± 15 seconds. They take 10 ± 5 minutes to shop. Twenty per cent will then use an express checkout counter. The rest use one of three normal checkout counters, for which they form a common queue. It takes 2 ± 1 minute to checkout at the normal counters and 60 ± 30 seconds to checkout at the express counter. Measure the waiting lines at the two different types of counter. Also, find the distribution of the time spent in the supermarket for all types of customers. Initialize for 10 customers and then simulate for 500 terminations.

8-3 A garage has space for only three cars in its workshop. Cars are brought for service at the rate of one every 60 ± 30 minutes. They are serviced, one at a time, taking 40 ± 25 minutes. If there is not room for a car when it arrives, it is sent to another workshop, where it will wait for as long as is necessary for service. Work is slower in the second shop, taking 90 ± 40 minutes. It also takes 10 minutes to transport cars to the second workshop, and another 10 minutes to bring them back. Find the proportion of cars sent to the second workshop and the distribution of the time to complete service, including delays and transfer times, for the individual shops and the combined shops.

8-4 A bus route has an intermediate checkpoint between its origin and destination, breaking the route into two sections. A dispatcher is placed at the checkpoint and told to delay buses by a full 2 minutes if there are more than two buses in the second segment. If necessary, a bus could be delayed more than once. Assume that buses start from the origin every 5 minutes and that the times taken to cover the sections are 4 ± 3 minutes for the first and 9 ± 6 for the second. Measure the distribution of time required to complete the journey, and the time from first reaching the dispatcher to the end. Initialize for 10 transactions and simulate for 500.

8-5 Customers arrive in a department store at the rate of one every 10 ± 5 seconds. There are two sections; initially customers are equally likely to go to either. Twenty per cent of those finishing at section 1 must then go to section 2. Similarly, 50 per cent who finish at section 2 then go to section 1. (It is possible for one customer to go around more than once.) Customers can be served only one at a time in each section. Section 1 takes 12 ± 4 seconds and section 2 takes 15 ± 5 seconds. Find the distribution of interarrival times at the two sections, and the distribution of the time to finish shopping completely. Initialize for 10 transactions and simulate for 500.

8-6 Parts are being turned out at the rate of one every 5 ± 3 minutes. They go through some general processing that takes 10 ± 6 minutes and must then be individually inspected by a single inspector, who takes 4 ± 2 minutes. Every 30 ± 5 minutes the inspector is called away for 10 ± 2 minutes. Any part he was inspecting at that time must begin inspection again, and does so as the next part when he returns. Find the distribution of the time needed to complete inspection, including delays due to restarting, and also find the distribution of the time needed to complete inspection, including delays due to restarting, and also find the distribution of time that the interrupted parts must wait before they start being inspected again. Initialize for 10 transactions and simulate for 500.

8-7 In the example of Exercise 4-8, measure the distribution of the interarrival time at the beginning of the third corridor. Also measure the distribution of time to reach either platform. Initialize for 10 transactions and simulate for 500.

8-8 In the example of Fig. 5-4, discussed in Sec. 5-11, arrange to collect the following statistics as each new part first enters the system:
(a) The number of parts in stage 1 at that time
(b) The number of parts that have completed their processing since the last new part arrived
Tabulate the statistics in separate tables. Initialize with 10 transactions and simulate for 500.

8-9 Produce a set of delay curves, similar to those of Fig. 8-7, for the case of a two-server system in which the service time is uniformly distributed with mean 20 and spread 10, and the interarrival time is exponentially distributed. Use $\rho = 0.2, 0.4, 0.6, 0.8$, and 0.9. Design a system of this type for which the probability of no delay is at least 0.2, and the probability of the delay exceeding 40 seconds is less than 0.05.

8-10 In the disk file example of Sec. 7-7, measure the distribution of the total time to read a record, and the total time from the point at which the disk arm has been positioned. Also measure the distribution of the number of rotations that a transaction must wait (excluding those that do not wait at all) by measuring the transit time spent while waiting for extra rotations and tabulating in time units of 18 milliseconds, which is the disk rotation time.

9

FUNCTIONS

Except for a brief introductory example given in Sec. 3-6, action times have been either a constant or a uniformly distributed random variable. It is essential to be able to model cases where the action time is a nonuniform random variable and also where its value depends upon either the particular transaction being processed or upon the conditions prevailing in the system. The functions that are described in this chapter provide an important means of meeting these needs.

Unlike general-purpose scientific programming languages, GPSS does not provide basic mathematical functions, such as the sine or logarithm function. It does provide simple computational ability in the form of the variable statements that will be described in Chap. 11. It is not practical, however, to use these to evaluate functions from numerical approximations, such as power series. Instead of describing functions mathematically, GPSS uses the method of approximating functions by a series of short straight-line segments.

There are two reasons for this choice. First, the high accuracy that can be obtained with fuller mathematical capabilities is generally much greater than is needed for the type of system simulation carried out with GPSS. In particular, an inherent upper limit to the accuracy of GPSS results from the fact that time is expressed in integral units. Second, by far the greatest need for nonlinear functions in system simulation is to generate random numbers from nonlinear probability density functions. As will be discussed in Sec. 9-1, the commonest way of generating such numbers is to evaluate an inverted cumulative distribution. Even when the probability density function can be expressed as a mathematical function, the cumulative distribution, which is its integral, often cannot be expressed simply, and an inverted cumulative distribution is very unlikely to exist as a simple mathematical expression.

The exponential function, described in Sec. 9-2, is a notable exception. The inverted cumulative distribution is the logarithm function. The normal distribution, described in Sec. 9-3, however, is an example in which neither the cumulative distribution nor its inverted form can be expressed in simple mathematical form. The other theoretical distributions commonly used in statistics and operations research suffer the same fault. Having simple mathematical functions available as subroutines is not helpful, therefore. The theoretical, as well as the experimentally observed, distributions need some form of approximation.

Section 9-1 describes the general method by which GPSS generates random numbers that are an approximation to any required nonuniform distribution, either discrete or continuous. Sections 9-2 and 9-3, respectively, describe specifically the generation of exponentially and normally distributed random numbers that are widely used in system simulation.

There are six modes in which GPSS functions can operate. Section 9-4 describes the method of defining and encoding all the modes. The two most common, *continuous numeric* and *discrete numeric*, are described in Sec. 9-5. GPSS functions use pairs of values to define points, and, if the function is to approximate continuous functions, they interpolate between the points. Without interpolation, they are simply tables of values and they are frequently used solely for the purpose of presenting such tables. The *list numeric mode* of the functions, described in Sec. 9-6, also operates in this manner.

Two other modes, *discrete attribute* and *list attribute*, can be used to supply the numbers of entities that were named at the time of constructing the model and were not numbered until the time of assembly. The description of these two modes is deferred until Sec. 11-9. The sixth mode of functions, called the *entity mode*, is also associated with the assembly program. It allows different types of entity to be assigned the same number when they have been given the same name at the time of building the model. That mode is described in Sec. A2-5 of Appendix 2. Finally, the use of functions to supply operands for the TRANSFER block is described in Sec. 9-10.

9-1
Generating Nonuniformly Distributed Random Numbers

Appendix 1 describes the method by which uniformly and continuously distributed random numbers are generated by special subroutines within

GPSS. The most widely used method of generating nonuniformly distributed random numbers is based on the use of functions with the uniformly and continuously distributed generators used as input.

To produce a *discrete* random variable from the output of these generators means, in effect, dividing the interval from 0 to 1 into numbered parts, where the lengths of the parts represent the proportion of the times the random variable takes the different discrete output values. The value the output takes is then the value associated with the interval into which the uniformly distributed number happens to fall. The simplest example is when a choice must be made randomly between two alternatives. When the first alternative is taken on, say, 60 per cent of the choices, a random, uniformly distributed number between 0 and 1 will be compared with the value 0.6. If it is less than or equal to 0.6, the first choice is taken. If it is greater than the 0.6, the second choice is taken.

As another example, suppose that in the machine shop simulation discussed in Sec. 2-1 the types of parts are distributed with the probabilities shown in Table 9-1. Shown in the third column of the table is the cumulative probability. Since the part type must take one of the values $1, \ldots, 5$, the sum of all the probabilities is equal to 1. The values given in this column mark the ends of the intervals into which the range of 0 to 1 must be broken. If the uniformly distributed random number falls between 0 and 0.10, the part is type 1; if it is between 0.10 and 0.35, it is type 2, and so on. As examples, the following list shows, on the right, the output derived from using the uniformly distributed numbers on the left:

```
0.325    2
0.048    1
0.689    4
0.025    1
0.999    5
```

To illustrate the generation of *continuous but nonuniformly* distributed random numbers, consider the data of Table 9-2, which show the results of

Table 9-1 Distribution of Part Types

Part type	Probability	Cumulative probability
1	0.10	0.10
2	0.25	0.35
3	0.22	0.57
4	0.28	0.85
5	0.15	1.00

Table 9-2 Distribution of Machining Times

Machining time (min)	Number of parts	Cumulative distribution
0–2	31	0.031
2–4	131	0.162
4–6	352	0.514
6–8	316	0.830
8–10	148	0.978
10–12	22	1.000

measuring the time that it takes to machine 1000 parts. Although the times can be any nonnegative value up to a limit of, say, 12 minutes, the data have been collected to the nearest 2 minutes. Column 2 shows the number of parts whose machining time fell into each 2-minute range. Dividing these figures by 1000, the total number of parts, and accumulating the results gives the cumulative distribution shown in the last column. These figures are plotted in Fig. 9-1, and an approximation is made to the continuous distribution by joining the points with straight lines.

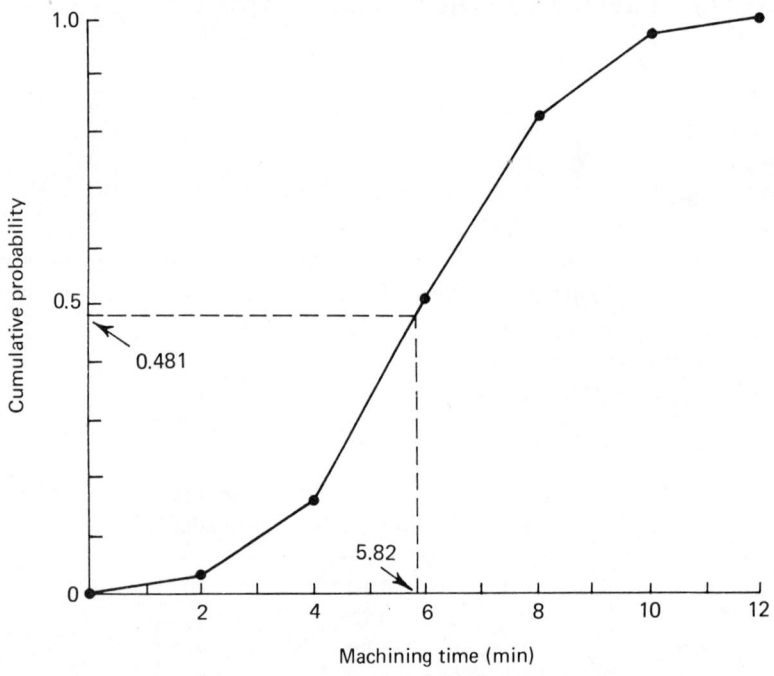

Figure 9-1. Distribution of machining times.

If it were sufficient to generate the machining times to an accuracy of 2 minutes, the method used for discrete random variables could be used to choose between the six ranges of values shown in Table 9-2. The midrange values could then be associated with each choice. For example, the cumulative probability is 0.162 that the time is less than or equal to 4 minutes, and 0.514 that it is less than or equal to 6 minutes. Given that the uniformly distributed random number input fell in the range 0.162 to 0.514, the value of 5 minutes might be taken as output. Since it is known that the variable is continuous, however, interpolation can be used to get a higher accuracy. That is, the output can be judged to lie between 4 and 6 minutes at a point proportional to the way the input falls between 0.162 and 0.514. Suppose that the input value is 0.481. This falls 91 per cent of the distance between the tabulated input values 0.162 and 0.514; so the output will be 5.82 minutes, which is at 91 per cent of the range between 4 and 6 minutes.

The process consists, therefore, of marking off the uniformly distributed random number along the vertical axis of Fig. 9-1 and reading off the corresponding value on the horizontal axis as indicated by the dotted line of the figure. In other words, an inverted form of the cumulative distribution is produced. Figure 9-2 shows the inverted cumulative distribution of the ma-

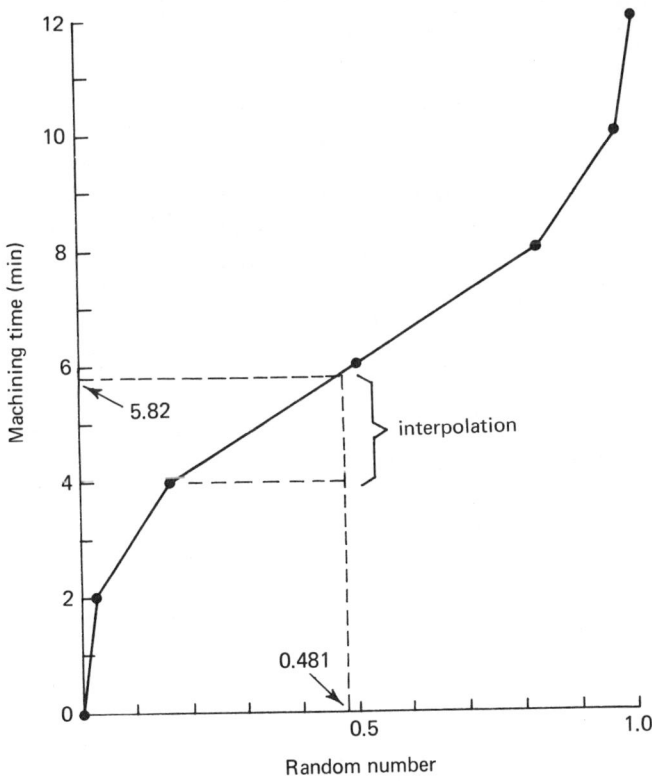

Figure 9-2. Inverted distribution of machining times.

chining time, and the dotted line repeats the same example using 0.481 as an input, but here the direction of reading is from the horizontal to the vertical axis.

To carry out the same process in a computer, a table is constructed for the points of the inverted cumulative distribution, as shown in Table 9-3. The two columns of Table 9-2 have been reversed, so that the values of the cumulative distribution appear in the first column labeled as input, and the machining times at which the points are defined appear in the second column, labeled as output. Interpolation between the tabulated points requires knowing the slope of the output with respect to the input. Since these values do not change, it is convenient to compute these slopes once and list them as the third column of figures in Table 9-3. The values are the slopes per unit input, and they are stored on the line that corresponds to where that slope begins. Thus, the first line of the table indicates that the inverted cumulative distribution begins at zero and slopes upward (positively) at the rate of 64.6 minutes per unit input, until the second line shows that the slope changes at 0.031 to 15.3, and so on.

Table 9-3 Generating a Continuously Distributed Machining Time

Input	Output	Slope
0.000	0	64.6
0.031	2	15.3
0.162	4	5.69
0.514	6	6.32
0.830	8	13.5
0.978	10	91.0
1.000	12	—

Repeating the previous example of 0.481 as input, a search from the beginning of the table shows that 0.481 is between the two tabulated input values of 0.162 and 0.514. The output is therefore $4 + (0.481 - 0.162) \times 5.69 = 5.82$. The method previously described for generating discrete random variables is essentially the same as the one just described. Because of its discrete nature, the cumulative distribution of the part type would be a staircase function, as shown in Fig. 9-3. When this cumulative distribution is inverted, it appears as shown in Fig. 9-4. This can be described in a computer, as shown in Table 9-4, which is similar to Table 9-3, differing in that there is no column of figures for a slope and therefore no interpolation. If the number for the input falls between two tabulated values, the output at the higher of the two is taken and no interpolation is made.

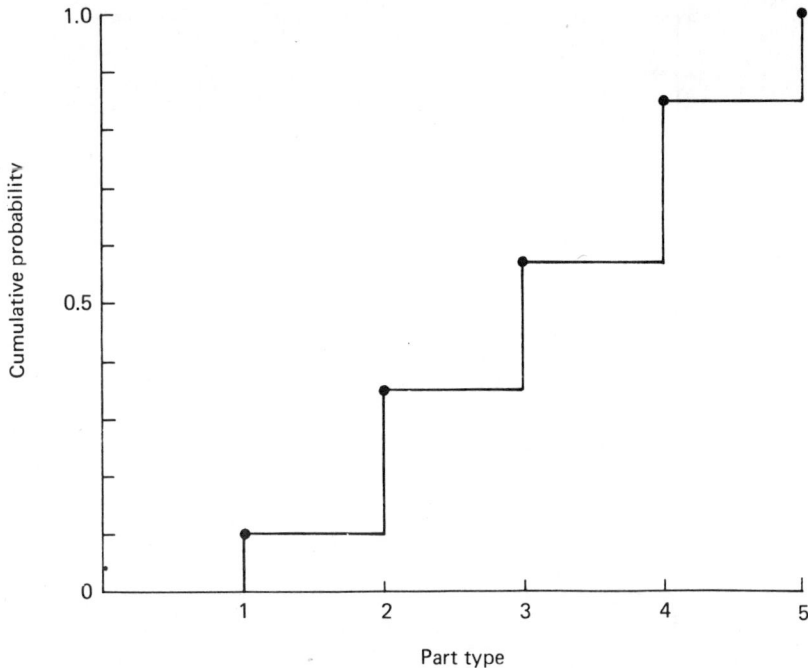

Figure 9-3. Cumulative discrete distribution.

The straight line graph for machining times given in Fig. 9-2, and its numerical equivalent in Table 9-3, is only an approximation to a continuous function that would change slope smoothly. The approximation can be improved by using more points in the table. Note that it is not necessary for the points to be spaced at uniform intervals in the way the time units are spaced in the present case. For a given number of points, it is better to place the points closer together in sections where the slope is changing rapidly and stretch them farther apart where the slope changes slowly. It is also possible

Table 9-4 Generating a Discrete Part-Type Number

Input	Output
0.00	0
0.10	1
0.35	2
0.57	3
0.85	4
1.00	5

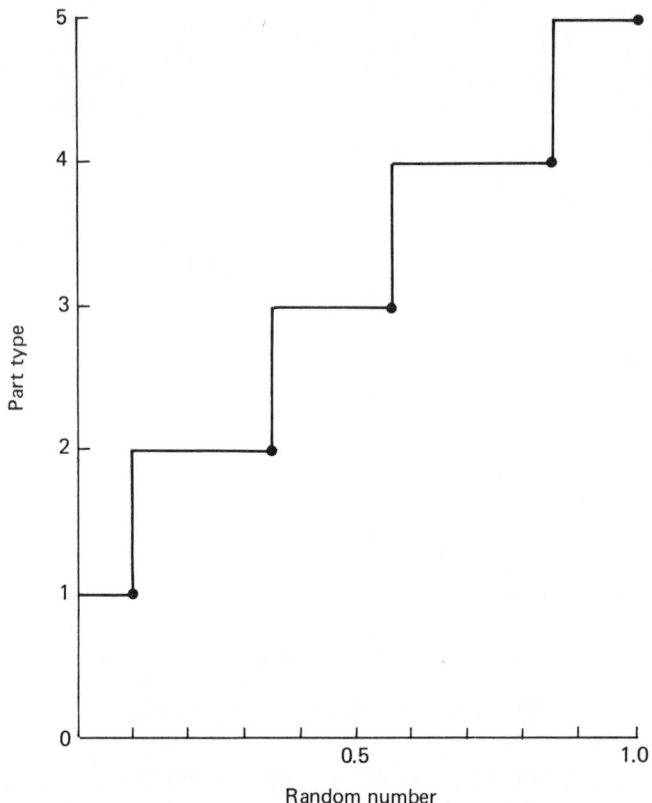

Figure 9-4. Inverted cumulative discrete distribution.

to use more complex interpolation methods than the simple linear method just described. Ideally, the number of points and their spacing should be chosen to keep the maximum difference between the true curve and the straight line approximations below a given percentage of the true value. This can involve a tedious amount of calculation and it is usually good enough to judge the approximation by eye, possibly at the expense of using a few more points than are really necessary, and so increasing the table search time slightly.

9-2
Exponential Distribution

Table 9-5 shows a set of values which can be used to generate random numbers that have a particular continuous distribution called the *exponential distribution*. It will be noticed that, unlike Table 9-3, the values are not uniformly spaced.

The exponential distribution is frequently used to represent interarrival times, such as the times between the arrival of jobs in a machine shop, when the arrivals are random. It is often found that when these times are measured

Table 9-5 Table for Generating an Exponentially Distributed Random Variable (mean = 1)

Input	Output	Slope	Input	Output	Slope
0	0	1.04	0.90	2.30	11.0
0.1	0.104	1.18	0.92	2.52	14.5
0.2	0.222	1.33	0.94	2.81	18.0
0.3	0.355	1.54	0.95	2.99	21.0
0.4	0.509	1.81	0.96	3.20	30.0
0.5	0.690	2.25	0.97	3.50	40.0
0.6	0.915	2.85	0.98	3.90	70.0
0.7	1.20	3.60	0.99	4.60	140
0.75	1.38	4.40	0.995	5.30	300
0.80	1.60	5.75	0.998	6.20	800
0.84	1.83	7.25	0.999	7.0	3333
0.88	2.12	9.00	0.9997	8.0	—

and plotted as a distribution, they are quite well represented as being exponentially distributed. A reasonably accurate simulation of a random arrival pattern can be generated from uniformly distributed random numbers using Table 9-5.

The output of Table 9-5 gives a distribution with a mean of 1. In the context of arrivals, this means that if we use the output to represent interarrival times (in units, say, of minutes), the average time between arrivals is 1 minute, which, in turn, implies an arrival rate of one per minute. If the mean time between arrivals needs to be some other value, say 20 minutes, the output of Table 9-5 can be multiplied by 20. Note, however, that this is a specific property of the exponential distribution. In general, multiplying a distribution by a scale factor distorts the form of the distribution.

Table 9-6 shows how arrival times would be generated, assuming exponentially distributed interarrival times and a mean interarrival time of 20 minutes. The first column is a set of uniformly distributed random numbers. Column 2 is the output of Table 9-5 using the method described for producing nonuniformly distributed numbers. The third column multiples the output by 20 to get exponentially distributed numbers with a mean of 20. Finally, column 4 accumulates the figures of column 3 line by line to give the actual arrival times.

Testing whether a particular set of data corresponds to an exponential distribution is a topic more appropriate for discussion in a textbook on engineering statistics (see 18, p. 202). A simple test, however, is to rank the data in increasing size and plot the values against rank on semilogarithmic graph paper. Figure 9-5 shows such a plot for the interarrival times computed in column 3 of Table 9-6. This special graph paper automatically

Table 9-6 Calculation of Arrival Times

Uniformly distributed random numbers	Exponentially distributed random numbers (mean = 1)	Interarrival times (mean = 20)	Arrival times (min)
0.100	0.104	2.08	2.08
0.375	0.470	9.40	11.48
0.084	0.087	1.74	13.22
0.990	4.600	92.00	105.22
0.128	0.137	2.74	107.96
0.660	1.086	21.72	129.68
0.310	0.370	7.40	137.08
0.852	1.963	39.26	176.34
0.635	1.915	38.30	214.64
0.737	1.333	26.66	241.30

places the data plotted on the vertical scale at a distance equal to their logarithm. The same results would be obtained by taking the logarithms of the data and then plotting on ordinary linear graph paper.

If the data have been sampled from an exponential distribution, the points will lie close to a straight line. If this appears to be the case, a simple estimate of the mean value can be made by averaging the measured values. In the present case, even though the data are known to come from an exponential distribution with a mean of 20, the average interarrival time is 24.14. This small sample apparently has an unusually high number of values greater than the population mean. A larger sample would no doubt bring the average closer to the expected value of 20. As large a sample as is reasonably practical should be used, since the accuracy of the estimate improves with the sample size.

9-3
Normal Distribution

Another frequently used distribution is the normal distribution. This is characteristic of a variable that should have a specific value but is subject to random errors, usually due to a number of independent minor causes, each of which may equally well be positive or negative. A typical example is provided by a machining operation intended to produce parts of a standard size. Differences in such factors as metal hardness, tool setting, and tempera-

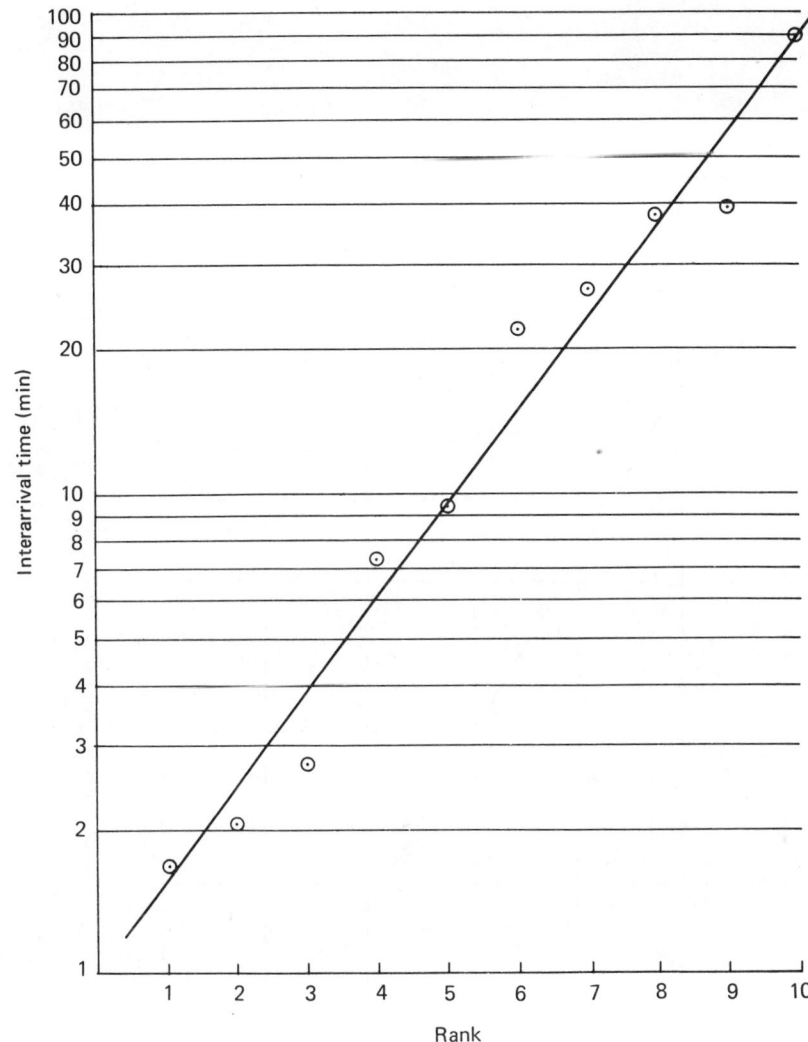

Figure 9-5. Interarrival times on semilogarithmic paper.

ture cause random errors, and in these circumstances it will frequently be found that the size is normally distributed.

Unlike the exponential distribution, which can be characterized by one parameter, the mean, the normal distribution is specified by two parameters, a mean and a standard deviation. (The exponential distribution also has a standard deviation, but its value is always equal to the mean.) Just as semilogarithmic paper can be used to plot exponentially distributed data as a straight line, so also is there a special form of graph paper, called probability paper, that will turn a plot of a cumulative normal distribution into a straight line. Figure 9-6, for example, shows the data of Table 9-2 for machining time plotted on probability paper. The horizontal axis shows the cumulative dis-

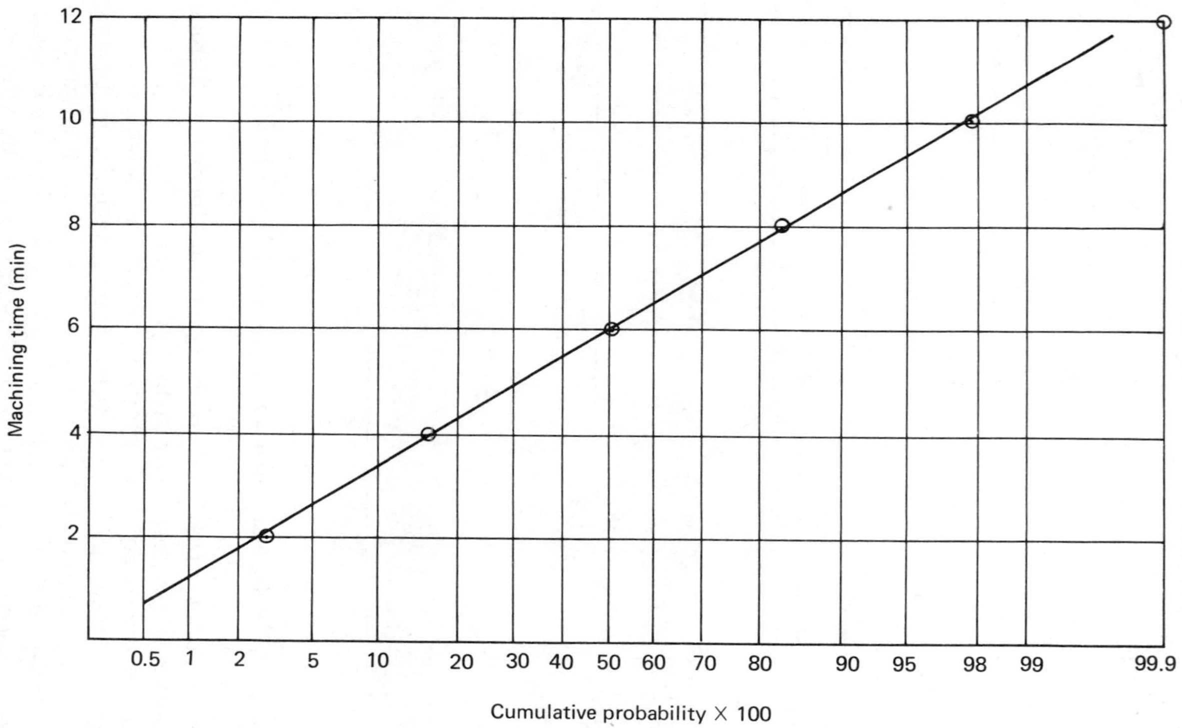

Figure 9-6. Machining times on probability paper.

tribution multiplied by 100 to give a percentage. The vertical scale shows machining time. The result is very close to a straight line, indicating that the data is from a normal distribution. The 50 per cent point of the graph corresponds to the mean of the distribution, μ. The standard deviation, σ, is such that for a true normal distribution, 16 per cent of the cumulative data should fall at or below the point corresponding to $\mu - \sigma$ and, similarly, 84 per cent should fall at or above the $\mu + \sigma$ point. Given an estimate of the mean from the 50 per cent point, either of the other two points can be used to estimate the standard deviation. Better still, both can be used and the results averaged. In the data of Fig. 9-6 the values correspond closely to an estimated mean of 60 seconds and a standard deviation of 20 minutes.

Plotted on linear graph paper, a cumulative normal distribution has a characteristic ogive shape similar to the curve of machining time given in Fig. 9-1. The relations just given for the points used to estimate the mean and standard deviation also apply to this type of graph. Once it is decided to accept the data as being normally distributed, the best estimates of the mean, M, and standard deviation, S, from the observations are given by

$$M = \frac{1}{n} \sum_{i=1}^{n} x_i$$

$$S = \left\{ \frac{1}{n-1} \sum_{i=1}^{n} (M - x_i)^2 \right\}^{1/2}$$

Table 9-7 gives a set of numbers from which a variable with a normal distribution can be derived. In this case the output will have a mean of 0 and a standard deviation of 1. This particular form of the normal distri-

Table 9-7 Table for Generating a Standard Normal Variable

Input	Output	Slope	Input	Output	Slope
0	−5.0	33,333	0.57926	0.2	2.63
0.00003	−4.0	756	0.65542	0.4	2.84
0.00135	−3.0	206	0.72575	0.6	3.21
0.00621	−2.5	30.2	0.78814	0.8	3.76
0.02275	−2.0	11.3	0.84134	1.0	4.59
0.06681	−1.5	6.22	0.88493	1.2	6.22
0.11507	−1.2	4.59	0.93319	1.5	11.3
0.15866	−1.0	3.76	0.97725	2.0	30.2
0.21186	−0.8	3.21	0.99379	2.5	206
0.27425	−0.6	2.84	0.99865	3.0	756
0.34458	−0.4	2.63	0.99997	4.0	33,333
0.42074	−0.2	2.52	1.0	5.0	—
0.50000	0	2.52			

bution is referred to as the standard normal distribution and the output is usually denoted by z. A variable x that has a normal distribution but with a mean of μ and a standard deviation of σ is derived by first computing the variable z and then converting to x with the formula

$$x = z\sigma + \mu$$

For example, suppose that a normal variate is needed with a mean of 60 and a standard deviation of 20 and that the input to Table 9-7 from a uniformly distributed random number generator is 0.765. Table 9-7 shows this value to lie between the tabulated inputs of 0.726 and 0.788. The output at the point 0.726 is 0.6 and the slope at that point is 3.21. Therefore, the standard normal output is $z = 0.6 + (0.765 - 0.726) \times 3.21 = 0.725$. Applying the equation for the value of x gives

$$x = 20 \times 0.725 + 60 = 74.5$$

The following list shows five worked values, including the one just computed:

Input	z	x
0.765	0.725	74.5
0.649	0.384	67.7
0.196	−0.861	42.8
0.094	−1.332	33.4
0.802	0.853	67.0

The figures of Table 9-7 truncate the normal distribution to a limit of five standard deviations from the mean. This means that, if the mean is less than five standard deviations above zero, it is possible for a negative output to occur. There are times when a check needs to be made before using the output.

9-4

Definition of Functions

There can be many functions in a GPSS model, each identified by name or number. The normal limit is 200. Each function is defined by two or more pairs of values relating an input x_i to an output y_i, and it can operate in one of six modes. For completeness, all the modes are listed below, together with the symbols by which they are indicated:

Continuous numerical valued	Cn
Discrete numerical valued	Dn
List numerical valued	Ln
Discrete attribute valued	En
List attribute valued	Mn
Entity	Sn

In each case the letter n is replaced by the number of points defining the function.

Continuous, discrete, and list numerical functions will be described in this chapter. Descriptions of the attribute modes will be deferred until Sec. 11-9. The sixth mode of function, the entity mode, is used in the assembly phase to control the assignment of entity numbers. A description is given in Appendix 2, but it will be better understood after reading Sec. 11-9, since the entity mode is closely associated with the attribute modes. Both the entity and list modes are examples of functions being used simply as tables of values.

The input to a function can be any one of the SNAs except the matrix savevalue SNA (see Secs. 4-10 through 4-12 and Appendix 5). Examples will be given in Sec. 11-8. We shall see, first, examples of functions that use as input a random number uniformly distributed between 0 and 1. This is one of the SNAs. It is denoted by RNn, where n takes one of the values 1, 2, . . . , 8 to select a random number generator. Other SNAs allow the input to be a parameter of a particular transaction or the value of some system variable, such as the current content of a storage.

The value of a function is indicated by FNj, or FN$NAME, where j is the number, or NAME is the name of the function. A function is itself an SNA and it is permissible to use one function as the input to another. Examples of this are given in Secs. 11-10 and 11-11.

9-5

Continuous and Discrete Functions

Figure 9-7 illustrates both a continuous and a discrete numerical valued function. In a continuous mode, the program interpolates linearly between the defined points, allowing the user to approximate any given curve by a series of straight line segments. In a discrete mode, the function is regarded as a "staircase" function. If x_i and x_{i+1} are two successive points at which the function is defined, an input in the range $x_i < x \leqslant x_{i+1}$ will result in the output y_{i+1}. In either mode, if the argument goes outside the range of definition, the output is the value defined at the end of the range.

9-6

List Functions

The list mode simply treats a function as a table of values. The input is assumed to be an integer j in the range 1 to n, and the program will extract the jth listed value of the table. A reference outside the range 1 to n causes an error stop.

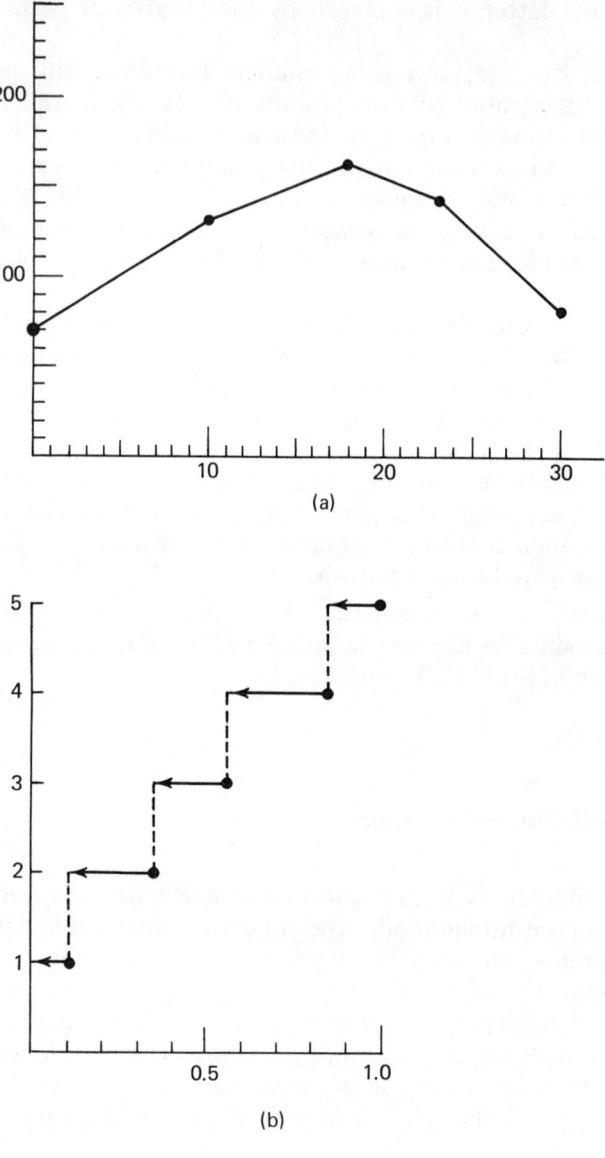

Figure 9-7. Continuous and discrete functions: (a) continuous; (b) discrete.

The same result can be obtained by using a discrete mode, defining the input values to be the integers $1, 2, \ldots, n$, but in that case the program will begin at the lowest defined input value and will search to find the jth value. A list mode function will execute more quickly by going directly to the jth value.

9-7

Specifying Functions

Any number of points (> 1) can be used to define a function. The range and the size of the intervals between points of continuous and discrete valued functions can vary freely, except that a function defined to have a uniformly distributed random number as input must have values of its input in the range 0 to 1. The x values must be given in increasing order of magnitude.

The x_i and y_i values that define a function can be nonintegral. In addition, the input values, x_i, can be negative. The great majority of GPSS variables can take only nonnegative integral values. In particular, all action times are zero or a positive integer. However, to increase accuracy, the input to a function can be fractional. The use of a uniformly distributed random number in the range 0 to 1 is a case in point. Later, when discussing FVARIABLE statements, we shall see ways in which floating-point calculations may be used, and these also may result in a nonintegral input to a function. Parameters and savevalues, which are SNAs that will be described later, can be both floating-point and negative. They are frequently used as function inputs.

At least two statements are needed to define a function. The first is a FUNCTION statement. It is immediately followed by one or more *function follower statements*. The format for the FUNCTION statement is shown in Table 9-8. The function follower statements carry the values of x and y that define the function. Values are given, without blanks, beginning in column 1, with commas between the x and y values, and slashes between successive pairs in the following manner:

$$x_1, y_1 / x_2, y_2 / \ldots x_n, y_n$$

Table 9-8 FUNCTION Statement Format

Field	Content
Location	Function name (or number)
Operation	FUNCTION
A	SNA to be used as input
B	Cn* for continuous numerical mode
	Dn for discrete numerical mode
	Ln for list numerical mode
	En for discrete attribute mode
	Mn for list attribute mode
	Sn for entity mode

*n is the number of points

Any number of points may be in one statement so long as the statement does not go beyond column 71. Any number of additional statements may be used but no one pair of x, y values may be split between two statements.

In the case of list mode functions, it is permissible to enter the pairs of values x_i, y_i, with $x_i = 1, 2, \ldots, n$. However, the program simply assumes the x values, so list function data statements may also be written in the form

$$, y_1 /, y_2 /, \ldots /, y_n$$

As examples, the two functions of Fig. 9-7 would be coded as follows:

```
    1 FUNCTION      RN1,C5
0,70/10,130/18,160/23,140/30,80
    2 FUNCTION      RN1,D5
.1,1/.35,2/.57,3/.85,4/1,5
```

Both these functions are using a random number as input and both are defined with five points.

The set of statements for a function can be placed anywhere in the input deck with one important exception. If a GENERATE block is to use a function, the definition of the function must appear ahead of the GENERATE block. This is because the program creates the first transaction for the GENERATE block as soon as it reads the block description, and the function must be defined at that time. The function description does not have to be immediately in front of the GENERATE block. A common practice of many users is to put all function definitions at the beginning of the problem description to avoid violating this rule inadvertently.

9-8

Evaluating Functions

Since the values defining a function can be fractional and, in the case of continuous functions, the program interpolates between defined values, the output of a function can be nonintegral. It is possible to use the output value of a function directly as an input to the block diagram—for example, as a block location or an entity number. (This technique, which can be used with any SNA, will be described later in Chap. 11.) However, every value used in a GPSS block diagram must be a positive integer or zero. Consequently, any function value used in the block diagram is automatically converted to an integer. All such conversions are made by *truncating* the value. That is, the fractional part of the value is dropped: the value is not rounded to the nearest integer.

Consider, for example, the function illustrated in Fig. 9-8. The input is a uniformly distributed random number between 0 and 1, and the function is given by the equation

$$y = 1 + 100x$$

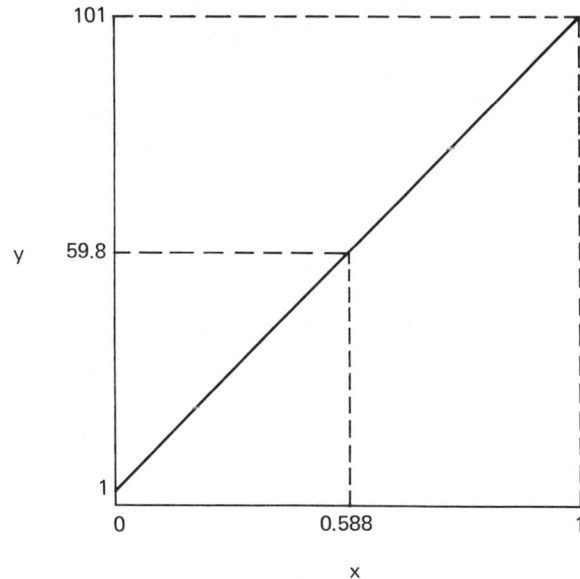

Figure 9-8. Evaluating a continuous function.

The coding for the function in GPSS would be

```
       1 FUNCTION    RN1,C2
0,1/1,101
```

The function, number 1, has random number generator 1 as input and it is a continuous function defined by two points. The two defining values are, $x = 0$, $y = 1$, and $x = 1$, $y = 101$.

Suppose that the generator gave as input the value $x = 0.588$. The computed output would be $y = 59.8$. If this output were to be applied directly to the block diagram—for example, as a facility number—it would first be truncated to the value 59. Similarly, the input value 0.995 would produce an output truncated to 100, and input 0.003 would produce 1.

As can be seen, the example provides a convenient way of choosing a random number between 1 and 100 with equal probability given to each value. Functions are often used for this purpose. The reason for biasing the function so that it does not pass through the origin is to exclude the value zero, which could result from the truncation when the function does go through the origin. Zero is usually an illegal number in GPSS.

There are two cases where the value of a function is not directly used in the block diagram. Instead, the value is used in a calculation. The function value is not then truncated, although the result of the calculation will be truncated if it is used in the block diagram.

One case is the computation of action times. If a function is specified in the B field of an ADVANCE or GENERATE block, the action time is derived by multiplying the function value by the mean value given in field A. The function value is left in floating-point form for the multiplication, and the result is then truncated. The ASSIGN block that will be described later (Sec. 10-6) is often used to assign an action time, and the same procedure is then used to calculate action times from functions.

The other case occurs when a function appears as a component in an FVARIABLE. An FVARIABLE is a mathematical statement describing a combination of two or more SNAs. An example will be given in the next section. FVARIABLEs are specifically designed to operate with floating-point numbers, so any function values they use are not truncated.

Note, however, that VARIABLE statements (to be described in Sec. 11-13) are similar to FVARIABLE statements but are designed to work with integers. A function value being used in a VARIABLE statement *will* be truncated before being used in the computation.

9-9

Shopping Example

As an example of how nonuniformly distributed action times are used, consider the following example. Shoppers drive to a supermarket, arriving with an exponentially distributed interarrival time that has a mean of 100 seconds. They first park their cars, and this is a normally distributed time with a mean of 100 seconds and a standard deviation of 50.

A sample of 1000 shoppers is taken and the time they take to shop is measured to the nearest second. The results are shown in Table 9-9. Section 9-1 discussed how random numbers with this distribution can be generated. The cumulative distribution, shown in the fourth column, has to be inverted. The numbers in column 4 become the x values, and the shopping times, 100, 200, . . . , 600, become the y values of a GPSS function. Generating the exponential and normal distributions was discussed in Secs. 9-2 and 9-3, and Tables 9-5 and 9-7 are in exactly the form needed for GPSS functions.

Table 9-9 Distribution of Shopping Time

Shopping time (sec)	Number of customers	Relative frequency	Cumulative distribution
1-100	123	0.123	0.123
101-200	250	0.250	0.373
201-300	384	0.384	0.757
301-400	139	0.139	0.896
401-500	71	0.071	0.967
501-600	33	0.033	1.000

All three functions are continuous, so there will be interpolation between the defined points; but it is not necessary for the user to compute the slopes needed in the interpolation: they are generated automatically by GPSS.

The input for all three functions is to be a uniformly distributed random number between 0 and 1. This is derived by using the SNA called RN_n, $(1 \leq n \leq 8)$, where n indicates one of eight random number generators. It is permissible to use the same generator for all three functions, since the successive output numbers of the generator are mutually independent; so the input to all three functions will be RN1.

The values of Table 9-7 give a standard normal variate which, in this case, needs to be converted to a normal variate with mean 100 and standard deviation 50. The conversion is made with the equation (see Sec. 9-3)

$$x = 50z + 100$$

This type of calculation is carried out in GPSS with variable statements, in this case, floating-point type. They are explained more fully in Chap. 11. In this instance, using the name SHOP to identify the variable and NORM to identify the normal function, the coding is

SHOP FVARIABLE   50*FN$NORM+100

Figure 9-9 shows a block diagram for the system. The exponential function is called EXP, and the shopping time distribution function, derived from Table 9-9, is called TIME. Programming of the problem and the results of a run are shown in Fig. 9-10. Note that the EXP function has been placed

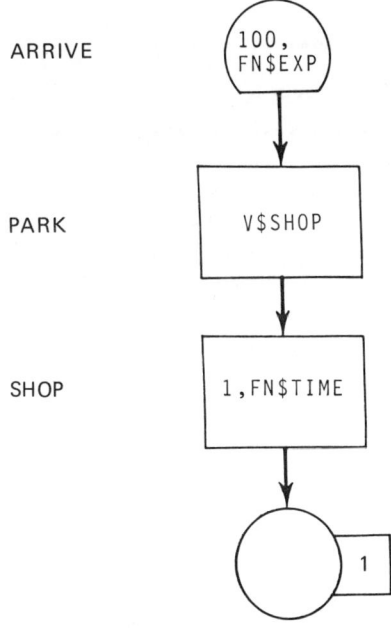

Figure 9-9. A shopping example.

```
*         A SHOPPING EXAMPLE
*
 EXP      FUNCTION     RN1,C24           INVERSE EXPONENTIAL FUNCTION
0,0/.1,.104/.2,.222/.3,.355/.4,.509/.5,.69
.6,.915/.7,1.2/.75,1.38/.8,1.6/.84,1.83/.88,2.12
.9,2.3/.92,2.52/.94,2.81/.95,2.99/.96,3.2/.97,3.5
.98,3.9/.99,4.6/.995,5.3/.998,6.2/.999,7/.9997,8
*
 NORM     FUNCTION     RN1,C25           INVERSE STANDARD NORMAL
0,-5/.00003,-4/.00135,-3/.00621,-2.5/.02275,-2/.06681,-1.5
.11507,-1.2/.15866,-1/.21186,-.8/.27425,-.6/.34458,-.4/.42074,-.2
.5,0/.57926,.2/.65542,.4/.72575,.6/.78814,.8/.84134,1/.88493,1.2
.93319,1.5/.97725,2/.99379,2.5/.99865,3/.99997,4/1,5
*
 TIME     FUNCTION     RN1,C7            SHOPPING TIME
0.0,0/0.123,100/0.373,200/0.757,300/0.896,400/0.967,500/1.0,600
*
1         GENERATE     100,FN$EXP        CREATE CUSTOMERS
2         ADVANCE      V$SHOP            PARK
3         ADVANCE      1,FN$TIME         SHOP
4         TABULATE     1                 TABULATE TOTAL TIME
5         TERMINATE    1
*
 SHOP     FVARIABLE    50*FN$NORM+1000   COMPUTES PARKING TIME
 1        TABLE        M1,1000,100,10
          START        50,NP             INITIALIZE SYSTEM
          RESET
          START        1000
```

```
RELATIVE CLOCK         94633  ABSOLUTE CLOCK        100433
BLOCK COUNTS
BLOCK CURRENT TOTAL    BLOCK CURRENT TOTAL    BLOCK CURRENT TOTAL    BLOCK CURRENT TOTAL
    1       0   1001
    2       9   1001
    3       2   1000
    4       0   1000
    5       0   1000
```

```
*****************************************
*                                       *
*              TABLES                   *
*                                       *
*****************************************
```

```
TABLE   1
ENTRIES IN TABLE    MEAN ARGUMENT    STANDARD DEVIATION    SUM OF ARGUMENTS
         1000           1238.068             130.000           1238069.000    NON-WEIGHTED

   UPPER       OBSERVED       PER CENT     CUMULATIVE     CUMULATIVE     MULTIPLE     DEVIATION
   LIMIT      FREQUENCY       OF TOTAL     PERCENTAGE     REMAINDER      OF MEAN      FROM MEAN
    1000           21           2.09           2.0           97.8          .807         -1.831
    1100          133          13.29          15.3           84.5          .888         -1.062
    1200          243          24.29          39.6           60.3          .969          -.292
    1300          331          33.09          72.7           27.2         1.050           .476
    1400          157          15.69          88.4           11.5         1.130          1.245
    1500           79           7.89          96.3            3.6         1.211          2.014
    1600           30           2.99          99.3             .6         1.292          2.784
    1700            6            .59         100.0             .0         1.373          3.553
REMAINING FREQUENCIES ARE ALL ZERO
```

Figure 9-10. Coding and output for shopping example.

ahead of the GENERATE block because the function must be defined when the assembler reads the GENERATE block.

As shown in Fig. 9-10, the value of the FVARIABLE, denoted by V$SHOP, can be placed directly in field A of the ADVANCE block that represents the parking time. This is an example of a general principle that allows any SNA to be used in almost any operand field of a block. Variable statements are included among the SNAs. The general principle allowing SNAs to be used as operands is discussed more fully in Sec. 11-6.

9-10

Function Mode of TRANSFER Block

Transactions often need to be transferred to one of several locations. A random choice between two alternatives is made with the fractional mode, and a random choice among many alternatives can be made with the PICK mode, provided the probabilities of picking each path are the same. A more general way of choosing among many alternative locations is to use the function mode of the TRANSFER block.

To indicate this mode, the letters FN are placed in field A of the TRANSFER block. The B field carries a function number. If field C is used, it carries a number that is added to the value of the function. When a transaction enters the block, the function is evaluated and the value of field C, if used, is added. Should the result be nonintegral, the result is truncated to produce an integral value. The truncated value becomes the location to which the transaction is transferred.

Any mode of function can be used but, usually, either a discrete or list mode numerical valued function is used. With a discrete mode, the choice between the alternatives can be of unequal probability, by spacing the discrete points unevenly. With a list mode, the choice can easily be made to depend upon the transaction type by making a parameter act as input to the function.

In using the function mode of a TRANSFER block, the absolute values of the locations may not be known at the time of coding the problem. It is therefore permissible to give the symbolic names of locations as the dependent values of a function. Upon assembly, the program will substitute the specific location numbers.

As an example, suppose that there is a choice between four paths leading to locations called LOCA, LOCB, LOCC, and LOCD. The probabilities of going to these locations are, respectively, 0.2, 0.1, 0.4, and 0.3. The following TRANSFER block and discrete value function could be used:

```
            TRANSFER     FN,2
          2 FUNCTION     RN1,D4
    .2,LOCA/.3,LOCB/.7,LOCC/1,LOCD
```

Exercises

9-1 Design functions that will produce random numbers with the following probability density functions:
- (i) $f(x) = 0.0125$ $0 < x \leq 40$
       $f(x) = 0.025$ $40 < x \leq 60$
       $f(x) = 0$ elsewhere
- (ii) $f(x) = 0.0125$ $0 < x \leq 10$
       $f(x) = 0.0375$ $10 < x \leq 20$
       $f(x) = 0.025$ $20 < x \leq 40$
       $f(x) = 0$ elsewhere
- (iii) $f(x) = 1/15$ $0 < x \leq 5$
       $f(x) = 0$ $5 < x \leq 10$
       $f(x) = 2/15$ $10 < x \leq 15$
       $f(x) = 0$ elsewhere

9-2 Design functions that will produce random numbers with approximately the following probability density functions. In each case use 10 equally spaced intervals and do not attempt to minimize the errors:
- (i) $f(x) = x/10$ $0 < x \leq 20$
       $f(x) = 0$ elsewhere
- (ii) $f(x) = 40x$ $0 < x \leq 5$
       $f(x) = 40(1-x)$ $5 < x \leq 10$
       $f(x) = 0$ elsewhere
- (iii) $f(x) = \sin x$ $0 < x \leq 90°$
       $f(x) = 0$ elsewhere

9-3 Given a normal 365-day year, design two functions that produce a number, 1 through 12, to represent the month a person was born, assuming for the different functions that
- (a) Birthdates are uniformly distributed over the year.
- (b) The months of May and September both have 10 per cent more birthdays than would be expected from a uniform distribution.

9-4 Reprogram Exercise 4-2 on the assumption that the time to move between floors is exponentially distributed with the following mean values: floor 1 to 2, 20 seconds; floor 2 to 3, 30 seconds; and floor 3 to 4, 35 seconds.

9-5 The number of days to perform a certain job is uniformly distributed between 1 and 675. Jobs are created with exponentially distributed intervals having a mean of 30 days. Find the distribution of the intervals between the finishing of successive jobs. Initialize with 10 transactions and simulate for 500.

9-6 An Erlang distribution of mean value T and order k can be generated as the distribution of the total time to process a transaction through k successive stages when the time spent in each stage is independently and exponentially distributed with mean T/k. No transaction can begin processing until its predecessor has cleared all stages. There is no loss of time between stages. Generate and tabulate an Erlang distribution with a mean value of 200 and order 4. Initialize with 10 transactions and simulate for 500.

9-7 Reprogram Exercise 8-2 with the following modifications:
(i) The arrival time is exponentially distributed with a mean of 30 seconds,
(ii) Checkout times are normally distributed with a mean of 120 seconds and a standard deviation of 20 seconds for the normal counters, and a mean of 60 seconds and a standard deviation of of 10 seconds at the express counter,
(iii) Sampling of the time taken to shop by 800 shoppers gives the following results:

Shop time (min)	Number of shoppers
0-5	52
5-10	105
10-15	346
15-20	191
20-25	82
25-30	24

9-8 Parts are arriving with an interarrival time that is exponentially distributed and has a mean of 50 seconds. There are three types in the following proportions: A, 30 per cent; B, 20 per cent; and C, 50 per cent. A separate machine is to be used for each type and the simulation is to produce individual statistics for the three machines. The time to machine a part is normally distributed with a mean of 90 seconds and a standard deviation of 15 seconds for all types. Simulate the system, using a function as an SNA to supply the facility number.

9-9 Orders are received for one of five types of parts at the rate of one order every 3 ± 1 minutes. The table that follows shows the proportions of the parts and the time taken to fill each type of order. Orders of type A and B are picked up immediately as they are filled, but orders of type C, D, and E must wait 10 ± 5 minutes to be picked up. Find the distribution of time to complete delivery for all orders combined. Initialize with 10 transactions and simulate for 500.

Part type	Percentage	Service time (min)
A	40	5 ± 2
B	30	7 ± 3
C	15	10 ± 5
D	10	15 ± 8
E	5	20 ± 10

9-10 Messages arrive at a center with exponentially distributed interarrival times that have a mean of 50 seconds. Each message takes 10 ± 5 seconds to be recorded prior to processing. There are four types of messages and the time to process each type is normally distributed. The proportions of the types and the parameters of their processing times are as follows:

Type	Percentages	Mean (sec)	Standard deviation (sec)
A	50	30	10
B	30	40	15
C	15	60	20
D	5	100	30

Find the distribution of the time to complete processing for all types combined. Initialize with 10 transactions and simulate for 500.

10

PARAMETERS AND SAVEVALUES

As described so far, priority is the only attribute that distinguishes one transaction from another. In fact, transactions also have parameters that record other attributes. Values are given to parameters when a transaction enters an ASSIGN block. The meaning of the parameters is determined by the user. Transactions representing cars, for example, might use parameters for such data as origin or destination. A transaction representing an order in a job shop might use parameters to indicate part number, number of parts to be made, and so on.

Parameters are included among the SNAs and as such can be used to supply block fields. In this way, parameters can control the way blocks process individual transactions, providing a very powerful way of increasing the flexibility of a block diagram, particularly when there are repetitive sections in the model.

Other uses of parameters are to control transaction transfers through two modes of the TRANSFER block, the parameter and subroutine modes, and to control the execution of program loops through the use of LOOP and INDEX blocks.

Parameters are data that are directly accessible only to the transaction with which they are associated. There is also a need to record data more generally, either data that are collected during the simulation, or initialization data that are entered at the beginning of a run. The program provides savevalues for this purpose. The savevalues can occur singly or in the form of matrices. During a run, values are placed in them by the SAVEVALUE or MSAVEVALUE blocks, and they can be initialized by an INITIAL control statement. A matrix savevalue also needs a MATRIX control statement for its definition.

Parameters, savevalues, and matrices of savevalues can all exist in one of four data formats. They can be positive or negative integers occupying a fullword, halfword, or byte-sized space. They can also be positive or negative floating-point numbers. Following are the ranges of values and the numbers of the entities that are normally available:

fullword	$\pm 2^{31} - 1$	1000
halfword	$\pm 2^{15} - 1$	500
byte-sized	$\pm 2^{7} - 1$	800
floating-point	$\pm 2^{24} - 1$	100

Floating-point values have a wider range with some loss of precision. This chapter describes parameters and savevalues, and the five new block types just mentioned. The block diagram symbols for the block types are shown in Fig. 10-1.

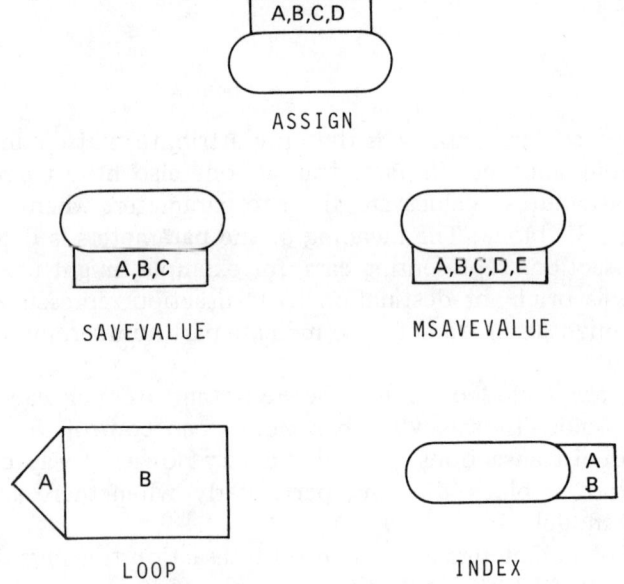

Figure 10-1. Block types 6.

10-1
Parameters

Transactions can have a total of 1020 parameters consisting of 255 in each of the four data formats. The number of each type is selected at the

GENERATE block creating the transactions (see Sec. 4-2). The parameters are numbered, beginning at 1, with a different sequence of numbers used for each type. The SPLIT block, to be described in Sec. 13-2, can also create transactions, and it, also, can select the number of parameters by type.

If there is more than one GENERATE block, the number of parameters can be chosen independently at each. Once the selection is made, the number of parameters cannot be changed during the simulation. However, the SPLIT block can create a copy with fewer parameters. An original, with a large number of unwanted parameters, can then be destroyed.

A number of block types are concerned with processing or using parameters. Table 10-1 lists, with two exceptions, all the block fields where the content is interpreted as a parameter number. Some of the block types have yet to be described. These fields must identify the parameter both by number and type. The notation used is kPx, where k is the parameter number and x is one of the following letters indicating the parameter type: F, fullword; H, halfword; B, byte-sized; and L, floating-point. For example, 10PF denotes the tenth fullword parameter, and 12PL denotes the twelfth floating-point parameter. This notation is called the *suffix notation*. Later, in Sec. 10-9, another notation for parameters, used when they are being referenced as SNAs, will be described.

The two exceptions to the suffix notation are in the ASSIGN block and the TRANSFER block operating in a parameter mode. In both these cases the parameter number is given in one field and the type in another.

Table 10-1 Block Fields That Use the Suffix Notation

Block	Operand(s)
ALTER	C, E
COUNT	A
FUNAVAIL	D
GENERATE	F, G, H, I
INDEX	A
LINK	B
LOOP	A
MARK	A
PREEMPT	D
REMOVE	D
SCAN	B, D, E
SELECT	A
SPLIT	C, D, E, F, G
UNLINK	D
TRANSFER	C (subroutine mode only)

10-2
Savevalues

The program provides savevalues in which to save numbers. They exist in the same four data formats as are used for parameters. The symbols used and the number of savevalues normally allowed are shown in Table 10-2.

Savevalues are most frequently used as temporary storages in which to hold values for later use. The values can be placed there by a SAVEVALUE block type. They can also be initialized by an INITIAL control statement. In addition, the values of nonzero savevalues are printed at the end of the simulation run, so that savevalues provide a way of extracting data from a simulation run.

Table 10-2 Types of Savevalues

Type	Symbol*	Limit
Fullword	XFj or Xj	1000
Halfword	XHj	500
Byte-sized	XBj	800
Floating-point	XLj	100

*j is the number of the savevalue.

10-3
Matrix Savevalues

The program also allows matrices of savevalues in any of the four data formats. Table 10-3 shows the symbols used to represent the different types of matrices and the normal limits on their numbers. Note the symbol for a fullword matrix, MX, which differs in form from the notation used for fullword parameters, PF, and savevalues, XF. The size of a matrix must be defined by a MATRIX control statement, which is described in the next section.

As with savevalues, matrices can be initialized with an INITIAL control statement, and the values of nonzero matrices are printed at the end of a run. An example of the output will be given shortly in Fig. 10-3.

Table 10-3 Types of Matrices

Type	Symbol*	Limit
Fullword	MXj(a, b)	25
Halfword	MHj(a, b)	25
Byte-sized	MBj(a, b)	25
Floating-point	MLj(a, b)	25

*j is the matrix number; a is the row number; and b is the column number.

10-4
MATRIX Control Statements

Each matrix must have a separate control statement to establish its size and type. The statement carries the matrix number, or name, in the location field, and the word MATRIX in the operation field. Field A contains MX, MH, MB, or ML to indicate the type of matrix. The numbers of rows and columns are given in fields B and C, respectively.

As an example, the following statement establishes matrix number 6 as having 10 rows and 5 columns of halfword size:

```
6 MATRIX     MH,10,5
```

The statement may appear anywhere in the input, and a new statement can redefine the size between simulation runs.

10-5
INITIAL Control Statements

The initial values of both savevalues and matrix savevalues are zero unless INITIAL control statements set them otherwise. RESET statements do not clear them, and CLEAR statements normally clear them but have the option of not doing so (see Sec. 3-16). The word INITIAL is placed in the operation field, and the location field is left blank. Beginning at column 19 and extending up to column 71, without blanks, the initial values of a series of savevalues or matrix savevalues can be specified. Ranges of contiguous entities that are to be set to the same value can also be indicated by naming the lower and upper values separated by a hyphen. The order in which the items are specified does not matter, and savevalues and matrix savevalues can be freely intermixed.

The item to be initialized is given first, using the notation of Table 10-2 or 10-3. The value to be taken follows, separated by a comma. A slash denotes the end of an item and another item can immediately follow. The following are examples:

```
INITIAL    XF1,40/XH3,50/MX3(4,5),-7
INITIAL    XB15,1/MH1-MH2(2-3,1-2),-2/XL5-XL10,1.5
```

The first statement initializes fullword savevalue 1 to 40 and halfword savevalue 3 to 50. It then initializes the fourth-row, fifth-column element of fullword matrix 3 to -7. The second example first initializes the byte-sized savevalue 15 to 1. In both halfword matrices 1 and 2, it then sets the elements (2,1), (2,2), (3,1), and (3,2) to the value -2, a total of eight initializations. Finally, it sets the floating-point savevalues 5 through 10 to 1.5.

INITIAL control statements can also set logic switches, as will be explained in Sec. 12-1. References to logic switches can be interspersed with references to savevalues and matrix savevalues.

10-6

ASSIGN Blocks

An ASSIGN block usually modifies a single parameter of the transaction entering the block. It can also modify the values of a consecutively numbered range of parameters, but each parameter must then be modified in the same way. Field A has either the number of the single parameter or a range of numbers, separated by a hyphen with no spaces. This field does *not* use the suffix notation; only the parameter numbers are given, and not the type. Field B, and possibly field C, specify the value to be used in modifying the parameters. Field D carries one of the notations PF, PH, PB, or PL to denote the parameter type. However, if field C is not used to define the modifying quantity, the information usually put in field D can be moved over to field C.

If field A only specifies a parameter number or range of numbers, the parameters are set equal to the modifying value. By following the parameter number immediately by a plus or minus sign (or, in the case of a range of values, following the rightmost digit of the range specification), the modifying value is added to or subtracted from the current value of the parameters.

The modifying value is supplied by field B. This may be an integer; usually, however, field B contains an SNA from which the value is to be derived. For the time being, only two sources, other than integers, will be discussed; these are functions and savevalues that are included among the SNAs. Functions are identified by the symbol FNj. Savevalues use the symbols of Tables 10-2 and 10-3, according to their type. Consider the following examples:

```
ASSIGN      1,1,PB
ASSIGN      2+,FN6,PF
ASSIGN      4-,XF6,PH
ASSIGN      5-10+,1,PB
```

The first example sets byte-sized parameter number 1 to be 1. In the second example, function 6 is evaluated and the result is added to fullword parameter 2. In the third example, fullword savevalue number 6 is evaluated and subtracted from halfword parameter 4. The last example adds 1 to each of the byte-sized parameters 5 through 10. Since field C was not needed in these examples, the definition of parameter type, which would otherwise be in field D, has been moved to field C. It could just as well have been left in field D with field C indicated to be blank.

A common use of ASSIGN blocks is to store an action time derived from a function in the same manner as action times are calculated from a mean and a modifier at an ADVANCE or GENERATE block. For this reason, if field C contains any entry other than the specification of the parameter type, its content is interpreted as a function number, and the content of field B is taken as a mean. The function indicated by field C is evaluated, and the result is multiplied by field B to get the value used to modify the parameter indicated in field A. The function output may be a floating-point number, in which case the product is computed as a floating-point number and the result is then truncated. This action is exactly the same as that used to create action times from functions at ADVANCE or GENERATE blocks.

The following example will place 5 times the value of function number 2 in fullword parameter 7. In this case the parameter type designation must be made in field D:

```
ASSIGN      7,5,2,PF
```

10-7

SAVEVALUE Blocks

A transaction entering a SAVEVALUE block modifies the value of a single savevalue or a range of savevalues. The savevalue number, or range of numbers, is given in field A. A range is specified by giving the lower and upper numbers, separated by a hyphen with no interspersed blanks.

The modifying value is indicated by field B. Field C identifies the type of savevalue with one of the symbols XF, XH, XB, or XL. If field A only contains the savevalue number or name, the savevalue is replaced by the value indicated in field B. If a plus or minus sign immediately follows the savevalue number, the value is added to or subtracted from the savevalue.

If a range is given in field A, all the specified savevalues are modified in the same way; and, if a plus or minus sign is used, it immediately follows the last digit that defines the range of values. If a number appears in field B, it is used as the modifying value. Field B, however, will frequently contain an SNA. The following are examples:

```
SAVEVALUE    6,10,XH
SAVEVALUE    TOTAL+,6,XF
SAVEVALUE    10-15,5,XB
SAVEVALUE    LOW-HIGH,1,XH
```

The first example sets halfword savevalue number 6 to 10. The second adds 6 to a fullword savevalue called TOTAL. The third example sets to the value 5 all the byte-sized savevalues numbered from 10 through 15. In the last example, a range of halfword savevalues is set to the value 1. In using this example it would be necessary to specify values for the symbols LOW and HIGH at assembly time, by using the EQU statement (see Appendix 2). The symbol HIGH must be assigned a higher value than LOW, and the program will then automatically reserve all the numbers in that range.

10-8

MSAVEVALUE Blocks

The MSAVEVALUE block modifies elements of a matrix savevalue in exactly the same way a SAVEVALUE block modifies savevalues. Field A gives the matrix number, possibly followed by a plus or minus sign. Fields B and C give the row and column, respectively, and field D has the modifying value. Field E must have one of the symbols MX, MH, MB, or ML, according to the matrix type. It is permissible to specify a range of values in either fields A, B, or C, so the modification can apply to a range of matrices, a range of row numbers, a range of column numbers, or any combination of the three. In each case the range consists of a consecutive set of numbers. In the case of specifying a range of matrix numbers, symbols may be used to identify the lower and upper limits of the range. The remarks made in Sec. 10-7 regarding the way the symbols are assigned numbers by an EQU statement then apply. The following are examples:

```
MSAVEVALUE    5,2,3,100,MX
MSAVEVALUE    20+,7,12,2,MH
MSAVEVALUE    1-3,1-5,1-4,0,MB
```

The first example puts 100 in the second row, third column of fullword matrix 5. The second adds 2 to the seventh row, twelfth column of halfword matrix 20. The last example sets to zero all elements in rows 1 through 5 and columns 1 through 4 of byte-sized matrices 1, 2, and 3—a total of 60 elements.

10-9
Use of Parameters as Operands

Parameters may be used to supply the value of many operands. By putting Pxj in a block field, where x is the parameter type and j is the number, the program will extract that parameter value from the transaction entering the block and use the result as the block operand. Similarly, a parameter may be used in evaluating functions and variables. This is, in fact, only one example of a general principle, to be discussed in the next chapter, which allows SNAs to be used in most fields. Using parameters this way is particularly useful because it makes a block operation depend upon the specific transaction entering the block.

Examples have already been seen where sections of coding have been identical, except for different values of some operands. The simple machine shop, shown in Fig. 3-1, needed five sections for dispatching the different parts to different destinations. The factory example of Fig. 5-4 needed three identical sections to represent machines, except that each section needed a different facility number. Such repetitive sections of coding can be eliminated by letting a parameter of the transaction supply the value to be used. The next section gives an example.

10-10
Communication System

As an example of parameters being used as operands, consider a communication system that sends messages from a center to one of five destinations, each connected to the center by a line of its own that carries one message at a time. Suppose that messages are generated at exponentially distributed intervals with a mean of 100 seconds and that the message lengths are normally distributed but with values that depend upon the destination. Table 10-4 gives the mean and standard deviation of the transmission times in columns 2 and 3. In column 4 it gives the probability of a message being sent to a given destination. The simulation is to collect a total of all the transmission times, by destination.

A five-row, two-column matrix of halfword size will be used with column 1 carrying the means and column 2 the standard deviations. The destination distribution, or message type, will be placed in a discrete mode function.

A block diagram for the system is shown in Fig. 10-2, and results of a run are given in Fig. 10-3. A series of transactions, which represents the messages, are generated, using the exponential function as function number 1. The message destination will be placed in halfword parameter number 1. Another halfword parameter, number 2, will carry the transmission time. After creation, the transactions go through two ASSIGN blocks. The first

Table 10-4 Message Characteristics

Destination	Mean	Standard deviation	Probability
1	200	50	0.4
2	400	40	0.2
3	450	40	0.2
4	800	60	0.1
5	750	30	0.1

selects the message type at random from function 2, which has the distribution of destination probabilities. When a transaction enters the second ASSIGN block, variable 1 is evaluated to derive a normally distributed number from the standard normal function, entered here as function 3. The standard normal value is turned to the desired value by multiplying by the appropriate standard deviation and adding the mean, derived from the matrix according to message type. This illustrates yet another use of parameters, that is, as components of a variable statement. This also is a role that can be taken by any SNA.

The transmission time selected from the matrix goes into halfword parameter 2. The transactions then go to a SEIZE block with field A set to PH1. Each transaction will therefore seize one of the facilities 1, 2, ..., 5, according to the message destination. Having seized a facility, the transaction goes to an ADVANCE block with PH2 in the A field, so that the action time, which represents the transmission time, is the value stored in parameter 2. When the transmission is complete, the facility is given up at a RELEASE block with PH1 in the A field.

To collect the transmission times, the transactions go to a SAVEVALUE block with PH1+ in field A and PH2 in field B. The program will add the transmission time in parameter 2 to one of the savevalues 1, 2, ..., 5, according to the message destination in parameter 1. The messages are then destroyed at a single TERMINATE block. The example should be compared with the model of Fig. 3-1, where the same operation of accumulating a total by part type and destroying the transactions required the separation of the transactions into five separate streams.

In the example, one SEIZE block is controlling five facilities. The usual rule applies that only one transaction at a time can use a given facility, but it is possible for up to five transactions to be simultaneously in the ADVANCE block.

This example depends on the reservation of specifically numbered facilities and savevalues so that they match the assigned parameter values. Often, this will be inconvenient. The EQU statement and the entity type of func-

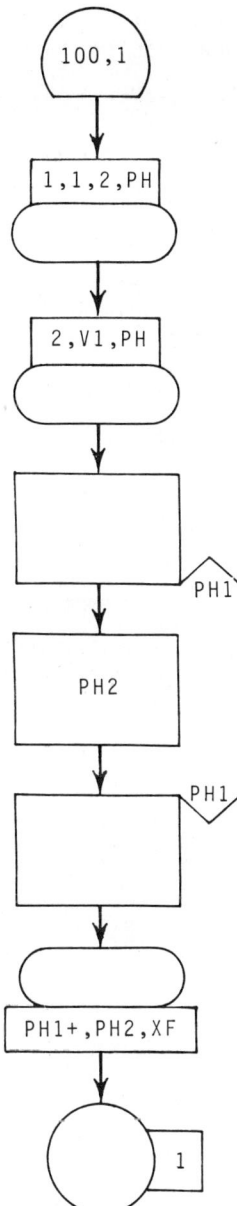

Figure 10-2. Communication system.

tion, used in the assembly phase and described in Appendix 2, Secs. A2-4 and A2-5, allow numbers to be assigned more freely. Another example is given in Sec. 11-6.

```
*       A COMMUNICATION SYSTEM
*
 1      FUNCTION     RN1,C24        EXPONENTIAL INTERARRIVAL TIME
.0,0/.1,.104/.2,.222/.3,.355/.4,.509/.5,.69/.6,.915/.7,1.2/.75,1.38
.8,1.6/.84,1.83/.88,2.12/.9,2.3/.92,2.52/.94,2.81/.95,2.99/.96,3.2
.97,3.5/.98,3.9/.99,4.6/.995,5.3/.998,6.2/.999,7.0/.9998,8.0
*
 2      FUNCTION     RN1,D6         MESSAGE TYPE DISTRIBUTION
0,1/0.4,1/0.6,2/0.8,3/0.9,4/1.0,5
*
 3      FUNCTION     RN1,C25        STANDARD NORMAL DISTRIBUTION
0.0,-5/0.00003,-4/0.00135,-3/0.00621,-2.5/0.02275,-2.0/0.06681,-1.5
0.11507,-1.2/0.15866,-1.0/0.21186,-0.8/0.27425,-0.6/0.34458,-0.4
0.42074,-0.2/0.5,0.0/0.57926,0.2/0.65542,0.4/0.72575,0.6
0.78814,0.8/0.84134,1.0/0.88493,1.2/0.93319,1.5/0.97725,2.0
0.99379,2.5/0.99865,3.0/0.99997,4.0/1.0,5.0
*
1       GENERATE     100,FN1        CREATE MESSAGES
2       ASSIGN       1,1,2,PH       SELECT MESSAGE TYPE
3       ASSIGN       2,V1,PH        SELECT TRANSMISSION TIME
4       SEIZE        PH1            GET TRANSMISSION LINE
5       ADVANCE      PH2            TRANSMIT
6       RELEASE      PH1            END TRANSMISSION
7       SAVEVALUE    PH1+,PH2,XF    INCREMENT TOTAL TRANSMISSION TIME
*                                   BY MESSAGE TYPE
8       TERMINATE    1
    1   FVARIABLE    MH1(PH1,2)*FN3+MH1(PH1,1)   TRANSMIT TIME
    1   MATRIX       MH,5,2         MATRIX OF TRANSMISSION TIME PARAMETERS
*
        INITIAL      MH1(1,1),200/MH1(1,2),50/MH1(2,1),400/MH1(2,2),40
        INITIAL      MH1(3,1),450/MH1(3,2),45/MH1(4,1),800/MH1(4,2),60
        INITIAL      MH1(5,1),750/MH1(5,2),30
*
        START        1000
```

```
RELATIVE CLOCK          95447   ABSOLUTE CLOCK        95447
BLOCK COUNTS
BLOCK CURRENT TOTAL     BLOCK CURRENT TOTAL    BLOCK CURRENT TOTAL    BLOCK CURRENT TOTAL
  1     0     1021
  2     0     1021
  3    18     1021
  4     0     1003
  5     3     1003
  6     0     1000
  7     0     1000
  8     0     1000
```

```
*******************************************
*                                         *
*              FACILITIES                 *
*                                         *
*******************************************
```

FACILITY	NUMBER ENTRIES	AVERAGE TIME/TRAN	AVERAGE UTIL. DURING-			CURRENT STATUS	PERCENT AVAILABILITY	TRANS NUMBER SEIZE	PREEMPT
			TOTAL TIME	AVAIL TIME	UNAVAIL TIME				
1	425	197.456	.879	.879	.000	A	100.0		
2	184	401.277	.773	.773	.000	A	100.0	17	
3	201	449.781	.947	.947	.000	A	100.0	9	
4	107	788.065	.883	.883	.000	A	100.0	15	
5	86	754.255	.679	.679	.000	A	100.0		

Figure 10-3. Coding and output for communication system.

```
***********************************************
*                                              *
*           FULLWORD SAVEVALUES                *
*                                              *
***********************************************
```

NUMBER	CONTENT	NUMBER	CONTENT	NUMBER	CONTENT	NUMBER	CONTENT	NUMBER	CONTENT
1	83919	2	73591	3	90355	4	84273	5	64866

```
***********************************************
*                                              *
*           HALFWORD MATRICES                  *
*                                              *
***********************************************
```

HALFWORD MATRIX   1

ROW/COLUMN	1	2
1	200	50
2	400	40
3	450	45
4	800	60
5	750	30

Figure 10-3. (continued)

10-11
Parameter Mode of TRANSFER Blocks

The parameter mode of the TRANSFER block allows a parameter to supply the location to which a transaction is to be sent. The A field of the block contains PF, PH, or PB, according to the type of parameter, and field B carries the parameter number. If field C is used, its value is added to the parameter value before making the transfer. The main purpose of this field is in connection with the use of subroutines, described in the next section.

Suppose that, in the communication system discussed in the previous section, the messages, after transmission, need to go to separate sections beginning at locations LOCA, LOCB, LOCC, LOCD, and LOCE. The following ASSIGN and TRANSFER blocks could be used, together with a list mode function whose values are the location symbols. The assembly program will change these symbols to location numbers:

```
        ASSIGN      4,FN3,PH
        TRANSFER    PH,4
            ...
      3 FUNCTION    PH1,L5
,LOCA/,LOCB/,LOCC/,LOCD/,LOCE
```

The ASSIGN block puts the value of function 3 in halfword parameter 4. The function input is halfword parameter 1 of the transaction entering the ASSIGN block, which contains the message destination. The location of the destination therefore goes into halfword parameter 4, and will be used at the TRANSFER block, which is in a parameter mode.

10-12

Subroutine Mode of TRANSFER Blocks

Another use of TRANSFER blocks is to permit the execution of a subroutine. A *subroutine* is a section of blocks detached from the main stream of the block diagram. On reaching certain points in the main block diagram, the transaction is to be transferred to the subroutine section and returned to the main stream after execution of the subroutine.

A special mode of the TRANSFER block, called the *subroutine mode*, is used for this purpose. It is indicated by putting the letters SBR in field A. Field B gives a location to which all transactions entering the block will be sent unconditionally. Field C indicates a parameter by number and type in which to place a return address. Only integer values are permitted.

A TRANSFER block in a subroutine mode is placed at the point in the main block from which the transaction is to execute the subroutine. At the time the transfer is made, the location of the TRANSFER block is placed in the parameter numbered in field C. At the end of the subroutine, the transaction is sent to a TRANSFER block in a *parameter* mode to return the transaction to the main stream. Field C of the parameter mode TRANSFER block is used to increment the value of the parameter—holding the address saved by the subroutine mode TRANSFER block.

For example, suppose that the main diagram is to be left at a location AAA to execute a subroutine beginning at BBB. Upon completion of the subroutine, the transaction is to continue from AAA. The following sequence of blocks would be used:

```
     AAA   TRANSFER    SBR,BBB,2PF
           ADVANCE     10
           ...
     BBB   ADVANCE     20
           ...
           TRANSFER    PF,2,1
```

A transaction entering the TRANSFER block at AAA is transferred to the location BBB, after the location number AAA is stored in fullword parameter 2. The subroutine begins at BBB. When the subroutine execution is finished, the transaction goes to the TRANSFER block in a parameter mode. This sends the transaction to the location AAA plus 1 because of the entry 1 in field C. The two ADVANCE blocks are used as examples; they are not obligatory.

10-13
LOOP Blocks

A frequent requirement is to arrange for a transaction to cycle around a loop of blocks a given number of times. A parameter can be used to carry a count of the number of cycles executed. The count needs to be decremented and tested for zero at the end of each cycle. The LOOP block is designed to carry out this operation.

When a transaction enters a LOOP block, the parameter indicated by field A is decremented by 1. If the result is not zero, the transaction is sent to the location given in field B. If the result is zero, the transaction goes to the next sequential block. Field B therefore identifies the beginning of the loop. An error stop will occur if the parameter value is initially zero or negative. Floating-point parameters cannot be used. Any numbered parameter can be used, but, if the LOOP block is used in conjunction with the INDEX block, described in the next section, parameter number 1 should be used.

10-14
INDEX Blocks

The initialization of a parameter to be used by a LOOP block can be done by an ASSIGN block, in which case any parameter can be used. If the user elects to use one of the number 1 parameters, the initialization can be done by an INDEX block. There is no significant difference in the time taken by either method. However, an INDEX block allows the initialization value to be constructed as the sum of two quantities, to provide extra flexibility.

When a transaction enters an INDEX block, either its fullword, halfword, or byte-sized parameter number 1 is initialized. The value used is the sum of the parameter numbered in field A and the content, if any, of field B. The fact that it is a parameter number 1 that is being initialized is implied. The type of parameter initialized is the same as the parameter indicated in field A. The notation used in field A must be the suffix notation, kPx.

If the initialization value, or part of it, is not being carried in a parameter of the transaction being initialized, there is no particular value in using an INDEX block over an ASSIGN block. If it is then used, it will be necessary to put in field A some parameter known to be zero, to establish the type.

10-15
Controlling Loops

To illustrate how loops are controlled by INDEX and LOOP blocks, consider the following example. A formula has been developed for forecasting the number of products to be made in a month. From experience, it is known that forecasts have been in error by a random variable with a known distribution. To test the formula, production will be simulated and the monthly production time measured. The experiment will be repeated 100 times to develop a statistical distribution of the monthly production time.

A model is shown in Fig. 10-4. A GENERATE block creates a single transaction which will cycle around two loops. An inner loop represents the making of each product, and the outer loop represents one month's production. An ASSIGN block places 100 in PH2, which will be used to control the number of months' production to be simulated. The transaction then goes to another ASSIGN block, called FORC, which places in halfword parameter 3 the forecast for one month, derived from a formula given here as variable 1. Another variable, number 2, computes the random error.

The transaction goes to an INITIAL block having 3PH in field A and V2 in field B. The result is that the sum of the forecast in PH3 and the calculation of an error term from variable 2 is placed in halfword parameter 1. The parameter is number 1 because that is implicit in the INDEX block action. It is of the halfword type because the field A reference mentions a halfword parameter.

The transaction goes to a SAVEVALUE block, called TIME, to add the production time for one part to fullword savevalue 1. The time is computed by variable 3. A more complete model might simulate the entire production process at this point. The first LOOP block is then entered. It decrements PH1 by 1 and, if the result is not zero, sends the transaction back to the SAVEVALUE block to compute and accumulate the time for the next product.

When the count in PH1 drops to zero, the transaction passes to the TABULATE block to enter, into table 1, the total time for the month's production. A second LOOP block checks the count in PH2 and, if it is not zero, sends the transaction back to FORC, after setting the accumulated total of time to zero. That begins the simulation of another month's production. A zero count at the second LOOP block terminates the run.

Note that, in this example, there are no times specified. This is an example of the type of application, mentioned in Sec. 1-4, where the step-by-step technique of a simulation program is being used simply to carry out a repetitive calculation in which execution time is not significant. In fact, this GPSS model will be executed at time equal to 1 because an initial zero time of zero at a GENERATE block is set to 1 (see Sec. 4-2).

10-16

Transaction and Savevalue SNAs

Having completed the description of transactions, the SNAs associated with them can now be given. They are as follows:

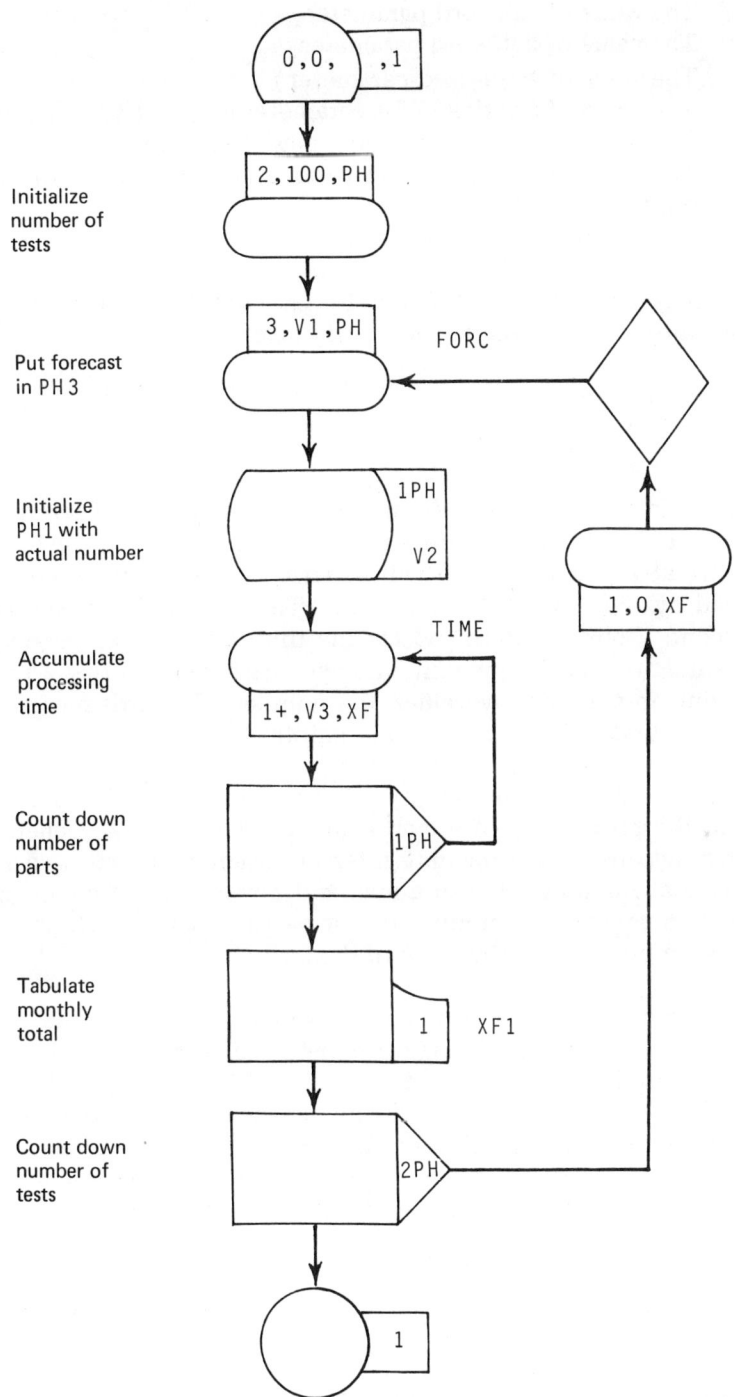

Figure 10-4. Controlling loops.

PFj   The value of fullword parameter j
PHj   The value of halfword parameter j
PBj   The value of byte-sized parameter j
PLj   The value of floating-point parameter j
M1   The mark time recorded in the mark time word
MPjPx   The mark time recorded in parameter j of type x (the type can only be F or H)
PR   The priority of the transaction

The symbols given in Tables 10-2 and 10-3 are the ones used to indicate the SNAs associated with savevalues and matrix savevalues.

Exercises

10-1   Records are being read from a poor quality tape. There is a chance of 1 in 50 that the record will be bad on the first reading. Up to two more attempts at reading will be tried and, if the record has not been read by then, it will be discarded. The probability of success on the second attempt is 0.8, and for the third attempt 0.5. Generate 1000 transactions at 1 time-unit intervals, each representing a record, and count, in separate savevalues, the number of records successfully read on the first, second, and third attempts.

10-2   Suppose that the probability of a woman being left-handed is 0.05 and the probability of a man being left-handed 0.04. Generate 1000 transactions at 1 time-unit intervals, each representing a marriage made at random between a man and a woman, and count in a two-by-two matrix the number of marriages that have men and women in each possible combination of dexterity.

10-3   A number of trials are made by tossing a fair coin that has a 50 per cent chance of coming down heads. If there is a head, the coin is tossed again, and so on, until it comes down tails. One trial is a run of heads. Simulate 1000 trials by generating transactions at 1 time-unit intervals and count the number of trials with a given number of heads. Save the counts in halfword savevalues beginning with the count of no heads in number 1. Also put the total number of tosses in fullword parameter 1.

10-4   Reprogram the simple machine shop shown in Fig. 3-1 and described in Sec. 3-6 as a single line of code.

10-5   Cars arrive at an inspection center with exponentially distributed interarrival times that have a mean of 7 minutes. The cars are of five types and they arrive in random order in the following proportions: A, 27 per cent; B, 25 per cent; C, 20 per cent; D, 15 per cent; and E, 13 per cent. Inspection for all types of cars takes 25 ± 10 minutes but a separate line is established for each type. Only one car of each type can be inspected at a time. Using a single stream of blocks, measure the waiting lines for inspection to begin and the distribution of time to complete inspection. Derive each measurement for the individual types of cars and for all types combined. Initialize for 50 cars and simulate for 1000.

10-6 Extend the communication system example of Sec. 10-10 in the following way. In addition to going to one of five destinations, the messages are also of four types with the following proportions: A, 20 per cent; B, 30 per cent; C, 25 per cent; and D, 25 per cent. The type is chosen randomly and independently of the destination. Collect in a matrix the total transmission time by destination and message type. Initialize with 50 transactions and simulate for 1000 transactions.

10-7 A series of messages are being read into a computer at the rate of one every 50 ± 10 milliseconds. Each must be examined by the CPU for 10 ± 5 milliseconds to determine its type. Ten per cent need only write a record on a disk unit. The other 90 per cent must read a record from the disk, wait for the CPU to process the record for 20 ± 10 milliseconds, and then write the record back on the disk. There is only one disk unit and it can only handle 1 read or write at a time. The CPU is not needed to either read or write on the disk unit. There is no interaction between reading in messages and accessing the disk unit.

Later, a more elaborate model of the disk unit will be made. For the time being, it is sufficiently accurate to represent the disk unit as a facility that needs to be held for 20 ± 10 milliseconds for each data transfer. Write a program for the system, representing access to the disk by a subroutine.

10-8 Transactions enter an ADVANCE block at the rate of one every 50 ± 20 milliseconds. At the block, they are processed for 5 milliseconds and then sent to a subroutine which, for the time being, can be represented as a process taking 10 milliseconds. There is a probability of 0.05 that there will be a type A error and a probability of 0.10 of a type B error. (The errors are mutually exclusive.) In the event of a type A error, the transaction is to be returned to the first ADVANCE block for a retry. In the event of a type B error, the transaction is to be destroyed. When transactions execute the subroutine with no error they are processed for an additional 15 ± 10 milliseconds by the main program. Simulate the processing of 1000 good executions and count the number of transactions that will have then been destroyed. It is to be assumed that only one transaction at a time can be processed.

10-9 Reprogram factory model 3 of Fig. 5-4, described in Sec. 5-11, using a single line of code for the machines. (For simplicity, assume that the machines are numbered in the order 3, 2, 1.)

10-10 A computer program has an entry section that takes 10 milliseconds. There is a probability of 0.20 that the entry section is extended by an additional 5 milliseconds. Whether it is extended or not, a loop is then entered where the number of cycles will be randomly and uniformly distributed between 1 and 100 (see Sec. 9-8). Each cycle takes 5 ± 2 milliseconds. When the loop is left, a final stage of processing takes 5 milliseconds. By generating 1000 transactions, measure the distribution of the time the program takes to execute a transaction. (There is no need to assume that only one transaction at a time can be processed.)

11
STANDARD NUMERICAL ATTRIBUTES

Standard numerical attributes, or SNAs, were briefly introduced in Sec. 4-10, where they were described as being items of data that make system attributes available to the user. As the various entities of GPSS have been described, the SNAs associated with them have been defined. A few more entities and their attributes remain to be described, but, at this point, we collect together information about the notation and definition of SNAs, and describe some of the uses they serve.

11-1
SNA Notation

Most SNAs are associated with one of the GPSS entity types. There are several instances of each type, so SNAs are identified by a one- or two-letter code to denote the type, followed by a number to indicate the particular instance that is intended. For example, the content of storage number 7 is referenced by the symbol S7, and the current length of queue number 13 is Q13. Some SNAs are unique, but the same format of a character and a number is used. For example, the clock time is denoted by C1, and the mark time of a transaction, carried in the mark time word, is referenced by M1. Another special case is the symbol PR, without a number, for the priority level of a transaction.

When describing SNAs for which there can be many instances, the notation used is SNAj, where SNA stands for the letters indicating the type, and *j* represents the particular instance. Instead of *j* being replaced by a number, a symbolic name may be used. As with locations, the symbols are from three to five characters, drawn from the alphabetic characters A through Z and the decimal digits 0 through 9. The first three characters must be alphabetic. To avoid confusion, however, the letters indicating the type must be separated from the symbolic name by a dollar sign, $. Thus the content of a storage called NEXT would be denoted by S$NEXT, and the value of a function called LNGTH would be given by FN$LNGTH.

There are some cases in which symbolic names may not be used. None of the attributes of a transaction, parameters, priority, or mark time, can take a symbolic name. In addition, the clock time, in either form, and the number of terminations to end simulation, cannot be addressed symbolically. Random number generators, also, cannot be named. The following list gives the SNAs that cannot have a symbolic name:

Pxj	Transaction parameter *j* of type *x*
M1	Mark time in the mark time word
MPjPx	Mark time in parameter *j* of type *x*
PR	Priority level of a transaction
C1	Relative clock time
AC1	Absolute clock time
TG1	Number of terminations to end simulation
RNn	Output of random number generator *n*

When there can be more than one instance of an SNA type, the number *j* can be given by another SNA. This is called indirect addressing, which is described later in Sec. 11-3. The notation used in that case takes the form SNA*SNAj, or SNA*SNA$NAME, where the first group of letters, SNA, indicates the type of SNA being defined, and the second group indicates the SNA type being used to provide the number of the SNA being defined. Although transaction parameters and random number generators cannot be named, they can be identified indirectly.

11-2

Principal SNAs

There are 42 different SNA types, not counting the multiple formats in which parameters, savevalues, and matrices can occur. An abbreviated listing giving the principal 22 SNAs is given in Table 11-1. They will be described here. The other 20 SNAs are statistical measures associated with the GPSS entities that are collected during the run and form part of the standard out-

Table 11-1 Principal SNAs

Type of entity	Symbol	Description
Transactions	Pxj	Parameter j of type x
	PR	Priority
	M1	Mark time in mark time word
	MPjPx	Mark time in parameter j of type x
Blocks	Nj	Number of transactions that entered block j
	Wj	Current number of transactions in block j
Facilities	Fj	Status of facility j (0 if free, 1 if busy)
Storages	Sj	Current content of storage j
	Rj	Space remaining in storage j
Queues	Qj	Length of queue j
Tables	TBj	Current mean value of table j
User chains	CHj	Number of transactions on chain j
Groups	Gj	Number of entries in group j
Functions	FNj	Value of function j
Savevalues	Xxj	Savevalue j of type x
	Mxj(a, b)	Row a, column b of matrix j, type x
Variables	Vj	Variable j (integer or floating-point)
	BVj	Boolean variable j
System	C1	Relative clock time
	AC1	Absolute clock time
	RNn	Random number from generator n ($n = 1, \ldots, 8$)
	TG1	Number of remaining terminations

put report. Appendix 5 brings together the description of all the SNAs, including a definition of the range of values they can take.

Each transaction can have four types of SNA. The value of its jth parameter of type x is denoted by Pxj. Its priority, as a number from 0 through 127, is denoted by PR. The mark time, when recorded in the mark time word, is denoted by M1. When recorded in the jth parameter of type x, it is denoted by MPjPx.

Note that the symbol for a parameter as an SNA is Pxj. This is consistent with other SNA types which are defined by a letter, or letters, for the type, followed by a postscript numbering the particular instance. In Sec. 10-1 it was pointed out that in fields that supply the program with a parameter number, another notation, kPx, is used. The number is indicated by the letter k and the letters Px are being used as a suffix that distinguishes between the four types of parameter. Table 10-1 lists the fields where this suffix notation is used.

There are two SNA types associated with the blocks. The symbol Nj is a count of the total number of transactions that have entered block j, and Wj is the count of the transactions currently located at block j.

The principal SNA associated with a facility is Fj, which is a Boolean variable. It takes the value 1 if the facility is busy and the value 0 if it is not. For storages, the SNAs Sj and Rj represent the current content of the storage and the remaining space in the storage. The SNA Qj is the current length of queue number j, and TBj is the current mean value of table number j.

In Chap. 14 we will introduce two ways of forming sets of transactions, user chains and groups. The current numbers of transactions in such sets are denoted by CHj for chains and Gj for groups.

We have already discussed functions, which are SNAs denoted by FNj. Savevalues are denoted by Xxj or Mxj(a,b), where x is the type and j the number. We have mentioned variables. One type, which can have either an integer or floating-point format, is denoted by Vj. There are also Boolean variables which are denoted by BVj.

References to the relative and absolute clock times are made by C1 and AC1, respectively, and the number by which the termination count is to be incremented before the simulation run ends is denoted by TG1. A request for a uniformly distributed random number is made by RNn, $n = 1, 2, \ldots, 8$, where n selects the generator. Normally the output is an integer between 0 and 999, inclusive. If, however, the reference is made for the input of a function, given in the A field of the FUNCTION definition statement, the value is automatically scaled to the range 0 to 0.999999.

11-3

Indirect Addressing

To extend the usefulness of SNAs, it is possible to allow the number of the SNA to be specified by another SNA. The number used with each execution of the SNA then depends upon the value of the second SNA and is therefore influenced by the prevailing conditions in the system. This general method of using SNAs is called *indirect addressing*.

Just as a special symbol, $, is needed to separate the name of an SNA type from a symbol used to define the number, so, also, is a special symbol needed to separate the name of an SNA type and the SNA used to specify the value. The special symbol used to indicate indirect addressing is an asterisk, *. For example, suppose that the content of one of several storages is needed and that the number of the intended storage is in halfword savevalue number 4. This will be indicated by the notation S*XH4. The general notation used to indicate indirect addressing is SNA*SNAj. The first SNA is called the *primary* and the second is the *secondary*. The secondary SNA may be specified symbolically, in which case the notation is SNA*SNA$NAME, where NAME stands for the symbolic name.

In the case of the suffix notation, kPx, the parameter number, k, may be given by another SNA, but it is not then necessary to use an asterisk. For example, the MARK block indicates in field A a parameter to be used for storing the mark time, so the field uses the notation kPx. Suppose that the parameter is to be of the fullword type and that its number is supplied by byte-sized savevalue number 6. The notation would be XB6PF. The savevalue might be identified by name, say PARN, in which case the notation would be XB$PARN$PF.

Indirect addressing may only be used to one level. For example, SNA*SNA*SNAj is illegal. There are also some restrictions on the use of SNAs for secondary addressing. They are stated here for reference purposes. The reader will probably find it easier to return to these exceptions when some experience in the use of indirect addressing has been gained. The SNAs to which the restrictions apply are functions, the matrix savevalues in any of their data formats, and variable statements, which are defined later in this chapter. Variable statements are denoted by Vj or BVj, depending upon their type, and the restrictions apply to both types. Variable statements are combinations of other SNAs, so the three types of SNA to which the restrictions apply are complex in the sense that they involve more than one item of data. For this reason they are called *multilevel SNAs*.

It is legal to use an SNA as an argument of a multilevel SNA. Further, the SNA used as an argument can usually be indirectly addressed. However, it is illegal in the definition of a multilevel SNA to use another multilevel SNA as a secondary SNA to provide an indirect address. The following examples of legal and illegal uses of multilevel SNAs will help explain the rules:

Legal Uses

```
        AAA     FUNCTION    PF*XH6,C4
                VARIABLE    XF*PB6+MH*PB3(5,6)
                ENTER       XH*MH1(PB4,PH*PB3)
```

Illegal Uses

```
        AAA     FUNCTION    PH*MH1(6,4),C4
                VARIABLE    XF*PF6+MH*FN4(5,6)
                ENTER       XH*MH1(V2,PH*PB3)
```

The first function definition is legally using XH6 as a secondary SNA to indicate which fullword parameter is to supply the function input. The second function definition is illegal because it is using MH1, which is a multilevel SNA, as a secondary SNA. The first variable statement has two elements, each of which legally uses a secondary SNA. The first term indicates the fullword parameter whose number is given in byte-sized parameter number 6. The second term indicates row 5, column 6 of the halfword matrix numbered in byte-sized parameter 3. The second variable statement is illegal because the matrix number is defined by FN4, which is a multilevel SNA. Last, the first ENTER statement says the storage number is to be supplied by the halfword savevalue whose number is given by an element of the halfword matrix number 1. The specific element is in the row numbered by byte-sized parameter 4, and the column is given by the halfword parameter numbered in byte-sized parameter 3. Although a matrix is a multilevel SNA, it is being used legally as a secondary SNA in an SNA that is not multilevel. Also, the row and column are being given by legal SNAs, neither of which is a multilevel SNA, even though the column is given by an indirectly addressed SNA. The second ENTER statement, however, is illegal because it uses a multilevel SNA, V2, to define the row of a multilevel SNA that is being used in a secondary role.

11-4

Uses of SNAs

The main purpose of the SNAs is to provide ways of describing how activities and system attributes depend upon the state of the system. A second important use is to provide ways of extracting statistics from the simulation, other than the standard output statistics. To these ends there are five ways SNAs may be used. They may be used as one of the following items:

(a) Block operands
(b) Indirect addresses
(c) Function arguments
(d) Function dependent variables
(e) Table arguments

These various uses will be described in subsequent sections.

11-5

SNAs as Block Operands

With certain exceptions and limitations to be given later, any field of a block type may be coded with an SNA. The value that will be used for that operand is the value of the SNA at the time a transaction enters the block. The use of parameters in this way has already been illustrated (Sec. 10-10). It was seen that parameters allow blocks to be generalized by letting the transaction supply its own block operands. The principle extends to any SNA, so that a block action can depend not only upon the particular transaction but also upon the prevailing conditions in the system.

Suppose, for example, the facility to be used in an operation needs to be periodically changed. The number of the facility might be stored in byte-sized savevalue number 1. The following coding would make a SEIZE block use the current choice and allow the choice to be changed by altering the content of the savevalue:

```
        SEIZE         XB1
```

The entity identified by the SNA does not have to be directly numbered; it could be named. If the savevalue in the above example were called FCYN, the coding would be

```
        SEIZE         XB$FCYN
```

Some other examples follow:

```
        DEPART        1,Q1
        ENTER         3,S6
        ENTER         6,R6
        ADVANCE       W16
        ASSIGN        2,F12,PB
```

The first removes from queue 1 the current content of queue 1; in other words, it empties queue 1. The next example adds the current content of storage 6 to storage 3, and the next example would fill storage 6. The ADVANCE block would make a transaction take one unit of time for every transaction currently waiting at block 16. The last example would set parameter number 2, which is byte-sized, to the value 1 if facility number 12 is currently busy, and to 0 if it is not.

In the case of matrices, it is permissible to use SNAs as the arguments, except that other matrix values may not be used. For example, suppose that the time to carry out a job depends upon the type of job, the day of the week, and the hour of the day. The type of job, the day, and the hour are stored in halfword savevalues called TYPE, DAY, and HOUR. There is a separate halfword matrix for each type of job, where the rows and columns, respectively, give the time for that job type on a given day and hour. The following coding could be used to extract the job time:

```
        ADVANCE       MH*XH$TYPE(XH$DAY,XH$HOUR)
```

Care must be taken if an SNA is used in fields that supply a parameter number, and therefore uses the suffix notation. If an SNA is used to supply a parameter number, it must be followed by the type suffix (see Sec. 11-3).

An SNA in a field is an alternative to providing a fixed integer value. It is convenient, therefore, to consider the positive integers, and zero, as being SNAs. This avoids having to state repeatedly that a field can contain an SNA or an integer. To make this more explicit, an integer, n, can be indicated by the symbol Kn.

Certain fields, listed below, can specify a range of entity numbers by giving the low and high numbers in the range, separated by a hyphen. The two limits can be specified as SNAs, not necessarily of the same type. For example, a range might be given as XB6-PH7. An error stop will occur if the upper limit is not greater than the lower limit. The fields that can accept ranges are as follows:

```
ASSIGN      A
FAVAIL      A
FUNAVAIL    A
MSAVEVALUE  A,B,C
SAVAIL      A
SAVEVALUE   A
SUNAVAIL    A
```

In addition, the INITIAL, CLEAR, RESET, and STORAGE control statements can all use a range in field A, but they are defined at assembly time.

The cases in which SNAs may not be used in a field are as follows:

(a) *Keyword fields.* Any field containing a keyword cannot be replaced with an SNA. These words are indicated in the text by uppercase letters. Examples are the words BOTH, ALL, and PICK in the TRANSFER block.

(b) GENERATE *block.* The GENERATE block is limited by the fact that the only SNAs it may use, other than a constant, are

```
FNj    Functions
Vj     Variable statements (described later)
Xxj    Savevalues of type x, except floating-point
RNn    A random number
Nj     A total transaction count
C1     Relative clock time
AC1    Absolute clock time
```

In addition, functions and variables used at a GENERATE block may only use these same SNAs. Field B of the GENERATE block is also subject to the condition specified in the next subsection.

(c) *Action times.* The B fields of the GENERATE and ADVANCE blocks are subject to special conditions. The fields can indicate either a spread or a function modifier. The selection of a function is indicated by using the notation FNj. In this case the letters FN are not being interpreted as an SNA but as an indicator of the function mode. The *j*th function will be evaluated and used to multiply field A to produce an action time, unless field A is blank, in which case, the function value is used directly as the action time. The function may also be named by FN$NAME. It may also be indicated indirectly by FN*SNAj or FN*SNA$NAME. In particular, if a function is to be used to define the number of the function to be used as a modifier, the notation would be FN*FNj or FN*FN$NAME.

This means that the SNA FNj cannot be used in the B field of a GENERATE or ADVANCE block to provide a spread. Any other legal SNA, however, would give the value of a spread.

(d) ASSIGN *block*. The ASSIGN block is often used with the B and C fields serving the same role as the A and B fields of a GENERATE block in creating an action time. The special conditions described in the previous subsection, however, do not apply. Field C of an ASSIGN block, if it contains a number, is treated as a function number whose value is to multiply field B, unless field B is a blank, in which case the function value is taken directly as the output. The fact that field C indicates a function does not have to be shown by using the letters FN. Any SNA in the C field of an ASSIGN block, including FNj, is interpreted as a function number whose value is used as a modifier to the mean indicated in field B.

If field C is not needed as a modifier to field B, it is permissible to move into field C the notation that would otherwise be in field D to indicate the type of parameter. That notation is one of the pairs of letter, PF, PH, PB, or PL, without a number. The absence of the number indicates to the program that field D has been moved into field C. If the notation Pxj appears in field C, where j is a number, or name, the program will interpret this as an SNA, and use the value of parameter j of type x as the number of a function to modify field B.

(e) TRANSFER *block*. The fractional mode of the TRANSFER block expects a decimal fraction of up to three digits in field A. If this field uses an SNA, the result is treated as a three-digit number representing parts per thousand. If the value falls below zero, or exceeds 999, the TRANSFER is treated as being unconditional.

In the ALL mode, SNAs are not allowed in any field.

(f) *Floating-point SNAs.* Only certain fields can accept the floating-point SNAs shown in Appendix 5. They are the B operand of an ASSIGN or SAVEVALUE block, the D operand of an MSAVEVALUE block, or the A and B fields of a TEST block (to be described in Sec. 12-5).

(g) *Matrix savevalues.* The following block fields cannot accept a matrix savevalue in any of its data formats:

COUNT	E
GENERATE	A-I
SELECT	E
SPLIT	D-G

11-6

SNAs in Indirect Addressing

Any fixed-point SNA can be used as a secondary SNA in indirect addressing. By far the greatest use of this feature, however, is with a parameter providing the secondary SNA. In this way, aspects of a system that depend upon a particular transaction type can be programmed with a general-purpose block diagram in which the transaction itself provides specific values. To illustrate the use of this technique, we first show an example where addressing is done directly by putting a parameter in a block field without indirect addressing.

Suppose that transactions represent parts that are of five types and each type is to be machined by a different facility. In addition, individual queues will be maintained for the facilities. Suppose that the part number is in halfword parameter 5. The following coding could be used:

```
          QUEUE          PH5
          SEIZE          PH5
```

However, this direct approach requires a careful reservation of the entity numbers to match the parameter values, and it requires that different types of entities, such as the queues and facilities in this example, be assigned exactly the same numbers for a given part type.

If the restriction that the same number be assigned to different entity types is acceptable, greater freedom to assign the numbers corresponding to a given parameter value can be gained by using the entity type function described in Appendix 2 (see Sec. A2-5). The function is used during the assembly phase to ensure that different types of entity are assigned the same number. The function would be defined and used in the present case as follows:

```
          QUEUE          FN$ENTN
          SEIZE          FN$ENTN
            ...
   ENTN   FUNCTION       PH5,S5,F,Q
   1,MACH1/2,MACH2/3,MACH3/4,MACH4/5,MACH5
```

The assembly program will assign specific values to the symbols MACH1 and following, which are not necessarily consecutive. The same symbol is applied to both a facility and a queue, in this case, allowing the parameter number to select both the queue and facility numbers.

Whichever of the previous two methods is used, the entity numbers will have been permanently assigned at the time of assembly. Indirect addressing allows the numbers to be changed dynamically. Suppose that the numbers of the facilities and queues are in byte-sized savevalues 1 through 5. The following coding, using the parameter in an indirect addressing mode, could be used:

```
          QUEUE          XB*PH5
          SEIZE          XB*PH5
```

The contents of the byte-sized savevalues can now be changed during a run to change the assignment of entity numbers. The savevalues have to be assigned the specific values 1 through 5. If consecutive numbering is still acceptable, the numbers can be moved to some other range, say 11 through 15, by using a variable statement indirectly, as follows:

```
          QUEUE         XB*V$SVNOS
          SEIZE         XB*V$SVNOS
          ...
   SVNOS  VARIABLE      10+PH5
```

Complete freedom in assigning the entity numbers independently, can be gained by using a matrix with the entities in different columns and the rows corresponding to part type. Suppose that the queue numbers are in column 1 and the facility numbers in column 2 of a matrix called PART. The following coding could be used:

```
          QUEUE         MH$PART(PB5,1)
          SEIZE         MH$PART(PB5,2)
```

11-7

Push-Down Lists

Another way of using SNAs indirectly, particularly parameters, is in the control of push-down lists. A *push-down list* is effectively a list of numbers with a last-in, first-out discipline. The list might represent a set of tasks to be performed. At any time a new task may be added to the list, possibly interrupting the task in progress, and the rule is that the last task must be finished before returning to previously acquired tasks. A parameter can be conveniently used to point to the current task in such a list.

For example, a model may have many subroutines, each represented by a separate segment of coding. Suppose that it is possible to call one subroutine from within another subroutine. Each entry to a subroutine requires that a return address be preserved. Allowing subroutines to be used within subroutines raises the problem of maintaining an open-ended list of return addresses. This list is a push-down list because the returns must be implemented in a last-in, first-out order.

The TRANSFER block in a subroutine mode (see Sec. 10-12) performs the task of transferring to a subroutine and saving a return address. Field C gives the parameter number that is to hold the return address. The parameters of the transaction representing the execution of the subroutines can be made to form a push-down list by the following coding:

```
          ASSIGN        3+,1,PB
          TRANSFER      SBR,AAA,PH*PB3
```

Byte-sized parameter 3 is being used as a counter to indicate how many levels of subroutines have been entered. Preceding each entry to a subroutine, it is incremented by 1 at the ASSIGN block. It will be decremented by 1 when the subroutine execution has been completed. The TRANSFER block sends the transaction to the entry point of the subroutine, here called AAA, and puts the return address in the halfword parameter indirectly addressed by byte-sized parameter 3.

Assuming that the return from the subroutine is to the block following that from which the entry was made, the return can be made by using

    TRANSFER   PH,PB3,1

Field B specifies the content of the halfword parameter indicated by the level counter in byte-sized parameter 3. Field C adds 1 to that value. At the point of return, AAA+1, the level counter is decremented by 1, as follows:

    AAA+1 ASSIGN   3-,1,PB

The decrementing of the counter could be done within the subroutine before returning. It is then necessary to save the return address temporarily, before decrementing the counter. If, for example, fullword parameter number 1 is available, this could be done as follows:

    ASSIGN   1,PH*PB3,PF
    ASSIGN   3-,1,PB
    TRANSFER   PF,1,1

The first ASSIGN block uses PB3, indirectly, to put the return address in PF1. The second ASSIGN block then decrements the counter in PB3. The TRANSFER block is in a parameter mode, and it sends the program back to the block following the point from which entry to the subroutine was made, because of the 1 in field C.

11-8

SNAs as Function Arguments

Any SNA, with the exception of matrix savevalues, may be used as the argument of a function. The selection is indicated in field A of the FUNCTION statement. The function will be evaluated with the value of that SNA at the time the evaluation is being made. This provides a very powerful way of introducing dependencies into the model. A common way of using this feature is to control the action time at a GENERATE or ADVANCE block. However, at a GENERATE block there are some additional restrictions on which SNAs may be used (see Sec. 11-5).

Some examples follow of how SNAs being used as function arguments introduce different kinds of dependencies:

(a) By using a uniformly distributed random number, RNn, as input to a function, any nonuniform distribution of action time can be generated. The method was explained in Sec. 9-1.

(b) Using clock time, C1 or AC1, as input to a function can make an action time depend upon the time of day and so simulate peak loads. However, it must be remembered that as the load increases, the interarrival time decreases, so an increase in load is associated with a decrease in the action time.

Suppose, for example, that the mean arrival rate is usually 5 per hour but that during the lunch hour, between 12:00 and 13:00 hours, the rate drops to 3 per hour. However, there are two peaks of 6 per hour in the hours immediately preceding and following the lunch hour. Suppose that the time unit is 1 minute and that the simulation covers a workday from 9:00 to 17:00 hours. The mean interarrival time is then as shown in Fig. 11-1, where the horizontal scale is minutes from the start of the day. The following coding can be used:

```
ARR     FUNCTION    C1,D5
120,12/180,10/240,20/300,10/480,12
        GENERATE    FN$ARR,FN$EXP
```

The function ARR provides the mean value of the interarrival time. The entry in the B field refers to the inverted exponential function defined in Sec. 9-2 and coded in Fig. 9-10. It is not shown here.

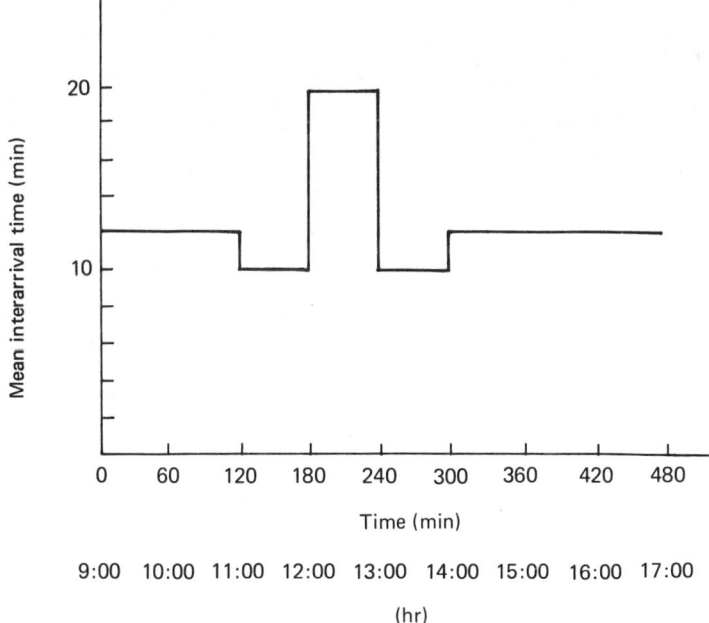

Figure 11-1. Mean interarrival time for system with peak loads.

Note that both the functions ARR and EXP must be defined ahead of the GENERATE block.

(c) Using the current content of a storage, Sj, or queue length, Qj, as input to a function can make the action time depend upon the load placed on a system. Suppose, for example, that the average service time at a counter is normally distributed but tends to decrease as the queue of waiting customers increases, reflecting the fact that the servers tend to work more quickly as the load increases. Let Fig. 11-2 represent the mean service time as a function of queue size. Suppose, for the sake of simplicity, that the standard deviation remains a constant 20 seconds. The following coding can be used:

```
          ADVANCE      V$SERV
SERV      VARIABLE     20*FN$NORM+FN$MEAN
MEAN      FUNCTION     Q1,C8
0,100/2,97/4,93/6,84/8,74/10,67/12,61/14,58
```

The function MEAN provides the mean value of the service time. The function NORM is the inverted standard normal function, described in Sec. 9-3 and coded in Fig. 9-10, but not shown here.

One function may use another as input, and examples will be given in Secs. 11-10 and 11-11. A function may not, however, use itself as input,

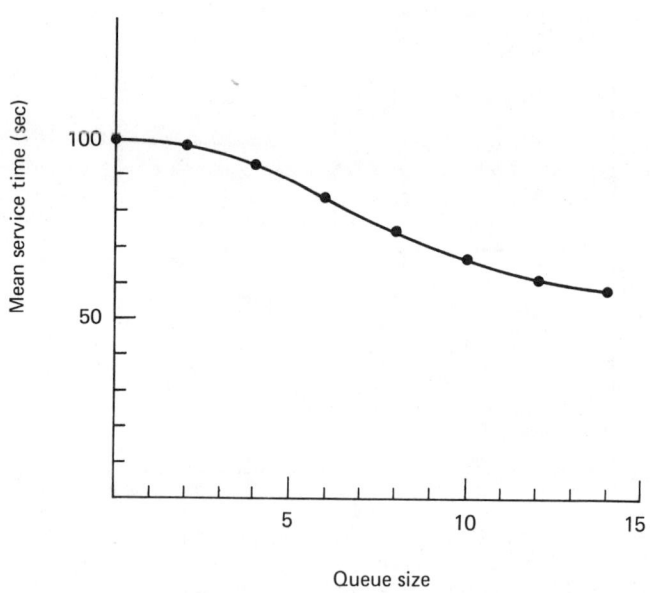

Figure 11-2. Mean service time in load-dependent service system.

either directly or indirectly. Such an attempt will cause an error labeled as a *cyclic definition*.

11-9
SNAs in Attribute Valued Functions

In addition to using SNAs as inputs to functions, the discrete attribute and list attribute modes of the functions allow any SNA, except matrix values, to be used as the output of the function. The SNA may be used as the y_i that defines any of the output values, and it does not have to be the same SNA for all values of y_i. As an example, suppose that a machining operation has the following probabilities for choosing a facility:

Facility number 1	0.2
Facility numbered in savevalue 6	0.3
Facility numbered in parameter 1	0.4
Facility numbered in parameter 2	0.1

Fullword entities are to be used. The following SEIZE block and discrete attribute function can be used:

```
            SEIZE       FN$FAC
    FAC     FUNCTION    RN1,E4
0.2,1/0.5,XF6/0.9,PF1/1.0,PF2
```

A discrete attribute function is evaluated in the same way as a discrete valued function but, as shown above, it is coded with the letter E instead of D in field B of the FUNCTION statement.

It would also be possible to use a list attribute function if, instead of making a random choice between the four possible facilities, the choice is stored as one of the numbers 1, 2, 3, or 4 in, say, byte-sized parameter 5. The coding would then be as follows:

```
            SEIZE       FN$FAC
    FAC     FUNCTION    PB5,M4
,1/,XF6/,PF1/,PF2
```

The list attribute mode is indicated by the letter M in the B field of the FUNCTION statement.

11-10
Ragged Tables

A matrix provides a way of executing a double-index table lookup, that is, of deriving an output dependent upon two inputs, since the matrix output depends upon the selected row and column. Sometimes the number of outputs for a given row is not constant. Such sets of data are often called *ragged tables*. If a matrix is used for a ragged table, the number of columns, j, must equal the largest number of items in any row. Other rows will be left with a number of unused cells.

The combination of functions used as outputs of functions provides a convenient way of forming ragged tables. As an example, in simulating a programming control system, entry points are needed to a number of subroutines representing different macros. The macros are organized as a number of types with a choice, by number, within the type. The following is a list of the macros and the addresses assigned to the entry points of the subroutines that represent them:

1 Storage Control
    1 GETMAIN   SCP02
    2 FREEMAIN   SCP07
2 Program Control
    1 LINK   PCP03
    2 RETURN   PCP04
    3 XCTL   PCP06
    4 LOAD   PCP08
    5 DELETE   PCP09
3 File Control
    1 GET   FCP03
    2 PUT   FCP04

Suppose that a transaction, which is to represent the execution of the macro, has the macro-type number, such as 1 for storage control, in byte-sized parameter 1, and the call within macro type, such as 2 for FREEMAIN, in byte-sized parameter 2. The following coding can be used:

```
      CALL    FUNCTION    PB1,M3
,FN$HSC/,FN$HPC/,FN$HFC
      HSC     FUNCTION    PB2,L2
,SCP02/,SCP07
      HPC     FUNCTION    PB2,L5
,PCP03/,PCP04/,PCP06/,PCP08/,PCP09
      HFC     FUNCTION    PB2,L2
,FCP03/,FCP04
        ...
              TRANSFER    FN,CALL
```

The first function, called CALL, is a list attribute type function having three other functions, HSC, HPC, HFC, as outputs. The macros-type number, in byte-sized parameter 1, will select one of these functions. Each of the output functions is a list type function that uses the call number, in byte-sized parameter 2, to select the transfer address. The functions are evaluated when the transaction enters the TRANSFER block shown last, which is in a function mode. The TRANSFER block could also have been coded as TRANSFER ,FN$CALL, which is in an unconditional mode, using the function CALL as an SNA. Both ways of programming are equally effective.

11-11
Stochastic Processes

Suppose that a system can be in one of several discrete states and is continually making a transition from one state to another. If the probability of going into any state depends upon the previous state but is independent of any state prior to that, the system changes are said to form a *Markov chain*. In general, the probability of the system being in any particular state depends upon the length of time the process has been in progress and the initial state from which it started. For most systems of practical interest, the probability of finding the system in any particular state tends to a limit with increasing time and is independent of the initial state. If the system has N states, it can then be described by an $N \times N$ transition probability matrix, (p_{ij}), giving the probability of a single transition taking the system from state i to state j, including the probabilities p_{ii} that the system will stay in the same state. The sum of the probabilities in any row of the matrix is then equal to 1, reflecting the fact that whatever state the system is in, the next transition must take it to one of the possible states. Systems having the properties just described are examples of *stochastic processes*.

Stochastic processes are widely used in many types of studies, including studies of social, biological, economic, and medical systems (14, 61, 72, 75, 80, and 88). Usually, experimental data provide estimates of the elements of the transition probability matrix, and the problem that arises is to determine what will be the long-term probabilities of the system being in any state.

Although the transition probability matrix is square, it is better, in GPSS, to use functions to form a double-index table similar to the ragged tables discussed in the previous section. Each row of the matrix, i, can then be represented by a function incorporating the probabilities of reaching state j from state i. The row functions are made the outputs of an attribute mode function that selects the function for a given row from the current state.

Consider the following example, discussed in (61). The data, based on a sample of 3500 families, show the probabilities of a son having a given occupation as a function of his father's occupation. For the purposes of the study, occupations were divided into seven general categories. Table 11-2 shows the transition probability matrix based on the data.

Table 11-2 Transition Probabilities for Occupations

Father's occupation	Son's occupation						
	1	2	3	4	5	6	7
1 Professional and higher administrative	0.388	0.146	0.202	0.062	0.140	0.047	0.015
2 Managerial and executive	0.107	0.267	0.227	0.120	0.206	0.053	0.020
3 Higher-grade supervisory and nonmanual	0.035	0.101	0.188	0.191	0.357	0.067	0.061
4 Lower-grade supervisory and nonmanual	0.021	0.039	0.112	0.212	0.430	0.124	0.062
5 Skilled manual and routine nonmanual	0.009	0.024	0.075	0.123	0.473	0.171	0.125
6 Semiskilled manual	0.000	0.013	0.041	0.088	0.391	0.312	0.155
7 Unskilled manual	0.000	0.008	0.036	0.083	0.364	0.235	0.274

Shown in Fig. 11-3 is a GPSS model of the stochastic process, together with an output based on a run of 10,000 transactions. The current state of the system is held in a savevalue called STATE, which is initialized to 1. A seven-valued list-type attribute function, called ROW, uses the current state as input to select as output one of the functions called ROWi ($i = 1, 2, \ldots,$ 7). The inputs, x_{ij}, for each of these functions are the successive cumulative totals of the probabilities p_{ij}, that is,

$$x_{ij} = \sum_{r=1}^{j} p_{ir}, \quad i,j = 1, 2, \ldots, 7$$

The function outputs are the numbers r, ranging from 1 to 7, which represent the new state to which the system changes. This replaces the value of STATE and is used to add 1 to a counter for the number of times the system goes to that state. To illustrate the way the entity-type function can be used to generalize the assignment of entity numbers, as was discussed in Sec. 11-6, an entity-type function, called CNT, is used to select the savevalue in which to accumulate the totals.

The two steps of selecting the new state and incrementing a counter are repeated by means of a LOOP block, here established for 10,000 repetitions. The results, divided by 10,000 to represent the probabilities of the system being in any state, are shown in Table 11-3 along with the observed values, reported in (61), and some equilibrium values predicted by other means and reported in (90).

```
* A STOCHASTIC SYSTEM
*
 ROW     FUNCTION    XF$STATE,M7       PICK FUNCTION FROM STATE
1,FN$ROW1/2,FN$ROW2/3,FN$ROW3/4,FN$ROW4
5,FN$ROW5/6,FN$ROW6/7,FN$ROW7
*
 ROW1    FUNCTION    RN1,D7            TRANSITIONS FROM STATE 1
.300,1/.534,2/.736,3/.798,4/.938,5/.985,6/1.0,7
*
 ROW2    FUNCTION    RN1,D7            TRANSITIONS FROM STATE 2
.107,1/.374,2/.601,3/.721,4/.927,5/.980,6/1.0,7
*
 ROW3    FUNCTION    RN1,D7            TRANSITIONS FROM STATE 3
.035,1/.136,2/.324,3/.575,4/.872,5/.939,6/1.0,7
*
 ROW4    FUNCTION    RN1,D7            TRANSITIONS FROM STATE 4
.021,1/.060,2/.172,3/.384,4/.814,5/.938,6/1.0,7
*
 ROW5    FUNCTION    RN1,D7            TRANSITIONS FROM STATE 5
.009,1/.033,2/.108,3/.231,4/.704,5/.875,6/1.0,7
*
 ROW6    FUNCTION    RN1,D7            TRANSITIONS FROM STATE 6
.000,1/.013,2/.054,3/.142,4/.533,5/.845,6/1.0,7
*
 ROW7    FUNCTION    RN1,D7            TRANSITIONS FROM STATE 7
.000,1/.008,2/.044,3/.127,4/.491,5/.726,6/1.0,7
*
 CNT     FUNCTION    XF$STATE,S7,XF   ASSIGNS SPECIFIC NUMBERS TO COUNTERS
1,CNT1/2,CNT2/3,CNT3/4,CNT4
5,CNT5/6,CNT6/7,CNT7
*
1        GENERATE    ,,,1,,2PF         CREATE A SINGLE TRANS.
2        ASSIGN      1,10000,PF        INITIALIZE LOOP COUNT
3        SAVEVALUE   STATE,FN$ROW,XF   PICK NEXT STATE
4        SAVEVALUE   FN$CNT+,1,XF      INCREMENT COUNT FOR THAT STATE
5        LOOP        1PF,*-2
6        TERMINATE   1
         INITIAL     XF$STATE,1
         START       1
```

RELATIVE CLOCK   1   ABSOLUTE CLOCK   1
BLOCK COUNTS
BLOCK CURRENT TOTAL   BLOCK CURRENT TOTAL   BLOCK CURRENT TOTAL   BLOCK CURRENT TOTAL
  1   0   1
  2   0   1
  3   0   10000
  4   0   10000
  5   0   10000
  6   0   1

```
*****************************************
*                                        *
*          FULLWORD SAVEVALUES           *
*                                        *
*****************************************
```

NUMBER	CONTENT	NUMBER	CONTENT	NUMBER	CONTENT	NUMBER	CONTENT	NUMBER	CONTENT
STATE	4	CNT1	229	CNT2	423	CNT3	866	CNT4	1330
CNT5	4079	CNT6	1798	CNT7	1275				

Figure 11-3. Coding and output for a stochastic process model.

Table 11-3 Comparison of Results for Distribution of Occupations

Occupation	Observed	Predicted	GPSS
1	0.029	0.023	0.023
2	0.046	0.042	0.042
3	0.094	0.088	0.087
4	0.131	0.127	0.133
5	0.409	0.409	0.408
6	0.170	0.182	0.180
7	0.121	0.129	0.128

11-12

SNAs as Table Arguments

The tables used so far have all used transit time, either by using M1 or MPjPx, in the A field of a TABLE statement. In fact, any SNA, except matrix values or floating-point SNAs, can be used. This allows a TABULATE block to gather a wide variety of statistical information, particularly since the SNA may be one of the variable statements, defined in the next section, that combine other SNAs.

For example, Fig. 11-4 shows to the left a simple chain of blocks that creates one transaction every T1 time units, sends it to a TABULATE block, and terminates it. This means that a sample of some statistic can be taken every T1 time units. The same effect can be achieved by creating a single transaction and injecting it into a closed loop where it will cycle at a fixed interval of time by going into an ADVANCE block on each cycle. One or more TABULATE blocks included in the loop will sample the statistics. In other cases, the transaction taking the sample may be held up (by a logic switch, described in the next chapter) and only released to take a sample when some system condition exists (see Sec. 8-15).

The right-hand side of Fig. 11-4 shows a storage, called MAC. Perhaps the statistic of interest is the number of transactions currently waiting to use the storage. Suppose that they wait in the ADVANCE block called AAA. The TABULATE block could then sample the SNA called W$AAA, the number waiting at block AAA. If the current number being processed is needed, the SNA called S$MAC could be used, or if the sum of these two numbers were needed, a variable can be defined as the sum and tabulated as an SNA.

In this case, the number waiting could be derived by defining a queue

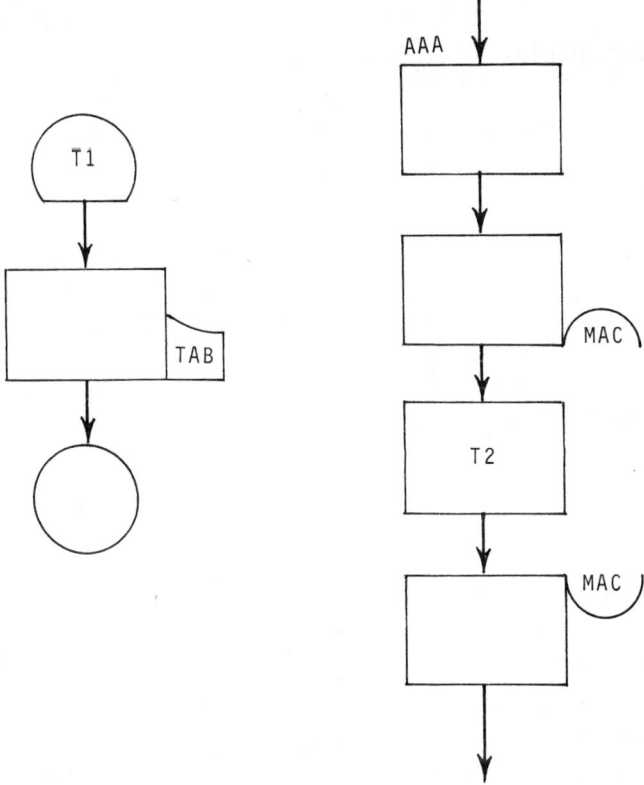

Figure 11-4. Sampling statistics.

and using the SNA Qj. However, this involves extra blocks that maintain the statistic continuously, whereas the method illustrated in Fig. 11-4 only computes the statistic when it is needed for tabulation purposes.

Special arrangements have been made for gathering some of the commonly needed statistics. In Secs. 8-14 and 8-15 we discussed two special modes of tabulation: one was to derive the interarrival time and the other the rate of arrival at any point in the block diagram. In addition, the incremental values of any SNA can be tabulated by putting a minus sign after the SNA in field A of the TABLE statement.

The QTABLEs, described in Sec. 8-11, also give a commonly needed statistic, the distribution of time spent on a queue. The QTABLEs can, in fact, be used to measure the distribution of time involved in many other types of delay. For example, the standard output gives the average time transactions spent using a facility or storage. If the distribution of the time is needed, the transactions can be entered in a queue, with a QTABLE, while they are using the facility or storage. The principle can obviously be extended to measure the distribution of time spent in any section of the block diagram marked by the points at which a transaction enters and leaves a queue.

11-13

Variable Statements

Individual SNAs may be combined to define a type of SNA called a *variable statement*. There are three types of variable statements. In one type, all operations in the calculation are carried out in integer arithmetic. These are called arithmetic variables, or simply variables, and are denoted by Vj. A second type, called floating-point variables, also denoted by Vj, operates with floating-point inputs. They will be described in Sec. 11-15. A third type of variable, called Boolean variables, will be described in Sec. 12-8. They are denoted by BVj. The normal limit for arithmetic and floating-point variables is 200, and they share the same number set. Boolean variables have a normal limit of 25 and they have a separate number set.

Arithmetic variables are formed by combining other SNAs mathematically with the following symbols representing the allowable operators:

addition	+
subtraction	-
multiplication	*
division	/
modulo division	@

Note that, in GPSS, division by zero is not illegal. Instead, it will result in the value 0 for both normal and modulo division.

Modulo division means that the remainder from the division of two numbers will be retained. For example, the division of 35 by 11 normally gives a quotient of 3 and a remainder of 2. In an arithmetic variable, division, represented by 35/11, would give 3 as the result, and modulo division, represented by 35@11, would give a result of 2. Modulo division provides a useful way of producing a number that will cycle through a series of values 1 to n. The expression ABCD@n can only have as remainder one of the numbers $0, 1, \ldots, (n-1)$, so the expression ABCD@n+1, where *ABCD* takes the successive values $0, 1, \ldots$, will result in the cyclic sequence $1, 2, \ldots, n, 1, 2, \ldots$.

Arithmetic variables are defined by putting the variable number, or name, in the location field, and the word VARIABLE in the operation field. The expression defining the variable begins in column 19 and can continue up to and including column 71 with no intervening blanks. The expression is evaluated from left to right with multiplication, division, and modulo division taking precedence over addition and subtraction. For example, an expression of the form S1*S2-S3 is interpreted as (S1*S2) - S3. There can be up to five levels of parentheses to group terms that are to be treated as one element. The parentheses occurring in the definition of matrix savevalues are not included in this count of five.

The following are examples of variable statements:

```
1 VARIABLE    S5+S16+XF6*Q7
5 VARIABLE    PF5+MH3(2,3)*(Q1-Q2)
```

The first defines variable 1 as the sum of the contents of storages 5 and 16 plus the length of queue 7 multiplied by the value of fullword savevalue 6. The second defines variable 5 as the fullword parameter 5 plus the difference of queues 1 and 2 times the value of row 2, column 3 of the halfword matrix number 3.

The individual terms of an arithmetic variable can be positive or negative and the result can be positive or negative. If any term is a floating-point number, it will be truncated before entering the calculation. It is permissible to include integers in the expression: for example, 5*S6 will give five times the content of storage 6. The program will also accept symbols of the form Kn as a representation of the integer n. Thus, K5*S6 also gives five times the content of storage 6.

11-14
Data Packing

In models using large amounts of data it is often helpful to pack the data so that more than one field of information is contained in one word. The packing might be done in a function or in savevalues. The packing will not only save space, it will sometimes save time by giving more than one field of information for a single access to the data base; however, the cost of decoding the packed information has to be considered. The decoding can be done using variable statements to carry out both normal and modulo divisions. The following is an example using packed data.

A computer system is receiving messages from a network of terminals coming from six areas. Each message requires access to one of five files which reside on disk units. The records are divided by area, so there are a total of 30 data sets. The computer system has three channels, and, for convenience, the data sets are allocated so that all the data for two areas are on one channel. The data sets are large so they are spread over several disk units and segments of more than one data set can be on each unit. However, if a data set is spread over more than one unit, it occupies a consecutively numbered set of units.

The number of disk units on a channel and the manner in which the data sets are spread over the units can be varied in an attempt to balance the load. The six areas are numbered 1 through 6, and are allocated to the channels as follows:

Area	Channel
1	1
2	1
3	2
4	2
5	3
6	3

Table 11-4 shows how the files for areas 1 and 2 are spread over 14 disk units attached to channel 1. Similar tables are drawn up for the other channels, but are not shown here.

Since the files are spread over consecutively numbered disk units, a convenient way of representing the allocation is to record the low number unit and the number of units over which the data set is spread, using two decimal digits for each number. Putting these two numbers together gives a four-digit number. For example, file 1 for area 1 exists on three disk units, 2, 3, and 4. This allocation can be represented by the number 0203. The first two digits form a number, A, representing the low-number disk, and the second two digits, B, represent the number of disk units involved. The value A can be derived as the quotient resulting from a normal division by 100, and B can be derived as the result of modulo division by 100.

Table 11-4 Distribution of Data Sets over Disk Units

File:	1		2		3		4		5	
Area:	1	2	1	2	1	2	1	2	1	2
Disk										
1			X				X			
2	X		X				X			
3	X						X			
4	X						X		X	
5							X		X	
6				X			X			
7				X			X			
8			X				X			
9		X	X				X			
10		X					X			
11		X					X		X	
12							X		X	
13					X		X			
14						X	X			

A halfword matrix, called FILES, can be used to store the coded numbers. The matrix row is selected by the area, and the column by the file number. Table 11-5 shows the values to which the matrix will be initialized.

Suppose that a simulation represents the execution of instructions that access the data. The number of the file to be accessed is in halfword parameter 3, and the area number is in byte-sized parameter 4. The program is to determine from these two numbers the channel and disk unit numbers. The channel number is to go into byte-sized parameter 8 and the disk unit number is to go into byte-sized parameter 9. It is assumed that each data access is uniformly distributed over the range of disks to which that item of data is assigned. The following coding can be used:

```
          ASSIGN      8,V$CHAN,PB
          SAVEVALUE   TEMP,MH$FILES(PB4,PH3),XF
          ASSIGN      9,V$FILEN,PB
            ...
CHAN      VARIABLE    PB4/2+PB4@2
FILEN     VARIABLE    XF$TEMP/100+(XF$TEMP@100)*RN1/1000
```

The variable CHAN divides the area number, in PB4, both normally and in a modulo mode. Both divisions give integer results. The modulo result is 0 when the area number is even, and 1 when it is odd. The value of CHAN is therefore 1 when PB4 is 1 or 2, 2 when PB4 is 3 or 4, and 3 when PB4 is 5 or 6. The first ASSIGN block places this result in byte-sized parameter 8.

The next statement takes a value from the matrix FILES and places it in a fullword savevalue called TEMP. The area number, in PB4, is selecting the row, and the file number, in PH3, is selecting the column. The first two decimal digits of the number, A, give the lowest numbered disk. The second two decimal digits, B, give the number of disk units.

To select randomly between the B disk units means picking one of the numbers $A, A + 1, A + 2, \ldots, A + B - 1$, with equal probability given to each number. If B is multiplied by a uniformly distributed random number, between 0 and 1, the result is one of the numbers $0, 1, 2, \ldots, B - 1$, with equal probability, because the result is truncated to the next lowest

Table 11-5 Values of Matrix Called FILES

	1	2	3	4	5
1	0203	0102	0602	0107	0402
2	0903	0802	1302	0807	1102
3	0204	0102	0702	0108	0403
4	0904	0902	0902	0904	1102
5	0206	0104	0902	0110	0603
6	1104	1102	1102	1104	1302

integer. Adding A to the result gives a file number. The variable FILEN carries out the calculations just described. Note that the SNA RN1 is not being used as the input to a function so its value is in the range 0 to 999. It is divided by 1000 to bring it into the range 0 to 1. The second ASSIGN block puts the value of the variable FILEN in byte-sized parameter 9.

The intermediate step of storing the value of the matrix temporarily is not needed in principle: it would be permissible to use MH$FILES(PB4,PH3) in place of XF$TEMP in the variable statement FILEN. However, there is a practical problem. With the matrix SNA being used, the variable statement will extend beyond column 71. It must be shortened, and the use of TEMP is a convenient way of doing this. In addition, the method used is preferable from the point of view of execution time. There is only one access to the data, whereas the other method requires two accesses. Because the matrix SNA involves the evaluation of two other SNAs, its execution will be slow. Offsetting this is the need to execute the SAVEVALUE block. However, there will be a small gain in time.

11-15

Floating-Point Variable Statements

Floating-point variable statements are similar to arithmetic variables, but the individual terms of the statements are allowed to be floating-point numbers. One other difference is that modulo division is illegal for floating-point variables. Floating-point variables are distinguished from integer forms of variable statements by having the word FVARIABLE in the operation field, but they are still represented as an SNA by the symbol Vj, and they share the same sequence of numbers as the arithmetic statements. Examples of using FVARIABLES in connection with calculating normal distributions have been given in Secs. 9-9 and 10-10. All mathematical operations are carried out in floating-point form during the evaluation of an FVARIABLE, and the output will be a floating-point number. If the floating-point number is presented as a block field argument, other than those specifically dealing with floating-point numbers, the value will be truncated to an integer. This includes a floating-point variable in the B field of a GENERATE or ADVANCE block.

The principal original sources of floating-point numbers are functions. In addition, the statistical calculations concerned with means and standard deviations that appear in the standard output and are also defined as SNAs give their values in floating-point form. Appendix 5, which lists all the SNAs, indicates those that take floating-point form with an asterisk. Parameters, savevalues, and matrix savevalues all have floating-point forms for saving floating-point numbers, so they frequently form part of the input for floating-point variables. Floating-point variables may also form part of the input for other floating-point variables.

Fractional constants can be used in FVARIABLEs, and they can be expressed in exponent form. For example, 1.23E3 represents 1230 in exponent form.

Exercises

11-1   A random walk in one dimension is defined as a process in which an entity, starting from an origin, takes a number of steps each of which is of unit size and is equally likely to be forward or backward. It can be shown that the distance from the origin after N steps tends to a normal distribution with a mean of zero and a standard deviation of $\sqrt{N}$. Demonstrate this result by simulating a random walk of 500 steps and tabulating the displacement with 500 trials.

11-2   Orders are received for the manufacture of parts at the rate of one every 25 ± 10 minutes. The orders are for one of four types of part. Each order is for one type only and the number of parts to an order is uniformly distributed between 1 and 10, regardless of the part type. The parts are to be made individually and all parts for one order are to be finished before another order is started. The time for each part is normally distributed with a mean value, depending upon the part type. There is some variability that can be expressed as a standard deviation of 1 minute for all part types. Using a time unit of 10 seconds simulate the processing of 100 orders, assuming the following figures for the mean times and percentages of part types:

Type	Percentage	Mean time (min)
A	30	3
B	25	4
C	25	5
D	20	6

11-3   An electric utility company serves three classes of customers, private, commercial, and government. The commercial and government customers are allowed discounts. It is found that the number of units of electricity consumed a month by a customer is exponentially distributed, with the mean depending upon the type of customer. The relevant statistics for the customers are as follows:

Type	Percentage	Mean	Discount (per cent)
private	70	500	0
commercial	20	70,000	5
government	10	20,000	10

The basic rate schedule (before discount) depends upon the amount consumed, as follows: first 1,000 units, 0.075¢/unit; next 49,000 units, 0.050¢/unit; and beyond 50,000 units, 0.030¢/unit. Simulate the billing of 1000 customers, assuming that they are processed in random order, and tabulate the distribution of the amount of the bill by type of customer.

11-4 A one-way tunnel for cars is 750 feet long. It is found that the average speed at which cars travel depends upon the number of cars in the tunnel, x, according to the following formula:

$$\text{speed} = \frac{15,000}{x + 1000} \text{ ft/sec}$$

Assuming that cars arrive with interarrival times that are exponentially distributed with a mean of 1 second, simulate the passage of 1000 cars. Use a time scale of $\frac{1}{10}$ second. Assign the car speed when it enters the tunnel, and do not attempt to adjust the speed of a car once it has entered the tunnel.

11-5 Messages are being sent over a circuit at the rate of 10 characters a second. The message sizes are normally distributed with a mean of 900 characters and a standard deviation of 150 characters. In addition to the transmission time, there is a uniformly distributed delay, with a mean of 10 seconds and a spread of 2 seconds, needed to establish the circuit for each message. The circuit is tied up during this delay. Messages arrive with an exponentially distributed interarrival time having a mean of 100 seconds. Using a time unit of 1 second, simulate the transmission of 500 messages, counting the total number of characters transmitted.

11-6 An office has a backlog of 20 jobs at the beginning of a day. New jobs arrive at the rate of one every 40 ± 10 minutes. There are four clerks working in the office, and the time to complete a job is normally distributed with a mean of 25 minutes and a standard deviation of 4 minutes. Once every hour, a supervisor will estimate the amount of work outstanding, measured in man-hours, by assuming that each job will need 25 minutes and each job in progress is half finished. Arrange to simulate the system for one day of 8 working hours. (Use a GENERATE block with a zero time and a count of 20 in field D to create the initial load.)

11-7 A manufacturing process has three stages of production, each followed by an inspection. The probability of rejection at the end of the three stages are, in order, 0.1, 0.15, and 0.05. Assume that each stage takes 1 time unit, and generate jobs at the rate of one every time unit. Initialize the system with five terminations and then sample the system every 100 time units. Tabulate the number of failures that occur from all stages during the sampling period. Run the simulation for 50 samples.

11-8 The following transition probability matrix describes the movement of people between three broad categories of employment. Find the long term steady-state distribution between the three occupations [see (61), p. 17].

		1	2	3
1	nonmanual	0.594	0.396	0.009
2	manual	0.211	0.782	0.007
3	farm	0.252	0.641	0.108

12

TESTING
SYSTEM CONDITIONS

So far, the only factor we have discussed that can stop the flow of transactions is the unavailability of facilities or storages. We introduce now a third type of entity, logic switches, whose main function is to help control the flow of transactions. As their name implies, logic switches have two states, on and off, or set and reset. Depending upon their setting, transactions can be allowed to flow or be blocked. In this respect logic switches are similar to facilities, which can play the same role by being seized or free. The program does not, however, keep statistics on logic switches, so it is able to process logic switches faster than facilities. Any time a facility is being used and there is no interest in the facility statistics, it is probably better to use a logic switch. Although a logic switch may often be used in this way to represent a physical entity of the system, logic switches frequently represent some condition of the system or its environment which needs to be recorded and tested.

There can be many logic switches (normally 1000), each identified by name or number. One block type, LOGIC, is concerned with setting or resetting logic switches; it does not, however, block transactions. Another block type, GATE, can test the status of a logic switch and, if necessary, block the flow of transactions. The GATE block can also test the status of a facility or storage and control the flow of transactions accordingly. The GATE block can appear anywhere in the block diagram; that is, it does not have to be near the block that controls the entity it is testing. It can therefore control the flow of transactions at a point remote from the place at which the entity is used.

One other block type, TEST, compares the values of a pair of SNAs and controls the flow of transactions according to the outcome. The comparison may be between two simple SNAs, but complex conditions can be constructed by using variable statements to combine SNAs before the comparison is made.

Two other block types are designed to examine a range of entities or conditional statements. The COUNT block will find how many entities meet a specified condition—for example, how many facilities are currently busy. The SELECT block will identify a specific entity that meets some condition—for example, it will find a storage that is empty or identify the shortest queue. The COUNT block does not directly control the flow of transactions; it simply collects the information on which to base a decision. The SELECT block, however, can control transaction flow directly.

The five block types that have been mentioned will be described in this chapter. The chapter will also describe Boolean variables that are similar to the variables described previously in Sec. 11-13 but that are concerned with the status of GPSS entities rather than numerical values.

The block diagram symbols for the blocks to be described are shown in Fig. 12-1. The GATE block has four modes of operation, depending upon the type of entity involved. A different flag is used for each mode, as shown in Fig. 12-1. One of the modes, the match mode, will not be described until Sec. 13-8. The "X" appearing in the symbols represents control characters selected from lists to be explained later.

12-1

Logic Switches

Logic switches are two-state entities that are either set or reset. Normally, all logic switches are initially reset. However, the INITIAL control statement, previously mentioned in connection with savevalues (Sec. 10-5), can also be used to set logic switches at the beginning of a simulation run. Beginning in column 19, the INITIAL statement gives the switches to be set with the notation LSn, where n is the number of the switch to be set, or LS$NAME, when it has the name NAME. Several switches can be named in one statement, separated by slashes (/), and a group of consecutively numbered switches can be indicated by LSn_1-LSn_2, where the range is identified by number or name. For example, the following statement will set logic switches 5, 9, 12, 13, 14, and 15:

        INITIAL   LS5/LS9/LS12-LS15

There are no embedded blanks. There can be many such statements, and one INITIAL statement can mention both logic switches and savevalues.

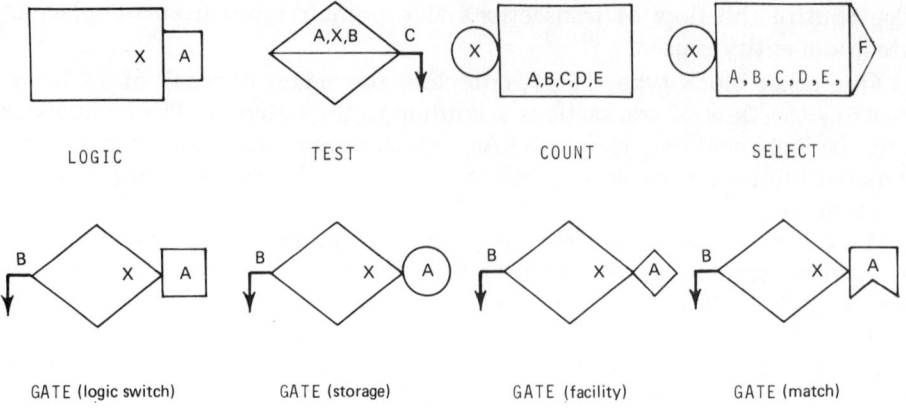

Figure 12-1. Block types 7.

No statistics are kept on logic switches. However, the program prints a list of the switches that are set at the end of a simulation run. They may therefore be used to report that some event or system condition occurred during the run.

12-2
LOGIC Blocks

The status of a logic switch is controlled by transactions entering a LOGIC block. Field A of the block identifies the logic switch. The transaction can either set or reset the switch, or it can invert the current status of the switch. If the switch is already in the desired state, no action is taken.

The choice of mode is made by following the word LOGIC in the operation field by one blank and one of the letters S, R, or I for set, reset, or invert. When drawing block diagrams, it is customary to write the letter in the block to indicate what choice has been selected.

The LOGIC block always allows a transaction to enter, so it cannot cause blocking by itself. The GATE block, described in the next section, can test a logic switch and cause blocking.

12-3
GATE Blocks

When a transaction *attempts to enter* a GATE block, the program tests the status of a logic switch, facility, or storage for one of several conditions. It can also test whether a transaction is waiting to be matched. The match option will be described in Sec. 13-8. The conditions that can be tested, and the operator codes used to indicate them, are shown in Table 12-1.

The choice of condition is made by following the word GATE in the operation field by a blank and the appropriate characters, as shown in Table 12-1. The characters therefore begin in column 13. The particular entity number, or name, is carried in field A.

The test is made at the time the transaction attempts to enter the block. If the condition is true, the transaction will enter the block and then attempt to proceed to the next sequential location. If the condition is not true, there are two modes of operation, according to whether field B is blank or not.

(a) If field B is blank and the condition is not met, the transaction will *not* enter the GATE block. Instead, it will wait until the condition does become true and then enter the block. It will then proceed to the next sequential location.

(b) If field B is not blank and the condition is not met, the transaction *will* enter the block and then proceed to the location indicated by field B.

Normally a transaction that enters a GATE block immediately moves out of the block, either to the next sequential block or to the location in

Table 12-1 Logical Operators

Operator	Condition
U	Facility in use
NU	Facility not in use
I	Facility interrupted
NI	Facility not interrupted
FV	Facility available
FNV	Facility not available
SE	Storage empty
SNE	Storage not empty
SF	Storage full
SNF	Storage not full
SV	Storage available
SNV	Storage not available
LR	Logic switch reset
LS	Logic switch set
M	Match (GATE block only)
NM	No match (GATE block only)

field B. If it is unable to leave immediately, its presence in the block will not affect the operation of the block on subsequent transactions. There may be many transactions waiting in a GATE block; similarly, there may be many waiting to enter the block. When the condition that causes the blocking changes, all waiting transactions are eligible for movement. If only one should move, the method to be discussed in Sec. 12-6 can be used. If a transaction was selected to go to the location named in field B but must then wait in the GATE block, the decision is not reconsidered if the condition tested by the GATE changes while the transaction is waiting to move.

12-4
Shipping Example

As an example, suppose that the movement of ships is subject to the following rules. A ship will not set sail unless there is a high tide. When the ship does set out, it travels for 6 ± 2 hours before selecting a route. It prefers to go to a particular port and will do so if it knows there is a free berth at that time. If not, it goes to another destination.

Figure 12-2 shows a block diagram. On the left is a closed loop of blocks simulating the change of tide. A logic switch, number 1, is set at high tide and reset at low tide. A GENERATE block, after an offset time of 6 hours (field C), creates a single transaction (field D), which is injected into the closed loop. The transaction sets the switch and then waits in an ADVANCE block for 12 hours to reset the switch. Twelve hours later it is transferred to execute another cycle of the loop, and it continues in this manner for the rest of the simulation.

To the right, another GENERATE block creates a transaction, representing a ship, every 15 ± 10 hours. This will not leave until there is a high tide because the GENERATE block leads to a GATE block that tests for switch 1 to be set. There is no alternative path; so, if the tide is low, the ship will have to wait, and, in doing so, it will delay the preparation of the next ship for departure. When the ship does set sail, it goes to an ADVANCE block for 6 ± 2 hours, and then checks if a storage called PORT1, representing the prime destination port, which can accommodate 5 ships, has free space. If so, the ship proceeds on that course, taking 40 ± 10 hours. If not, it goes to the alternative destination, which is not simulated in this model.

Note that the test of the storage does not affect the storage content. The ship has not reserved a berth, and when it reaches the port, the space might be taken by a transaction, coming from the third GENERATE block, that represents other shipping lines competing for the space. Also, with this simple representation of the tide changes, a single LOGIC block could have been used with the transaction that controls the tide, inverting the switch every 12 hours. Coding and results of a run are shown in Fig. 12-3.

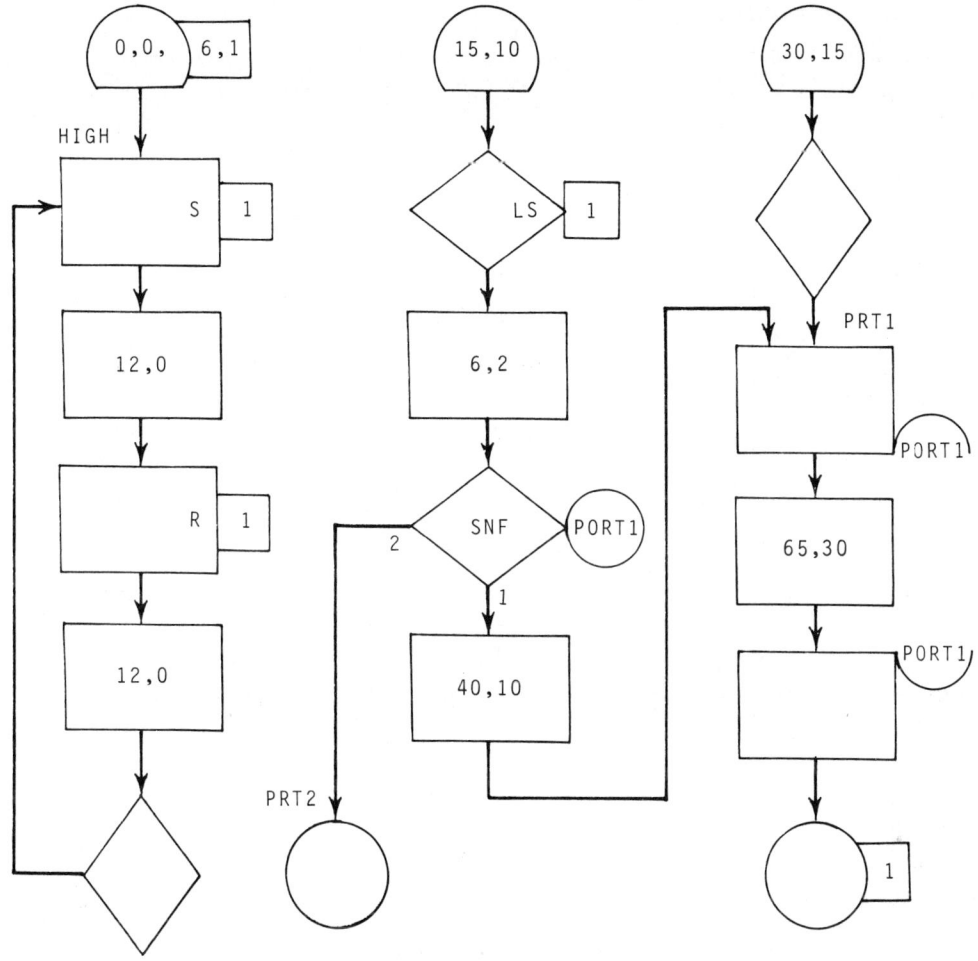

Figure 12-2. A shipping example.

12-5
TEST Blocks

The TEST block is similar to a GATE block, but, instead of testing the status of an entity, it tests a relationship between two SNAs. Since the SNAs include variable statements, which can be functions of other SNAs, the TEST block can introduce very complex conditions. The relationships that can be tested and the symbols used to indicate them are shown in Table 12-2. As in the case of a GATE block, the symbol follows the block name separated by a blank. The two SNAs to be compared are placed in fields A and B, with A being the left-hand operand. The operands may be floating-point, but

```
        *      A SHIPPING EXAMPLE
        *
 1             GENERATE      ,,6,1              CREATE A SINGLE TRANSACTION AFTER 6
        *                                       HOURS TO CONTROL THE TIDES
 2      HIGH   LOGIC S       1                  SET TIDE HIGH
 3             ADVANCE       12,0               WAIT 12 HOURS
 4             LOGIC R       1                  SET TIDE LOW
 5             ADVANCE       12,0               WAIT 12 HOURS
 6             TRANSFER      ,HIGH              CYCLE
        *
 7             GENERATE      15,10              CREATE A SHIP
 8             GATE LS       1                  TEST FOR HIGH TIDE
 9             ADVANCE       6,2                SET OUT TO SEA
10             GATE SNF      PORT1,PRT2         TEST IF PORT 1 HAS A BERTH
11             ADVANCE       40,10              SAIL TO PORT 1
12      PRT1   ENTER         PORT1              ENTER BERTH
13             ADVANCE       65,30              WAIT IN PORT 1
14             LEAVE         PORT1              LEAVE PORT 1
15             TERMINATE     1
        *
16             GENERATE      30,15              RIVAL LINE SHIPPING
17             TRANSFER      ,PRT1
        *
18      PRT2   TERMINATE                        GO TO PORT 2
        *
               STORAGE       S$PORT1,5          CAPACITY OF PORT 1

               START         1000
```

```
RELATIVE CLOCK          16079   ABSOLUTE CLOCK         16079
BLOCK COUNTS
BLOCK CURRENT TOTAL    BLOCK CURRENT TOTAL    BLOCK CURRENT       BLOCK CURRENT TOTAL
   1      0      1       11      2     470
   2      0    670       12      0    1004
   3      0    670       13      4    1004
   4      0    670       14      0    1000
   5      1    670       15      0    1000
   6      0    669       16      0     536
   7      0    875       17      0     536
   8      0    875       18      0     405
   9      0    875
  10      0    875
```

```
                        *********************************************
                        *                                           *
                        *                 STORAGES                  *
                        *                                           *
                        *********************************************
                                       AVER UTIL DURING
STORAGE  CAPACITY  AVERAGE   ENTRIES   AVERAGE    TOTL  AVAL  UNAVL  CURRENT   PCNT    CONTENT
                   CONTENT             TIME/UNIT  TIME  TIME  TIME   STATUS    AVAIL   CURR  MAX
PORT1       5      4.069      1004     65.168     .813  .813  .000      A      100.0    4    5
```

Figure 12-3. Coding and output for shipping example.

floating-point and fixed formats may not be mixed. Field C can give an alternative location to which the transaction is sent when the tested condition is not true. The modes of operation are the same as for a GATE block. If field C is not used, the transaction will enter the block if the tested condition is true, and will wait to enter the block if it is not true. With field C specifying an alternative location, the transaction always enters the block and then leaves by way of the next sequential block, if the condition is true,

Table 12-2 Conditional Operators

Symbol	Relationship
L	Less than
LE	Less than or equal
E	Equal
NE	Not equal
G	Greater than
GE	Greater than or equal
MAX	Maximum (SELECT, ALTER, REMOVE, and SCAN blocks only)
MIN	Minimum (SELECT, ALTER, REMOVE, and SCAN blocks only)

and by way of the alternative location, if it is not. Should the transaction become blocked inside the TEST block, its presence does not influence the block action, and the transaction does not change its course if the condition it found to be untrue becomes true while it is blocked.

As an example, suppose that the test is to see if queue 6 is longer than queue 5. The following block will carry out the test:

```
      TEST G      Q6,Q5
```

As a second example, suppose that the test is to see if the combined residual space in storages 1 and 2 is sufficient to accommodate the contents of queues 1 and 2 plus twice the content of queue 5. If it is not, the testing transaction is to go to location AAA. The following TEST block and two variable statements could be used:

```
      TEST GE     V1,V2,AAA
      ...
    1 VARIABLE    R1+R2
    2 VARIABLE    Q1+Q2+2*Q5
```

In the shipping example of Fig. 12-2, suppose that the choice between destinations is made by selecting the one with more space, preferring port 1 if there is equality. Assume that storage 2 represents the second port. Then the GATE block testing for the SNF condition would be replaced by the following block:

```
      TEST GE     R1,R2,PRT2
```

As will be explained in Appendix 6, keeping a transaction blocked by a TEST block is an undesirable condition because the program must continually check for a change in the condition. One way of avoiding blocking, when there may be several conditions causing the block, is to use the SIM mode of the TRANSFER block, to be described in Sec. 12-7.

12-6
Single and Multiple Releases With GATE and TEST Blocks

If a GATE or TEST block is preventing several transactions from moving, all the transactions will be released simultaneously when the blocking condition changes. It may be desired to move only one or a fixed number of the transactions. It is then important to remember the rule that each transaction moves as far as it can before the program turns its attention to another.

Figure 12-4 shows an arrangement that will allow only one transaction to move. Transactions wait in the ADVANCE block for logic switch 1 to be set. When it is set, by some transaction elsewhere in the block diagram, all transactions in the ADVANCE block are free to move. However, the first to move through the GATE block immediately passes into the LOGIC block to reset switch 1. The remaining transactions in the ADVANCE block do not move because the GATE condition has reverted to not true.

In Fig. 12-5, transactions are similarly waiting in an ADVANCE block for space to become available in storage 1. The storage has been filled by trans-

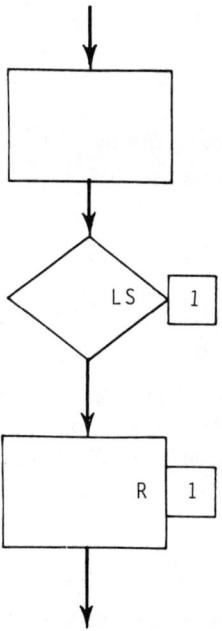

Figure 12-4. Releasing one transaction at a time.

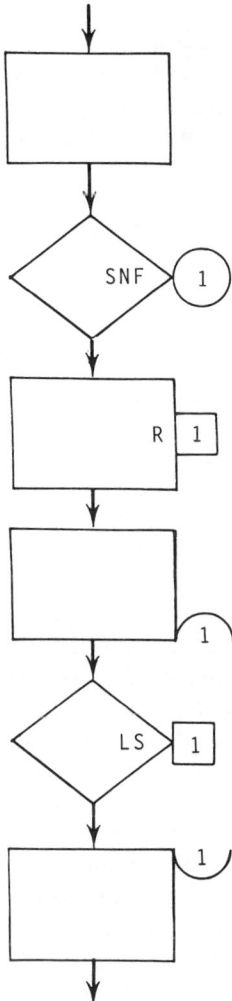

Figure 12-5. Releasing batches of transactions.

actions that are in the ENTER block waiting for switch 1 to be set. When the switch is set, all transactions in the ENTER block are released, and, in this example, they all move before any transaction in the ADVANCE block moves. After emptying the storage, the program finds that all the transactions waiting in the ADVANCE block can move because the storage is no longer full. It begins to move the transactions into the ENTER block. In doing so, the logic switch is reset so that the transactions cannot go beyond the ENTER block. As a result, only a number of transactions equal to the storage content can move before the GATE block testing for space in the storage again cuts off the flow. The arrangement therefore moves transactions in batches.

Some care needs to be exercised in the last example because it assumes that all transactions are at the same priority level. That being so, the transactions that are released when the logic switch is set move first because they were previously processed ahead of the others. A transaction with a higher priority could alter the order of processing.

Another way of releasing a measured number of transactions is to put the waiting transactions on one of the user chains described in Chap. 14: they can then be unlinked with a count control. When the transactions must wait for some time, this method is more efficient because it takes the waiting transactions off the current events chain.

12-7

Simultaneous Mode of TRANSFER Block

Sometimes a string of GATE and TEST blocks is needed to represent a set of conditions that should be tested simultaneously. From the point of view of the model the tests are simultaneous, but the program must execute them in sequence by moving a transaction through the string. What can happen is that several conditions are satisfactory and the transaction proceeds down the string until it meets a blocking condition. It waits for that blocking condition to change and then proceeds to test the remaining conditions. By the time it reaches the end of the string, some of the conditions tested earlier may have changed. All that can be assured is that each condition was at one time satisfied; but it is by no means certain that they are all satisfied simultaneously.

One mode of the TRANSFER block is designed for these circumstances. Called the *simultaneous* mode, and denoted by SIM in the A field, it operates with a *delay indicator* that exists in every transaction but that is not under the direct control of the user. Initially, the delay indicator is reset. Whenever the transaction is delayed, the indicator becomes set. Upon entering a TRANSFER block in a SIM mode, the indicator is tested. If it is not set, the transaction goes to the location given in field B, usually the next sequential block. If the indicator is set, the transaction goes to the location given in field C, and the indicator is reset.

The usual way of using the block is to place it at the end of a string of blocks representing conditions that must be satisfied simultaneously. The C field names the first block in the string. A transaction that reaches the TRANSFER block with the indicator reset has not been delayed, so the conditions of the string are met simultaneously. If the indicator is set, there has been a delay; the transaction is therefore sent back to retest the string. If, in fact, all conditions are satisfied simultaneously, the transaction will immediately return to the TRANSFER block but this time with the indicator remaining reset. It is possible that the transaction may have entered the string with the indicator set by some delay outside the string conditions, in which case the transaction may have to do a superfluous cycle of the string.

The indicator is also reset whenever the transaction goes into an ADVANCE block with nonzero action time, the supposition being that this delay was intentional. As a result, any string of blocks meant to test simultaneous conditions should not contain such blocks.

As an example, suppose that in the shipping example of Fig. 12-2 the conditions to be met for leaving port are the following:

(a) There must be a high tide.
(b) The harbor pilot must be available.
(c) A berth in the preferred destination port must be available.

Suppose that the pilot is represented by facility number 1. The section of a block diagram shown in Fig. 12-6 will accomplish the test.

The transaction representing the ship cannot pass through the TRANSFER block in a SIM mode to reach the sea unless the three preceding GATE

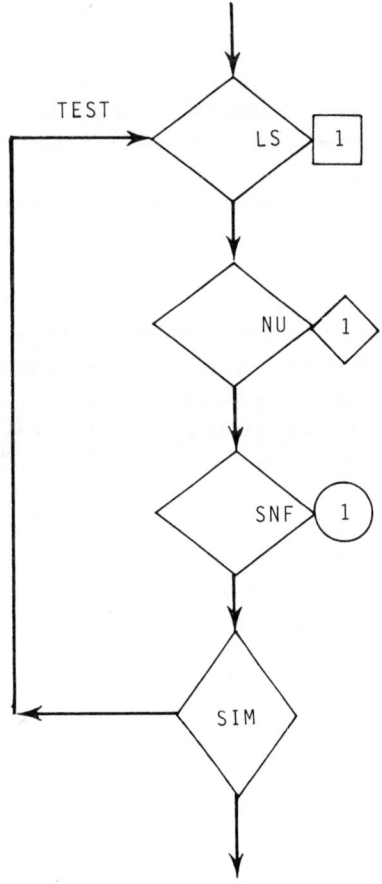

Figure 12-6. Testing simultaneous conditions.

blocks all pass the transaction without delay. The conditions tested are (1) that logic switch 1 is set, representing high tide; (2) that facility 1 is available, meaning that the harbor pilot is free; and (3) that storage 1 has some space, meaning that the destination port has free space.

12-8
Boolean Variable Statements

In addition to the calculations carried out by arithmetic and floating-point variable statements, it is also possible to perform logical calculations in Boolean algebra. The terms in such calculations represent conditions that are either true or false, denoted by 1 or 0, respectively. Terms are combined by requiring that two should either both be true, which is referred to as an AND condition, or at least one should be true, which is referred to as an OR condition.

The normal limit for Boolean variables is 25. Each is given a number or name, which appears in the location field. The word BVARIABLE appears in the operation field. The statement defining the variable begins in the operand field and continues, with no embedded blanks, to a limit of column 71.

The terms of a Boolean statement are formed from the logical and conditional operators shown in Table 12-3. Note that the logical operators differ somewhat from those of Table 12-1 that are used for the GATE block. The operators that relate to a facility begin with the letter F. In addition, the operators for the availability of facilities and storages and matching are not included. The conditional operators, however, are the same as those of Table 12-2 which are valid for the TEST block.

Each of the logical operators gives the value 1 or 0, according to whether the condition it describes is true or false, respectively. The conditional operators are placed between two SNAs marked off by single quotes. The term is evaluated from left to right as in the case of a TEST block. For example, S5'GE'S7 will test if the content of storage 5 is greater than or equal to the content of storage 7. If this condition is true, the term will be evaluated as 1, and if it is not true, the value is 0.

Components of a Boolean statement are combined by the operator *, representing an AND condition, and by + for an OR condition. If the two terms joined by * are both true, the combination is true and is evaluated as 1. If either (or both) is false, so also is the combination, which is then evaluated as 0. For a + operator, the combination is true and evaluated as 1 if either (or both) is true; it is false and evaluated as 0 only if both terms are false. For example, consider the following Boolean variable:

```
1   BVARIABLE    FU5*S5'GE'S7
```

Table 12-3 Operators for Boolean Variables

Logical operators		Conditional operators	
FUj	facility j in use	L	less than
FNUj	facility j not in use	LE	less than or equal
FIj	facility j interrupted	E	equal
FNIj	facility j not interrupted	NE	not equal
SEj	storage j empty	G	greater
SNEj	storage j not empty	GE	greater than or equal
SFj	storage j full		
SNFj	storage j not full		
LRj	logic switch j reset		
LSj	logic switch j set		

This will take the value 1 only if facility 5 is in use and if the content of storage 5 is greater than or equal to the content of storage 7. If either (or both) of these conditions is not true, the Boolean variable value is 0. If the symbol * in the previous statement is changed to +, then the variable is 1 if either (or both) condition is true, and 0 only if both are false.

Boolean variables are read from left to right, and they may contain up to five levels of parentheses to group terms, not including parentheses used in defining matrices. For example,

```
         2 BVARIABLE    SNF1*(Q1'L'R2+Q2'G'S6)
```

is read as "storage 1 is not full and either queue 1 is less than the remaining space in storage 2 or queue 2 is greater than the content of storage 6."

Testing whether a Boolean variable is 1 or 0 provides a way of testing for complex conditions. In particular, the type of operation carried out by the TRANSFER block in a SIM mode can be done with a Boolean variable. In the shipping example of the previous section, the multiple test illustrated in Fig. 12-6 could be made with the following code:

```
           TEST E       BV1,1
             ...
         1 BVARIABLE    LS1*FNU1*SNF1
```

As was pointed out in Sec. 12-5, this method will be more time-consuming if transactions remain blocked by the TEST block for long periods. Another example of the use of Boolean variables will be found in Sec. 14-4.

12-9
COUNT Blocks

The purpose of a COUNT block is to examine the logical status of a range of entities or to evaluate a series of conditional statements, and detect how many meet a specified condition. There are two modes of operation: a logical mode, in which the behavior is similar to a GATE block, and a conditional mode, in which it is like a TEST block.

To define the block, the word COUNT is placed in the operation field. For a logical mode one of the operators shown in Table 12-1, except M and NM, follows in the operation field, separated by one blank. The operator therefore begins in column 14. The range of entity numbers to be searched is formed by putting the lower limit in field B and the upper limit in field C. Field A is used to give the number of a parameter that is to receive the result of the count. For example, to count how many storages in the range 1 through 12 are full, the following block would be used:

```
        COUNT SF    3PF,1,12
```

The result will be placed in parameter number 3 of fullword size. Note that the suffix mode of designating the parameter number must be used.

In the conditional mode of the COUNT block, one of the operators shown in Table 12-2, except MAX and MIN, is placed in the operation field, beginning in column 14. The A, B, and C fields serve the same function as in the logical mode. Fields D and E are also used. The type of SNA to be examined is placed in field E. This can be any SNA except matrix savevalues. Only the symbol for the SNA is used. Field D carries the quantity that is to be compared with the SNAs being searched. The order should be carefully noted. The operation being carried out, when read from left to right, is

Field E 'comparison' Field D.

Consider the following examples:

```
        COUNT GE    2PF,1,10,20,R
        COUNT L     2PF,1,5,XF6,V
```

The first will count how many of the storages 1 through 10 have residual space of 20 or more units. The second counts how many of the arithmetic variable statements numbered 1 through 5 have a value less than the value of fullword savevalue 6. In both examples the count will be placed in fullword parameter 2.

12-10
SELECT Blocks

The SELECT block performs the same type of search as the COUNT block in a conditional mode, and its fields A through E are used in the same way.

However, instead of counting the number of entities that meet the stated condition, the SELECT block extracts the number of the first entity it finds that meets the condition. The selected number is placed in the parameter indicated in field A. If none of the examined entities meets the condition, the transaction making the selection can be sent to an alternative location indicated in field F. If the selection is successful or if field F is left blank, the transaction goes to the next sequential location.

As an example, the two blocks shown below will look for a storage in the range 6 to 10 which has at least 100 units of space left, and will take space in the first such storage that can be found. If no storage meets this condition, the transaction goes to location ABCD.

```
SELECT  GE    2PF,6,10,100,R,ABCD
ENTER         PF2
```

Any of the logical or conditional operators of Tables 12-1 or 12-2 can be used and, as in the COUNT block, the operator is separated by one blank. This means the operator begins in column 15.

There are two important additions to the list of operators. The words MAX or MIN may be used. The program will then select the number of the entity which has the maximum or minimum value of the SNA being searched. In this case, field D is left blank, since the comparison is not being made to a specific number. In addition, field F is inoperative, since a maximum or minimum will always be found, including a possible value of zero. When more than one entity has the same value of the maximum or minimum, the program will select the number of the first that it encounters, that is, the lowest number.

Suppose, for example, that a transaction is to join the shortest of five queues, numbered 1 through 5. The following blocks would be used:

```
SELECT MIN    1PH,1,5,,Q
QUEUE         PH1
```

12-11

Gasoline Filling Station Example

To illustrate the use of COUNT and SELECT blocks, consider the following example of a gasoline filling station. Normally, there are five active pumps. The rate of arrival for cars is one every 50 ± 20 seconds. Arriving cars select the pump with the shortest queue. If there is more than one with the minimum value (which may be zero), a car will take the lowest numbered one. It takes 180 ± 60 seconds to service a car and, for the sake of simplicity, it is assumed that the number of gallons of gasoline needed is uniformly distributed between 1 and 16.

A separate storage tank is used by each pump, each able to hold 1000 gallons. The station manager checks the contents every hour. If he finds that two or more tanks have dropped below 500 gallons, he fills those tanks to capacity. If not, he waits 1 hour before checking again.

A block diagram for the system is shown in Fig. 12-7. The left-hand string of blocks represents the movement of cars. Immediately following the GENERATE block that creates transactions representing cars arriving at intervals of 50 ± 20 seconds, an ASSIGN block places in parameter 2 the number of gallons needed. The figure comes from function 1. There is then a SELECT block that puts in parameter 1 the number of the shortest queue, selected from queues 1 through 5. Parameter 1 is used to select that queue for the car. After servicing the car with a facility representing the pump, the appropriate number of gallons is removed from the tank for that pump.

The right-hand side of Fig. 12-7 is a loop of blocks representing the filling of the tanks. A single transaction is injected into the loop by a GENERATE block, using field D. The transaction goes immediately to a section of the block diagram concerned with filling the tanks. It enters an INDEX block to have parameter 1 set to 5, and then goes round a loop once for each tank that has less than 500 gallons. A TEST block checks the contents of the tanks. If a tank has less than 500 gallons, it is filled by using the indirectly addressed SNA R*PH1 in the B field of an ENTER block. The A field has PH1. Since halfword parameter 1 has the tank number, the action is to place in a tank the amount by which it is empty, thereby filling the tank.

A LOOP block counts the cycles. Initially all tanks are empty, so the first step is to fill all tanks. The transaction then goes to an ADVANCE block to wait 1 hour before using a COUNT block to see how many tanks are low. The count goes into parameter 2, and a TEST block checks for the count to be greater than or equal to 2. If it is not, the transaction returns to the ADVANCE block to wait another hour. When there are two or more low tanks, the transaction again enters the loop for filling tanks but, this time, will only fill those that have fallen below 500 gallons.

The coding of the problem and the results of a run are shown in Fig. 12-8.

12-12

Simulating Time Constraints

Transactions are often subject to some time constraint; for example, a transaction might wait no more than 100 time units for a facility to become available. It is possible for the transaction to test periodically whether the facility is available and give up waiting if the time limit is exceeded; but, unless the check is made at every time unit, the expiration of the time limit cannot be accurately detected, and, obviously, this method can be very time-consuming. In the case where the transaction is to be destroyed if the time limit is exceeded, the method illustrated in Fig. 12-9 can be used.

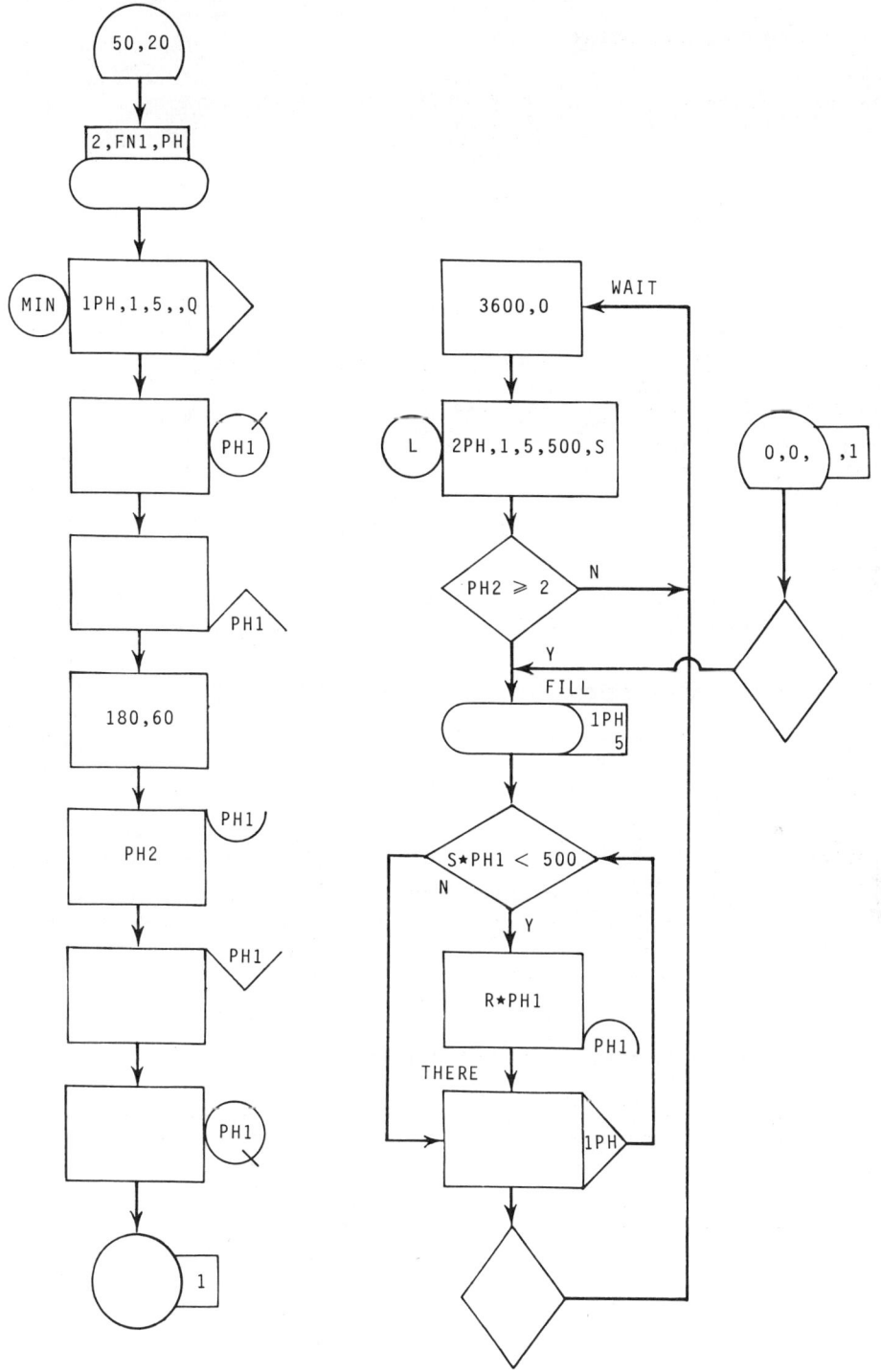

Figure 12-7. Filling station example.

```
         *      EXAMPLE OF FILLING STATION
         *
 1              GENERATE      50,20              CREATE CARS
 2              ASSIGN        2,FN1,,PH          AMOUNT OF GASOLINE NEEDED
 3              SELECT MIN    1PH,1,5,,Q         FIND SHORTEST QUEUE
 4              QUEUE         PH1                JOIN QUEUE
 5              SEIZE         PH1                GET PUMP
 6              ADVANCE       180,60             FILL UP
 7              LEAVE         PH1,PH2            REMOVE GASOLINE
 8              RELEASE       PH1                RELEASE PUMP
 9              DEPART        PH1                LEAVE STATION
10              TERMINATE     1
         *
11              GENERATE      ,,,1               CREATE 1 TRANS TO REPRESENT MANAGER
12              TRANSFER      ,FILL
13       WAIT   ADVANCE       3600               WAIT 1 HOUR
14              COUNT L       2PH,1,5,500,S      COUNT NO. OF HALF-EMPTY TANKS
15              TEST GE       PH2,2,WAIT         ARE THERE TWO OR MORE?
16       FILL   INDEX         1PH,5              INITIALIZE INDEX
17       CYCLE  TEST L        S*PH1,500,THERE    IS THIS TANK HALF-EMPTY?
18              ENTER         PH1,R*PH1          FILL THE TANK
19       THERE  LOOP          1PH,CYCLE
20              TRANSFER      ,WAIT
         *
                STORAGE       S1-S5,1000         SET CAPACITIES OF ALL TANKS
         *
         1      FUNCTION      RN1,C2             USED TO PICK AMOUNT OF GASOLINE NEEDED
         0,1/1,17
         *
                START         1000
```

RELATIVE CLOCK   50124   ABSOLUTE CLOCK   50124
BLOCK COUNTS

BLOCK	CURRENT	TOTAL	BLOCK	CURRENT	TOTAL
1	0	1004	11	0	1
2	0	1004	12	0	1
3	0	1004	13	1	14
4	0	1004	14	0	13
5	0	1004	15	0	13
6	4	1004	16	0	5
7	0	1000	17	0	25
8	0	1000	18	0	16
9	0	1000	19	0	25
10	0	1000	20	0	5

****
*   *
*   FACILITIES   *
*   *
****

FACILITY	NUMBER ENTRIES	AVERAGE TIME/TRAN	AVERAGE UTIL. DURING- TOTAL TIME	AVAIL TIME	UNAVAIL TIME	CURRENT STATUS	PERCENT AVAILABILITY	TRANS SEIZE	NUMBER PREEMPT
1	250	177.871	.887	.887	.000	A	100.0	5	
2	235	179.944	.843	.843	.000	A	100.0	8	
3	215	177.041	.759	.759	.000	A	100.0	9	
4	188	182.085	.682	.682	.000	A	100.0		
5	116	180.913	.418	.418	.000	A	100.0	4	

Figure 12-8. Coding and output for filling station example.

```
*******************************************
*                                          *
*                 STORAGES                 *
*                                          *
*******************************************
```

					AVER	UTIL DURING				CONTENT
STORAGE	CAPACITY	AVERAGE CONTENT	ENTRIES	AVERAGE TIME/UNIT	TOTL TIME	AVAL TIME	UNAVL TIME	CURRENT STATUS	PCNT AVAIL	CURR MAX
1	1000	705.006	2883	12257.281	.705	.705	.000	A	100.0	689 1000
2	1000	730.356	2778	13177.964	.730	.730	.000	A	100.0	738 1000
3	1000	688.270	2020	17078.656	.688	.688	.000	A	100.0	223 1000
4	1000	697.472	2365	14782.289	.697	.697	.000	A	100.0	816 1000
5	1000	771.755	1587	24375.218	.771	.771	.000	A	100.0	624 1000

```
*******************************************
*                                          *
*                  QUEUES                  *
*                                          *
*******************************************
```

QUEUE	MAXIMUM CONTENT	AVERAGE CONTENT	TOTAL ENTRIES	ZERO ENTRIES	PERCENT ZEROS	AVERAGE TIME/TRAN	$AVERAGE TIME/TRAN	TABLE NUMBER	CURRENT CONTENT
1	2	.929	250		.0	186.315	186.315		1
2	2	.850	235		.0	181.310	181.310		1
3	1	.759	215		.0	177.041	177.041		1
4	1	.682	188		.0	182.085	182.085		
5	1	.418	116		.0	180.913	180.913		1

$AVERAGE TIME/TRANS = AVERAGE TIME/TRANS EXCLUDING ZERO ENTRIES

Figure 12-8. (continued)

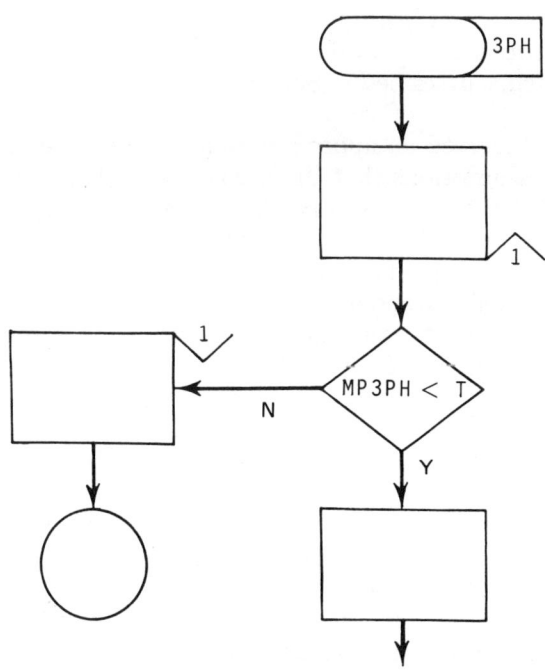

Figure 12-9. Limiting the time a transaction waits for a system change.

The transaction is marked at the block that precedes the SEIZE block so that the time the transaction first wanted the facility is recorded. Halfword parameter number 3 is being used in this example. The transaction stays in the MARK block until it can get the facility by entering the SEIZE block. At that point a check is made to see if the time the transaction waited exceeded the time limit. The check is made at a TEST block that could use a variable to compute the waiting interval, or a savevalue could be used to save the transit time before making the test. If the time limit is exceeded, the transaction is destroyed, after giving up the facility it just seized.

This simple method, however, does not detect when the time limit expired, so, if the transaction is to be diverted to some other line of action at that time, the system will not be simulated accurately. That case requires another method using chains, which will be given in Sec. 14-6. The present method will also give false statistics on waiting times because some transactions will stay in the queue longer than they should. That fault is also corrected by the method of Sec. 14-6.

Exercises

12-1 Parts are being produced at the rate of one every 50 minutes. They are processed for a time of 40 ± 35 minutes and packed 20 to a box. Simulate the system, assuming that it takes no time to pack the boxes. Arrange for a separate transaction to represent each box, apart from transactions representing the parts.(Compare with the model of Fig. 5-6, which is described in Sec. 5-12.)

12-2 Section 7-7 discussed an approximation for the time to move a disk arm on the assumptions that the access is equally likely to be to any track and that the arm starts from the track it last read. The time is approximated by a normal distribution truncated so that it cannot be less than a given quantity. Assume the normal distribution to have a mean of 25 and a standard deviation of 10. Show how to program an ADVANCE block for the access time when the minimum value of the time is 11 time units.

12-3 Pieces of metal that are sprayed with paint are to be dried in an oven. The oven has room for 10 parts and it takes 15 minutes for a part to dry. Parts are sprayed at the rate of one every 4 ± 3 minutes. If there is room in the oven, parts are placed in the oven immediately; otherwise, they wait for space to become available. However, the parts are not automatically taken out at the end of 15 minutes. Instead, an operator checks the oven every 5 minutes and removes any parts that are finished at that time. Simulate the operation of the process for 8 hours.

12-4 As part of a study of the time taken by ambulances to respond to emergency calls, a simulation model is to calculate the distance to be covered and derive the response time on the assumption of an average speed of 45 mph (66 ft/sec). The streets serviced form a rectangular grid of 10 avenues crossed by 100 streets. The length of a block along the avenues is 1000 feet and along the streets is 200 feet. Assume that when an emergency call is made the ambulance that responds is randomly located at any intersection with equal probability being given to each intersection. The calls are made from any intersection randomly selected in the same manner. Simulate the dispatching of 1000 calls, and tabulate the time to respond.

12-5 Two programming groups are generating jobs for a single computer at the rate of one job every 5 ± 3 minutes for each group. For the first hour, and thereafter for every other hour, group A has priority over group B. For the other hours, both groups are given the same priority. The priority of a job is assigned as soon as it arrives at the computer center and is not subsequently changed. Assume that jobs from both groups take 4 ± 3 minutes to run and that there is no delay between jobs when jobs are waiting. Simulate 10 hours of operation, and measure the difference in the response time for the two groups.

12-6 There are 10 people in an office, each with a telephone. They call each other at a rate that results in a call being generated somewhere in the office every 2 ± 1 minutes. A new call is equally likely to come from anybody not already busy and it is equally likely to go to anybody, irrespective of whether he is busy or not. If the person being called, however, is busy, the call is immediately abandoned. Assume that calls last 12 ± 10 minutes, and simulate for 1000 completed calls, counting the number of calls abandoned because the called party was busy. (Note that there cannot be more than 5 calls simultaneously in progress. Stop generating new calls while this condition exists.)

12-7 A reservoir with a capacity for 50,000 gallons receives water from rainfalls that occur at intervals that are exponentially distributed with a mean of 5 days. The amount of rain accumulating from a rainfall is normally distributed with a mean of 25,000 and a standard deviation of 5000 gallons. Should the reservoir become full, the excess water will overflow to waste. The amount of water drawn from the reservoir each day is also normally distributed with a mean of 4000 and a standard deviation of 500 gallons. Assume that the reservoir initially holds 40,000 gallons, and simulate the system for 100 days. Simulate to the nearest day and arrange to withdraw a day's demand before adding any rainfall collection. Although it is unlikely to happen, arrange that, if there is not enough water to fill the demand for a day, the reservoir is emptied.

12-8 If a random variable is sampled N times, the range is defined as the difference between the maximum and minimum values that occur in the sample. The standard deviation of the range is a measure that is used in the application of statistical control techniques. Assume the variable to be normally distributed, and tabulate the standard deviation of the range for $N = 2, 3, \ldots, 10$. Use a normal distribution with a mean of zero and standard deviation of 1000, and tabulate the SNA called TDj (see Appendix 5). For each value of N, use 500 repetitions to estimate the standard deviation [see E. L. Grant, *Statistical Quality Control* (3rd Ed.), McGraw-Hill Book Company, New York, 1964, p. 561].

12-9 Telephone traffic between two cities can go by one of many routes. Each route consists of from one to three successive segments, each of which has 50 circuits. Orders are issued for groups of N circuits between the cities. A simulation study is planned to estimate the probabilities of orders being filled to a given level. The simulation is to generate 1000 orders and take each through the process of attempting to assign circuits but without actually taking the circuits. A route is selected at random and it can have one, two, or three segments with probabilities 0.5, 0.3, and 0.2, respectively. Any segment can have from 1 to 50 free circuits and the order is for 1 to 20 circuits. In both cases the distribution is uniform. If any segment of the route does not have enough free circuits to satisfy the order, the minimum number available from any segment of that route is taken and the rest of the order goes unfilled. Simulate the attempts to fill 1000 orders and count, in a matrix, the number of times an order for N circuits would have found C circuits ($C = 0, 1, \ldots, N$). Include an extra row and column in which to accumulate the row and column totals and a grand total.

12-10 An office is reached by five consecutively numbered telephones. Incoming calls arrive at the rate of one every 100 seconds with an exponentially distributed interarrival time. Calls last for a time of 25 ± 15 seconds. Each call is made by way of the lowest numbered line that is available at the time the call is placed. If all lines are busy, the call is abandoned. Use a facility to represent each line and simulate the completion of 100 calls (not including the abandoned calls). Arrange to sample the system every 500 seconds to tabulate the number of calls in progress.

13

SYNCHRONIZATION OF EVENTS

In this and the next chapter we discuss three ways in which sets of transactions can be processed. We look first at *assembly sets*, which are sets of transactions created by making a number of copies from a single original transaction. The next chapter discusses groups and chains of transactions, which are two ways of forming sets from transactions that already exist in the block diagram.

The main point of generating assembly sets is to model systems where there are entities that can be processed independently. But, at certain points, two or more of the entities must either be brought together or synchronized; that is, one or more entities must reach a certain stage in the processing before others are allowed to proceed. A typical example is the operation of assembly lines where the components of a product can be manufactured independently, but they must be available, in given numbers, at specific points for assembly.

The SPLIT, MATCH, ASSEMBLE, and GATHER block types, described in this chapter, are concerned with assembly sets. Their block diagram symbols are shown in Fig. 13-1.

13-1
Assembly Sets

Every transaction created at a GENERATE block forms an assembly set, initially of only that one member. New members are created when the

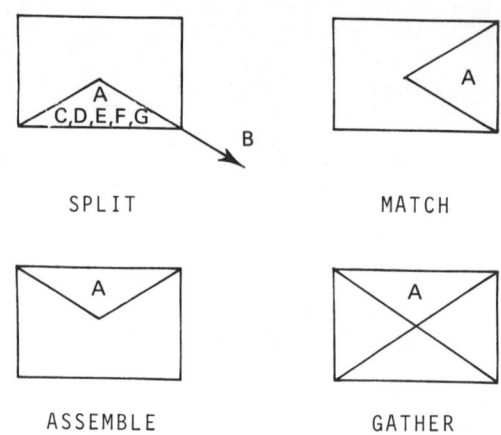

Figure 13-1. Block types 8.

transaction enters a SPLIT block and generates one or more copies that become members of the same assembly set. Any of the copies, or the original transaction, can enter a SPLIT block and create more copies that also become members of the assembly set. The process can be continued indefinitely. Every transaction is therefore a member of one and only one assembly set. There is no specific limit on how many assembly sets can exist or on the number of members in any one set. The only effective limit is the upper limit on the number of transactions that can exist in the model simultaneously.

The MATCH block can synchronize the movement of two members of the same assembly set by ensuring that a pair from the set have both reached specific, and usually different, points of the block diagram before either is allowed to proceed. The GATHER and ASSEMBLE blocks arrange that a specific number of assembly set members are collected at one point. The GATHER block then allows the collection to proceed, but the ASSEMBLE block destroys all but one transaction before allowing that one to proceed.

Each transaction is given a number that is not usually apparent to the program user. The transaction numbers are used to link the members of an assembly set. If an error stop occurs or the user calls for a listing of transactions, either by using the PRINT block (to be described in Sec. 15-2) or by using the snap option of the START statement (Sec. 3-13), then the transactions are listed. A column headed "TRANS" gives the transaction number and another column, headed "ASSEM SET," gives the number of another transaction in the assembly set. That member, in turn, lists the next member, and so on. The list is closed by having the last member in the set refer to the first. In fact, there is no identifiable first and last member; beginning with any member, the trail of numbers identifies all members. If a transaction has not arisen from a SPLIT block or itself caused copies to be created at a SPLIT block, it is the sole member of a set and the number in the column headed "ASSEM SET" will be its own number. Figure 13-2 is an example of how an assembly set is listed. In this case there are four members, transaction numbers 6, 12, 21, and 32.

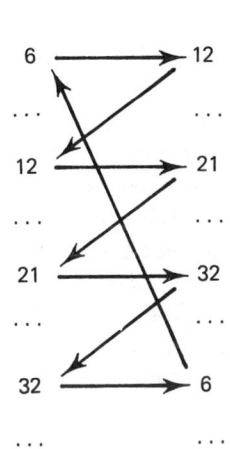

Figure 13-2. Assembly-set listing.

13-2

SPLIT Blocks

For each transaction entering a SPLIT block, the program creates as many copies as are indicated in field A, including the possibility of no copies. The SPLIT block is the only block, other than the GENERATE block, that can create transactions.

The original transaction to enter the block goes to the next sequential block. The copies go to the location indicated in field B. For example, consider the following blocks:

```
            SPLIT     XH$COUNT,AAA
    BBB     ADVANCE
              . . .
    AAA     ADVANCE
```

When a transaction enters the SPLIT block, a number of copies equal to the current value of the halfword savevalue called COUNT will be sent to AAA; the original will go to BBB. If the savevalue happened to have the value 5, there will be a total of six transactions after the entry to the SPLIT block: five at AAA and one at BBB. The location AAA can be the same as BBB. Otherwise, it is not necessary to name the location following the SPLIT block, as has been done here.

All copies are created as soon as the block is entered. Both the total block count, Nj, and the current block count, Wj, are incremented by 1 for the original and for each copy. The current count is decremented by 1 as each transaction leaves the block. The value of field B is computed separately as each copy leaves, so it is possible to use an SNA in field B to control the destinations of the individual copies.

If field C is used, it gives the number and type of a parameter that will be used to give serial numbers to both the original transaction and the copies. If that parameter of the original transaction contained X (which is usually zero) at the time of entering the block, that parameter will contain $X + 1$ when the original has been processed, and the copies will contain $X + 2$, $X + 3$, and so on. This provides a simple way of distributing the copies by sending them to a TRANSFER block in a function mode (see Sec. 9-10). An example will be shown in Sec. 13-7. The notation needed in this field is kPx, where the type may not be floating-point.

The mark time and the priority of the original transaction are given to the copies. Their values may become different in the course of subsequent processing. If no fields beyond C are used, the copies have the same number of parameters of all types as the original, and the values are set to be the same as the parameters of the original. Fields D, E, F, and G may be used to specify the number of parameters of each type the copies are to have. The method for specifying the numbers is exactly the same as that used at a GENERATE block (see Sec. 4-2). If the number of parameters is reduced, those that remain are still set to the value of the corresponding parameters of the original. If the number of parameters is increased, the extra parameters are set to zero.

If the original transaction has seized or preempted a facility, it remains in control of the facility, and it alone may give up the control. A copy that subsequently gets control of a facility is the sole transaction that has control.

As the copies are created, they become the last members of their priority class. They will be processed in the same instant at which they were created, after the program has finished processing the original transaction and any other transactions in the same priority class that are ahead of the copies. If, for any reason, it is desirable to reverse the order of processing the copies and the original, the method described in Sec. 6-8 can be used.

13-3

MATCH Blocks

MATCH blocks serve to synchronize the movement of pairs of transactions that belong to the same assembly set. They usually operate in pairs, referred to as *conjugates*. However, a MATCH block can be its own conjugate, in which case it operates like a GATHER block with a count of two (see Sec.

13-5). Field A is the only field used by the MATCH block. It gives the name, or number, of the conjugate block, each block of the conjugate pair cross-referring to the other. In block diagrams, the relationship between the two conjugate blocks is sometimes indicated by joining them with a dotted line.

The purpose of the block is to delay the first transaction that arrives at either of the conjugate blocks until another member of the same assembly set arrives at the other conjugate. When this condition is met, both transactions can proceed. A transaction waiting for the matching condition is placed on the match chain and temporarily removed from the current events chain (see Appendix 6). While on the chain, the transaction remains at the MATCH block, and both the total and current block counts of that block are incremented by 1.

The action of the block is therefore different for the early- and late-arriving transactions. When a transaction enters a MATCH block, the program searches the assembly set of the transaction to see whether another member of the same set is on the match chain, waiting at the conjugate block. If not, the transaction that just arrived is the early one, and the program places it on the match chain to await the arrival of an appropriate transaction at the conjugate block.

If the transaction arriving at a MATCH block is the late arrival, then, upon searching the assembly set, the program will find another member of the same assembly set waiting at the conjugate block. The program will update the total and current block counts for the new arrival and reactivate the transaction at the conjugate block by transferring it from the match chain to the current events chain, where it becomes the last member of its priority class.

The program then continues processing the late arrival until that transaction cannot move farther at the current clock time. The status change flag will have been reset by the return from the match chain (see Appendix 6), so the program will recommence the scan of the current events chain. The transaction that was reactivated will therefore be processed at the same clock time, although it is possible that other, higher priority, transactions will be processed first. If it is important that the reactivated transaction be processed ahead of the reactivating transaction, the method described in Sec. 6-8 should be used.

Once two transactions have been matched, they play no further part in the action of the MATCH blocks, even if either or both become blocked and are unable to leave their MATCH block. The same pair of conjugate blocks can therefore repeatedly match different pairs from the same assembly set and may concurrently be operating with any number of different assembly sets. (If after leaving a MATCH block, a transaction reenters the block or its conjugate, that is a separate event which starts a new matching process.)

If a transaction is preempted on a facility while it is in a matching condition, it will not be returned to the current events chain until both the matching condition is met and the preemption is removed.

13-4

Simulation of Wait Operation of Control Programs

A typical use of MATCH blocks is in the simulation of computer operating systems that control real-time events. When a computer program wants to read or write a record from, say, a disk file, access to the file is usually under the control of an operating system.

Typically, the time to get the record could be 30 milliseconds, if the channel giving access to the item of data is available. If it is not, the time can be increased by the need for one or more disk rotations, each adding about 15 milliseconds (see Sec. 7-7). Since a computer might be capable of executing several hundred instructions per millisecond, it would be extremely inefficient to hold up the computer while waiting for a data access. Control programs are designed to suspend the programming task calling for the data and to assign the computer to some other task during the wait. When the item of data is finally reached, it is read in by the control program, and the suspended task is reactivated. It may have to wait further for the computer to finish the task on which it was engaged at the time the data arrived, and it may have to wait for the completion of other tasks that have higher priority or have been waiting longer.

Figure 13-3 illustrates how the control program action can be simulated. The computer processing unit is represented by a facility called CPU. It is seized by the transaction representing the current, active task. When the model is to simulate the execution of a read or write operation, the transaction goes to a SPLIT block creating a single copy. The copy goes to a segment of blocks representing the access to the data, which is not shown in Fig. 13-3, but the model of Fig. 7-9 is a typical example.

The original transaction, which controls the facility CPU, goes to a RELEASE block to give up the facility, and then goes to a MATCH block, here called WAIT1. The programming task has then entered the wait state and is no longer active. Some other transaction, representing a task that has been waiting for the computer to become available, can take over control.

Eventually, the copy transaction will have completed the access to the data and will arrive at the MATCH block called WAIT2. Both transactions can then advance from their MATCH blocks. Usually, the copy transaction will be terminated, while the original will contend for the facility CPU to continue its processing task.

13-5

GATHER Blocks

GATHER blocks are used to collect a number of members of the same assembly set before allowing them all to proceed. The number to be gathered

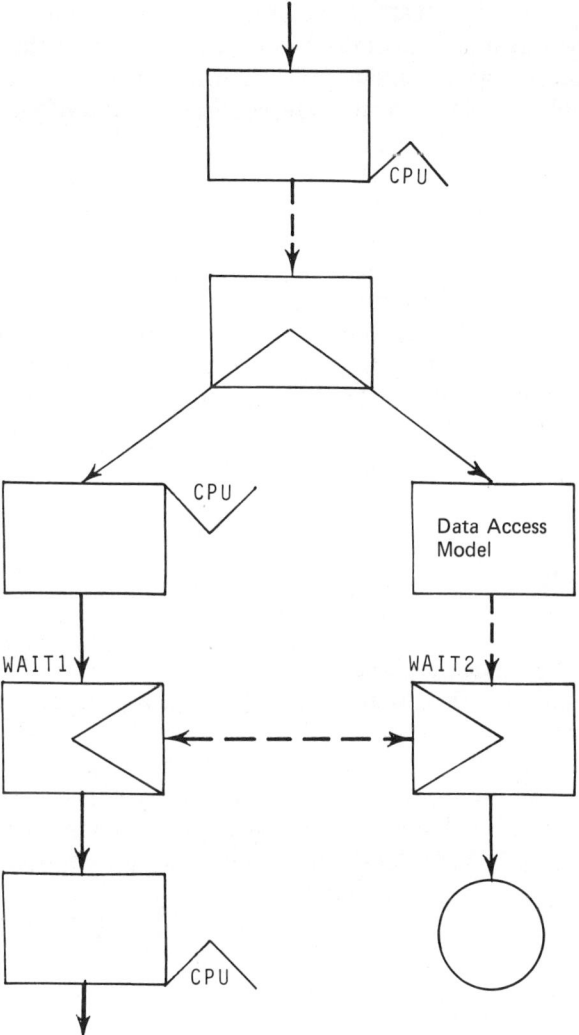

Figure 13-3. Simulation of a wait operation.

is indicated in field A, which is the only field used by the block. A zero or negative value for field A will cause an error stop.

The first transaction of an assembly set to arrive at a GATHER block initiates a counter for that assembly set and is then placed on the match chain. Subsequent arrivals of the same assembly set decrement the counter by 1 and also join the match chain. When an arrival brings the counter to zero, that last transaction is also placed on the match chain, and the program proceeds to return the completed set to the current events chain.

As transactions rejoin the current events chain, they do so in the order in which they arrived on the match chain, and they become the last members of their priority class. The scan of the current events chain is recommenced so that all the reactivated transactions will be processed at the clock instant in which the count was completed. The transactions attempt to go to the next sequential block. If they cannot leave, they do not affect the gathering of another group at the same GATHER block, either of the same assembly set or of any other assembly set. The total and current block counts are affected by each individual transaction entering and leaving a GATHER block.

Should any transaction be preempted on a facility it controls while at a GATHER block, it will not return to the current events chain until both the gather count is complete and the preemption is removed. This does not, however, stop the other members of the assembly set moving.

An error stop will occur if a transaction entering a GATHER block is the only member of its assembly set.

13-6
ASSEMBLE Blocks

The ASSEMBLE block operates in the same way as a GATHER block except that all but the first transaction of the group of transactions being assembled is destroyed upon arrival. The first arrival is placed on the match chain; subsequent arrivals are destroyed. The first arrival returns to the current chain when the count is complete. Only the initial transaction affects the total and current block counts. The ASSEMBLE block is the only block, other than the TERMINATE block, that can destroy transactions.

13-7
Furniture Factory Example

As an example, consider a small factory that makes armchairs. Because of the variations in wood finish and upholstery, the armchairs are not kept in stock but are made to order. Manufacturing is carried out by three separate departments making the frames, the cushions, and the cushion covers. There are two cushions and two cushion covers to each chair. Each department can begin work on an order independently, once a shop order has been issued.

After manufacture of the parts, the cushions must be covered, and the frame and its cushions must be brought together for assembly and packing. The packing, however, does not start until a shipping order, prepared by the accounting department, has been received.

The times required for the various operations are as follows:

Operation	Time (min.)
Interarrival time of customer orders	60 ± 45
Make a frame	60 ± 15
Make a cushion	45 ± 15
Make a cover	30 ± 15
Inspect covered cushions	15
Assemble and finish chairs	45 ± 15
Prepare a shipping order	120 ± 45

Figure 13-4 is a block diagram of the model. A time unit of 15 minutes is used. A GENERATE block creates transactions representing customers' orders. They go to a SPLIT block that produces five copies of the original, so that there is a total of six transactions for each order. The original transaction goes to the accounting department. The copies represent the shop orders for the frame, two cushions, and two covers. Halfword parameter 1, which is initially zero for the original transaction, is used to carry a sequence number, 1 through 6, by using the C field to carry 1PH. Field D of the SPLIT block is not used, so the copies have the same number of transactions as the original, which, since fields F through I of the GENERATE block were not used, means that they have 12 halfword parameters—the same as the original transaction.

The copies go to a TRANSFER block in a function mode. The function is in the list mode, using halfword parameter number 1 as input, and having the locations to which the various copies should go, as arguments. The pair of transactions that represent the cushions go to the same ADVANCE block and, for the sake of simplicity, they are shown as being processed simultaneously. The pair of covers is treated in a similar manner.

The original transaction goes to the next sequential location, which has been called PAPER, so that the function to be used for transferring the copies can have its definition completed. If it were not convenient to continue the processing of the original transaction at the next sequential block, all transactions could be sent to the TRANSFER block in a function mode for dispersal.

Following the splitting of the original transaction and the transfer of the copies, four ADVANCE blocks represent activities of the different departments, performed independently of each other. The transactions that represent the cushions and the covers pass to a GATHER block arranged to receive four copies. When all four have arrived, they all pass to an ADVANCE block with a time of 1 to represent inspection (here carried out simultaneously on each item). They then pass to an ASSEMBLE block arranged to

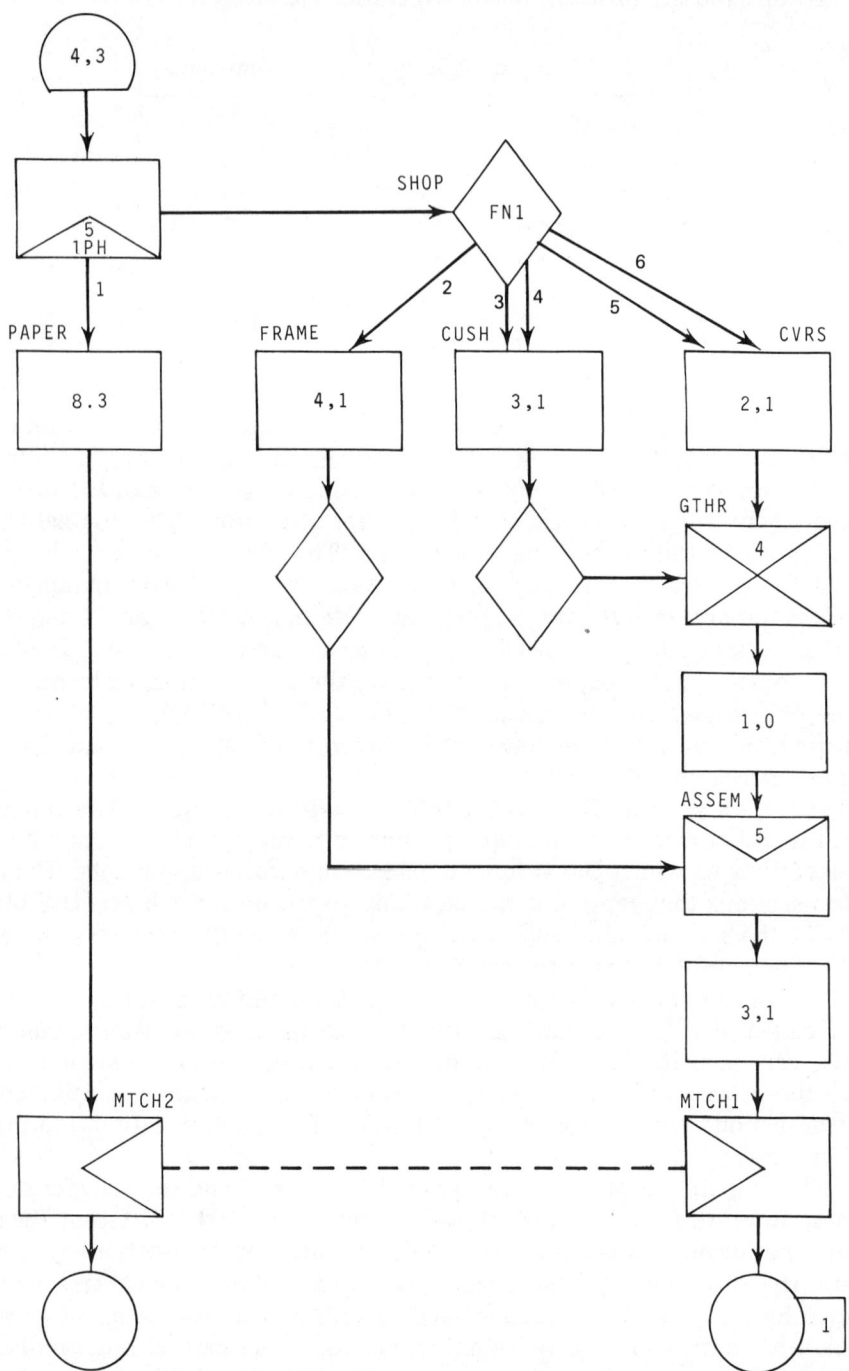

Figure 13-4. Furniture factory model.

process five members of the same assembly set. The transaction representing the frame also comes to this block.

When five transactions from the same assembly set arrive at the ASSEMBLE block, the parts for one chair have been completed, and assembly begins. Four copies are destroyed, and one copy, representing the assembled chair, goes to an ADVANCE block to expend the assembly time. The finished chair then goes to a MATCH block and, if necessary, waits for the transaction at the conjugate MATCH block which represents the shipping order from the accounting department. Following a match, both transactions proceed independently. Both transactions could have been gathered or assembled, but, in a larger model, the two transactions would need to follow different routes. Figure 13-5 is a listing of the problem and the results of a run.

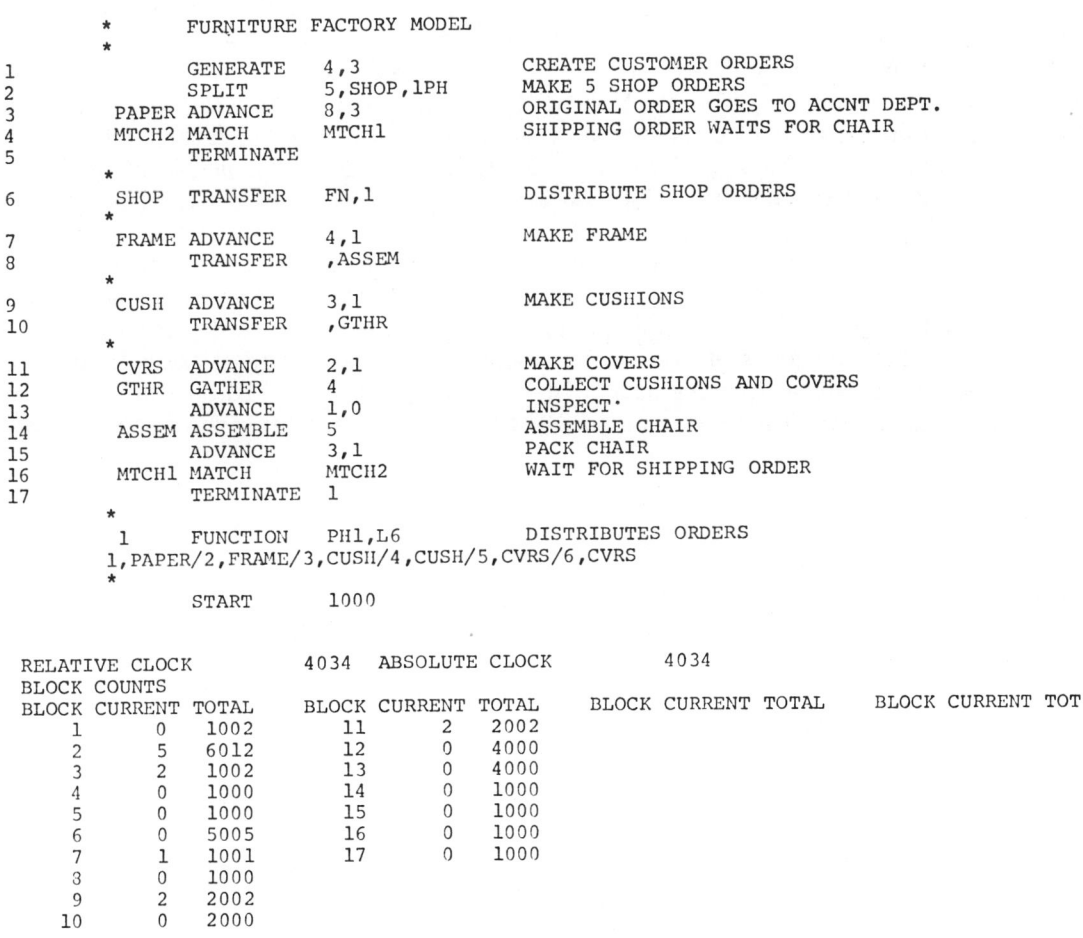

Figure 13-5. Coding and output of furniture factory example.

13-8
GATE Block in Match Mode

In Sec. 12-3 we discussed the use of GATE blocks when the tests involve the status of a logic switch, facility, or storage. There is another mode of operation in which the condition tested is whether a transaction of the same assembly set as the transaction making the test is waiting to be matched. Figure 12-1 shows the block diagram symbol for this mode of operation of the GATE block. A transaction will be in a matching condition if it has arrived at a MATCH, ASSEMBLE, or GATHER block, and is waiting on the match chain. In the case of a MATCH block there can only be one such transaction for each assembly set. In the case of the ASSEMBLE block also, there can be only one, which is the first to arrive at the block. In the case of a GATHER block there could be many waiting.

The condition to be tested can either be that there is a transaction waiting or that there is not one waiting. The first condition is denoted by the symbol M, and the second by NM. The characters indicating the choice follow the word GATE in the operation field, separated by one blank, so they begin in column 13. The location of the block which is to be tested is placed in field A. Field B can carry an alternative location to which the testing transaction will be sent if the test condition is not met. The action of the block in response to the test is the same as that described in Sec. 12-3 for the other modes.

Suppose, for example, that in the furniture factory it was decided not to start the assembly until the shipping order from the accounting department has arrived at the shipping department. Further, if the order has not arrived when the parts are ready for assembly, the parts are put aside for half an hour before checking again. The blocks shown in Fig. 13-6 could be placed immediately in front of the ADVANCE block representing the assembly time.

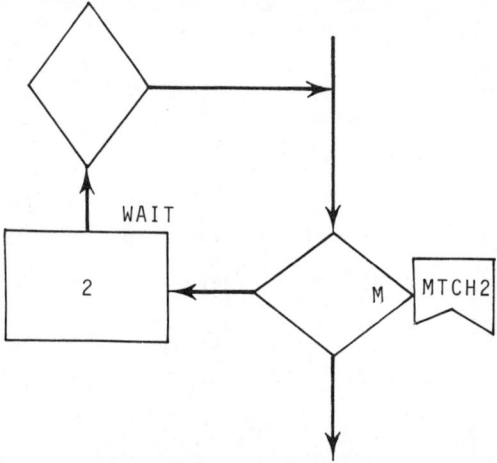

Figure 13-6. GATE block in a match mode.

The GATE block is coded as follows:

```
GATE M     MTCH2,WAIT
```

When the ASSEMBLE block releases a transaction, to represent the fact that all parts for a chair are ready for assembly, the transaction goes to the GATE block. If the transaction representing the shipping order for this chair is waiting at the MATCH block called MTCH2, the transaction representing the parts proceeds to the ADVANCE block for assembly. If not, the transaction is sent to the ADVANCE block called WAIT to wait half an hour before coming back to try again.

Transactions that are kept waiting at a GATE block in a match mode slow down the execution of the program (see Appendix 6). Keeping transactions in this condition for any length of time should be avoided.

Exercises

13-1 Family groups consisting of a mother and children arrive at a gathering where the children are to be given presents. The number of children in each family is uniformly distributed between 1 and 5, and the groups arrive with exponentially distributed intervals having a mean of 5 minutes. Upon arrival, the children proceed individually to get their presents, taking a normally distributed time with a mean of 10 and standard deviation of 2 minutes. The mothers wait outside until all their children have finished, and the families then leave. Simulate the arrival and departure of 50 families.

13-2 Customers will wait for a service for a length of time that is randomly and normally distributed with a mean of 100 and a standard deviation of 20 seconds. A choice is made for each individual. They arrive at exponentially distributed intervals with a mean of 20 seconds. The service is by a single server taking a normally distributed time that has a mean of 95 and a standard deviation of 15 seconds. Using a SPLIT and GATE block, simulate the system by assigning the time a customer is prepared to wait upon arrival and by checking whether the time has been exceeded when the customer would have reached the head of the queue. Remove the customer at that point if the limit has been exceeded. Make sure that all transactions eventually leave the system.

13-3 Two door-to-door salesmen move simultaneously down two parallel avenues that are intersected by a number of cross streets. They agree to wait for each other at each crossing before moving into the next block. The time taken by each salesman to cover a block is normally distributed with a mean of 10 and a standard deviation of 2 minutes. Simulate until both salesmen have completed 20 blocks.

13-4 Extend the previous problem by tabulating the waiting time of the salesmen at the crossings. Use a single table and ignore the order of arrival.

13-5 A party of 100 people has been taken to a football game in four buses, each of capacity 25. When the game is over, each person returns independently to the bus that brought him to the game. The time taken to reach a bus is normally distributed with mean values of 10, 12, 15, and 18 minutes for the four buses. In each case the standard deviation is 2 minutes. When a bus is full, it leaves, and arrives home after a drive that is normally distributed with a mean of 80 and a standard deviation of 5 minutes. Begin a simulation from the time the game finishes and find the time at which the last bus arrives home.

13-6 The task-dispatching algorithm of a program operating system is to be simulated in the following manner. A single transaction is created to represent each job the dispatcher is to handle. A job consists of a number of consecutive tasks. At the time a transaction is created to represent a job, a copy is also made. Dispatching consists of sending the copy to a location that should depend upon the particular task but for the purposes of this exercise, all tasks can be represented by an ADVANCE block taking 500 ± 200 milliseconds. The original transaction requires 50 milliseconds to perform the dispatching. It must then wait for completion of the dispatched task before dispatching the next task for that job, if any. New jobs arrive every 250 milliseconds. Simulate the completion of 100 jobs under the conditions that only one task in the system at a time can be dispatched but, having been dispatched, there is no limit on how many tasks can be running simultaneously. Assume the number of tasks to a job to be randomly and uniformly distributed between 1 and 5.

14

MANAGEMENT OF SETS

Transactions can be organized into sets by becoming members of user chains or by joining groups. In addition, sets of numbers can be formed into groups. Usually, these numbers will identify GPSS entities other than transactions, such as facilities or storages.

Transactions are put on a chain by entering a LINK block. They are then made inactive until they are removed from the chain by some other transaction entering an UNLINK block. In contrast, when a transaction joins a group, by entering a JOIN block, it may continue to move through the block diagram, remaining in the group until it terminates, removes itself by entering a REMOVE block, or is removed by another transaction entering a REMOVE block. The path taken by a transaction can be made to depend upon its group membership by entering the transaction into an EXAMINE block. Transactions in a group can be examined for a particular attribute by a transaction entering a SCAN block, or an attribute of group members can be changed by a transaction entering an ALTER block. The attribute concerned in the operation of the SCAN and ALTER blocks is either the value of a transaction parameter or the transaction priority. The transaction that scans or alters the group may or may not be a member of the group.

The way the program controls transactions in a group is to keep a list of transaction numbers. An option that is available for the JOIN, REMOVE, and EXAMINE blocks is to operate in a numeric mode where the list is not transaction numbers but any numeric values the user cares to nominate.

The user might, for example, want to keep a list of all facilities that are currently busy. The JOIN and REMOVE blocks operating in the numeric mode will enter and remove the numbers of busy facilities, and the EXAMINE block will check whether a particular number is in the list. The SCAN and ALTER blocks do not operate in the numeric mode.

Figure 14-1 shows the block diagram symbols for the seven block types just mentioned. They will be discussed in this chapter. Again, the "X" in the block diagram system represents control symbols.

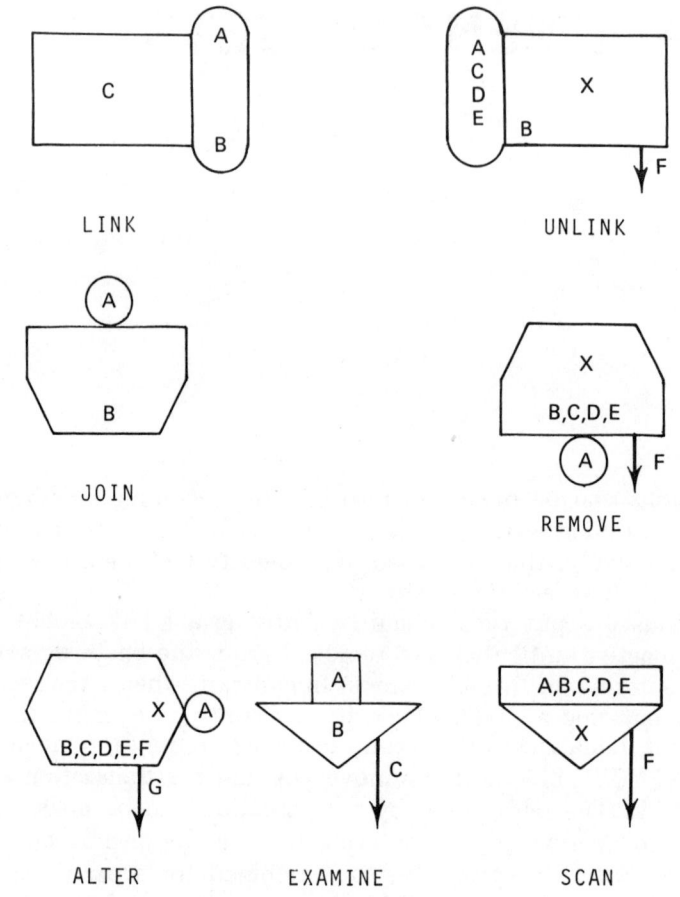

Figure 14-1. Block types 9.

14-1
User Chains

There are normally 100 user chains, but there is no limit on the number of transactions that can be on a chain. When transactions join a user chain,

282   Management of Sets / Ch. 14

they are removed from the current events chain. They do not increment the current block count SNA which, therefore, is always zero. It is not possible for a transaction to be on more than one user chain at a time.

The order in which the transactions are linked and unlinked to and from the chains can be controlled. The conditions under which transactions may be unlinked and the count of how many may be removed at any time are also user options. Consequently, user chains can be used to implement various scheduling rules or to introduce a more complex queuing discipline than simple FIFO, inherent in the way GPSS handles transactions that are delayed. A secondary use of chains is to save computing time in problems where a high proportion of the transactions will be delayed.

14-2
LINK Blocks—Without Use of Field C

Field C of the LINK block is used when the user chain is to control queues. It provides a way for the chain to schedule the unlinking of transactions for itself. Without this option, the user must make some arrangement for a transaction, not on the chain, to control the dispatching of transactions. The use of the field C option is described in Sec. 14-5. In this section we discuss the case when only fields A and B of the LINK block are used.

Transactions entering a LINK block join the user chain identified in field A. Field B determines the ordering on the chain. It offers three alternatives:

(a) The word FIFO, meaning first-in, first-out, links a transaction to the end of the chain.
(b) The word LIFO, for last-in, first-out, links a transaction to the beginning of the chain.
(c) By using kPx, where x is the parameter type indicator F, H, or B, but not L, and k is a parameter number, the transactions are placed in ascending order of the kth parameter of type x. Transactions that have the same parameter value will be kept in FIFO order within that set. There is no facility for sequencing transactions directly in descending order of parameter values. However, the BACK option of the UNLINK block, described in the next section, achieves the same effect by removing transactions in the reverse order to which they are linked.

Note that in deciding upon the order of linking transactions the priority of the transactions is ignored. A set of transactions linked in FIFO order on a user chain is not necessarily in the same order as it would be kept automatically by the program on any system chain. The user chain discipline is strictly FIFO, while the discipline the program automatically invokes is by priority and FIFO within priority class.

The block to which transactions will go when they are unlinked is specified by the UNLINK block. When drawing block diagrams, a dotted line is often used to connect the LINK block to that future destination.

14-3

UNLINK Blocks

A transaction entering an UNLINK block removes transactions from the chain identified in field A. Field B gives the location to which the unlinked transactions are to be sent, and field C gives a count of how many are to be removed. Field C may contain the word ALL, in which case all transactions that meet the conditions for being removed are unlinked. Fields A, B, and C must be specified. The rest of the fields are optional. If field D is left blank, transactions will be removed from the beginning of the chain. If field D contains the word BACK, the transactions are removed from the end of the chain.

Field D may also be used to select one of three matching modes in which certain conditions must be met before a transaction can be removed. When these options are being used, only the transactions that meet the matching condition are counted by field C. The three matching modes are as follows:

(a) *A parameter in field D but field E blank.*

If field D is used, it identifies a parameter, using the suffix notation kPx, where k is the number and x is the type. Floating-point type may not be used. With field E blank, the specified parameter of both the transaction that entered the UNLINK block and the transactions on the chain are compared. If they are equal, the linked transaction is removed.

(b) *A parameter in field D with an SNA in field E.*

Field D identifies a parameter, subject to the same notation rules given in subsection (a), and field E contains an SNA, which may be a constant. The parameter of the *linked* transaction is matched with the value of the SNA. If the match is satisfactory, the linked transaction is removed. The conditional operator by which the comparison is made is given in the operation field, separated by a blank from the word UNLINK. It can be any of the operators given in Table 12-2. If no operator is specified, an equality condition is assumed. The parameter of the linked transaction is the left-hand operand of the comparison. For example,

UNLINK GE   6,AAA,10,2PF,S5

can unlink up to 10 transactions from chain 6 and send them to location AAA. To be unlinked, a transaction must have the value of fullword parameter 2 greater than or equal to the current content of storage 5. Using field E without specifying field D will result in an error stop.

If the SNA in field E involves a parameter or uses PR, the attributes of the transaction in the UNLINK block are implied.

(c) *A Boolean variable in field D with field E blank.*

If field D contains BVj, where j is a Boolean variable number, transactions will be removed only if the Boolean variable is true. If the Boolean variable refers to parameters or uses PR, it is the values associated with the linked transaction that are used. An example will be given in the next section.

Field F is another optional field. When it is used, it contains a location. The transaction that entered the UNLINK block goes to that location if it finds the chain empty or if it finds no match when using any of the matching modes. If the transaction is successful in removing any transaction or if field F is left blank, it goes to the next sequential location.

14-4

Simulating Scheduling Rules With User Chains

To illustrate the use of chains for dispatching, suppose that a machine can operate on several part types. A series of orders for different quantities of a part type are collected, and batches of the orders are dispatched whenever the machine becomes idle. The simulation is to test various dispatching rules. Figure 14-2 shows a block diagram for the system, and Fig. 14-3 shows the results of a run.

On the right is a string of blocks processing the orders. A transaction, representing an order, is created every 60 ± 20 minutes. Parameter 1 will represent the part type, and parameter 2 will give the number of parts. Suppose that there are 5 types of parts and that there may be up to 10 parts to an order. For simplicity, assume that the part-type number and the number of parts are uniformly distributed.

The transactions go through two ASSIGN blocks to assign values randomly. The blocks use two continuous linear functions that select an integer at random from the appropriate range, using the method described previously in Sec. 9-8. The transactions then go to a LINK block, where they join chain 1 in FIFO order to await dispatching. When they are dispatched, they will go to the ADVANCE block called JOBQ to await their turn for using facility number 1, representing the machine. It is assumed that each part will take 10 time units, and variable 1 makes the action time of the ADVANCE block that represents the machining equal 10 times the number of parts, recorded in parameter 2.

The blocks to the left of Fig. 14-2 form a closed loop for a single transaction which controls the dispatching. A GENERATE block creates the trans-

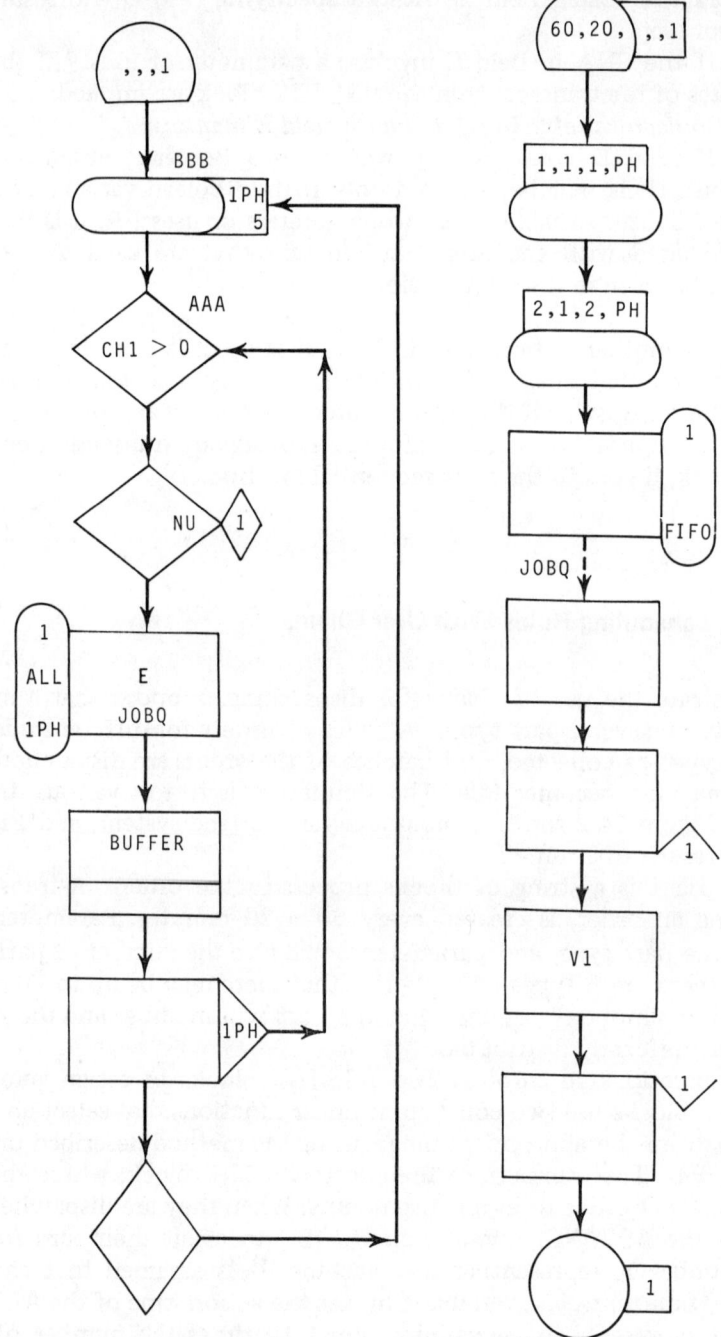

Figure 14-2. Implementing scheduling rules with user chains.

```
         *       IMPLEMENTING SCHEDULING RULES WITH USER CHAINS
         *
1                GENERATE    ,,,1              CREATE A SINGLE CONTROL TRANS.
2        BBB     INDEX       1PH,5             INITIALIZE INDEX
3        AAA     TEST G      CH1,0             ARE THERE ANY WAITING JOBS?
4                GATE NU     1                 IS MACHINE IDLE?
5                UNLINK E    1,JOBQ,ALL,1PH    DISPATCH ALL PARTS OF ONE TYPE
6                BUFFER                        WAIT TILL UNLINKED TRANS. MOVES
7                LOOP        1PH,AAA
8                TRANSFER    ,BBB
         *
9                GENERATE    60,20,,,1         CREATE JOBS
10               ASSIGN      1,1,1,PH          ASSIGN PART NO.
11               ASSIGN      2,1,2,PH          ASSIGN QUANTITY TO BE MADE
12               LINK        1,FIFO            WAIT FOR DISPATCHING
13       JOBQ    ADVANCE                       BUFFER
14               SEIZE       1                 GET MACHINE
15               ADVANCE     V1                MACHINE A NUMBER OF PARTS
16               RELEASE     1                 RELEASE MACHINE
17               TERMINATE   1
         *
         1       VARIABLE    10*PH2            MACHINING TIME
         *
         1       FUNCTION    RN1,C2            SELECTS PART NO.
         0,1/1,6
         *
         2       FUNCTION    RN1,C2            SELECTS NO. OF PARTS
         0,1/1,11
         *
                 START       1000
```

RELATIVE CLOCK   60227   ABSOLUTE CLOCK   60227
BLOCK COUNTS

BLOCK	CURRENT	TOTAL	BLOCK	CURRENT	TOTAL	BLOCK	CURRENT	TOTAL	BLOCK	CURRENT	TOTAL
1	0	1	11	0	1002						
2	0	426	12	0	1002						
3	1	2126	13	0	1000						
4	0	2125	14	0	1000						
5	0	2125	15	0	1000						
6	0	2125	16	0	1000						
7	0	2125	17	0	1000						
8	0	425									
9	0	1002									
10	0	1002									

```
                    *******************************************
                    *                                         *
                    *             USER CHAINS                 *
                    *                                         *
                    *******************************************
```

USER CHAIN	TOTAL ENTRIES	AVERAGE TIME/TRANS	CURRENT CONTENTS	AVERAGE CONTENTS	MAXIMUM CONTENTS
1	1002	56.595	2	.941	5

```
                    *******************************************
                    *                                         *
                    *             FACILITIES                  *
                    *                                         *
                    *******************************************
```

FACILITY	NUMBER ENTRIES	AVERAGE TIME/TRAN	AVERAGE UTIL. TOTAL TIME	DURING-AVAIL TIME	DURING-UNAVAIL TIME	CURRENT STATUS	PERCENT AVAILABILITY	TRANS SEIZE	NUMBER PREEMPT
1	1000	54.319	.901	.901	.000	A	100.0		

Figure 14-3. Coding and output of scheduling example.

action at the beginning of the run and injects it into the loop. Whenever the machine completes one batch of orders, the dispatching transaction will go to an UNLINK block to select the next batch. A number of different dispatching rules will be discussed later. Usually they involve scanning through the part-type numbers.

The dispatching transaction first goes to an INDEX block to set halfword parameter number 1 to 5. It will cycle the inner loop of Fig. 14-2 five times and then be sent by the LOOP block, at the bottom of the inner loop, to be reinitialized for an additional five cycles. It will not start on a cycle unless there are transactions waiting to be dispatched, which is determined by a TEST block checking that CH1, the number of transactions on chain 1, is greater than zero. It then waits for any previously dispatched batch to be completed by using a GATE block to test for facility number 1 to be free. When conditions are right, it enters the UNLINK block to dispatch one or more orders.

After entering a transaction into an UNLINK block, the program will normally continue to process that transaction before turning its attention to the transactions that are unlinked. In the present case, that could lead to the dispatching transaction going around its loop endlessly, because the unlinked transactions will not have seized facility 1 before the dispatching transaction leaves the UNLINK block and tests for the next cycle. Inserting a small time delay after the UNLINK block will prevent this. Alternatively, the program must be forced to process the unlinked transactions ahead of the unlinking transaction. The method discussed previously in Sec. 6-8 can be used here.

The dispatching transaction goes to a BUFFER block so that, after unlinking transactions, the program will pause to look for higher-priority transactions before continuing with the dispatching transaction. It will be noticed that the order transactions have been created with a priority of 1. This ensures that they will be processed during the rescan before the scan returns to the dispatching transaction in the BUFFER block, which has a priority of zero. If any transactions have been unlinked, the first one will have seized the facility before the dispatching transaction moves out of the BUFFER block.

If the system should be empty of transactions, as it is initially, the dispatching transaction will stop cycling. As soon as any transaction joins the chain, so that CH1 is greater than zero, it begins cycling again.

Various scheduling rules can be implemented by the coding used for the UNLINK block. If the dispatching rule were to send a given number of orders in each batch, regardless of their type, the count would be placed in field C, and field D would be blank. For example, the following coding for the UNLINK block will dispatch four orders in each batch, regardless of type, unless there are fewer than four, in which case it dispatches all that there are:

```
UNLINK      1,JOBQ,4,FIFO
```

Fields C and D call for four transactions to be dispatched from the beginning of the chain. In this particular case, where the dispatching does not involve the part number, there is no need to index the loops: a continuous cycling of the inner loop is sufficient.

Suppose, however, that the rule is that all outstanding orders for a given part are to be dispatched and the part types are searched in the reverse sequence, 5, 4, ..., 1. The UNLINK block would then be coded as follows:

       UNLINK   1,JOBQ,ALL,1PH

Field D now refers to a parameter but field E is blank, so the first matching mode is being used, as described in Sec. 14-3(a). This is the specific case illustrated in Fig. 14-2 and given in the coding of Fig. 14-3. With this coding of the UNLINK block, the halfword parameters of the dispatching transaction and the order transactions will be compared and all linked transactions for which there is a match are dispatched.

Suppose that it is not convenient to scan the part-type numbers in reverse sequence order. In fact, the sequence needs to be freely changeable. Suppose that the desired order is placed in byte-sized savevalues numbers 5, 4, ..., 1. The dispatching transaction can use the second matching mode, described in Sec. 14-3(b). The UNLINK block is now coded as follows:

       UNLINK E   1,JOBQ,ALL,1PH,XH*PH1

The differences from the previous case are that field E now carries an SNA, and a conditional operator has been added to the operation field. The effect of the E field entry is to make the program compare parameter 1 of the linked transactions (field D) with a savevalue selected indirectly by parameter 1 of the sequencing transaction (field E). This parameter value cycles through the numbers 1 through 5 (in reverse order); the order in which the part types are sequenced is thus controlled by the contents of the five savevalues. Since an equality condition is being used in this case, it is not essential to include the operator; if no operator is given, the program assumes equality.

Finally, we illustrate the Boolean variable option of the UNLINK block, which is the third matching method. Suppose that in the previous scheduling example the completed orders are held until the customer who placed the order comes to collect them. The transactions for the completed orders would then be placed on a user chain, number 2, by a LINK block following the RELEASE block of Fig. 14-2. Transactions representing customers coming to pick up their orders would then be routed to an UNLINK block. Suppose that the order transactions carry a number representing the customer in parameter number 3. If the customer takes all his completed orders, the first or second matching modes could be used to unlink all transactions with parameter number 3 equal to the customer number. More complex conditions for picking up orders can be implemented by using the Boolean variable mode.

Suppose, for example, that the customer, number 12, say, wants to pick up part types 2 and 4 on this trip. The following Boolean variable, evaluated for an order transaction, will be true if the transaction represents an order from customer number 12 and is for part number 2 or 4.

```
1 BVARIABLE   PH3'E'12*(PH2'E'2+PH2'E'4)
```

The UNLINK block at which the customer transaction unlinks the order transactions and sends them to LOCA would then be coded:

```
       UNLINK       2,LOCA,ALL,BV1
```

14-5

LINK Blocks—Using Field C

The term *queuing discipline* refers to the way entities are selected for service when the system conditions force some entities to wait for service. It usually implies that the waiting entities form a line according to some rule and service goes next to the entity at the beginning of the line. If the queuing discipline is to be by priority, with a FIFO rule within each priority class, GPSS can implement the discipline automatically because it uses this basic rule for ordering transactions on all its chains, except the user chains. If another discipline is needed, the transactions are placed on a user chain in the order required by the discipline. They must then be dispatched, one at a time, from the beginning of the chain. Under these circumstances, field C of the LINK block provides a way in which the transactions can be scheduled for unlinking without the need of a special control loop, as used in the previous section.

Suppose that the required service is simply to use a facility. When there is a queue, the dispatching can be controlled in the way shown in Fig. 14-4. As each dispatched transaction releases the facility, it enters an UNLINK block to dispatch the first transaction on the chain. The dispatched transaction goes to ABCD to seize the facility. The UNLINK block is therefore coded as follows:

```
       UNLINK       1,ABCD,1
```

However, when there are no transactions waiting for service, some way is needed to dispatch the next arrival and so start up this dispatching process. It will be recalled that the dispatch control loop used in the previous section included the logic of detecting the first arrival after an empty period and restarting the scan.

The field C option of the LINK block provides this capability automatically. The location to which the transactions are to be dispatched is placed in this field, in addition to being in the customary B field of the UNLINK block. (The B and C fields, however, do not have to refer to the same

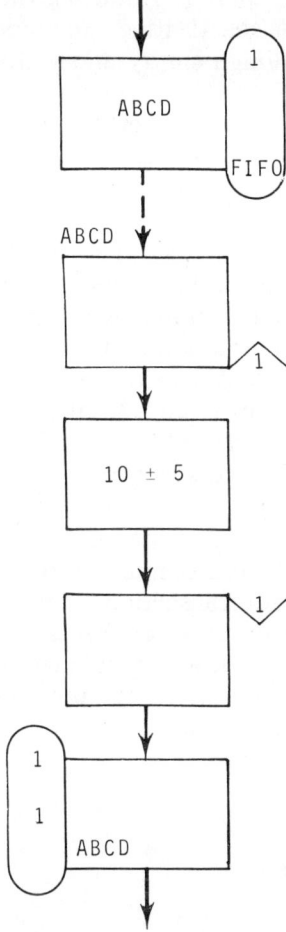

Figure 14-4. Field C option of the LINK block.

location.) If a transaction entering a LINK block finds that the chain is empty and that no transaction from the chain is currently being serviced, the program immediately sends the transaction to the location given in field C.

To control the conditions, there is an indicator associated with each chain showing whether the chain is active or inactive. Whenever there are transactions on the chain, or a transaction has been dispatched for servicing but has not yet completed the service, the chain is set to active. New arrivals will then be linked to the chain without making use of the field C option. When the program finishes processing a dispatched transaction, it tries to unlink a successor. If it finds the chain empty, it resets the chain to inactive, indicating that the system is quiescent. The next arrival on the chain, finding the chain inactive, will set the chain active and immediately transfer to the location given in field C, thereby restarting the dispatching. If another transaction arrives before this reactivating transaction finishes its service, it will find the chain active although empty and will wait to be dispatched by the transaction ahead of it.

The condition that determines whether to make the chain inactive at the time an unlinking is attempted is that the chain be empty, that is, $CHj = 0$. Suppose that the UNLINK block were to use a matching mode. If the program then finds that there is no match and yet there is some transaction on the chain, it will not make the chain inactive. The field C option, therefore, is effective only for controlling queuing disciplines where the transactions are linked in the order in which they are to be served and where service next goes to the first transaction on the chain.

Although the program will dispatch queues with FIFO discipline without the need for a user chain, there is an advantage to using a chain for this standard discipline. It ensures that only one transaction is dispatched. The way the program automatically processes transactions that are delayed, waiting for, say, a facility, is to put the waiting transactions on a delay chain. When the facility is released, all delayed transactions are reactivated. Only one will get the facility and the rest must be returned to the delay chain. When there are many delayed transactions, this can be time-consuming. Using a user chain with the field C option can save time by dispatching only one transaction at a time. Note, however, this will be exactly equivalent to the automatic dispatching carried out by the program only if all transactions have the same priority (see Sec. 14-2).

14-6

Limiting Waiting Time on Queues

When a queue forms for some kind of service, new arrivals do not always choose to join the queue, or, if they do, they may abandon the queue before getting service. The term *balking* is used to describe this behavior. New arrivals may refuse to join the queue if it exceeds a given size, or their behavior may be prescribed by a probability function that decides whether they join as a function of queue length. Balking at the time of arrival is simulated by the methods of testing system conditions that were described in Chap. 12.

When balking is caused by a time limit on waiting, other methods are needed. A version of this discipline was discussed in Sec. 12-12, where it was assumed that the balking transaction was to be destroyed. It is then possible to measure the waiting time when service is about to be offered and destroy the transaction if the time limit is exceeded. If, however, the transaction is to be diverted rather than destroyed, it must be removed from the queue at the time of balking.

The unlinking of a transaction from a chain provides the only general method of displacing a transaction from a set without examining the transactions individually. It is, in fact, possible to displace transactions with a PREEMPT or FUNAVAIL block, but then each potentially displaceable transaction must be in control of a facility on which it can be interrupted; this method is therefore practical for only a few transactions at a time.

With a chain, the method illustrated in Fig. 14-5 can be used. It is necessary to force an event to occur when the time limit expires. The transaction is therefore sent to a SPLIT block, after marking the time the transaction is to enter the queue in, say, halfword parameter number 3. The original transaction joins the chain AAA at a LINK block, while a copy goes to an ADVANCE block to expend the time the transaction is prepared to wait on the chain. The queuing discipline on the chain and the method of removing transactions from the chain when service is offered are not relevant here.

When the copy leaves the ADVANCE block, it must look for a transaction on the chain that entered at the time the copy was created. It is not possible to search a chain for another member of an assembly set. The simplest test would be to see whether a transaction on the chain matches the mark time

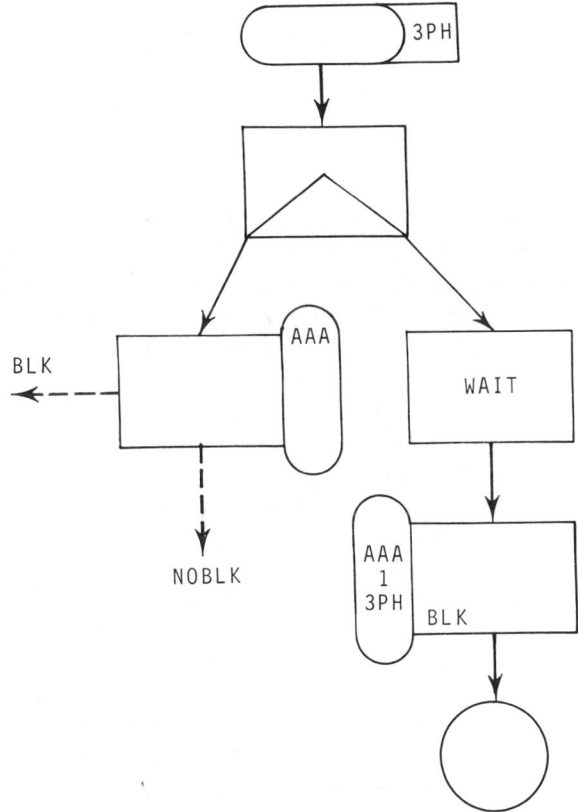

Figure 14-5. Time limit on waiting in a queue.

in 3PH. The UNLINK block would then use the first of the match modes described in Sec. 14-3 and be coded as follows:

UNLINK   AAA,BLK,1,3PH

A match will send the transaction on the chain to BLK, representing a balking transaction. If there is no match, the transaction will have left to receive service by way of NOBLK. Whichever condition occurs, the copy goes to a TERMINATE block to be destroyed.

If two transactions join the queue simultaneously and they happen to have exactly the same balking time, this method could allow a copy to unlink a transaction that is not its original. Since the assembly-set properties of the pairs of matching transactions are not being used, this presents no difficulty: all the transactions that are to balk simultaneously will be displaced at the correct clock instant. If for any reason the order in which the transactions that joined the queue simultaneously is to be maintained when they balk simultaneously, it will be necessary to use some identification on the individual transactions, unless the queuing discipline is FIFO. In that case, both the originals and the copies maintain their order of arrival.

14-7

Groups

A second way in which transactions can be organized as sets is to place them in a group. Normally there can be up to 25 groups, which can be identified by number or name. There is no limit to the number of members in a group, nor is there a limit on the number of groups that one entity can join.

There are two modes of operation. In a transaction mode the group members are transaction numbers. In a numeric mode the entries are numbers whose significance is the user's choice. A group simply provides a convenient way of keeping a list of numbers. The numbers in the group, however, are unique. An attempt to enter a number that is already in the list will cause no action. For this reason, the numeric mode is particularly useful for keeping lists of GPSS entity numbers. The user might, for example, want a list of all storages that ever reached their full capacity. A transaction that is refused entry to a storage can enter the storage number in a group. If more than one transaction is refused entry to the same storage, only the first will actually enter the number, so there is no need to check for double counting. Part of the standard output report is a list of all the numbers in the group at the time the program ended, together with a statement of which mode applied to the group. An example will be shown in Fig. 14-8.

The choice of mode is made by the first block to reference the group during the simulation run. Once made, the choice cannot be changed, and an attempt to enter the group in the other mode will cause an error stop.

Three block types that are associated with groups, JOIN, REMOVE, and EXAMINE operate in either mode. Two others, SCAN and ALTER, operate in the transaction mode only.

Unlike transactions that join a chain, the transactions that join a group are not made inactive; they continue to move freely and independently. In fact there is no direct way of knowing where a group member is located. The program merely keeps a list, in FIFO order, of the numbers of the transactions in the group. For this reason, group operations on transactions should be used sparingly because the program has to scan the transactions listed in the group.

14-8

JOIN Blocks

Field A of a JOIN block identifies a group. When operating in a transaction mode, that is the only field used. A transaction entering the block will become a member of the group. The same transaction cannot be entered in a group twice. No action is taken if the transaction is already in the group. A transaction may, however, belong to more than one group. Transactions are listed in the order in which they join the group.

When the block is to operate in a numeric mode, field B identifies the source of the number. It may contain an SNA value, and the value may be given either directly or indirectly. If that number is already in the group, no action is taken.

14-9

REMOVE Blocks

The REMOVE block takes either transactions or numbers out of a group according to whether the group has been established as being in the transaction or numeric mode. When it removes transactions, it does not change their locations or alter their status in any other way. In both modes, field A identifies the group to be examined. Both modes also have an option in which field F can contain a location. The transaction entering the REMOVE block will be sent there if it does not succeed in fully meeting the specified conditions. It will also go there if it finds the group empty or it finds no suitable transaction when it has been coded in an ALL mode. When field F is blank, the transaction goes to the next sequential location, as it always does when its action is successful.

Some, or all, of fields B through E may be used in a variety of ways to select one of several options, which differ according to whether the group is operating in a transaction or a numeric mode. Descriptions of the options follow:

(A) *Transaction Mode*

In a transaction mode there are four options, which may use fields B, D, or E. Field C is not used in this mode. The options are as follows:
(1) *Self Removal.* If fields B, D, and E are all left blank, so that only field A, and possibly F, are used, the transaction entering the REMOVE block removes itself from the group.
(2) *Count Control.* If field B is used but not D or E, the number of transactions indicated by field B are taken from the group in the order in which they were listed. If there are not enough transactions to fill the count, they are all removed. The word ALL may also be used in field B to empty the entire group.
(3) *Parameter or Priority Control.* If fields B, D, and E are all used, transactions are removed according to the value of one of their parameters or their priority. Field B contains a count of how many are to be removed, including the possibility of ALL. Field D gives the parameter of the group members to be examined. The notation kPx must be used and the type cannot be floating-point. If the attribute to be examined is the priority of the transactions in the group, field D contains the letters PR.

Field E gives an SNA to be compared with the parameter or priority. Reference to a parameter or the use of PR in the SNA implies the attributes of the transaction in the REMOVE block. A conditional operator, chosen from the list given in Table 12-2, is placed in the operation field beginning in column 15, that is, one blank from the word REMOVE. The use of the operators MAX and MIN is described in the next subsection.

When comparing parameter values or priority against the SNA in field E, exactly the same rules apply as for the UNLINK block operating in the second matching mode. (They were described in Sec. 14-3.) The parameter value is the left-hand operand: if no operator is given, equality is assumed. The following are some examples:

```
REMOVE LE   10,5,,6PB,1
REMOVE      2,ALL,,5PF,XF6,AAA
REMOVE G    4,3,,PR,1,ABCD
```

The first example removes from group 10 five transactions that have a value less than or equal to 1 in byte-sized parameter 6. If there are less than five such transactions, they will all be removed. In this example, because field F is not used, the transaction entering the REMOVE block will go to the next location whatever the outcome. The second example removes from group 2 all transactions whose fullword parameter 5 equals the value of fullword savevalue 6. Because equality is being tested, it is not necessary to put operator E in the operation field. If there are no transactions in the group with fullword parameter 5 equal to fullword savevalue 6, the transaction will go to location AAA; otherwise, it continues to the next sequential location. The last example removes, from group 4, three transactions with priority greater than 1. If the program does not find three such transactions, the transaction that entered the REMOVE block will go to location ABCD.

(4) MAX *and* MIN *Operations.* As indicated in Table 12-2, the operator used in the operation field can be MAX or MIN. In that case, the program will find the transaction that has the largest or smallest value of a parameter or priority. Field D selects the parameter to be examined, using the notation rules of the previous subsection, or it contains PR for priority. Fields B, C, and E are not used in this mode. If the maximum or minimum is attained by more than one transaction, the first one encountered will be selected. If the group is empty and field F is used, the transaction will be sent to the location given in field F. The following are examples:

```
REMOVE MAX 6,,,4PF
REMOVE MIN 7,,,V$TYPE$PH,,ABCD
```

The first example removes, from group 6, the transaction with the largest value of fullword parameter 4. The transaction entering the REMOVE block continues to the next location. In the second example, the program removes, from group 7, the transaction with the minimum value of the halfword parameter whose number is given by a variable called TYPE. In this case, the transaction entering the REMOVE block will go to location ABCD if the group happens to be empty.

(B) *Numeric Mode*

The REMOVE block, operating on a group in the numeric mode, uses fields A and C, and possibly F. The group specified in the field A is searched for the numeric value indicated by field C. If that number is found, it is removed from the group. If it is not in the group, the transaction goes to the location in field F, if one is specified. Otherwise, it goes to the next sequential location. For example,

```
REMOVE     3,,V6,,,ABCD
```

Variable 6 will be evaluated and group 3 will be searched to see if this number is in the group. If so, the number is removed and the transaction goes to the next sequential location. If not, the transaction goes to ABCD.

14-10
EXAMINE Blocks

An EXAMINE block selects the path of a transaction, depending upon a group membership. It can operate on groups in either a transaction or numeric mode. In both modes, field A gives the group number to be examined and field C gives the location to which the transaction will go if the membership condition is not met. The transaction goes to the next sequential location if the condition is met.

If the group being searched consists of transactions, only fields A and C are used. The condition to be met is that the transaction is itself a member of the group. If the group is in a numeric mode, field B must also be specified. The condition to be met is that the value given by field B must be a member of the group.

14-11
SCAN Blocks

The SCAN block operates only on groups of transactions. It allows a transaction, not necessarily in the group, to scan a group for the first transaction that has a parameter value or a priority, meeting a given condition. Having located such a group member, the program can extract the value of any parameter or the priority of that member. Either type of information can be extracted, regardless of the scanning criterion, and, if a parameter value is extracted, it does not have to be the same parameter as was used to conduct the scan: it does not even have to be of the same type. Whichever type of information is extracted, the value is placed in one of the parameters of the transaction that entered the SCAN block.

Field A must be given to identify the group to be searched, and field B must have either the parameter number to be searched or the letters PR for priority. The notation kPx must be used, and the parameter cannot be a floating-point type. The SNA to be compared with the transaction attribute is placed in field C. Reference to a parameter or to PR in the SNA implies the attributes of the transaction in the SCAN block. The operator to be used follows the word SCAN in the operations field, beginning in column 13. The rules for the comparison are the ones previously given in Sec. 14-3. The operators MAX or MIN can be used, in which case field C is left blank.

Fields D and E, which go together, are optional. If they are left blank, the program checks only whether a transaction with the indicated attribute value exists in the group. When D and E are used, they result in the extraction of an attribute from the identified transaction. Field D gives a parameter number or the letters PR specifying the item of data to be extracted. Field E gives the parameter number of the scanning transaction that is to receive the extracted value. Both fields use the notation kPx, but the type may not be floating-point. Field F is optional, and it indicates an alternative exit to which the transaction entering the SCAN block will be sent if no transaction meeting the condition is found. If field F is not used, the transaction goes to the next sequential block, as it does if the scan condition is met. The following are some examples:

```
         SCAN E      10,6PB,V2,,,ABCD
         SCAN GE     5,PR,4,,,ABCD
         SCAN L      2,7PH,FN6,5PB,1PH,ABCD
         SCAN G      4,PR,7,5PB,1PH,ABCD
         SCAN MAX    3,2PH,,PR,1PF,ABCD
```

The first example scans group 10 to see if there is a transaction whose byte-sized parameter 6 is equal to the value of variable 2. If there is, the transaction that entered the SCAN block goes to the next sequential location; if not, it goes to ABCD. In this example, it is not essential to include the operator E; a blank in column 13 will default to E. The second example searches group 5 for a transaction whose priority is greater than or equal to 4. The scanning transaction continues to the next sequential location if there is a match, and goes to ABCD if there is not. The third example scans group 2 for a transaction with the seventh halfword parameter less than the value of function 6. If there is such a transaction, the value of its fifth byte-sized parameter is placed in halfword parameter 1 of the transaction that entered the SCAN block. The next example is similar. It checks group 4, looking for a transaction whose priority is greater than 7. It also puts the value of the fifth byte-sized parameter in halfword parameter 1. The last example searches group 3 to find the transaction that has the greatest value of halfword parameter 2 and puts the priority of that transaction in fullword parameter 1. In the last three examples, the scanning transaction goes to the next location if a match is found and to location ABCD if it is not. In the last example, failure to find a maximum means that the group is empty.

14-12

ALTER Blocks

The ALTER block, like the SCAN block, operates only on groups of transactions. It will change the value of a parameter or the priority of a given number of members in the group. Field A identifies the group, and field B gives a count of how many members are to be changed. Field B may also contain ALL to change all members. The identity of the parameter to be changed is placed in field C, using the notation kPx, or, if the priority is to be changed, field C contains PR. The new value the parameter or priority is to take is given in field D. The parameter being altered may not be in floating-point form.

All fields A through D must be given (with the one exception mentioned below). Fields E and F are optional. If they are omitted, the program searches all members of the group. If fields E and F are used, they select which transactions are to be searched. Field E contains a parameter number (or the letters PR) indicating which attribute of the group members is to determine whether they are included in the search. The parameter or priority is compared with the SNA given in field F, using a conditional operator given in the operation field, beginning in column 14. The rules given in Sec. 14-3 are used in the comparison. If the SNA in field F involves a parameter or PR, it is the attribute of the transaction in the SCAN block that is used. Only those transactions that meet the condition affect the count in field B. It is permissible to use the operators MIN or MAX, in which case fields B and F are not used.

Field G is an alternative exit option. When it is used, it gives a location to which the transaction entering the ALTER block will be sent if it finds no transaction to alter. If it is not used, the transaction goes to the next sequential location, as it always does when it is successful. The following are examples:

```
ALTER      6,ALL,PR,2
ALTER      5,12,4PB,V6,,ABCD
ALTER GE   4,ALL,3PF,5,1PB,XF6,ABCD
ALTER MAX  4,,PR,5,1PH
```

The first example changes the priority of all members of group 6 to the value 2. The second example changes the value of byte-sized parameter 4 of the first 12 transactions of group 5 to the value given by variable number 6. If there are fewer than twelve, all are changed. The transaction entering the ALTER block proceeds to the next location, unless the group is empty, in which case it goes to ABCD. The third example searches group 4 for transactions whose byte-sized parameter number 1 equals the value of fullword savevalue 6. The third fullword parameter of all such transactions is changed to 5. If no such transactions are found, the transaction entering the ALTER block goes to ABCD, even though the group may not be empty. The last example changes, to the value 5, the priority of the transaction in group 4 which has the maximum value of halfword parameter 1.

14-13

Allocation of Manpower Example

To illustrate the use of groups, consider the following example. A company that leases equipment employs 16 servicemen and has 20 customers. Calls for service arrive at the rate of about 4 a day. It takes about 2 days to complete service and about 1 day to travel between the customer premises and the company offices.

Once a day, the office manager looks at the accumulation of service requests, and allocates his manpower accordingly. If he finds that a man has already been assigned to a customer, the manager tells the man to stay with the customer for the new call. Otherwise, he assigns any man who is free and waiting in the office. If there is nobody in the office, he assigns one of the men traveling back to the office. As soon as that man arrives at the office, he immediately leaves for the new call. If all men are assigned, the manager leaves the request for the next day.

Each serviceman will be represented by one transaction, and parameter 1 of the transaction will carry the number of the customer to whom he is assigned. Normally, a serviceman is in one of three states. A group will be defined for each state and, as the serviceman goes from one state to another, the transaction will change groups. The group definitions are as follows: Group 1, waiting at the office for assignment; Group 2, assigned to a customer; and Group 3, traveling back to the office. While waiting in the office, the transactions will also be placed on chain 1.

A matrix, number 1, of 20 rows and 2 columns will be used to count the customer calls. Column 1 will carry the number of calls awaiting the assignment of a serviceman. Column 2 will carry the current number of calls already given to a serviceman assigned to a customer, but not yet completed.

The block diagrams of Figs. 14-6 and 14-7 represent the system. Figure 14-6 shows, on the left, a string of three blocks that will create the customer calls. A time unit of 1 hour, and an 8-hour day will be used. For the sake of simplicity, the interspersion of nights between the days will be ignored. Calls arrive at the rate of about 4 a day, so a GENERATE block is used to create a transaction representing a call every 2 ± 1 hour. The transaction goes to an MSAVEVALUE block where it increments column 1 of one of the matrix rows picked at random. It then goes to a TERMINATE block that will count the number of calls and stop the simulation on the count.

The closed loop of blocks in Fig. 14-6 represents the movement of the servicemen. A GENERATE block injects 16 transactions of priority level 1 into the loop. The transactions immediately join group 1 to represent the fact that they are waiting at the office, and they are then linked to chain 1 to await assignment. When they are assigned, they go to the REMOVE block called ASSD, which takes them out of group 1. The following JOIN block puts them in group 2 to indicate that they have been assigned to a customer. An ADVANCE block with a time of 8 ± 4 represents the time to reach the customer, and another ADVANCE block, called WORK, with a time of 16 ± 8 represents the time to complete a call.

When a call is completed, the count of calls assigned for that customer is decremented by 1, and, if the result is not zero, the transaction returns to the block WORK to service another of that customer's calls. When all outstanding calls for that customer are completed, the transaction is removed from group 2 and immediately placed in group 3, representing the fact that the serviceman is now traveling back to the office.

A travel time of 8 ± 4 is expended in an ADVANCE block. Should the serviceman be reassigned while he is returning to the office, parameter 1 will have been set to the new customer number, and the transaction will have been removed from group 3, leaving the transaction temporarily out of all groups. When he arrives back at the office, an EXAMINE block checks

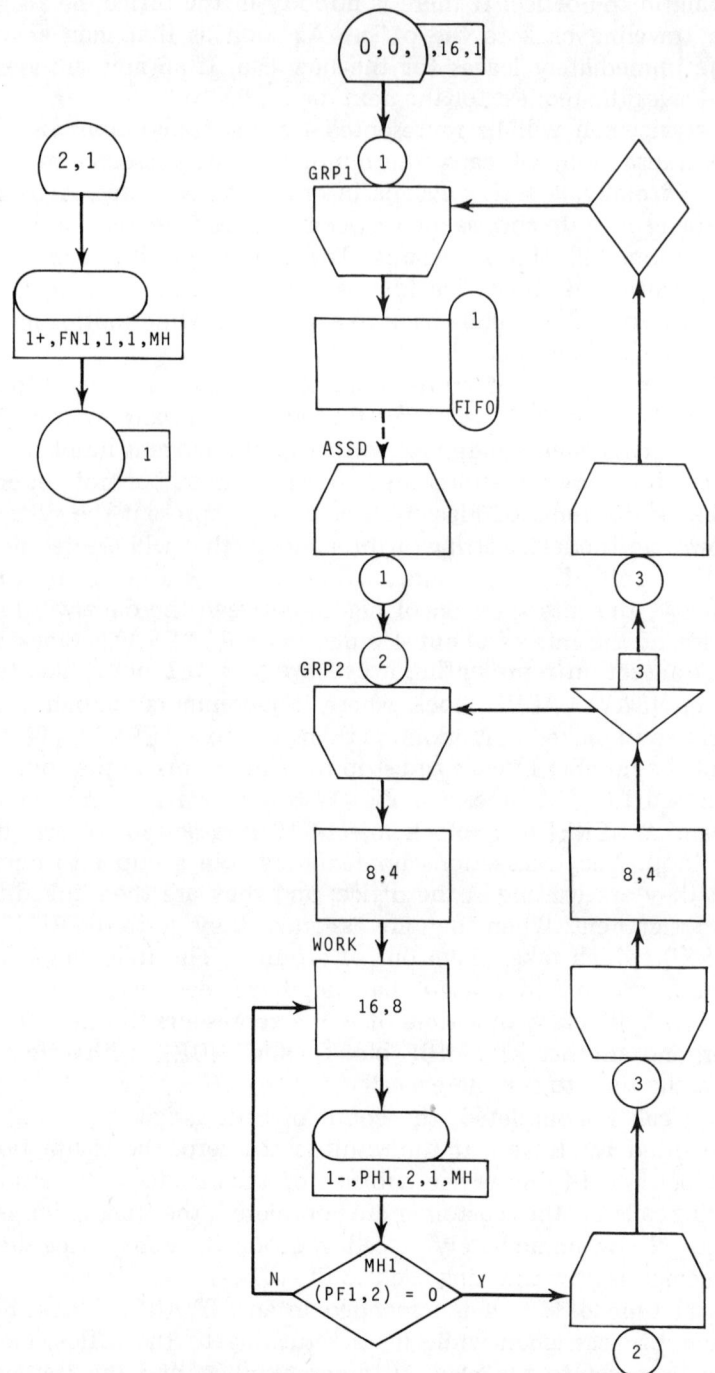

Figure 14-6. Allocating manpower 1.

whether the transaction is in group 3. If so, it is removed from group 3 and entered in group 1 to await reassignment. If, however, the transaction is not in group 3, it immediately goes to the JOIN block called GRP2 to proceed to its new assignment.

Figure 14-7 shows a block diagram for controlling the assignment of ser-

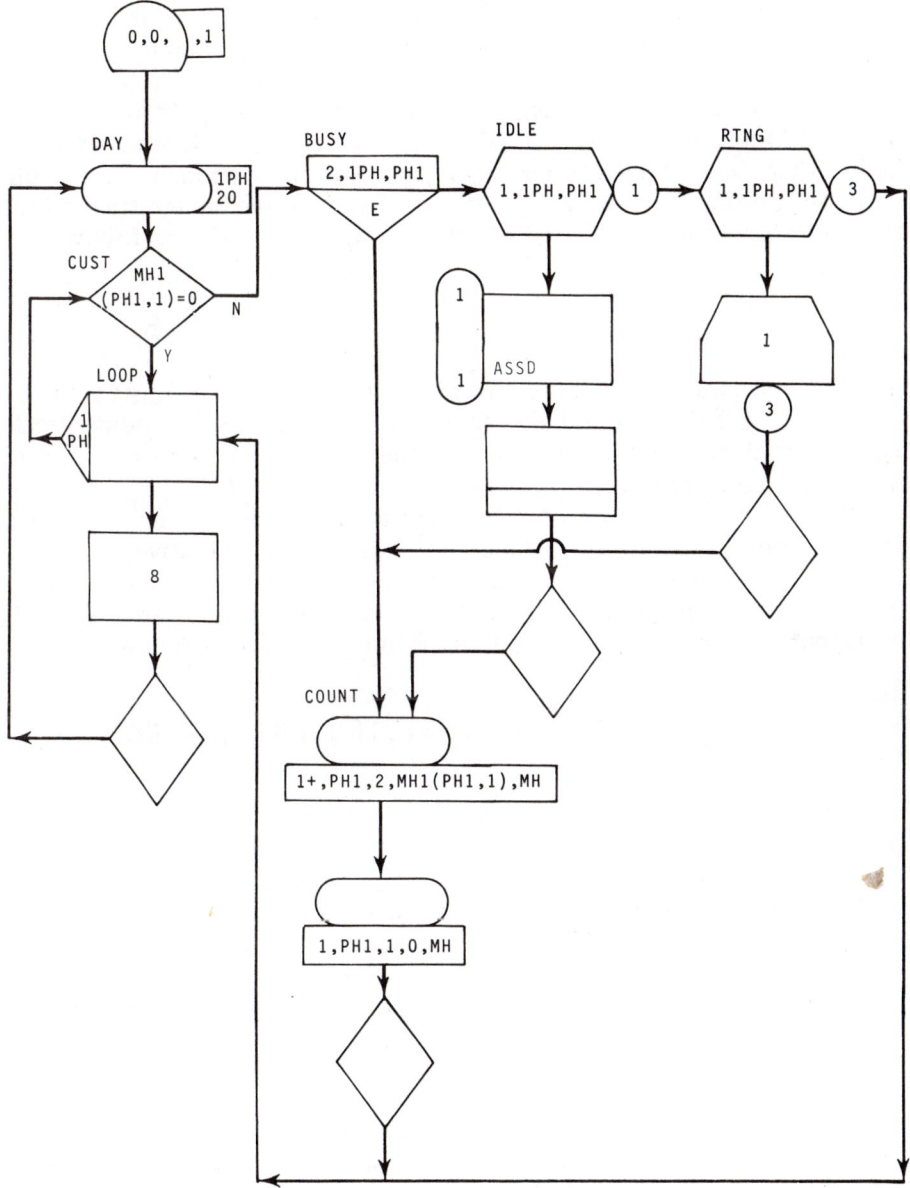

Figure 14-7. Allocating manpower 2.

vicemen. A single control transaction is injected into the diagram by a GENERATE block. Each day the transaction will cycle through the column of blocks shown to the left, once for each customer. It goes first to an INDEX block that sets parameter 1, representing customer number, to the value 20. The sequence in which customers will be scanned will be 20, 19, ..., 1. A TEST block sees if there are any new calls from the customer. If not, the transaction goes to a LOOP block called LOOP, to index to the next customer, until all customers have been examined. The transaction then waits 1 day and returns to the INDEX block to begin another cycle.

When there is a new customer call, the transaction goes to the next column of blocks headed by a SCAN block called BUSY. Here it will check whether there is a serviceman already assigned to the customer. To do this, it must scan group 2, looking for a transaction with parameter 1 set to the current customer number. The SCAN block is therefore coded as follows:

```
        BUSY    SCAN            2,1PH,PH1,,,IDLE
```

If there is such a transaction, the control transaction goes to an MSAVEVALUE block, called COUNT, to add the count of new calls to the count of calls assigned for this customer. It then sets the new call count to zero and returns to the LOOP block.

If the control transaction does not find a serviceman assigned to the customer, it goes from the SCAN block, by way of the alternative exit, to an ALTER block called IDLE. Looking for an idle serviceman waiting in the office, it will search group 1 for a transaction and alter its parameter 1 to the current customer number. The ALTER block is coded as follows:

```
        IDLE    ALTER           1,1,1PH,PH1,,,RTNG
```

If the control transaction does assign an idle serviceman, it goes to an UNLINK block to remove the transaction from chain 1 and then goes to a BUFFER block. Because the transactions representing the men are of higher priority, this ensures that those transactions are moved before the control transaction continues. When the control transaction continues, it goes to the block called COUNT to adjust the call counts and return to LOOP. If there are no idle servicemen, the control transaction will use the alternative exit of the ALTER block called IDLE to go to another ALTER block called RTNG. Here, it looks for a returning serviceman by locating the first transaction in group 3. If it finds one, the transaction has its parameter 1 set to the current customer number. The control transaction then removes it from group 3, and returns to the block COUNT. If there is no returning serviceman, the control transaction goes to LOOP, and the calls are left outstanding until the next day.

Figure 14-8 shows the coding for the problem and the results of a run.

```
        *       ALLOCATING MANPOWER
        *
1               GENERATE      2,1                   GENERATE A CALL
2               MSAVEVALUE    1+,FN1,1,1,MH         ADD TO CUSTOMER NEW CALL COUNT
3               TERMINATE     1
        *
        *       LOOP CONTROLLING MOVEMENT OF SERVICEMEN
4               GENERATE      ,,,16,1               CREATE 16 TRANSACTIONS
5       GRP1    JOIN          1                     JOIN GROUP 1
6               LINK          1,FIFO                LINK TO CHAIN 1
7       ASSD    REMOVE        1                     LEAVE GROUP 1
8       GRP2    JOIN          2                     JOIN GROUP 2
9               ADVANCE       8,4                   TRAVEL TO CUSTOMER
10      WORK    ADVANCE       16,8                  SERVICE CALL
11              MSAVEVALUE    1-,PH1,2,1,MH         REDUCE COUNT OF OUTSTANDING CALLS
12              TEST E        MH1(PH1,2),0,WORK     TEST FOR MORE CALLS
13              REMOVE        2                     LEAVE GROUP 2
14              JOIN          3                     JOIN GROUP 3
15              ADVANCE       3,4                   TRAVEL BACK TO OFFICE
16              EXAMINE       3,,GRP2               IS TRANSACTION IN GROUP 3?
17      BBB     REMOVE        3                     YES-REMOVE FROM GROUP 3
18              TRANSFER      ,GRP1                 RECYCLE
        *
        *       CONTROL GROUP
19              GENERATE      ,,,1                  CREATE A SINGLE CONTROL TRANSACTION
20      DAY     INDEX         1PH,20                INITIALIZE FOR CUSTOMER LOOP
21      CUST    TEST E        MH1(PH1,1),0,BUSY     ANY MORE CALLS FOR THIS CUST?
22      LOOP    LOOP          1PH,CUST              NO-MOVE TO NEXT CUSTOMER
23              ADVANCE       8                     NO MORE CUSTOMERS-WAIT ONE DAY
24              TRANSFER      ,DAY                  START NEXT DAY
        *
        *       LOOK FOR A SERVICE MAN ASSIGNED TO THIS CUSTOMER
25      BUSY    SCAN E        2,1PH,PH1,,,IDLE      SCAN GROUP 2 FOR A MAN
26      COUNT   MSAVEVALUE    1+,PH1,2,MH1(PH1,1),MH  FOUND-TRANSFER CALL COUNT
27              MSAVEVALUE    1,PH1,1,0,MH          SET OUTSTANDING CALL COUNT TO ZERO
28              TRANSFER      ,LOOP
        *
        *       LOOK FOR AN IDLE SERVICE MAN
29      IDLE    ALTER         1,1,1PH,PH1,,,RTNG    ASSIGN FIRST MAN IN GROUP
30              UNLINK        1,ASSD,1              UNLINK FROM CHAIN
31              BUFFER                              WAIT FOR MAN TO TRANSFER
32              TRANSFER      ,COUNT                CHANGE COUNTS
        *
        *       LOOK FOR A RETURNING SERVICE MAN
33      RTNG    ALTER         3,1,1PH,PH1,,,LOOP    ASSIGN FIRST MAN TO GROUP 3
34              TRANSFER      ,COUNT                CHANGE COUNTS
        *
        1       FUNCTION      RN1,C2                SELECTS CUSTOMER NUMBER
        0,1/1,21
        *
        1       MATRIX        MH,20,2
        *
                START         1000
```

RELATIVE CLOCK   2010   ABSOLUTE CLOCK   2010
BLOCK COUNTS

BLOCK	CURRENT	TOTAL	BLOCK	CURRENT	TOTAL	BLOCK	CURRENT	TOTAL	BLOCK	CURRENT	TOTAL
1	0	1000	11	0	982	21	0	5040	31	0	591
2	0	1000	12	0	982	22	0	5040	32	0	591
3	0	1000	13	0	507	23	1	252	33	0	3
4	0	16	14	0	507	24	0	251	34	0	3
5	0	521	15	2	507	25	0	924			
6	0	521	16	0	505	26	0	924			
7	0	519	17	0	505	27	0	924			
8	0	519	18	0	505	28	0	924			
9	4	519	19	0	1	29	0	522			
10	8	990	20	0	252	30	0	519			

Figure 14-8. Coding and output of manpower allocation example.

```
****************************************
*                                      *
*              USER CHAINS             *
*                                      *
****************************************
```

USER CHAIN	TOTAL ENTRIES	AVERAGE TIME/TRANS	CURRENT CONTENTS	AVERAGE CONTENTS	MAXIMUM CONTENTS
1	521	15.917	2	4.125	16

```
****************************************
*                                      *
*           HALFWORD MATRICES          *
*                                      *
****************************************
```

HALFWORD MATRIX   1

ROW/COLUMN	1	2
	ROWS 1-2, COLUMNS 1-2 ARE ZERO	
3	0	2
4	0	1
	ROWS 5-6, COLUMNS 1-2 ARE ZERO	
7	0	1
8	0	0
9	1	2
10	0	1
11	0	0
12	0	1
13	0	2
14	0	0
15	0	2
16	1	1
17	0	1
18	0	1
19	0	0
20	0	1

```
****************************************
*                                      *
*                GROUPS                *
*                                      *
****************************************
```

CURRENT MEMBERS OF GROUP   1
TRANSACTION MODE

         14   5

CURRENT MEMBERS OF GROUP   2
TRANSACTION MODE

          8   9   16   2   4   6   11   7   13   18   12   15

CURRENT MEMBERS OF GROUP   3
TRANSACTION MODE

         10   17

Figure 14-8. (continued)

14-14

Group and Chain SNAs

The only SNA associated with a group is the current number of members in the group. For chains, there are five SNAs, each of which is a statistic which, in addition to being available as an SNA, is printed as part of the standard GPSS output. Figure 14-3 shows an example of the user chain output statistics. The chain and group SNAs are defined as follows:

Gj   The number of members of group j
CHj   The current number of transactions on chain j
CAj   The average number of transactions on chain j
CMj   The maximum number of transactions on chain j
CCj   The total number of transactions that joined chain j
CTj   The average time transactions have spent on chain j

To derive these statistics the program maintains a cumulative time integral of the contents of each chain, in the same manner as it does for a storage or queue (see Sec. 5-21 and Fig. 5-8). The average number of transactions on the chain, CAj, is this time integral divided by the relative clock time, and the average time a transaction spends on a chain, CTj, is the integral divided by the total count, CCj.

Exercises

14-1   Reprogram the problem of Sec. 14-4 so that the system will dispatch batches of jobs consisting of jobs collected in their order of arrival until the total processing time first exceeds 500 time units.

14-2   A terminal feeds messages into a computer at the rate of one every 10 ± 5 seconds. They can have priorities of 0 to 4 with equal probability for each value. The computer processes the messages one at a time, in priority order, and it spends 11 + 4 seconds on each message. At 60-second intervals a control program interrupts the computer and raises the priority of all waiting messages by one level except that priorities may not go higher than four. The interruption takes 2 seconds and any interrupted message continues with its processing after the interruption. Simulate the processing of 100 messages.

14-3   Messages are being generated for transmission over a network at the rate of one every 50 ± 20 time units. They appear at random on one of 50 lines with an equal probability of being on any one line. For a message to be transmitted a polling system has to read the message. The polling system scans the lines, looking for messages by cycling around the lines in sequence. It takes 1 second to scan a line whether it has a message or not. While waiting to be polled, transactions representing the messages wait on a chain, and, when they have been read, they go to a location called READI. There can be more than one message waiting on a line, in which case, the system takes only one on each scan. Simulate the reading of 500 messages.

14-4 Transactions represent fragments of core space (i.e., blocks of contiguous bytes). The low address of the fragments is in PF1, the number of bytes is in PF2, and the high-order address is in PF3. The total available space is 100,000 bytes, numbered from 1 to 100,000. When a transaction represents a fragment that is free, it is put on a chain called FREE. When it has been assigned, it is transferred to a chain called BUSY. Both chains have fragments ordered by low-order address. When a fragment is released, the transaction returns to the FREE chain, except that it may be merged with another transaction or transactions that have adjoining addresses.

When a request is made for a fragment, the first fragment, starting from the low-address end, that is big enough to satisfy the request is used. If the fragment is too large, the desired amount is taken from the bottom and the rest is returned to FREE. Assume that a request is made for a fragment every 100 ± 50 time units and that the amount requested is randomly and uniformly distributed between 100 and 10,000 bytes. The fragment is returned after 500 ± 200 time units. A request that cannot be satisfied stops further requests from being generated until it is satisfied. Beginning with the whole of core as a single, free fragment, simulate the use and return of 500 fragments.

14-5 A study is being made of an airport when it is temporarily closed to traffic. Aircraft, however, are still arriving at the rate of one every 5 ± 2 minutes. They are stacked at 1000-foot intervals beginning at 5000 feet and extending up to 15,000 feet, so that a maximum of 11 aircraft can be stacked. Because of fuel shortages aircraft will only wait 10 ± 5 minutes before leaving for another airfield. Any aircraft that cannot join the stack immediately goes to the other airfield.

About 20 per cent of the arriving aircraft are light aircraft. If a hole has been left in the stack by an aircraft that has left, a light aircraft will take the lowest hole. (The stack is not pushed down to fill the holes.) The other aircraft are commercial airliners and they are not allowed to take a hole; they must go to the top of the stack. Simulate a period of 4 hours.

14-6   A car rental agency has cars renting for $5, $6, and $7 per hour. Customers arrive at the rate of one every 5 ± 2 minutes. Their choice of price is distributed as follows: $5/hr, 50 per cent; $6/hr, 30 per cent; and $7/hr, 20 per cent. If a car is not available at the requested price, any customer will take a cheaper price but nobody will take a higher price. If there is no suitable car, the customer leaves. Cars are used for 2 ± 1 hours, after which they are returned to stock and are immediately available for rehiring. Assume that there are initially 10 cars of each type, all of which are initially free. Simulate the operation of the rental agency for 100 hours.

14-7   Extend Exercise 12-4 in the following way. There are five ambulances, and calls arrive at the rate of one every 250 seconds with an exponentially distributed interarrival time. When an ambulance arrives at the scene of a call, it spends 60 ± 30 seconds attending to that call and then remains at the scene until it is dispatched again. The dispatching rule is that the call goes to the ambulance nearest the call which is currently unassigned. If all ambulances are busy, the call waits for the first to become available.

15

MODEL CONTROLS

This chapter describes a number of block types and features of GPSS concerned more with the control and modification of models, and their input and output data, rather than with language features designed to describe systems.

A pair of block types, TRACE and UNTRACE, are used mainly in the course of debugging models. Another block type, PRINT, is also used, mostly in the preliminary stages of model development. It can be used to obtain partial data dumps when certain events occur, rather than using the SNAP feature of the START statement, which gives complete dumps based on run length control. Two other block types to be described are the EXECUTE and CHANGE blocks, which can make dynamic, or temporary, changes to models during a simulation run, often avoiding the necessity of making permanent changes of models between successive runs.

A number of features are designed to assist the user with large models or in studies requiring a series of models. A WRITE block allows transactions created in one run to be saved. The JOBTAPE and REWIND control statements allow the transactions to be used in a later run, possibly with a different model. The READ/SAVE feature allows an entire model to be saved and restarted at a later time. An UPDATE feature can be used to control and modify the input data statements that define the model.

Figure 15-1 shows the block diagram symbols for the six block types to be described in this chapter.

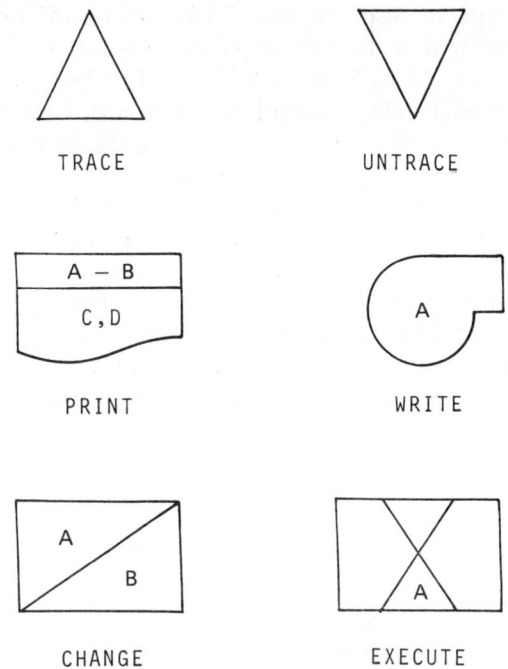

Figure 15-1. Block types 10.

15-1
TRACE and UNTRACE Blocks

The purpose of the TRACE and UNTRACE blocks is to track the movement of transactions as they go from block to block. Upon entering a TRACE block, an indicator within the transaction is turned on. It is turned off when the transaction enters an UNTRACE block. No operands are needed for either block type. A transaction can go through more than one TRACE block, and it can go through an UNTRACE block without previously going through a TRACE block. Whenever a transaction that has its trace indicator turned on enters any block (except an UNTRACE or TERMINATE block), the program prints a message describing the transaction and its movement.

The program first prints a single line message of the following form:

TRANS 1 FROM 2 TO 3 CLOCK 4 TERMINATIONS TO GO 5

The first figure is the transaction number. The next two are block locations, and the next is the clock time at which the transfer occurred. The last figure shows how many units are left for the termination counter to end the run. The line is followed immediately by a printout of the full details of the transaction, as it appears when the program prints an error dump or lists the transaction in response to a SNAP option. Figure 3-8 shows how this output appears, and a description of the output is given in Sec. 3-21.

The purpose of the TRACE and UNTRACE blocks is, of course, to help the user debug a model. They should be used with care because it is very easy to produce an excessive amount of output. In addition, since outputs are written in chronological order, a large number of messages generated by many different transactions can be very confusing. It is often a good idea to inject a single transaction into the block diagram in the manner illustrated in Fig. 15-2. Only that transaction goes through a TRACE block, and it is injected into the block diagram at a point where a detailed analysis will be useful. An UNTRACE block marks the end of the section being analyzed. The fact that the normal stream of transactions passes through the UNTRACE without having been through a TRACE block causes no difficulty.

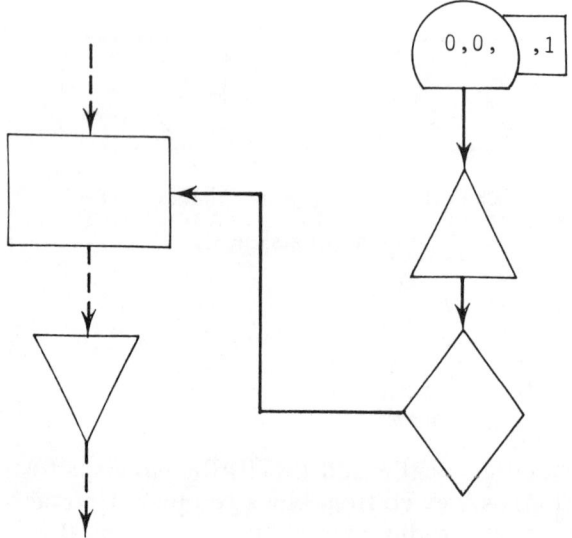

Figure 15-2. Using TRACE and UNTRACE blocks.

15-2
PRINT Blocks

The PRINT block allows statistical information about any one type of GPSS entity or any chain to be printed during the execution of a run. There can be several PRINT blocks. A message is printed every time a transaction enters a PRINT block. Field C contains one of the mnemonics shown in Table 15-1 to identify the entity or chain type. For those items marked with an asterisk, a complete list is always given and fields A and B should be left

Table 15-1 PRINT Block Mnemonics

Mnemonic	Meaning
MOV*	Current events chain
FUT*	Future events chain
I*	Interrupt chain
MAT*	Matching status chain
C*	Relative and absolute clock time
B or N or W*	Block counts
S	Storage statistics
Q	Queue statistics
F	Facility statistics
U	User chain statistics
T	Table statistics
X or XF	Contents of fullword savevalue
XH	Contents of halfword savevalue
XB	Contents of byte-sized savevalue
XL	Contents of floating-point savevalue
MX	Contents of fullword matrix
MH	Contents of halfword matrix
MB	Contents of byte-sized matrix
ML	Contents of floating-point matrix
LG	Status of logic switches
CHA	User chain listing
G	Current members of group

*Full list will always be printed

blank. For all other entities, fields A and B can contain a lower and upper limit, respectively, of the entity numbers to be printed. If they are blank, the complete set is printed. To print a single entity, the same entity number is given in both fields. The information that is printed is the same as would appear in the case of a standard output. If field D is left blank, a separate page will be used for each printed message. Any alphanumeric character in field D will suppress the page skipping. The following are examples:

```
          PRINT        1,10,F
          PRINT        5,5,F
          PRINT        ,,S
          PRINT        MOV
```

The first example prints the statistics for facilities 1 through 10. The second prints the statistics for facility 5 only. The third example prints the statistics for all storages, and the last example prints details of all transactions on the current events chain.

As with the TRACE and UNTRACE blocks, care should be exercised in using the block, because of the possibility of producing large amounts of output.

15-3

CHANGE Blocks

When a transaction enters a CHANGE block, any block in the diagram can be permanently changed into a copy of any other block in the diagram. Field A identifies the block to be changed, and field B identifies the block to be copied. The blocks are identified by giving their locations. The field B block remains unchanged. The current count, W_j, of the field A block is unchanged, but the total count, N_j, is set to zero. It is also possible to redefine blocks by placing block statements between START statements but that means stopping and restarting the run.

The CHANGE block can often save execution time when a model passes through a number of phases, each requiring the resetting of some system parameter—for example, a model representing a production line that periodically changes the type of part being produced. It is possible to use SNAs to check a logic switch and determine which phase is current, but this check takes time. The CHANGE block can interchange two blocks to establish the new values until a further change becomes due.

Suppose, for example, that a model represents the processing of four types of transactions and that the processing time is constant but depends upon the part type, stored in byte-sized parameter 1. One way of modeling the system, which does not use the CHANGE block, selects the time at an ADVANCE block from, say, a function in a list mode. The coding would be as follows:

```
     AAA    ADVANCE      FN1
            1 FUNCTION   PB1,L4
     1,5/2,10/3,15/4,20
```

If the part types were randomly interspersed, this would be a reasonable way of programming the problem, but suppose that the production is organized in batches by part type. During each batch, every transaction will be evaluating FN1 and deriving exactly the same value. The time it takes to evaluate the function could be saved by making a transaction that schedules the change of part type also change the ADVANCE block. Suppose that the scheduling transaction has the part type in byte-sized parameter 1; that transaction can then schedule the change of part-type production as follows:

```
            CHANGE      AAA,FN$TYPE
     TYPE   FUNCTION    PB1,L4
  1,PRT1/2,PRT2/3,PRT3/4,PRT4
     ...
     PRT1   ADVANCE     5
     PRT2   ADVANCE     10
     PRT3   ADVANCE     15
     PRT4   ADVANCE     20
```

When the scheduling transaction enters the CHANGE block, it replaces the ADVANCE block at AAA, which represents the machining time, by one of the four ADVANCE blocks, PRTj, each of which gives the time for one of the part types. As a result, the transactions representing the parts do not have to carry the part-type number as a parameter and do not have to spend time looking up the machining time.

The interchanged blocks do not have to be the same type, as in this example.

15-4
EXECUTE Blocks

A transaction entering an EXECUTE block will perform the operation of any other block in the block diagram, except a GENERATE block, without diverting the executing transaction from its normal path, or changing the block that is executed. The A field identifies the block to be executed by giving its location.

For example, in the model of the previous section, which changed an ADVANCE block according to the part type, suppose that the processing involves using a facility, called MACH. It could be that an occasional, urgent job of any type might need to break into the routine processing. Let byte-sized parameter 1 of the transaction represent the type of urgent task. The transaction could be passed through the following blocks:

```
     PREEMPT     MACH
     EXECUTE     FN$TYPE
     RETURN      MACH
```

The function TYPE is the one given in the previous section.

The transaction that enters the EXECUTE block will proceed to the next sequential location unless the block it executes causes a transfer—for example, a TRANSFER or TEST block.

Certain conditions that would have delayed the transaction if it had actually been in the executed block will delay the transaction, but it remains at the EXECUTE block for the period of the delay. The conditions causing a delay are as follows:

(a) The executed block is an ADVANCE block with a nonzero time.
(b) The executed block is a SEIZE block and the facility is seized in the same clock instant at which the execution occurs.
(c) The executed block is a MATCH, ASSEMBLE, or GATHER block, and the matching conditions are not satisfied.

15-5

WRITE Blocks

There are times when a user wants to save transactions that were created in one run for use in a later run. This can be done with WRITE blocks. Whenever a transaction enters a WRITE block, a copy of the transaction is written into any of three output data sets referred to as jobtapes 1, 2, or 3. The choice is made by putting JOBTAn, where n is 1, 2, or 3, in field A. There can be many different WRITE blocks referring to the same jobtape. After writing the output, the program continues to process the transaction that entered the WRITE block by moving it to the next location. The jobtape feature described in the next section is used to enter the transactions into a subsequent run, not necessarily using the same model.

The main use of the WRITE block is to create a set of transactions that can be preserved and used repeatedly in several different runs or different models. The purpose could be to provide an unvarying set of transactions for different models and so reduce the variance between the models to that due only to differences in system structure. Alternatively, the purpose may be to preserve a particular pattern of arrivals resulting from some special set of circumstances or some special system organization, and so avoid having to recreate the pattern on each run.

The output resulting from the entry of a transaction into a WRITE block consists of at least one record of 416 bytes. If there are a large number of parameters specified for the transaction, extra records may be needed. Each is 416 bytes, and, if the maximum number of 1020 parameters is specified, the output extends to seven separate records.

Details of the data layout in the first record are shown in Table 15-2. It is not necessary that a jobtape data set be produced by a WRITE block. Any program can be used to create a data set, if it follows the format of Table 15-2 for the first record and the format described below for subsequent records. The data set is closed by a final 416 byte record for which the first 16 bytes are END OF FILE JOBT. The remaining 400 bytes are not examined.

The first record begins, in the first word, with an interarrival time that is the interval between the transaction's entry into the data set and that of its

Table 15-2 First Record of WRITE Block Output

Word Number	Bytes	Content
1	1–4	Interarrival time
2	1–4	Transit time
3	1	Not used
	2	Priority
	3	Not used
	4	Not used
4	1	Number of floating-point parameters
	2	Number of byte-sized parameters
	3	Number of fullword parameters
	4	Number of halfword parameters
5 and over	—	Parameter values

predecessor. The first arrival carries the value 0. Usually there is only one WRITE block referring to a given jobtape, and the interarrival time is the interval between arrivals at that block; but if there is more than one such block, arrivals are considered to be consecutive within the set of blocks referring to the data set.

The second word stores a transit time computed as the difference between current clock time and mark time, just as though the transaction had entered a TABULATE block in an M1 mode immediately prior to entering the WRITE block. The priority is stored in the third word, and the fourth word indicates how many parameters of each type there are in the transaction.

Listing of the parameter value begins in word 5 of the first record and, if necessary, continues through the extra records. Parameters are listed in the following order:

halfword	2 bytes/parameter
fullword	4 bytes/parameter
floating-point	4 bytes/parameter
byte-sized	1 byte/parameter

The different parameter types immediately follow each other, except that the first parameter of each type starts on a fullword boundary (i.e., at multiples of 4 bytes beginning with word number 5). For example, a transaction having 5 halfword, 10 fullword, and 12 byte-sized parameters would need 64 bytes of space for recording parameter data. It would begin listing parameters at byte 17 (word 5) and continue to byte 80. The rest of the 416-

byte record would be blank. Bytes 27 and 28 would be blank in order that the fullword parameter listing starts at byte 29, which is the beginning of the eighth word.

If extra records are needed, the parameter information simply continues directly from one record to the next. The rule given above ensures that no one parameter is split between two records. The last record may have a number of unused, trailing bytes that fill the block size: they are unexamined.

Assembly set membership is lost when transactions are written on a jobtape. Upon entering the transactions in a later run, each behaves as though it were just created at a GENERATE block.

Execution of a JOB statement or an END statement will cause the end of file (EOF) record to be written on all active jobtapes and, if the output device is a tape, it will be rewound and unloaded. Execution of a CLEAR statement will write an EOF record but will not reposition the data set or unload a tape. A run following the CLEAR statement that uses a WRITE block will create a second data set.

15-6

JOBTAPE Control Statements

A JOBTAPE control statement is used to attach a jobtape data set that has been prepared either by a WRITE block or by some special program. The statement presupposes that a model has already been loaded. It normally appears after the input statements defining the model or after a READ statement that can load a model (see next section).

Each jobtape needs a separate control statement carrying the word JOBTAPE in the operation field. There can be three jobtapes, and the A field identifies the particular jobtape with the notation JOBTAn, $n = 1, 2,$ or 3. The B field must carry a location name or number identifying the point at which the transactions are to enter the model. It can be any block other than a GENERATE block. There can be GENERATE blocks coexisting with jobtapes, but they are not necessary.

With only fields A and B being used, the program enters transactions in accordance with the interarrival times preserved in the transaction records. The first transaction is initialized into the model and subsequent transactions arrive as their interarrival interval is expended. Even if transactions are blocked at their point of entry, the program continues to enter transactions.

If field C or D contains a number between 1 through 999999, the arrival times are modified. The C field is an offset time that delays the entry of the first transaction. If no C field is specified, the first transaction's entry time is offset to 1, in order to start the clock. The D field, when used, gives a positive integral multiplier that is used to scale up every interarrival time of transactions coming from that jobtape. A blank in field D implies a 1.

If an EOF is reached during the running of any model, the program stops reading from that jobtape. After finishing a run, if the program reads a JOB or END card, it will reposition all jobtape data sets to their beginning, irrespective of whether they had reached an EOF. In the case of tapes, this means that the tapes are rewound to the preceding EOF or to the beginning of the tape. On reading a CLEAR statement, the program will skip records to reach the EOF on all data sets that have not already reached their EOF.

More than one JOBTAPE control statement can refer to the same jobtape. The program then assumes that there are multiple data sets on the file. The first JOBTAPE statement will initially position the jobtape to the beginning of the first data set. Reading a second JOBTAPE statement immediately positions the jobtape to the beginning of the second data set. Any subsequent JOBTAPE statement similarly advances the jobtape by one data set. For example, the following coding will select the third data set for entry at the location called ENTER:

```
JOBTAPE      JOBTA1
JOBTAPE      JOBTA1
JOBTAPE      JOBTA1,ENTER
```

Note that it is not necessary to complete field B if the only purpose of the JOBTAPE statement is to skip a data set.

15-7

REWIND Control Statements

A REWIND control statement causes the program to reposition a jobtape to the beginning of its first data set, but it does not disconnect the jobtape. The statement has the word REWIND in the operation field and identifies a jobtape in field A with one of the entries JOBTAn, $n = 1, 2,$ or 3. Used in conjunction with the JOBTAPE statement, it can arrange for any data set on a jobtape to be used repeatedly in a run.

For example, suppose that the three JOBTAPE statements of the previous section had been given in order to use the third data set, and it is then decided to go back to the second data set. The following statements would have to follow the run that used the third data set:

```
REWIND       JOBTA1
JOBTAPE      JOBTA1
JOBTAPE      JOBTA1,ENTER
```

The REWIND statement resets the jobtape to the beginning of the first data set, the first JOBTAPE statement skips over the first data set, and the second JOBTAPE statement attaches the second data set to enter transactions at the location ENTER.

15-8

SAVE Control Statements

Another desirable feature is to be able to save a model and later reload it to continue the simulation. This can be done with the SAVE and READ control statements. A SAVE statement will write out a copy of a model, and the READ statement (described in the next section) can reload the model for a later run. Separate data sets are defined for the SAVE and READ functions. Two physically separate data sets must be attached to use both features simultaneously. If only one feature is used, only its data sets need be attached. The *Operator's Manual* (42 or 43) describes the procedures for attaching the data sets.

The SAVE statement carries the word SAVE in the operation field, and it may have an entry in the A field. Upon encountering a SAVE statement, the program should have loaded a model, and it may also have run the model for some period of time. The SAVE statement has one of two purposes.

(a) If a SAVE statement is placed after the statements that define a model (or part of a model) but before a START statement, the program will save the assembled model before it is executed. If, in fact, the only purpose of the run were to save the assembled model, a START statement need not be used. When a model has been satisfactorily debugged, this allows the READ statement to reload the model without the need for reassembly.

(b) If a SAVE statement is placed after a START statement, the model will be run and then saved. The program will have written the usual output report on the normal system output device. Using the READ statement, it is possible to restart the run from the point at which it was saved.

There can be many SAVE statements in a run and they could be used for either of the above purposes. If the A field of the SAVE statement is left blank, each SAVE statement, subsequent to the first, will cause the later SAVE output to be written over the output of the earlier SAVE statement. A SAVE statement with a nonblank A field will cause a separate record to be written.

As a rule, if the SAVE statement is being used to avoid reassembling the model, there will be only one SAVE statement and its A field will be left blank. The coding needed to save a model (and then run it) would be as follows:

```
JOB
Model
SAVE
START          1000
```

When SAVE statements are being used to save a model after a run, the purpose is usually to break a long run into a number of parts, so that, if the job has to be terminated before completion, the entire run is not lost. Used for this purpose, field A would usually be left blank. For example, suppose that a run is planned for 10,000 terminations. Instead of making a single run, it would be better to make a job of, say, 10 runs in the following way:

```
START      1000
SAVE
START      1000
SAVE
...
START      1000
```

There would be ten START statements, each calling for a run of 1000, and nine interspersed SAVE statements. As each group of 1000 terminations is completed (except the last), the program reads a SAVE statement to save the model, and restarts the model from where it stopped. Since field A of each SAVE statement is blank, only the latest model is saved. In the event that the job is permaturely ended, the record provides a checkpoint from which the job can be restarted in a later run.

If field A of all the SAVE statements had not been left blank, there would be nine separate records in the data set at the end of the job. This might be done, for example, if the purpose were to examine the statistical outputs to decide when a system has passed through its initialization phase and have available a convenient, fully loaded model from which to start subsequent runs. Alternatively, a nonzero A field would be used when several runs are being made with one loading of the GPSS program and several runs need to save a model.

Each output produced by a SAVE statement consists of a single binary record. When a JOB or END statement is read, the data set is closed with an EOF and the output device is repositioned to the beginning.

As mentioned previously in Sec. 3-12, the SIMULATE control statement has an option allowing a maximum execution time to be specified in field B. In addition, the C field can contain the word SAVE. If the time limit is reached during the execution of a run, the program will then perform the SAVE function automatically when it terminates the run.

15-9

READ Control Statements

A data set produced by using the SAVE statement in one run can be attached as the READ data set in a subsequent run, and used to reload the model saved in the earlier run. The READ statement calls for the model to be loaded. It has the word READ in the operation field and it may have a positive integer in the A field.

The data set could contain several records, each being a separate model. When the A field of the READ statement is blank (or 0), the program uses the first, and possibly only, record. When it is not blank, the program skips over the number of records indicated by field A. For example, suppose that there were four models saved and that the third model is to be loaded and run. The following coding would be used:

```
        SIMULATE
        READ        2
        START       1000
        END
```

A model can be modified after it has been loaded, but all such modifications must be in absolute form. Any block redefinition statements must be preceded by an ABS statement and followed by an ENDABS statement. Other types of statements, such as table definitions and INITIAL statements, need not be preceded by an ABS statement, but they may not use symbols. Functions must be entered in the assembled format (see Appendix 2).

For example, suppose it is known that the saved model has, at location 125, a SEIZE block using facility number 7. The facility is to be changed to number 10. In addition, fullword savevalue number 15 is to be initialized to 100. The following coding would be used, assuming the model to be the first or only one in the data set:

```
        SIMULATE
        READ
        ABS
125     SEIZE       10
        ENDABS
        INITIAL     XF15,100
        START       1000
        END
```

If the run that saved the model used any of the following features, the same features must be specified by using the same or equivalent statements at the time of loading the model:

```
        JOBTAPE
        REALLOCATE
        AUXILIARY
        LOAD
```

The last three features will be described later in Chap. 16. The statement for the LOAD feature must precede the READ statement that loads the model. Statements reestablishing any jobtapes follow the READ statement and precede the START statement. The REALLOCATE and/or AUXILIARY statements precede the START statement. Any of these statements that have to be used must be identical to the original statement used when the model was produced, except that the B fields of the JOBTAPE statements, which specify a location, must be in absolute form.

15-10
UPDATE Feature

To avoid handling large decks of input cards, provision is made for creating and updating data sets of input statements. Use of this feature requires the definition of sequential data sets called DDMASTER and DDNWMAST for the old and new master files [see the *Operator's Manual* (42 or 43) for details].

A file is initially created by preceding the input, at the time of loading a model, by a control statement with the word CREATE in the operation field. To update the data set, a control statement with the word UPDATE in the operation field precedes the statements giving details of the update. The control statement can have the words PUNCH, or NOASSEMBLE, or both in the A and B fields of the operand segment. The first calls for the updated deck to be punched in assembly form. This option requires the definition of a third data set called DDPUNCH. The other option suppresses the assembly phase, which otherwise occurs at the end of the update. If neither punching nor assembling is needed, the word NOASSEMBLE appears in the A field. Three control statements, REPLACE, DELETE, and ADD, make changes to an existing data set, and a control statement, ENDUPDATE, terminates the updating deck. The statement numbers, which appear at the right of a listing after assembly, are used to identify the statements to be modified. Only one set of update statements is allowed for each run, and it must precede the first JOB statement.

The statement DELETE A-B removes the statements numbered A through B inclusive. Note that the two numbers, A and B, are separated by a dash and not a comma. The statement ADD   A inserts, at a point immediately following statement A, all the statements that follow the ADD statement until another ADD, DELETE, REPLACE, or ENDUPDATE statement is read. The REPLACE   A statement removes statement A and then acts like an ADD statement; that is, it inserts statements that follow the REPLACE statement. The first replaces A and the others, if any, follow A, until another REPLACE, ADD, or ENDUPDATE is met.

16

MODIFYING THE GPSS PROGRAM

When using large, complex models, the normal facilities of GPSS can eventually be exceeded. The HELP block is a means for associating with the GPSS programs routines written by the user in Basic Assembler Language, FORTRAN, or PL/1. The purpose is either to introduce some processing which is impossible or difficult to execute in GPSS language, or to substitute for a segment of GPSS coding a compact subroutine that will either speed up the execution of the program or save space.

The use of space within GPSS is not usually a concern for the user because GPSS has a tabular structure with preassigned default values. When models become large, the user can readjust the assignments with the REALLOCATE statement and can, at the expense of execution time, extend the model indefinitely onto external storage by the use of the AUXILIARY control statement.

One other control statement available to the user is the LOAD statement, which can control which modules of the total GPSS programming system remain resident in core. Under certain circumstances this can increase the speed of problem execution.

16-1
HELP Blocks

The HELP block allows a user to associate with the GPSS program a routine that has been written by the user in Basic Assembler Language,

FORTRAN, or PL/1. There can be many such user routines, each associated with an individual HELP block. Basic Assembler Language routines can coexist with either FORTRAN or PL/1 routines, but FORTRAN and PL/1 routines cannot be used in the same model.

When a transaction enters a HELP block, control is passed to a routine named in field A. The other fields can identify information to be made available to the user's routine. While the routine is being executed, the clock and all transaction movement is suspended, unless the routine itself makes such changes. The user's routine is responsible for returning control to GPSS, at which time the GPSS program continues progress of the transaction that entered the HELP block.

The HELP block provides a powerful extension of GPSS. However, its use requires much greater programming skill than does GPSS alone. If the user's routine is to use or modify any internal GPSS data, it is necessary to know the names and data structures of the GPSS tables. There are many of these tables, and their structures are often complex. For this reason, the reader is referred to the *User's Manual* (41) for the necessary details of the table structures. This section will give a general description of how HELP blocks are used and what GPSS facilities are made available for the routines.

The reader is cautioned that the HELP block is an extension of, rather than a substitute for, GPSS. Careful thought should be given to the full capabilities of GPSS before deciding that a HELP block is needed because some function cannot be performed in GPSS. The principal circumstances that justify the use of a HELP block are that (1) a large model has been constructed and (2) either there is insufficient room to expand the model, or the execution time is too great. The HELP block can then consolidate the action of groups of blocks that do not interact directly with other parts of the block diagram and so save both space and execution time. The HELP block may also be used to carry out complex analyses of GPSS data that either cannot be done in GPSS or would require an excessive amount of GPSS programming—for example, such operations as matrix multiplication or inversion.

To use a HELP routine it is necessary to

(1) Code the routine.
(2) Assemble or compile the routine independently of GPSS.
(3) Link-edit the resulting object decks with GPSS.
(4) Test and debug the HELP routines.
(5) Code the HELP blocks and insert at the appropriate points of the block diagram.

The Basic Assembler Language version of the HELP block is the most powerful version: it gives access to virtually any element of the internal GPSS data, which can then be either read or changed. Up to six specific SNAs may be named in the B-G fields of the HELP block, and the program will pass the values of these SNAs directly to the HELP routine by placing them in a 25-word array established by the HELP routine. In addition, the array contains addresses that give access, directly or indirectly, to the tables for the different GPSS entities and to a number of internal GPSS routines that perform such functions as adding or removing a transaction to or from the current events, future events, or interrupt chains, creating a transaction, or storing or reading parameter values.

The FORTRAN and PL/1 versions each exist in one of three forms, referred to as A, B, or C. The A version provides one-way communication in which the GPSS program makes available to the HELP routine up to six SNA values. The B version provides two-way communication. Up to six savevalues, which must be either fullword or floating-point, can be specified. The program will provide the values of these savevalues to the HELP routine and will allow the HELP routine to change the values. The C version provides two-way communication in a manner similar to the Basic Assembler Language version of the block. Up to six SNA values can be supplied directly to the HELP routine and the addresses of tables for most GPSS entities are given, but there is no access to GPSS internal routines.

The HELP routines normally reside on external storage and are called into core when needed for execution. If a routine is used frequently, the LOAD feature, described in Sec. 16-5, should be used to keep the routine permanently in core.

16-2
Allocation of Storage Space

The GPSS program establishes a table for each type of GPSS entity. Each table allocates a fixed number of bytes to each entity, and its size is chosen to accommodate a given number of entities. Three standard versions of the program are made available. The selection is made by including a parameter, A, B, or C, in the control statement that loads the GPSS program. Core requirements for the three versions are 52K, 104K, and 178K bytes. They have different allocations of table sizes. Table 16-1 shows the allocations for the three versions.

Several types of entity cannot be specified in a fixed number of words. The space needed for tables and functions, for example, depends upon the number of elements. The program still allocates a fixed number of bytes for each entity to contain basic information about the entity. The variable part of the definition is placed in a block of storage called "Common," for which the program also allocates a fixed amount of space according to the version being used. The amounts of Common are shown in Table 16-1, and a series of footnotes in the table show how to calculate the total amount of Common storage that will be used by a particular model.

Table 16-1 Standard Entity Allocations

Entity type	Mnemonics	Byte allocation	Entity options A	B	C
Transactions[a]	XAC	16[b]	100	600	1200
Blocks	BLO	12[c]	80	500	1000
Facilities	FAC	28[d]	28	150	300
Storages	STO	44[d]	20	150	300
Queues	QUE	32	35	150	300
Logic switches	LOG	6	100	400	1000
Tables	TAB	48[e]	15	30	100
Functions	FUN	32[f]	20	50	200
Variables[a]	VAR	48[g]	20	50	200
Boolean variables[a]	BVR	32[h]	5	10	25
Fullword savevalues	FSV	4	100	400	1000
Halfword savevalues	HSV	2	50	200	500
Byte-sized savevalues	BSV	1	100	400	800
Floating-point savevalues	LSV	4	25	50	100
User chains[a]	CHA	24	20	40	100
Groups[a]	GRP	4[i]	5	10	25
Fullword matrices	FMS	24[j]	5	10	25
Halfword matrices	HMS	24[k]	5	10	25
Byte-sized matrices	BMS	24[l]	5	10	25
Floating-point matrices	LMS	24[m]	5	10	25
Macros[a]	MAC		50	50	50
Common[a] (expressed in bytes)	COM		5600	14400	25600

[a] These items are not allowed on AUXILIARY statement.
[b] Add 24 bytes of Common for every active transaction plus additional bytes for parameters (2 bytes per halfword parameter, 4 bytes per fullword parameter, 1 byte per byte-sized parameter, 4 bytes per floating-point parameter).
[c] Add 4 bytes of Common for each block with more than one operand specified; add 12 bytes per block operand when any field contains a matrix savevalue SNA.
[d] Add 16 bytes of Common for each equipment entity which uses the unavailable feature.
[e] Add 4 bytes of Common for each frequency class.
[f] Add 4 bytes of Common for each point of an L- or M-type function. Add 8 bytes of Common for each set of coordinates of a D- or E-type function. Add 12 bytes of Common for each set of coordinates of a C-type function.
[g] See "Core Allocation for GPSS Arithmetic Variables" in Chapter 4 of *User's Manual* for additional bytes of Common required.
[h] See "Core Allocation for GPSS Boolean Variable Entities" in Chapter 4 of *User's Manual* for additional blocks of 36 bytes of Common required.
[i] Add 36 bytes of Common when first value is joined to group; additional blocks of 36 bytes are obtained each time current contents of group exceed a multiple of 15.
[j] Add 4 bytes of Common for each msavevalue.
[k] Add 2 bytes of Common for each msavevalue.
[l] Add 1 byte of Common for each msavevalue.
[m] Add 4 bytes of Common for each msavevalue.

Source: Reproduced with permission of IBM Corporation from *General Purpose Simulation System—V User's Manual*.

The REALLOCATE control statement, described in the next section, allows the user to rearrange the table sizes. There is no loss of efficiency in running a model when the allocated space exceeds the space needed for the model; so there is no need to reallocate any space if all the numbers of all the entities used by the model will fit into one of the standard versions of the program.[†] If some entity types exceed the standard limit while others are below their limit, the REALLOCATE statement may be able to arrange a trade-off that keeps the model within bounds.

If this reallocation of space is still unable to meet the needs of the model, the AUXILIARY statement, described in Sec. 16-4, can expand the model to virtually any size by arranging that space is provided for most types of entity on some external storage device, such as a disk file. Table 16-1 marks with a superscript [a] those entities that cannot be expanded in this way. A penalty is paid for using external storage space because extra processing time is needed to gain access to the external data.

16-3

REALLOCATE Control Statements

The REALLOCATE control statement will allow the user to rearrange the space allocated for the GPSS entities listed in Table 16-1. The statement carries the word REALLOCATE in the operation field. Successive pairs of fields can then be used to reallocate an entity type. Field A gives the mnemonic of the first entity type, selected from the second column of Table 16-1; the B field gives the new number of entities; fields C and D can specify the reallocation of another entity type; and so. Commas are used as delimiters for all fields. Entries may not go beyond column 71. However, more than one REALLOCATE statement may be used, but an entity-type specification cannot be split between two statements. There is no restriction on the order in which the entity types are redefined, but multiple reallocation of the same entity will cause an error stop. Any entity type that is not redefined is given the number of the standard allocation of Table 16-1.

It is the user's responsibility to ensure that the total amount of space allocated to all entities following the reallocation does not exceed the total amount of space allocated to tables by the standard version. Any increase in space needed to expand the numbers of any entities must be equaled or exceeded by the space released by diminishing the size of other entities. Column 3 of Table 16-1 shows how many bytes are allocated in the fixed-sized tables for each entity type. Suppose, for example, that the user has

---

[†] This statement applies to a program not operating in a virtual environment. When operating in a virtual environment the amount of paging can be decreased by reducing the tables sizes to the maximum size needed; thereby minimizing the number of pages needed to carry the model.

selected the C option of the program and wants to extend the number of facilities to 500 and the number of Boolean variables to 30. The increase over the standard allocation is 200 facilities and five Boolean variables. Since these require 28 and 32 bytes for each entity in their respective tables, the two changes need a total expansion of 5760 bytes. At least this much space must be made available by reducing the assignment of space to other entities. Perhaps 10 user chains and 50 queues are sufficient for the model. Reducing these two entity type allocations to those sizes will save 90 user chains and 250 queues, which saves 10,160 bytes. The difference from the amount needed (4400 bytes) can be allocated to Common, but it is not essential to do so. (In the case of the DOS version of the program, all such unassigned space is automatically allocated to Common, although it will not be an error to assign it specifically.) The control statement needed for the example just given would be;

```
REALLOCATE FAC,500,BVR,30,CHA,10,QUE,50,COM,30000
```

This control statement follows the JOB control statement, or begins the input when a single job is being run.

16-4
AUXILIARY Control Statements

The AUXILIARY control statement allows the user to specify that some, or all, members of certain GPSS entity types are to be stored on an auxiliary disk file, which must be attached to provide the auxiliary storage. The procedure for its attachment is given in the *Operator's Manual* (42 or 43). The purpose of the feature is to accommodate models that are too large to fit into the space allocated by the selected option of GPSS, even after space has been reassigned by REALLOCATE control statements.

Reference to records that are on the auxiliary storage requires that the records be read into core storage; there is thus a loss of time in executing the model. Use of the auxiliary feature therefore requires careful planning to minimize the lost time. Only entities that are infrequently referenced should be put on the auxiliary storage.

There are 15 entity types that can be allocated to auxiliary storage. They are the entities listed in Table 16-1 which are not marked by [a]. One statement is needed to allocate each entity type. The operation field carries the word AUXILIARY. The A field identifies the entity type to be assigned, using the mnemonics given in Table 16-1. The B field carries the total number of the entity type, both those to be retained in core and those on auxiliary storage. This number does not have to equal the standard number, so the AUXILIARY statement can incorporate the function of reallocating space by either increasing or decreasing the number of entities. It is not necessary to use a REALLOCATE control statement in conjunction with the change, but it will not cause an error to do so, provided the REALLOCATE statement is consistent with the implicit reallocation of the AUXILIARY statement.

The C field specifies how many of the entities are to reside permanently in core. The number must be less than or equal to field B and it may be zero, except for the case of block entities, when the value must be at least 1. If n entities are to reside in core, then *they will always be the first n entities*. Entities numbers $n + 1$ up to the value given by field B will be placed on the auxiliary storage.

In writing the entity data on the auxiliary storage, the program forms records from groups of entities. Field D of the AUXILIARY control statement specifies how many entities will be grouped into one record. If field D contains the number m and field C specified that n entities are to remain in core, the program begins with entity number $n + 1$ and takes successive groups of m entities to form each record. The last record may contain less than m entities, in which case it will be filled with trailing blanks.

The records formed for each type of entity are of fixed size. However, the space needed for individual entities may not be constant. The record size must be such that it will accommodate the largest size of any group of m entities formed according to the rules just given.

Of the 15 types of entity that can be placed on auxiliary storage, the queues, logic switches, and savevalues use a fixed amount of space, and the program is able to compute for itself how many bytes are needed to store m entities. In the case of facilities and storages, the space is fixed, unless the unavailability feature is used, in which case, an extra 16 bytes of Common are needed for each entity using the feature. If any entity of either type uses the feature, the program assumes that all entities of that type use the feature, and it computes the block size accordingly.

Four entity types, blocks, tables, functions, and matrices, have space taken from Common. The amount depends upon the individual entity definitions. It is the user's responsibility to compute (from Table 16-1) the largest size reached by any of the blocks of m entities. A separate calculation is made for each entity type to be assigned to auxiliary storage. The program will compute for itself the fixed amount of space (exclusive of Common) by multiplying the number of entities per block, m (given in field D) by the number of bytes in column 3 of Table 16-1. The user must then place in field E a number greater than or equal to the largest number of extra bytes that must be taken from Common for the sets of m entities. That number, added to the number computed from field D, becomes the fixed record size allocated for the entity type. Field E is used only when assigning blocks, tables, functions, or matrices to auxiliary storage.

One further constraint is that the user must ensure that the number of entities grouped in a record is such that the fixed record size, whether computed automatically or supplied by the user, does not exceed the capacity of a single track, unless the program is being run under OS/360 with the track overflow option (not supported by DOS/360). In the interest of efficiency, however, track overflow should be avoided. Consider two examples, which assume the C option:

```
AUXILIARY   HSV,1200,200,500
AUXILIARY   FMS,25,5,5,1380
```

The first example specifies 1200 halfword savevalues, which is a reallocation from the standard number of 500. The first 200 are to stay in core. The remaining 1000 are formed into records of 500 savevalues, in this case, forming two records of 1000 bytes each. There is no need to use field E. The second example leaves the number of fullword matrices to be 25 but specifies that only the first 5 remain in core. The remaining 20 are to be placed on the auxiliary storage in records that group five matrices to a record. Suppose that matrices 6 through 10 are defined as follows:

```
 6  MATRIX   MX,5,10
 7  MATRIX   MX,6,12
 8  MATRIX   MX,2,3
 9  MATRIX   MX,10,10
10  MATRIX   MX,5,10
```

The total number of elements in this group of five matrices is 278; consequently they will need 1112 bytes of Common. The fixed space for five fullword matrices is 120 bytes, so these five matrices need a total of 1232 bytes. Assume that a similar calculation is made for each of the other three groups of five consecutively numbered matrices from numbers 11 through 25, and the results give smaller total values. Then field E must contain a number at least as big as 1112. In fact, the E field has 1380, so the matrices on the auxiliary storage will actually be formed into four records of 1500 bytes each.

16-5
LOAD Statements

The GPSS program itself consists of a number of different modules. [They are described in the *Operator's Manual* (42 or 43).] During the sequence of operations involved in reading, assembling, loading, executing, and reporting statistics for a problem, different modules are involved. They are loaded as required and replaced when their function has been performed. A Control module remains permanently resident. During execution of the problem, the Execution module is resident in core. When the normal statistical output report is to be written, the Execution module is replaced by the Normal Output module and the Graphic Output module is added if the output editor feature is used.

The latter two modules are used not only when the run ends but also when the TRACE feature is used and when a PRINT block or the SNAP option calls for an output. If outputs are needed for any of these reasons or if a restart is called for, the program normally loads the output modules and then reloads the Execution module to continue the simulation. A similar procedure is followed whenever a transaction enters a HELP block. Each routine associated with a HELP block forms a separate module, which is normally loaded only when needed.

The loading of the Output or HELP modules, followed by a reloading of the Execution module, can significantly slow the running of a problem, if it is required frequently. The LOAD statement is designed to avoid the loss of time involved in loading modules by giving the user the option of requesting that the Output modules or HELP modules remain resident.

The statement has the word LOAD in the operation field and, beginning in Column 19, can name the modules to be retained in core. Each name is separated by a comma, and names may extend up to, but not beyond, column 71. As many as 10 modules can be loaded and, if necessary, more than one LOAD statement can be used, but no one module description can be split between statements. (The LOAD statement will, in fact, load any of the GPSS modules but only in the case of the ones described is there any significant gain.) The names used for the modules that have been mentioned are as follows:

Module	OS/360	DOS/360
Normal Output	DAG06	DAR06
Graphic Output	DAG07	DAR07

The HELP routine modules are identified by the names given to the routines by the user. For example, the following statement would keep the Normal Output module and two HELP routines, called HELP1 and INVER, resident when using OS/360:

```
LOAD            DAG06,HELP1,INVER
```

The order of naming the modules is irrelevant. If the Graphic module is loaded, the Normal Output module must also be loaded.

It is the user's responsibility to ensure that there is sufficient core storage to accept the extra modules. The Normal Output modules require approximately 27,000 bytes of core, and the Graphic module combined with the Normal Output module requires approximately 37,000 bytes.

The LOAD statement can appear anywhere in the input, following any use of REALLOCATE, AUXILIARY, or UPDATE, and preceding the START statement.

APPENDIX

1

RANDOM NUMBER GENERATORS

Not all discrete system simulations involve random processes, but a substantial proportion do. It is necessary, therefore, to have an understanding of how random numbers are generated and used in digital computers.

A1-1

Random Numbers

Random numbers can be either continuously or discretely distributed. Consider a machine shop where parts arrive to be processed. The parts can be one of five types, chosen at random. The pattern of arrivals can be described by measuring the interval between successive arrivals. That number may also vary randomly. The time to machine each part could also be a random variable. The type of part is a discrete random variable, since it can take only one of the values 1, 2, . . . , 5 on each choice. The interarrival time and the processing time, however, are continuous random variables, since the former can, in theory, take any positive value and the latter will vary over some range of reasonable values.

A1-2

Continuous Uniformly Distributed Random Numbers

Many methods have been used to generate random variables. The one most commonly used in digital computers bases the generation of both continuous and discrete random variables on random numbers that are continuously and uniformly distributed between 0 and 1. Subroutines that produce such numbers are readily available. Their outputs are a series of numbers, each of which is equally likely to take any value between 0 and 1. The theory of these generators is quite complex, although the subroutines themselves are usually quite small and easy to use. See (3) for an extensive bibliography on the generation of random numbers.

The generation method that is used in GPSS is based on a general method called the *multiplicative congruence method*. This employs a reiterative procedure that produces one random number from the previous random number. Given one number, C_i, the next number, C_{i+1}, is derived by multiplying C_i by a constant, λ, and taking the remainder after dividing by another constant P. The procedure is described by the equation

$$C_{i+1} = \lambda C_i \pmod{P}$$

The process is started with an initial value C_0. With proper selection of the constants involved, it is possible to produce numbers that are random and uniformly distributed to a high degree of statistical significance.

It is apparent, however, that the process is completely determined. If the process is started with the same C_0, exactly the same sequence of numbers will result. In addition, because the numbers are finite in size, eventually one output will be exactly the same as some previous output, and, consequently, the numbers will cycle through the same set of numbers as occurs between the two identical outputs. With a well-designed generator, however, the length of such cycles is several hundred thousand numbers.

A1-3

GPSS Random Number Generators

GPSS contains eight independent random number generators, referenced by the SNA RNn, $n = 1, 2, \ldots, 8$. There is, in fact, one common subroutine being used to produce eight streams of numbers independently. The output of each generator is either a floating-point number, uniformly distributed between 0 and 0.999999, or an integer, uniformly distributed between 0 and 999.

The user does not directly specify which type of output occurs. If the request for a random number is made as the argument of a function, the output is automatically in floating-point form. All other references will produce a random integer.

The implementation of the multiplicative congruence method used in GPSS takes the lower 31 bits of the product λC_i and treats it as a positive binary fraction between 0 and 1. This is equivalent to using the divisor 2^{31} on the 63-bit number produced by the multiplication (when executed on 32-bit word-sized computers such as the IBM 360/370 systems). It also offers a simple procedure, because the lower 31 bits are simply the lower word of the two-word product. (The bit occuring at position 32 is a sign bit and it may be necessary to invert it to get a positive number.)

Usually the numbers C_{i+1} produced by the process are the random number outputs. In the GPSS implementation, however, there are two variations from this usual practice. Whereas the number required to continue the generating process is derived as described, the output is derived from the middle 32 bits of the product. If a floating-point output is needed, these bits are divided by 10^6 and the remainder treated as a fraction. If an integer is needed, the middle bits are divided by 10^3 and the remainder treated as an integer. In addition, since there are eight generators, there are eight λ constants. To add a further randomizing effect, the particular λ used on each iteration of the generation process is selected randomly from among the eight.

To carry out the process there are three 8-word arrays. The generator number, n, indicated in RNn, selects one column of these arrays. One array, called the *base number array*, contains the set of numbers λ_n. The second array, called the *multiplier array*, successively contains the values $C_{i,n}$. The third array, called the *index array*, contains a random three-bit number which selects the base number to be used. Suppose that the nth generator is being accessed and that the index array for that generator holds the number r, ($0 \leqslant r \leqslant 7$). The program selects the rth member of the base number array and multiplies it by $C_{i,n}$. It makes $C_{i+1,n}$ the lower 31 bits of this product. It selects three bits from the high-order end of the product and puts these in the nth number of the index array so that the number r for the nth generator has been reselected. The output is derived from the middle 32 bits of the product in the manner described above.

Initially, all words of the index array contain zero, so the first reference to any of the eight generators will use the same value, λ_0. In addition, unless the user selects otherwise, in a manner to be described shortly, the initial values of the multiplier array words, $C_{0,n}$, are set to 37. Under these circumstances, all eight generators will produce exactly the same sequence of numbers, although, depending upon how many times they are referenced, they will be at different points along the sequence.

To produce different sequences the user must supply other values of C_0, using an RMULT statement. This has the word RMULT in the operation field, and fields A through H supply the value of C_0 to the successively numbered generators. A blank field will leave unchanged the value of C_0 for the corresponding generator. (The GPSS manuals refer to these initial values, C_0, as "multipliers." They also use the term "seed" in referring to the fixed numbers, λ, in the base array. Elsewhere, these two terms are often reversed, so that the number C_0 is called a seed and λ is called a multiplier. We will continue to follow the notation of the GPSS manuals.)

When the program is initially loaded or when a JOB statement has just been read, the initial values are set to be 37. If an RMULT statement is used, it must precede all block statements. It must also precede the CLEAR statement (because the CLEAR statement may need to reference a generator in order to create an initial transaction at a GENERATE block). The use of a CLEAR, or RESET, statement does not reset the values of the multipliers. If another run were started without using an RMULT statement, the last value of the multiplier left from the run just completed becomes the initial value for the following run. This, in fact, is a simple way of getting multiple runs in which different sequences or random numbers are used. If the user wants to repeat exactly the same sequence of numbers as were used in the previous run, the initial value must be reset to 37 by the RMULT statement.

The purpose of providing eight independent random number generators is to give the user the ability to repeat some sequence of a random process exactly, while varying some other sequence. For example, the interarrival time of transactions might be produced from one generator while the other system action times are produced from another. Repetitive runs could then be made changing the sequence of numbers used for the action times while maintaining the same transaction timing sequence. This, of course, will usually be an artificial constraint, and, eventually, a series of runs should also be made in which all times use different numbers in different runs. Initially holding the interarrival times invariant, however, will give the user some insight into how much of the variability occurring in the system is intrinsic to the system itself, and how much extra variability is introduced by the randomness of the arrivals.

When using this technique, random number generator 1 should not be used for the invariant values. The GPSS program itself uses generator number 1 in the random and PICK modes of the TRANSFER block. A change in the pattern of transaction movements can change the sequence of numbers.

An analysis of the statistical properties of the GPSS random number generators will be found in (96) [also reproduced in (21)].

APPENDIX 2

GPSS ASSEMBLY PROGRAM

The prime functions of the assembly program are to check that input statements are correctly completed and to translate symbolic references to locations and entities into numbers. The basic format for input statements consists of the following main fields, named for the role they play when being used to describe a block:

Columns	Field name
2-6	Location
8-18	Operation
19-71	Operands

Column 1 is normally blank, but an asterisk in that column indicates a Comments statement that is listed in the output but that does not otherwise affect the program. Column 7 is also usually blank. The operands, which begin in column 19, are written in free form, with the individual entries being separated by commas. No embedded blanks are allowed. A blank terminates the operands list and anything appearing after the blank is treated as a remark. Input statements other than block definitions follow the same format with the information serving special purposes according to the nature of the control statement. The only exceptions are the Comments statement, which has just been described, and a function follower statement, which gives the data defining a function by beginning in column 1 and continuing, without blanks, possibly to column 71.

Inputs made by punched card are usually in the fixed format just described. In addition, there is a free format mode of input that is particularly useful for entering input from a terminal, since it minimizes the number of characters to be transmitted. With that format, the location field begins in column 1, and a single blank has the effect of terminating one field and starting the next. If there is no entry in the location field, there is an initial blank. There can, in fact, be more than one blank separating fields, so long as operands begin before column 21, when they are to appear, and remarks do not start before column 21, if there are no operands. For those block types that have a control character, or characters, in the operation field, such as TEST E, the single blank separating the control character is still used. The program recognizes that this is not intended to end a field.

As an example of the free form of input, Fig. A2-1 shows the input for the simple machine shop example, discussed in Chap. 3. It should be compared with Fig. 3-2, which shows the input for the same example in fixed format.

A2-1

Symbols

All symbolic names consist of from three to five characters drawn from the alphabetic characters A through Z and the digits 0 through 9. *The first three characters must be alphabetic.* Embedded blanks are not allowed. The following are examples of legal symbols:

    MACH   LOCC1   AAA   EXIT2   REJ

The following are examples of illegal symbols:

    AB   12M   BRANCH   NO   WY   NO.WY   XX5

Mixtures of symbolic names and absolute numeric values are allowed for both locations and entities. The program assigns numbers to symbolic locations in the order in which they are encountered in the input, normally beginning at 1 and assigning successive numbers that have not been preempted by the absolute assignments.

A2-2

Relative Addressing

Addressing relative to a symbolic or numeric reference is allowed in both a positive and negative direction. If, for example, the symbol AAA is assigned

```
        SIMULATE
*
        EXP FUNCTION RN1,C24 INVERTED EXPONENTIAL FUNCTION
        0,0/.1,.104/.2,.222/.3,.355/.4,.509/.5,.69
        .6,.915/.7,1.2/.75,1.38/.8,1.6/.84,1.83/.88,2.12
        .9,2.3/.92,2.52/.94,2.81/.95,2.99/.96,3.2/.97,3.5
        .98,3.9/.99,4.6/.995,5.3/.998,6.2/.999,7/.9997,3
*
        TYPE FUNCTION RN1,D5 DISTRIBUTION OF PART TYPES
        .1,1/.35,2/.57,3/.85,4/1.0,5
*
        NORM FUNCTION RN1,C25 INVERTED STANDARD NORMAL FUNCTION
        0,-5/.00003,-4/.00135,-3/.00621,-2.5/.02275,-2/.06681,-1.5
        .11507,-1.2/.15866,-1/.21186,-.8/.27425,-.6/.34458,-.4/.42074,-.2
        .5,0/.57926,.2/.65542,.4/.72575,.6/.78814,.8/.84134,1/.88493,1.2
        .93319,1.5/.97725,2/.99379,2.5/.99865,3/.99997,4/1,5
*
        BRCH FUNCTION PH1,L5 SEPARATES PARTS
        1,LOC1/2,LOC2/3,LOC3/4,LOC4/5,LOC5
*
*       SIMULATION OF SIMPLE MACHINE SHOP
*
         GENERATE XH$ARR,FN$EXP CREATE PARTS
         ASSIGN 1,FN$TYPE,PH PICK TYPE
         QUEUE WAIT JOIN QUEUE
         ENTER MACH GET MACHINE
         DEPART WAIT LEAVE QUEUE
         ADVANCE V$TIME MACHINE PART
         LEAVE MACH GIVE UP MACHINE
         TABULATE TRTM TABULATE TIME IN SYSTEM
         TRANSFER FN,BRCH BRANCH BY TYPE
*
        LOC1 SAVEVALUE 1+,1,XH ADD 1 TO COUNT OF TYPE 1 PARTS
         TERMINATE 1 DESTROY TRANSACTION
*
        LOC2 SAVEVALUE 2+,1,XH
         TERMINATE 1
*
        LOC3 SAVEVALUE 3+,1,XH
         TERMINATE 1
*
        LOC4 SAVEVALUE 4+,1,XH
         TERMINATE 1
*
        LOC5 SAVEVALUE 5+,1,XH
         TERMINATE 1
*
        TIME VARIABLE 20*FN$NORM+60 COMPUTES MACHINE TIME
         STORAGE S$MACH,3 NUMBER OF MACHINES
        TRTM TABLE M1,0,20,12 TABLE FOR TRANSIT TIME
         INITIAL XH$ARR,25 SET MEAN ARRIVAL TIME
*
         START 10,NP INITIALIZE WITH 10 PARTS
         RESET            WIPE OUT STATISTICS
         START 500 RUN FOR 500 PARTS
         END
```

Figure A2-1. Simple machine shop example input in free form.

the value 36, then AAA+2 and AAA-3 will denote blocks 38 and 33, respectively. Note that there are no blanks. The symbol * used in a field that should supply a location is interpreted as the current location, and it can be used in relative addressing. For example, TRANSFER ,*+5 transfers control to the location five ahead of the block.

A2-3

Symbolic Entities

An operand that refers to an entity may contain a symbol. Each type of entity has its own sequence of numbers. The same symbol can be used for two or more different types of entity, or for an entity and a location. The numeric values assigned to the multiply used symbol are independent. If the user wants them to have the same value, the Equate statement, or the entity-type function, described in Sec. A2-5, must be used.

A2-4

EQU and SYN Statements

The Equate statement carries EQU in the operation field and a symbol, which is to be assigned a specific value, in the location field. The value the symbol is to assume is the A operand. There follow one or more fields identifying the type of entity for which that symbol is to be assigned the specific value. For example,

```
          LINE    EQU           6,F,Q,XH
```

will assign the number 6 to the symbol LINE used to identify a facility, a queue, and a halfword savevalue. As many types of entity as desired can be defined, so long as the statement does not go beyond column 71. The characters representing the types of entity are shown in Table A2-1. Note that they are not all the same as the symbols used when describing the entities as SNAs.

Blocks of numbers may also be reserved by an Equate statement, using the following notation:

```
          COUNT   EQU           20(15),XF
```

This statement will reserve the 15 fullword savevalues numbered 20 through 34 and associate the symbol COUNT with number 20. The others can be reached by a relative address, such as COUNT+3.

A2-5

Entity Functions

It is often necessary to control dynamically which entity is to be used according to some SNA; for example, use a different queue and facility to represent a communication channel according to message type. The message type might be represented by a parameter, say, byte-sized parameter 4. If

Table A2-1 Symbols Representing Entities in Equate Statements and Entity Functions

Symbol	Entity
F	Facilities
S	Storages
Q	Queues
X or XF	Fullword savevalues
H or XH	Halfword savevalues
XB	Byte-sized savevalues
XL	Floating-point savevalues
M or MX	Fullword matrices
Y or MH	Halfword matrices
MB	Byte-sized matrices
ML	Floating-point matrices
T	Tables
V	Variables
L	Logic switches
C	User chains
Z	Functions
B	Boolean variables
G	Groups

it were convenient to reserve the numbers 1 through 4 for both the facilities and queues, the parameter could be used directly to supply the entity numbers, but it can be inconvenient to make such special assignments of numbers. An entity-type function is provided to allow entity numbers to be assigned more freely.

The function definition statement of an entity-type function uses the letter S, followed by the number of points, in field B. Beginning in field C there are symbols, selected from Table A2-1, denoting the entity types to be assigned values. The coding can extend to column 71. The function follower statement gives either the number to be assigned for the selected entities or, more commonly, a symbol that can then be assigned a value. In the example just discussed, suppose that there are four message types. The following entity function might be used:

```
      COMM    FUNCTION    PB4,S4,F,Q
1,COMM1/2,COMM2/3,COMM3/4,COMM4
```

During assembly, the symbols COMM1, COMM2, etc., will be assigned values, not necessarily consecutive. The following coding could then be used in the model:

```
          ASSIGN       1,FN$COMM,PH
          QUEUE        PH1
          SEIZE        PH1
```

The ASSIGN block places in halfword parameter 1 the value assigned to one of the symbols COMMj, depending upon the current value of byte-sized parameter 4. The next two blocks then use that number to select a facility and a queue according to message type (see Sec. 11-6 for another example).

A2-6

Symbolic SNA References

An SNA can be named symbolically by using the symbol for the SNA type followed by a $ sign and the symbolic name to be given to the SNA. For example, a function called NAME is denoted by FN$NAME.

Certain operands in some block types refer to a parameter. Because there are four types of parameters, the type must be indicated by attaching a suffix, using the following notation: PF, fullword; PB, byte-sized; PH, halfword; and PL, floating-point. Table 10-1 lists the operand fields where this notation must be used. If the parameter is directly numbered, the suffix immediately follows the number. If the entity is named, the suffix follows the name, separated by a $ sign. For example, it might be decided to store the clock time in fullword parameter 5, using the MARK block. The block would then be coded as

```
          MARK         5PF
```

If the parameter number to be used were to be selected by an SNA, say, halfword savevalue number 6, the coding would be

```
          MARK         XH6$PF
```

If the savevalue were named, say, MTP, the coding would be

```
          MARK         XH$MTP$PF
```

In a number of block definition and control statements it is possible to give a range of values. Section 11-5 gives a list of fields where this is possible. The range can be given symbolically if the symbols are assigned values with an Equate statement. For example,

```
          INITIAL      XH$FIRST-XH$LAST,0
  FIRST   EQU          10,XH
  LAST    EQU          19,XH
```

This will set all 10 halfword savevalues numbers 10 through 19 to zero and associate the symbol FIRST with number 10 and LAST with number 19.

A2-7
Macros

A macro is a segment of coding that is expected to be used, with different operands, in many places. It is named and defined once with as many as 10 fields of information left unspecified. The macro can then be used, or called, at any point in a model by a MACRO statement which gives specific values to be used in the fields that were left unspecified at the time of the definition. The action of the assembly program upon encountering a MACRO statement is to replace the statement with a copy of the coding that defines the macro, completing the unspecified fields with the values supplied by the MACRO statement.

Each macro definition is preceded by a control statement having the word STARTMACRO in the operation field and the name to be given the macro in the location field. The definition is concluded with another control statement that simply has the word ENDMACRO in the operation field. Between these two statements there can be any number of GPSS block definition or control statements, including other macros, subject to some limitations to be explained shortly. Fixed format coding must be used for macros.

The fields of information to be supplied at the time the macro is called are marked by entering the symbols #A, #B, etc., up to a limit of 10, which, if it were used, would result in the sequence ending with #J. The alphabetic sequence of these fields, which cannot contain gaps, refers to the order in which the values will be supplied at the time of calling. The fields do not have to appear in any particular order within the defining statements and the same symbol can be used more than once, in which case, the same value will be supplied to each occurrence.

Definitions of macros must appear at the beginning of a model, except that they must follow any use of the REALLOCATE, AUXILIARY, UPDATE, or LOAD statements. They may follow or precede a SIMULATE statement. When there is more than one macro, the order of loading is irrelevant, except that a macro that appears in the definition of another macro must precede the macro in which it appears.

When the macro is to be used in the model, a statement with the word MACRO in the operation field is used. The macro name appears in the location field. In the operands field is a list of the values needed to supply all the undefined fields of the macro. They are separated by commas and their number must exactly match the number of operands given in the definition.

As an example, suppose that a machine tool is represented by a facility. A model is to be built in which there are several different machine tools, each of which has a separate machining time. A macro could be constructed in which, say, the A field supplies the facility number and the B and C fields supply a mean and spread from which to calculate an action time. Suppose that the waiting line at each machine is to be measured and that it is convenient to use the same number for the queue and facility associated with each machine. The name of the macro is merely used for identification. It does not become a location symbol. If, as occurs in this example, it is necessary to identify a location within the macro, that location must be supplied as one of the items in the calling sequence. For the example just discussed, the following macro could be used:

```
MACH    STARTMACRO   #A,#B,#C,#D
#D      QUEUE        #A
        SEIZE        #A
        DEPART       #A
        ADVANCE      #B,#C
        RELEASE      #A
        ENDMACRO
```

The name of the macro is MACH. The first undefined field is the location of the first block, and, in spite of being first, this will be supplied by the D field of the calling sequence. The A field will supply a facility and a queue number, and the B and C fields supply the mean and spread at the ADVANCE block. The list in the operands field of the STARTMACRO statement is treated as remarks. It is not necessary to give such a list, but it helps the user to remember what items must be specified when calling the macro.

Suppose now that a process is to be represented by two machines in sequence followed by a third machine chosen at random between two other machines, with equal probability of each being chosen. The process could be described in terms of the macro as follows:

```
MACH    MACRO       FIRST,20,5,STG1
MACH    MACRO       SECD,45,20,STG2
        TRANSFER    .5,STG3A,STG3B
MACH    MACRO       THIRD,50,30,STG3A
        TRANSFER    ,AWAY
MACH    MACRO       FOUR,30,10,STG3B
```

As indicated, symbolic notation can still be used. Figure A2-2 shows, on the left, the macro definition followed by the process description given above, with some other blocks and control statements added to complete the model. The right side of the figure shows the code that results from the assembly phase that has expanded the macros.

The definition of one macro can include other macros. The internal macros may themselves include macros within their definition, so that there are three levels of macros, but the process cannot be extended any further. However, there is no limit on how many macros can be used internally at the second and third levels. Figure A2-3 may help to explain these rules. Level 0 indicates a macro to be defined by using other macros. The definition includes, at level 1, any number of other macros: in this case, there are two. They may be interspersed with other GPSS statements. Each of these

```
*          MACRO EXAMPLE                              *          MACRO EXAMPLE
*                                                     *
MACH   STARTMACRO  #A,#B,#C,#D                        MACH   STARTMACRO  #A,#B,#C,#D
#D     QUEUE       #A                                 #D     QUEUE       #A
       SEIZE       #A                                        SEIZE       #A
       DEPART      #A                                        DEPART      #A
       ADVANCE     #B,#C                                     ADVANCE     #B,#C
       RELEASE     #A                                        RELEASE     #A
       ENDMACRO                                              ENDMACRO
*                                                     *
       GENERATE    100                      1                GENERATE    100
MACH   MACRO       FIRST,20,5,STG1          2         MACH   MACRO       FIRST,20,5,STG1
MACH   MACRO       SECD,45,20,STG2          3         STG1   QUEUE       FIRST
       TRANSFER    .5,STG3A,STG3B           4                SEIZE       FIRST
MACH   MACRO       THIRD,50,30,STG3A        5                DEPART      FIRST
       TRANSFER    ,AWAY                    6                ADVANCE     20,5
MACH   MACRO       FOUR,30,10,STG3B                          RELEASE     FIRST
AWAY   TERMINATE   1                                  MACH   MACRO       SECD,45,20,STG2
       START       10                       7         STG2   QUEUE       SECD
                                            8                SEIZE       SECD
                                            9                DEPART      SECD
                                           10                ADVANCE     45,20
                                           11                RELEASE     SECD
                                           12                TRANSFER    .5,STG3A,STG3B
                                                      MACH   MACRO       THIRD,50,30,STG3A
                                           13         STG3A  QUEUE       THIRD
                                           14                SEIZE       THIRD
                                           15                DEPART      THIRD
                                           16                ADVANCE     50,30
                                           17                RELEASE     THIRD
                                           18                TRANSFER    ,AWAY
                                                      MACH   MACRO       FOUR,30,10,STG3B
                                           19         STG3B  QUEUE       FOUR
                                           20                SEIZE       FOUR
                                           21                DEPART      FOUR
                                           22                ADVANCE     30,10
                                           23                RELEASE     FOUR
                                           24         AWAY   TERMINATE   1
                                                             START       10
```

Figure A2-2. Coding and assembly of macro example.

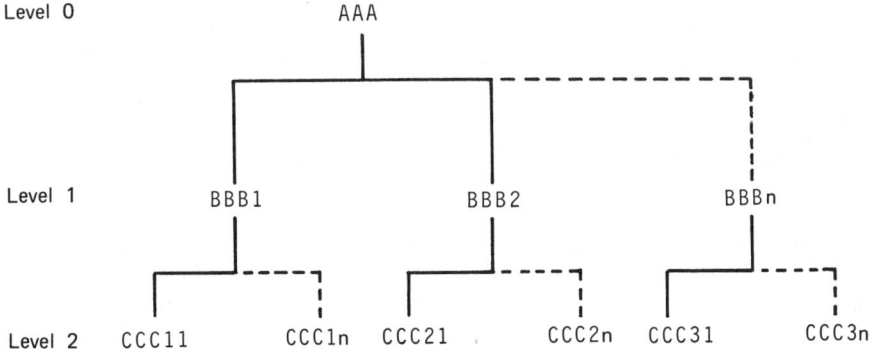

Figure A2-3. Multilevel macro rules.

level 1 macros can include, at level 2, any number of other macros: in this case, there is just one to each. Suppose, for simplicity, that each macro at the lowest level consists of a single ADVANCE block. The example illustrated in Fig. A2-3 would then be coded as shown on the left of Fig. A2-4, which also shows the expansion of the coding upon assembly.

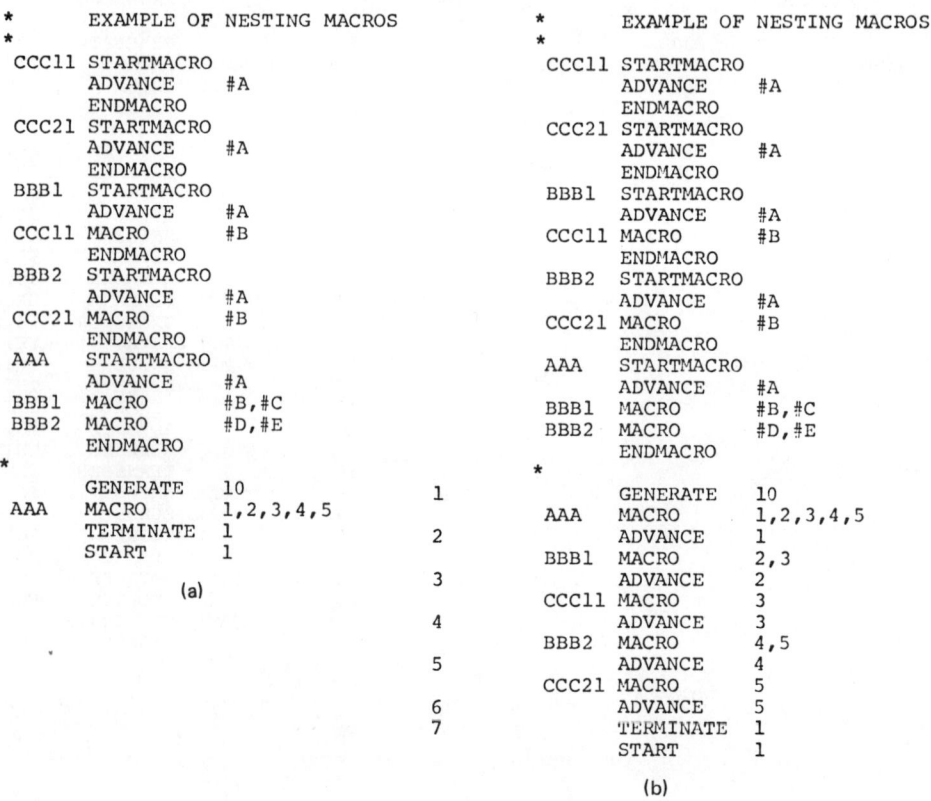

Figure A2-4. Coding of multilevel macro example.

A2-8

Absolute Statements

A number of control statements are designed to permit the mixing of absolute and symbolic statements. Absolute statements cannot use any symbols but otherwise follow the normal format, except that function follower statements have a fixed format, illustrated in Fig. 3-4 and described in Sec. 3-11. All blocks must also be given a specific location even though they are loaded in sequential order, because the location counter is frozen while reading absolute statements (see Sec. 7-5 for an example).

When statements in absolute format are to be loaded, the segment, or segments, of such code are preceded by a control statement with the word ABS in the operation field. They are followed by another control statement with the word ENDABS in the operation field. All statements between this pair of control statements are passed without processing by the assembly program. In particular, the location counter is not advanced. If the absolute statements are interspersed with normal symbolic statements, it may be necessary to reset the location counter. A control statement with the word ORG in the operation field will set the location counter to the value given in field A. It may also be necessary to leave sections of block numbers to be filled in later. A control statement with the word ICT in the operation field will increment the location counter by the amount given in field A.

A2-9
Redefinition of Statements

In the course of assembling a problem it is possible to use two or more statements that refer to the same entity or use the same location. In the case of multiply defined control statements, read within a single run, it will be the last one that is effective. What is often done is to define an entity, or use a location, in one run and then redefine it in a subsequent run. The redefinition statement will follow the START statement of the first run. At the time of assembly, the program resolves all the symbols it encounters within one job, regardless of the run in which they occur.

An example of when multiply defined entities might be used would be a series of runs in which an action time at an ADVANCE block is to be changed between runs. The first run would include the ADVANCE block with a symbolic location and the first value the action time is to take. Following the START statement that controls the first run will be another statement for an ADVANCE block using the same location and the second value of the action time. A second START statement follows that statement and any others used to redefine the model between the runs. This procedure can be followed for as many runs as necessary. At assembly time, all these ADVANCE blocks will be given the same location, but, to be sure that this was the intention of the user, the program prints a warning that a location has been multiply defined, but the simulation is not stopped.

An absolute statement can also use a location that has been used previously. This is, in fact, a common use of absolute statements. Certain blocks of a model that have been assembled, for which the assigned numbers are now known, may need to be modified in a later run. This is frequently done when a model has been saved by using the SAVE feature and the user wants to make some modifications after recovering the model with a READ statement.

Redefinition can change the block type, but there is a restriction on blocks that deal with transactions in assembly sets. A MATCH, ASSEMBLE, or GATHER block may be redefined only if the current transaction count at the block is zero. If a GENERATE block is redefined, any transaction waiting to enter the system at that block is removed. If a new GENERATE block is entered, an initial transaction is created to represent the next arrival at that block, based on the clock time at the point of redefinition.

Matrices, tables, variables, functions and storage capacities may all be redefined. In the case of redefining storage capacity, an error will occur if the new capacity is less than the current content at the time of redefinition.

A2-10

Listing Control Statements

As was described in Sec. 3-11, the normal sequence of events followed in producing output from a run is to list first the input statements defining the problem, then give the symbol tables followed by the input in assembled form, and finally give the output report. When a completed model is being repeatedly rerun or when sections of a model have been satisfactorily debugged, all this output is not needed. A statement with the word UNLIST in the operation field will cause all following statements in both the input and the assembly listing to be omitted, until either a statement with the word LIST in the operation field is met or the end of the input is reached. If the word ABS is placed in the A field of the UNLIST statement, only the assembly listing is affected. The LIST statement has no operands. Both the LIST and UNLIST statements are themselves listed.

Another control statement with the word NOXREF in the operation field will cause the cross-reference, or symbol, tables to be suppressed. It can appear anywhere in the input ahead of the START statement.

APPENDIX 3

BLOCK STATEMENT FORMATS

BLOCK STATEMENT FORMATS

OPERATION	A	B	C	D	E	F	G	H	I	BLOCK SYMBOL
ADVANCE	Mean time [k, SNAj, SNA*SNAj]	Spread [k, SNAj, SNA*SNAj] Function modifier FNj, [FN*SNAj]								A, B (rectangle)
ALTER G GE L LE E NE MIN MAX	Group no. k, SNAj, SNA*SNAj	Count ALL k, SNAj, SNA*SNAj	Member attribute to be altered PR or kPx, SNAjPx, SNA*SNAjPx	Value to replace attribute k, SNAj, SNA*SNAj	Matching transaction attribute [PR or kPx, SNAjPx, SNA*SNAjPx]	Matching SNA [k, SNAj, SNA*SNAj]	Alternate exit [k, SNAj, SNA*SNAj]			B, C, D, E, F (hexagon with A circle and G exit)

[ ] Indicates optional operand

{ } Indicates that one of the items within the braces must be selected

† Block operand where PL, XL, or ML is a valid SNA.

349

BLOCK STATEMENT FORMATS

OPERATION	A	B	C	D	E	F	G	H	I	BLOCK SYMBOL
ASSEMBLE	No. of transactions to assemble k, SNAj, SNA*SNAj									
ASSIGN	Parameter no. k, SNAj, SNA*SNAj [±]	SNA to be assigned k, SNAj, SNA*SNAj †	No. of function modifier [k, SNAj, SNA*SNAj]	Parameter type Px	The parameter type operand may optionally be coded as the C operand if a function modifier is not specified.					
BUFFER										
CHANGE	"From" block no. k, SNAj, SNA*SNAj	"To" block no. k, SNAj, SNA*SNAj								
COUNT G, GE L, LE E, NE U, NU I, NI SNE, SE SNF, SF LR, LS	Parameter in which to place count kPx, SNAjPx, SNA*SNAjPx	Lower limit k, SNAj, SNA*SNAj	Upper limit k, SNAj, SNA*SNAj	Comparison value [k, SNAj, SNA*SNAj]	[SNA mnemonic to be counted]					
DEPART	Queue no. k, SNAj, SNA*SNAj	No. of units [k, SNAj, SNA*SNAj]								
ENTER	Storage no. k, SNAj, SNA*SNAj	No. of units [k, SNAj, SNA*SNAj]								
EXAMINE	Group no. k, SNAj, SNA*SNAj	Numeric value–numeric mode [k, SNAj, SNA*SNAj]	Alternate exit k, SNAj, SNA*SNAj							

BLOCK STATEMENT FORMATS

OPERATION	A	B	C	D	E	F	G	H	I	BLOCK SYMBOL
EXECUTE	Block no. k, SNAj, SNA*SNAj									
FAVAIL	Facility no. or range k, SNAj, SNA*SNAj									
FUNAVAIL	Facility no. or range k, SNAj, SNA*SNAj	Remove or continue option [RE CO]	Alternate block no. [k,SNAj, SNA*SNAj]	Parameter no. [kPx, SNAjPx, SNA*SNAjPx]	Remove or continue option [RE CO]	Alternate block no. [k,SNAj, SNA*SNAj]	Remove or continue option [RE CO]	Alternate block no. [k,SNAj, SNA*SNAj]		
			Options for controlling transactions		Options for preempted transactions		Options for delayed transactions			
GATE {LS LR}	Logic switch no. k, SNAj, SNA*SNAj									
GATE {NI I NU U FV FNV}	Facility no. k, SNAj, SNA*SNAj	Next block if condition is false [k, SNAj, SNA*SNAj]								
GATE {SE SF SNE SNF SV SNV}	Storage no. k, SNAj, SNA*SNAj	Next block if condition is false [k, SNAj, SNA*SNAj]								

App. 3 / Block Statement Formats

BLOCK STATEMENT FORMATS

OPERATION	A	B	C	D	E	F	G	H	I	BLOCK SYMBOL
GATE {M / NM}	Match block no. k, SNAj, SNA*SNAj	Next block if condition is false [k, SNAj* / SNA*SNAj]								(diamond with X, A, →B)
GATHER	No. to be gathered k, SNAj, SNA*SNAj									(rectangle with X, A)
GENERATE	Mean time [k, SNAj, SNA*SNAj]	Spread [k, SNAj, SNA*SNAj, function modifier FNj, FN*SNAj]	Initialization interval [k, SNAj, SNA*SNAj]	Creation limit [k, SNAj, SNA*SNAj]	Priority level [k, SNAj, SNA*SNAj]	Fullword, halfword, byte & floating point parameters in any sequence kPx, SNAjPx, SNA*SNAjPx				(circle A,B with C,D,E,F,G,H,I)
	Note 1: Operands A–I may be a constant, FNj, Vj, Xj, XFj, XBj, XHj, RNj, C1, AC1, or Nj. Likewise, elements of functions or variables specified are restricted to these SNAs.									
HELP {A B C APL1 BPL1 CPL1'}	Help routine name When using HELPB or HELPBPL1, the B-G operands reference either fullword or floating-point (floating-point) or XF (fullword) suffix should be used with each operand.	B-G operands SNA values to be passed to help routine k, SNAj, SNA*SNAj								(shape with A, B,C,D,E,F,G)
INDEX	Parameter no. kPx, SNAjPx, SNA*SNAjPx	Increment k, SNAj, SNA*SNAj								(shape with A, B)
JOIN	Group no. k, SNAj, SNA*SNAj	Numeric quantity [k, SNAj, SNA*SNAj]								(shape with circle A, B)

BLOCK STATEMENT FORMATS

OPERATION	A	B	C	D	E	F	G	H	I	BLOCK SYMBOL
LEAVE	Storage no. k, SNAj, SNA*SNAj	No. of units [k, SNAj, SNA*SNAj]								B, A (with A in upper-left corner)
LINK	User chain no. k, SNAj, SNA*SNAj	Ordering of chain LIFO, FIFO or parameter number kPx, SNAjPx, SNA*SNAjPx	Alternate block exit [k, SNAj, SNA*SNAj]							C, with A on top, B on right
LOGIC S R I	Logic switch no. k, SNAj, SNA*SNAj									(X)A symbol
LOOP	Parameter no. kPx SNAjPx, SNA*SNAjPx	Next block if $P_xj \neq 0$ k, SNAj, SNA*SNAj								B, A
MARK	Parameter no. [kPx, SNAjPx, SNA*SNAjPx]									A (dashed top)
MATCH	Conjugate MATCH block no. k, SNAj, SNA*SNAj									Triangle with A
MSAVEVALUE	Matrix no. or range k, SNAj, SNA*SNAj [±]	Row no. or range k, SNAj, SNA*SNAj	Column no. or range k, SNAj, SNA*SNAj	SNA to be saved k, SNAj, SNA*SNAj †	Msavevalue type H, MH, MX, MB, ML					A,B,C,D,E

BLOCK STATEMENT FORMATS

OPERATION	A	B	C	D	E	F	G	H	I	BLOCK SYMBOL
PREEMPT	Facility no. k, SNAj, SNA*SNAj	Priority option [PR]	Block no. for preempted transaction [k, SNAj, SNA*SNAj]	Parameter no. of preempted transaction [kPx, SNAjPx, SNA*SNAjPx]	Remove option [RE]					B, C, D, E / A
PRINT	Lower limit [k, SNAj, SNA*SNAj any SNA except MX, MH, MB, ML]	Upper limit [k, SNAj, SNA*SNAj any SNA except MX, MH, MB, ML]	Entity mnemonic	Paging indicator [Any alphameric character]						A — B / C, D
PRIORITY	Priority no. k, SNAj, SNA*SNAj	[BUFFER]								A / B
QUEUE	Queue no. k, SNAj, SNA*SNAj	No. of units [k, SNAj, SNA*SNAj]								A / B
RELEASE	Facility no. k, SNAj, SNA*SNAj									A

BLOCK STATEMENT FORMATS

OPERATION	A	B	C	D	E	F	G	H	I	BLOCK SYMBOL
REMOVE ⎡G⎤ ⎢GE⎥ ⎢L⎥ ⎢LE⎥ ⎢E⎥ ⎢NE⎥ ⎣MAX⎦ MIN	Group no. k, SNAj, SNA*SNAj	Count ⎡k, SNAj,⎤ ⎢SNA*SNAj⎥ ⎣ALL⎦	Numeric quantity ⎡k, SNAj,⎤ ⎣SNA*SNAj⎦	Transaction attributes for comparison ⎡PR, or kPx,⎤ ⎢SNAjPx,⎥ ⎣SNA*SNAjPx⎦	Comparison SNA ⎡k, SNAj,⎤ ⎣SNA*SNAj⎦	Alternate exit ⎡k, SNAj,⎤ ⎣SNA*SNAj⎦				
RETURN	Facility no. k, SNAj, SNA*SNAj									
SAVAIL	Storage no. or range k, SNAj, SNA*SNAj									
SAVEVALUE	Savevalue no. or range k, SNAj, SNA*SNAj [±]	SNA to be saved k, SNAj, SNA*SNAj †	Savevalue type X, XF, H, XH, XB, XL							
SCAN ⎡G⎤ ⎢GE⎥ ⎢L⎥ ⎢LE⎥ ⎢E⎥ ⎢NE⎥ ⎣MAX⎦ MIN	Group no. k, SNAj, SNA*SNAj	Transaction attribute for comparison PR or parameter no. kPx, SNAjPx, SNA*SNAjPx	Comparison value for B operand k, SNAj, SNA*SNAj	Desired attribute PR or parameter no. kPx, SNAjPx, SNA*SNAjPx	Parameter no. in which to place D operand value ⎡kPx,⎤ ⎢SNAjPx,⎥ ⎣SNA*SNAjPx⎦	Alternate exit ⎡k, SNAj,⎤ ⎣SNA*SNAj⎦				

App. 3 / Block Statement Formats

BLOCK STATEMENT FORMATS

OPERATION	A	B	C	D	E	F	G	H	I	BLOCK SYMBOL
SEIZE	Facility no. k, SNAj, SNA*SNAj									
SELECT G,GE L,LE E,NE U,NU I,NI SE,SNE SF,SNF LR,LS MIN,MAX	Parameter in which to place entity kPx, SNAjPx, SNA*SNAjPx	Lower limit k, SNAj, SNA*SNAj	Upper limit k, SNAj, SNA*SNAj	Comparison value [k, SNAj, SNA*SNAj]	SNA mnemonic [to be examined]	Alternative exit [k, SNAj, SNA*SNAj]				
SPLIT	No. of copies k, SNAj, SNA*SNAj	Next block for copies k, SNAj, SNA*SNAj	Parameter for serial numbering [kPx, SNAjPx, SNA*SNAjPx]	No. of fullword, halfword, byte, & floating-point parameters in any sequence [k,Px, SNAjPx, SNA*SNAjPx]	[kPx, SNAjPx, SNA*SNAjPx]	[kPx, SNAjPx, SNA*SNAjPx]	[kPx, SNAjPx, SNA*SNAjPx]			
SUNAVAIL	Storage no. or range k, SNAj, SNA*SNAj									
TABULATE	Table no. k, SNAj, SNA*SNAj	Weighting factor [k, SNAj, SNA*SNAj]								
TERMINATE	Termination count [k, SNAj, SNA*SNAj]									

BLOCK STATEMENT FORMATS

OPERATION	A	B	C	D	E	F	G	H	I	BLOCK SYMBOL
TEST {E, NE, GE, LE, G, L}	First SNA k, SNAj, SNA*SNAj †	Second SNA k, SNAj, SNA*SNAj †	Next block if relation is false [k, SNAj, SNA*SNAj]							A X B with arrow to C (diamond)
TRACE										triangle
TRANSFER	Selection mode With ALL selection mode a block name of number is the only valid operand	Next block A₁ [k, SNAj, SNA*SNAj]	Next block B₁ [k, SNAj, SNA*SNAj]	[Indexing factor]						A, D, B (diamond)
UNLINK {G, GE, L, LE, E, NE}	User chain no. k, SNAj, SNA*SNAj	**Next block for the unlinked transaction (s)** k, SNAj, SNA*SNAj	Transaction unlink count ALL or k, SNAj, SNA*SNAj	[Parameter no. kPx, SNAjPx, SNA*SNAjPx, or BACK, or BVj, BV*SNAj]	Match argument [k, SNAj, SNA*SNAj]	Next block B [k, SNAj, SNA*SNAj]				rectangle with X, A C D E, B, F
UNTRACE										triangle
WRITE	Job tape no. {JOBTA1, JOBTA2, JOBTA3}									A (circle shape)

APPENDIX 4

CONTROL STATEMENT FORMATS

CONTROL STATEMENT FORMATS

OPERATION	A	B	C	D	E	F	G	H
AUXILIARY	Entity Mnemonic	Total Allocation k	Number to reside in core k	Number of entities constituting each direct access record k	Bytes in excess of basic bytes $[k]$			
BVARIABLE		Combinations of elements and operators: Elements k, SNA_i, $SNA*SNA_j$		Logical operators FU_j or F_j SF_j FNU_j SNF_j F_{ij} SE_j FN_{ij} SNE_j LR_j LS_j	Conditional operators 'G' 'NE' 'L' 'LE' 'E' 'GE'		Boolean operators + (or) * (and)	

[ ] Indicates optional operand

{ } Indicates that one of the items within the braces must be selected

CONTROL STATEMENT FORMATS

OPERATION	A	B	C	D	E	F	G	H
CLEAR	Savevalues or ranges not to be cleared [X, XF, XH, XB, XL, MX, MH, MB, ML]	Delimiter if multiple entries [,]						
END	(no operands)							
FUNCTION	Argument (independent variable) SNAj (any SNA except MX, MH, MB, or ML)	Function type and no. of points {C, D, E, L, M, S} n						
$x_1, y_1 / x_2, y_2 /$ etc.	(Note: Y values cannot be MX, MH, MB, or ML, and X and Y values must start in position 1.)							
INITIAL	Entity or range {X, XF, XH, XB, XL, MX, MH, MB, ML, LS}	Value k	Delimiter if multiple entries [/]					
JOB	No operands							
JOBTAPE	Jobtape no. {JOBTA1, JOBTA2, JOBTA3}	Next block for jobtape transactions [k, SNAj, SNA*SNAj]	Transaction offset time [k]	Scaling factor [k]				
LOAD	GPSS modules and/or user-written HELP routines to be loaded	Delimiter if multiple entries [,]						
MATRIX	Matrix format {MX, MH, MB, ML}	No. of matrix rows k	No. of matrix columns k					
NOXREF								

CONTROL STATEMENT FORMATS

OPERATION	A	B	C	D	E	F	G	H
QTABLE	Queue no. k	Upper limit of lowest frequency class k	Frequency class size k	No. of frequency classes k				
READ	No. of files to be skipped [k]							
REALLOCATE	Entity mnemonic to be reallocated	Total no. of entries k	Delimiter if multiple entries [,]					
RESET	Entity or range not to be reset	Delimiter if multiple entries [,]						
REWIND	Jobtape no. {JOBTA1, JOBTA2, JOBTA3}							
RMULT	Initial multiplier for RN1 [k]	Initial multiplier for RN2 [k]	Initial multiplier for RN3 [k]	Initial multiplier for RN4 [k]	Initial multiplier for RN5 [k]	Initial multiplier for RN6 [k]	Initial multiplier for RN7 [k]	Initial multiplier for RN8 [k]
SAVE	Reposition option [Any alphameric character]	Options at time expiration [SAVE REPLY]						
SIMULATE	Max. run length [k]	Supress printout [NP]	Snap interval [k]	Standard transaction printout [1]				
START	Run termination count k							

CONTROL STATEMENT FORMATS

OPERATION	A	B	C	D	E	F	G	H
STORAGE	Storage or range S_j	Capacity k	Delimiter if multiple entries [/]					
TABLE	Table argument k, SNA_j, $SNA*SNA_j$ RT, IA Any SNA except MX, MH, MB, ML, PL, XL	Upper limit of lowest frequency class k	Frequency class size k	No. of frequency classes k	Arrival rate time interval [k]			
VARIABLE FVARIABLE	Combinations of elements and arithmetic operators: Elements k, SNA_j, $SNA*SNA_j$			Arithmetic Operators + − / * @ (VARIABLE only)				

APPENDIX 5

STANDARD NUMERICAL ATTRIBUTES

STANDARD NUMERICAL ATTRIBUTES

ENTITY	SNA	DEFINITION	RANGE	MODIFIED BY	RESTRICTIONS/REMARKS
BLOCKS	N_j	The count of the total number of transactions to enter block j	$2^{24} - 1$		Value maintained automatically. The count is updated when a transaction successfully enters the block.
	W_j	The count of the number of transactions currently waiting at block j	$2^{15} - 1$		Value maintained automatically. For blocks followed by a blocking condition such as a GATE or a TEST block which the moving transaction is blocked from entering, W_j includes those transactions waiting to enter either the GATE, or TEST block.

* Except when used as the Y-value of an E- or M-type function (this does not apply to msavevalues) in a FVARIABLE statement or when saved in a floating-point parameter, savevalue, or msavevalue.

STANDARD NUMERICAL ATTRIBUTES

ENTITY	SNA	DEFINITION	RANGE	MODIFIED BY	RESTRICTIONS/REMARKS
FACILITIES	F_j	The in-use status of facility j	0 if not in use 1 if in use	SEIZE, RELEASE, PREEMPT, RETURN	Status maintained automatically. Those using FUNAVAIL and FAVAIL should review the effects of these blocks on the facility in use status.
	FR_j	Utilization in parts per thousand of facility j	0-1000		Value maintained automatically.
	FC_j	Total number of transactions to enter facility j	$2^{31} - 1$		Value maintained automatically.
	FT_j	Average transaction utilization time for facility j	$2^{31} - 1$ Truncated to integer*		Value maintained automatically.
FUNCTIONS	FN_j	The computed value of function j	$\pm 2^{31} - 1$ Truncated to integer except when used as function modifier in GENERATE, ASSIGN or ADVANCE blocks or as the argument of a function*		Defined by FUNCTION definition statement
GROUPS	G_j	The current number of members of group j	$2^{15} - 1$	JOIN REMOVE TERMINATE ASSEMBLE	Value maintained automatically.
MSAVEVALUES	$MX_j(a,b)$	The current contents of fullword msavevalue j, row a, column b	$\pm 2^{31} - 1$	MSAVEVALUE	
	$MH_j(a,b)$	The current contents of halfword msavevalue j, row a, column b	$\pm 2^{15} - 1$	MSAVEVALUE	
	$MB_j(a,b)$	The current contents of byte msavevalue j, row a, column b	$\pm 2^7 - 1$	MSAVEVALUE	
	$ML_j(a,b)$	The current contents of floating point msavevalue j, row a, column b	$\pm 2^{24} - 1$ Without loss of precision. Values may be larger but precision will be lost. Truncated to integer*	MSAVEVALUE	Can be used only as (1) the B operand of an ASSIGN or SAVEVALUE block, (2) the D operand of an MSAVEVALUE block, (3) an element of a FVARIABLE statement, or (4) an operand of a Test block in which two floating-point SNAs are being compared.

STANDARD NUMERICAL ATTRIBUTES

ENTITY	SNA	DEFINITION	MODIFIED BY	MODIFIED BY	RESTRICTIONS/REMARKS
QUEUES	Q_j	The current length or number of units in queue j	$2^{31} - 1$	QUEUE, DEPART	Value maintained automatically.
	QA_j	Average length or number of units in queue j	$2^{31} - 1$ Truncated to integer*		Value computed automatically.
	QM_j	Maximum length or contents of queue j	$2^{31} - 1$		Value maintained automatically.
	QC_j	Total number of units to enter queue j	$2^{31} - 1$		Value maintained automatically.
	QZ_j	Number of entries spending zero time units in queue j	$2^{31} - 1$		Value maintained automatically.
	QT_j	Average time each unit (including zero time transactions) spent in queue j	$2^{31} - 1$ Truncated to integer*		Value computed automatically.
	QX_j	Average time each unit (excluding zero-time transactions) spent in queue j	$2^{31} - 1$ Truncated to integer*		Value computed automatically.
SAVEVALUES	X or XF_j	The current contents of fullword savevalue j	$\pm 2^{31} - 1$	SAVEVALUE	
	XH	The current contents of halfword savevalue j	$\pm 2^{15} - 1$	SAVEVALUE	
	XB	The current contents of byte savevalue j	$\pm 2^7 - 1$	SAVEVALUE	
	XL	The current contents of floating point savevalue j	$\pm 2^{24} - 1$ Without loss of precision. Values may be larger but precision will be lost. Truncated to integer*	SAVEVALUE	Can be used only as (1) the B operand of an ASSIGN or SAVEVALUE block, (2) the D operand of an MSAVEVALUE block, (3) an element in a FVARIABLE statement, (4) an operand of a TEST block in which two floating-point SNAs are being compared, (5) the Y-value of an E- or an M-type function, or (6) the argument of a function.

STANDARD NUMERICAL ATTRIBUTES

ENTITY	SNA	DEFINITION	RANGE	MODIFIED BY	RESTRICTIONS/REMARKS
STORAGES	S_j	The current contents of storage j	$2^{31} - 1$	ENTER, LEAVE	Value maintained automatically.
	R_j	Number of available units or capacity remaining of storage j	$2^{31} - 1$	ENTER, LEAVE	Value maintained automatically.
	SR_j	Utilization in parts per thousand of storage j	0-1000		Value maintained automatically.
	SA_j	Average contents of storage j	$2^{31} - 1$ Truncated to integer*		Value computed automatically.
	SM_j	Maximum contents of storage j	$2^{31} - 1$		Value maintained automatically.
	SC_j	Total number of units to enter storage j	$2^{31} - 1$		Value maintained automatically.
	ST_j	Average utilization per unit of storage j	$2^{31} - 1$ Truncated to integer*		Value computed automatically.
SYSTEM ATTRIBUTES	RN_j ($1 \leq j \leq 8$)	A computed random number	An integer value from 0-999 unless used as the independent variable of a function. In that case the fraction is between 0 and .999999		
	C1	The current value of the relative simulator clock. Clock time relative to last reset or clear operation.	$2^{31} - 1$	RESET, CLEAR, JOB	Maintained automatically. Value reset to 0 at start of simulation run and by RESET, CLEAR, or JOB statement.
	AC1	The current value of the absolute simulator clock. Clock time since start of run or last clear operation.	$2^{31} - 1$	CLEAR, JOB	Maintained automatically. Reset to 0 at start of simulation run and by CLEAR or JOB statement.
	TG1	The number of terminations remaining in the model to satisfy START count.	$2^{31} - 1$	START TERMINATE	Maintained automatically.

STANDARD NUMERICAL ATTRIBUTES

ENTITY	SNA	DEFINITION	RANGE	MODIFIED BY	RESTRICTIONS/REMARKS
TABLES	TB_j	The mean value of table j.	$\pm 2^{31} - 1$ Truncated to integer*	TABULATE	Table frequencies are defined by TABLE statement. Value computed automatically.
	TC_j	Total number of entries in table j	$2^{31} - 1$		Value maintained automatically.
	TD_j	Standard deviation of table j	$2^{31} - 1$ Truncated to integer*		Value computed automatically.
TRANSACTIONS	PF_j	The current contents of fullword parameter j of the transaction currently being processed	$\pm 2^{31} - 1$	ASSIGN, INDEX, LOOP, MARK, SELECT, COUNT May possibly be modified by ALTER, SCAN, SPLIT, PREEMPT	
	PH_j	The current contents of halfword parameter j of the transaction currently being processed	$\pm 2^{15} - 1$	Same as PF_j	
	PB_j	The current contents of byte parameter j of the transaction currently being processed	$\pm 2^7 - 1$	Same as PF_j with the exception of MARK	PB_j may be referenced in a MARK block. SNAJPB cannot.
	PL_j	The current contents of a floating point parameter j of the transaction currently being processed	$\pm 2^{24} - 1$ With no loss of precision. Values may be larger but precision will be lost. Truncated to integer*	ASSIGN	Can be used only as (1) the B operand of either the ASSIGN or SAVEVALUE blocks, (2) the D operand of an MSAVEVALUE block, (3) an element in a FVARIABLE statement, (4) an operand of a TEST block in which two floating-point SNAs are being compared, (5) the Y-value of an E- or M-type function, or (6) the argument of a function.
	M1	The transit time of the transaction currently being processed	$2^{31} - 1$	MARK	M1 = current clock-mark time
	MP_jP_x	The intermediate transit time of the transaction currently being processed	$2^{31} - 1$	MARK ASSIGN (with C1 or AC1 as B operand)	MP_jP_x (where x is either F or H only) = current clock - $P_x j$ ($P_x j$ contains clock time placed there by a MARK block.)
	PR	Priority of transaction currently being processed	0-127	PRIORITY ALTER	Priority assigned when transaction created at GENERATE or SPLIT block.

STANDARD NUMERICAL ATTRIBUTES

ENTITY	SNA	DEFINITION	RANGE	MODIFIED BY	RESTRICTIONS/REMARKS
USER CHAINS	CH_j	The current count of the number of transactions on user chain j	$2^{15} - 1$	LINK UNLINK	Value maintained automatically.
	CA_j	The average number of transactions on user chain j	$2^{15} - 1$ Truncated to integer*		Value computed automatically.
	CM_j	The maximum number of transactions on user chain j	$2^{31} - 1$		Value maintained automatically.
	CC_j	The total number of transactions on user chain j	$2^{31} - 1$		Value maintained automatically.
	CT_j	The average time per transaction on user chain j	$2^{31} - 1$ Truncated to integer*		Value computed automatically.
VARIABLES and BOOLEAN VARIABLES	V_j	The computed value of variable j	$\pm 2^{31} - 1$ Arithmetic variable or 10^{-78} to 10^{75} if a floating point variable		Defined by VARIABLE statement.
	BV_j	The computed value of Boolean variable j	1 if statement true, 0 if false		Defined by BVARIABLE statement.

App. 5 / Standard Numerical Attributes

APPENDIX 6

GPSS SCANNING ALGORITHM

A6-1

GPSS Transaction Chains

All transactions must be on one, and only one, of the five transaction chains described below. In addition, some transactions that are on the current events chain may simultaneously be on one, and only one, of many auxiliary chains, called *delay chains*, which are described in the next section.

(a) *Future Events Chain.* All transactions that are due to move at some known time in the future, that is, ahead of the current clock time, are kept on the future events chain. This implies that all transactions on the future events chain are at an ADVANCE or GENERATE block (except that, when the rate mode of tabulation is being used, there will be a "dummy" transaction that is timing an interval for the tabulation; see Sec. 8-15).

The transactions are kept in chronological order. Those due to move at the same time are ordered by priority, which is assigned by the user. If they also have the same priority, they are kept in the order of their arrival on the chain.

(b) *Current Events Chain.* Transactions that should have moved, but cannot at the present time because of some blocking condition, are kept on the current events chain. They are kept in priority order, or in order of arrival for equal-priority transactions. (Transactions that have just become due for movement, but have not yet been tested, may also be present at some point in the scan.)

(c) *User Chains.* A program option, explained in Chap. 14, allows the user to construct a number of chains for his own use, principally for ordering transactions by some special queuing discipline. The transactions join a user chain when they enter a LINK block, at which time they are removed from the current events chain. They return to the current events chain when some other transaction removes them from the user chain by entering an UNLINK block.

(d) *Interrupt Chain.* Transactions that have seized a facility may lose control of the facility to another transaction that has entered a PREEMPT block. They are placed on the interrupt chain if they are due to have control of the facility returned to them. When the interrupting transaction enters a RETURN block, the interruption is removed and the transaction that was interrupted returns to the future events chain.

(e) *Match Chain.* Transactions arriving at a MATCH, GATHER, or ASSEMBLE block may have to wait in order to be synchronized with some other transaction. While waiting, they are placed on a match chain. They return to the current events chain when the matching condition is met.

A6-2

Delay Chains

When a transaction is on the current events chain, it may also be simultaneously on another type of chain, called a delay chain. The chain indicates the specific condition causing the transaction to be blocked. However, not all blocked transactions can be placed on a delay chain. The exceptions are described in Sec. A6-5.

Delay chains are associated with one of the three types of GPSS entities called facilities, storages, and logic switches. These entities can be in one of several states and a transaction can be blocked waiting for a particular entity to be in a particular state. GPSS builds a delay chain for transactions blocked by any condition on each facility, storage, or logic switch. When the program changes the status of any entity, it is able to detect whether the change has unblocked any transactions. The following list gives the condition for which transactions may be waiting while they are on a delay chain:

Facility in use　　　　　　Storage not empty
Facility not in use　　　　Storage full
Facility interrupted　　　　Storage not full
Facility not interrupted　　Storage available
Facility available　　　　　Storage not available
Facility not available　　　Logic switch set
Storage empty　　　　　　　Logic switch not set

A6-3
Simultaneous Events

There are occasions when a single entity can become involved in a string of concurrent events, all occurring at the same time. This can occur because some activity takes zero time, so that its beginning and ending occur at the same time, or the end of one activity can automatically imply the start of another activity for the same entity. Although these concurrent events are executed in a specific sequence they are logically simultaneous events.

Another cause of simultaneous events occurs when the movement of one transaction produces a change that unblocks some other transaction, or transactions. The movement of these unblocked transactions could, in turn, unblock other transactions and so on. The result is a cascading of events that are mutually simultaneous and also simultaneous with the concurrent events associated with the transaction responsible for the unblocking.

Maintaining the correct priority sequence of all these simultaneous events presents a difficulty. Blocked transactions, representing events that are waiting for a change of system status, are kept on the current events chain in order of their priority, and the chain is scanned from high to low priority. At some point in the scan, a transaction could move and, in doing so, cause a change that unblocks a higher-priority transaction. Because the unblocked transaction is of higher priority, it will have been passed by the scan. If the scan simply continues down the chain, some lower-priority transaction could take advantage of the change, either directly or indirectly through intermediate cascading events. Even if this does not happen, the higher-priority transaction that was passed in the scan will not become aware of the change until the next scan when the clock may have been advanced.

The difficulty is further complicated by new transactions that become current when the clock is updated, or transactions that are reactivated by being returned from the match or user chains. The priorities of these transactions need to be examined against the priorities of the blocked transactions.

To prevent violations of the priority rules, two actions are necessary. First, all new transactions arriving from the future events chain are merged, in priority order, with the blocked transactions on the current events chain before attempting to move them. Second, the scan should be restarted whenever a change of state occurs. The latter course of action would be very time-consuming. In GPSS almost all changes of state that unblock or reactivate a transaction, and therefore call for a rescan, can be detected. The program efficiency is greatly improved by rescanning only when these changes occur. There are, however, a few complex conditions where a change requiring a rescan is not detected. They are described and explained in Sec. A6-6.

A6-4
GPSS Scan of Events

A full description of the way GPSS scans the current events list and executes events will now be given.

When all the transactions that can be moved at a given time have been moved, there may be some left on the current events chain because they are blocked. There will be at least one transaction on the future events chain representing an event yet to come. If there is not, there will be an error stop. At the time of starting a run, the future events chain is initialized with one or more transactions.

After moving all transactions that can be moved at the current time, the program updates the clock to the block departure time of the first transaction on the future events chain. That transaction, and any others with the same block departure time, is transferred to the current events chain and merged in priority order with the transactions already on the chain. At this point, a flag signaling a change of status (explained shortly) will be turned off and the program will prepare to scan the current events chain.

All transactions on the current events chain are in one of two states, *active* or *inactive*. A flag in each transaction, called a *scan indicator*, is set off if the transaction is active. It is turned on, to make the transaction inactive, whenever the transaction is placed on one of the delay chains described in Sec. A6-2. New transactions arriving from the future events chain are initially set active. When the scan starts, therefore, there is at least one active transaction on the chain. The scan examines each transaction in priority order, looking for active transactions. When the program finds one, it transfers to some routine that will attempt to move the transaction. The routine is found interpretively. The transaction record holds the number of the block at which the transaction is located, and this can be used to find the type of block and supply the specific input parameters associated with the particular instance of the block type.

The program will attempt to execute all the concurrent events for the active transaction; that is to say, it will move the transaction through as many blocks as can be logically entered at the current clock time. In doing so, it may unblock or reactivate other transactions. It signals that fact by setting a flag called the *change status flag*. The setting of this flag will cause a rescan, without advancing the clock, to ensure that the unblocked or reactivated transactions are processed. Usually the rescan is not started until the current transaction has moved as far as it can.

Exceptions are made when continuation of the progress of the current transaction might violate priority rules. The program then immediately begins a rescan to be sure that no violations occur. If the transaction that caused the change can still be processed at the current clock time, that processing will be continued when the rescan eventually returns to the transaction.

A BUFFER block automatically forces an immediate rescan. An immediate rescan is also made when a transaction, entering either an ASSEMBLE or a GATHER block, completes a count of the number of transactions assembled by the block. Transactions are then reactivated by being brought from the match chain to the current events chain. They each become the last member of their own priority class. Because they might be in different priority classes, the program begins a rescan rather than continue processing the current transaction, which might be of a lower priority than one of the transactions being returned. (Although the MATCH block can also return a transaction from the match chain, a rescan is not immediately started. The occurrence of the match is regarded as a condition for the further advancement of the current transaction and the program continues to move the current transaction. A rescan is, however, made when the current transaction stops moving.)

The PRIORITY block changes the priority of a transaction entering the block. The program will not automatically execute an immediate rescan; but a BUFFER option allows the user to select that course of action.

In summary, once the scan begins moving a transaction, it will continue to move the transaction as far as is logically possible unless the transaction enters one of the following blocks, in which case it will immediately start a rescan:

(a) A BUFFER block
(b) A PRIORITY block with a BUFFER option
(c) An ASSEMBLE block that completes an assembly count
(d) A GATHER block that completes an assembly count

Entering the following blocks will cause the change status flag to be set, causing a rescan, but the rescan will occur only when the program has finished moving the current transaction as far as it can (the reason for the rescan is also given):

(a) A SEIZE, PREEMPT, RELEASE, RETURN, FUNAVAIL, or FAVAIL block because a facility has changed status
(b) An ENTER, LEAVE, SUNAVAIL, or SAVAIL block because a storage has changed its status
(c) A LOGIC block because a logic switch has changed its status

(d) A PRIORITY block, without a BUFFER option, because the transaction has changed its priority
(e) A MATCH block when it has found a matching condition and has returned a transaction to the current events chain
(f) An UNLINK block because the transaction has returned a transaction to the current events chain

The first three of these conditions for setting the change status flag involve a facility, storage, or logic switch. The program uses the delay chains associated with these entities to locate any transactions that have become unblocked because of the status change. Any such transactions are removed from the delay chains, and their scan indicators are set to active so that they will be processed in the rescan. Not all of them will necessarily be able to take advantage of the change, so they may be immediately returned to a delayed status by the rescan.

Eventually, the program will stop processing the current transaction and will return to the scan. At that time it checks the change status flag to see if the processing of the last transaction called for a rescan. If so, the program returns to the beginning of the scan, after turning off the change status flag. It will continue in this manner until either the current events chain is empty or the program is able to pass through the entire list without the need for a rescan. All events that can be processed at the current clock time are then complete (with the possible exceptions given in Sec. A6-6). The program returns to update the clock and start the scan again.

The program stops moving a transaction at the current clock time for one of the following reasons:

(a) The transaction moves into a nonzero time ADVANCE block, in which case it comes to represent a future event and will be moved to the future events chain. When it enters a zero time ADVANCE block, the program attempts to continue moving the transaction.
(b) The transaction leaves the system by being destroyed at a TERMINATE or ASSEMBLE block.
(c) The transaction is placed on a match chain by entering a MATCH, GATHER or ASSEMBLE block.
(d) The transaction becomes blocked. If the blocking is due to the status of a facility, storage, or logic switch, the transaction will be placed on a delay chain and have its scan indicator set to inactive.
(e) The transaction joins a user chain by entering a LINK block.

A6-5
Time-Consuming Blocking Conditions

The program can list in the delay chains only one blocking condition for each transaction. Sometimes there is more than one system change that can release a transaction. In that case, the program must leave the blocked transaction in an active state, and retry the transaction on each scan. If many transactions stay in this condition, the program will be slowed down by the need to retry their movement. These conditions should therefore be avoided as far as possible, or, at least, the time transactions spend in these conditions should be minimized. The following list gives the circumstances under which the conditions can arise.

(a) The TRANSFER block operating in a BOTH or ALL mode makes a choice between two or more alternative paths. If all choices are blocked, the opening of any one will release the transaction.

(b) The TEST block will hold a transaction as long as a relationship between two SNAs is not satisfied. The SNAs can depend upon many factors. There could be many changes of conditions that release the transaction.

(c) A GATE block operating in a match mode cannot detect when a transaction enters the conjugate MATCH block.

A6-6

Possible Violations of Simultaneity Rule

When the conditions described in the previous section exist, they tend to slow down the program. When the conditions are removed, they can also result in the program failing to detect a simultaneous event. In moving one transaction the program may unblock a higher-priority transaction by removing one of the conditions described in the previous section. It is unable, however, to set the change status flag to call for a rescan. Because the unblocked transaction is of higher priority, it will have been passed by the scan. Unless the transaction currently being scanned, or another transaction later in the scan, causes a rescan, the unblocked transaction will not become aware of the change until the next scan occurs.

At the very least, the transaction will not then move until some time later than it was entitled to move. It is even possible that some higher-priority transaction, which does not become due to move until the next scan occurs, can take advantage of the change ahead of the released transaction. The fact that the unblocked transaction may or may not move at the correct time, depending on whether or not there is a rescan, can also mean that two apparently identical runs give different results because of some slight rearrangement or because different random numbers reorder certain simultaneous events. For all these reasons the conditions described in the previous section should be avoided whenever possible and carefully monitored whenever they do occur.

APPENDIX

7

COMPARISON OF GPSS V AND GPSS/360

As the name implies there have been four preceding versions of GPSS produced by IBM. There have also been several versions produced for other manufacturers' equipment. The earlier IBM versions were the original GPSS (33), GPSS II (32), GPSS III (39), and GPSS/360 (35). The earliest two versions are now obsolete and were incompatible with GPSS V. GPSS III is obsolete but it was compatible with GPSS/360. GPSS V and GPSS/360 are compatible, with some exceptions to be noted below. GPSS V, however, has many extra features compared with GPSS/360.

The only difference in the block types occurs from the fact that GPSS V allows facilities and storages to be made unavailable and then returned to the available state. During a period of unavailability, statistics about the entity are not gathered. The main purpose is to simulate the effect of breakdowns in equipment. In GPSS/360 this had to be programmed by preempting a facility or artificially filling a storage, but the statistics were still gathered. There are four new block types in GPSS V for the purpose of switching facilities and storages between the available and the unavailable states (see Chap. 5).

When a GPSS/360 model runs under GPSS V, the results will be identical if the original model was run under GPSS/360 version 2. The earlier version of GPSS/360 had slightly different random number generators.

The following list gives the principal differences between the two versions that cause incompatibility. As can be seen, most are concerned with features that are not often used, and, when they are used, the coding relating to them is not extensive. The only exception is that the differences in the format options for parameters means that the two versions will be compatible only if both models use the default values for parameter formats (12 halfword).

(a) *Parameter Formats.* Whereas GPSS/360 allowed up to 100 parameters that were all either fullword or halfword, GPSS V has added byte-sized and floating-point parameters, and it allows any combination of the four formats up to a limit of 255 of each type. If no specification for the number of parameters was made in GPSS/360, a default value of 12 halfword parameters was assumed. Similiarly, omitting the specification of the parameters in GPSS V causes a default to 12 halfword parameters.

The possibility of more than one type of parameter coexisting in GPSS V makes it impossible to use the notation P*n, which in GPSS/360 indicated the use of the nth parameter in a block field. The full SNA Pxj, where x is the type and j is the number of a parameter, must be used in GPSS V. In addition, fields that specifically supply the number of a parameter (such as the A field of a MARK block) must, in GPSS V, indicate the type of parameter (see Sec. 10-1).

(b) *Savevalue and Matrix Formats.* Both savevalues and matrices of savevalues in GPSS V must specify one of the four parameter formats.

(c) *The PREEMPT Block.* In GPSS V the options available at a PREEMPT block are honored when the preempted transaction is on the future events chain or has just left an ADVANCE block (see Sec. 7-6). In GPSS/360 the options would be ignored under these circumstances.

(d) *HELP Routines.* The HELP routines in GPSS V can be written in FORTRAN and PL/I as well as in Basic Assembler Language. There have been some changes to the internal names of GPSS entities and routines [see the *Operator's Manual* (42 or 43)].

(e) *SNA Formats.* Some SNAs that in GPSS/360 were truncated are carried in floating-point in GPSS V (see Appendix 5).

(f) *The READ/SAVE Data Sets.* These data sets in GPSS V are separate, whereas in GPSS/360 they could be the same.

(g) *The Jobtape Format* has been changed (see Sec. 15-5).

(h) *Absolute Mode Input.* There is a difference in the format of the ABS mode input statement (see Sec. A2-8 of Appendix 2).

(i) *Program Size.* There has been a reduction in the number of entities allowed in the smallest standard allocation of entities, so that some models written for GPSS/360 may not load (see Table 16-1).

In addition to the inclusion of the availability feature and the expansion of parameter formats mentioned above, some of the other features of GPSS V that were not available in GPSS/360 are:

(a) Parts of a model can be stored on an external direct access device, such as a disk file (see Sec. 16-4).
(b) The GENERATE block may now use some SNAs that were not allowed in GPSS/360. They are RNn, C1, AC1, and Nj.
(c) The START control statement allows a computer time out limit to be set and provides for several operator actions if the limit is reached (see Sec. 3-13).

BIBLIOGRAPHY

General Bibliographies

1. IBM Corp., *Bibliography on Simulation* (Form 320-0924), White Plains, N.Y., 1966.

2. Malcolm, D. G., Bibliography on the use of simulation in management analysis, *Operations Res.*, Vol. 8, 1960, pp. 169–177.

3. Nance, R. E., and C. J. Overstreet, Jr., Random number generation: bibliography 29, *Computing Rev.*, Vol. 13, No. 10, 1972.

4. Naylor, T. H., Simulation and gaming: bibliography 19, *Computing Rev.* Vol. 10, No. 1, 1969. A listing of approximately 440 references on all aspects of simulation.

5. Shubik, Martin, Bibliography on simulation, gaming, artificial intelligence and allied topics, *J. Amer. Statist. Assoc.*, Vol. 55, 1960, pp. 736–751.

General Textbooks

6   Abraham, F. F., and W. A. Tiller (Eds.), *An Introduction to Computer Simulation in Applied Science*, Plenum Publishing Corporation, New York, 1972.

7   Chorafas, D. N., *Systems and Simulation*, Academic Press, Inc., New York, 1965.

8   Emshoff, J. R., and R. L. Sisson, *Design and Use of Computer Simulation Models*, Macmillan Publishing Co., Inc., New York, 1970.

9   Evans, G. W., G. F. Wallace, and G. L. Sutherland, *Simulation Using Digital Computers*, Prentice-Hall, Inc., Englewood Cliffs, N.J., 1967.

10 Fishman, G. S., *Concepts and Methods in Discrete Event Digital Simulation*, John Wiley & Sons, Inc., New York, 1973.

11 Gordon, Geoffrey, *System Simulation*, Prentice-Hall, Inc., Englewood Cliffs, N.J., 1969.

12 Hammersley, J. M., and D. C. Handscomb, *Monte Carlo Methods*, Methuen & Company Ltd., London, England, 1964.

13 Hollingdale, S. H. (Ed.), *Digital Simulation in Operations Research*, American Elsevier Publishing Company, Inc., New York, 1967.

14 Maisel, Herbert, and Guiliano Gnugnoli, *Simulation of Discrete Stochastic Systems*, Science Research Associates, Inc., Chicago, 1972.

15 Martin, F. F., *Computer Modeling and Simulation*, John Wiley & Sons, Inc., New York, 1968.

16 McLeod, John (Ed.), *Simulation: The Dynamic Modeling of Ideas and Systems with Computers*, McGraw-Hill Book Company, New York, 1968.

17 McMillan, Claude, Jr., and Richard Gonzales, *Systems Analysis: A Computer Approach to Decision Models* (Rev. Ed.), Richard D. Irwin, Inc., Homewood, Ill., 1968.

18 Miller, Irwin, and J. E. Freund, *Probability and Statistics for Engineers*, Prentice-Hall, Inc., Englewood Cliffs, N.J., 1965.

19 Mize, J. H., and J. G. Cox, *Essentials of Simulation*, Prentice-Hall, Inc., Englewood Cliffs, N.J., 1968.

20 Naylor, T. J., J. L. Balintfy, D. S. Burdick, and Kong Chu, *Computer Simulation Techniques*, John Wiley & Sons, Inc., New York, 1966.

21 Reitman, Julian, *Computer Simulation Applications: Discrete-Event Simulation for the Synthesis and Analysis of Complex Systems*, John Wiley & Sons, Inc., New York, 1971.

22 Rivett, Patrick, *Principles of Model Building—The Construction of Models for Decision Analysis*, John Wiley & Sons, Inc., New York, 1973.

23 Stephenson, R. E., *Computer Simulation for Engineers*, Harcourt Brace Jovanovich, Inc., New York, 1971.

24 Tocher, K. D., *The Art of Simulation*, D. Van Nostrand Company, New York, 1963.

Simulation Languages

25 Buxton, J. N., and J. G. Laski, Control and simulation language, *Computer J.*, Vol. 5, No. 3, 1962, pp. 194–200.

26 Buxton, J. N. (Ed.), *Simulation Programming Languages*, Proc. IFIPS Working Conf., Oslo, 1967, North-Holland Publishing Company, Amsterdam, Holland, 1968.

27 Clementson, A. T., Extended control and simulation language, *Computer J.*, Vol. 5, No. 3, 1966, pp. 215–220.

28 Connors, M. M., Claude Coray, C. J. Cuccaro, W. K. Green, D. W. Low, and H. M. Markowitz, The distribution system simulator, *Management Sci.* Vol. 18, No. 8, 1972, pp. 425–453.

29 Dahl, O. J., and K. Nygaard, SIMULA—an ALGOL-based simulation language, *Comm. ACM*, Vol. 9, No. 9, 1966, pp. 671–678.

30 Dewan, P. B., C. E. Donaghey, and J. B. Wyatt, OSSL—A Specialized Language for Simulating Computer Systems, *Proc. AFIPS 1972 Spring Joint Computer Conf.*, AFIPS Press, Montvale, N.J., 1972, pp. 799–814.

31 Dimsdale, B., and H. M. Markowitz, A description of the SIMSCRIPT language, *IBM Systems J.*, Vol. 3, No. 1, 1964, pp. 57–67.

32 Efron, R., and G. Gordon, A general purpose digital simulator and examples of its application: part 1—description of the simulator, *IBM Systems J.*, Vol. 3, No. 1, 1964, pp. 21-34.

33 Gordon, Geoffrey, *A General Purpose Systems Simulation Program*, Proc. EJCC, Washington, D.C., Macmillan Publishing Co., Inc., New York, 1961, pp. 87-104.

34 _____, A general purpose systems simulator, *IBM Systems J.*, Vol. 1, No. 1, 1962, pp. 18-32.

35 Gould, R. L., GPSS/360—an improved general purpose simulator, *IBM Systems J.*, Vol. 8, No. 1, 1969, pp. 16-27.

36 Granger, R. L., and G. S. Robinson, COMSL—A Communication System Simulation Language, *Proc. AFIPS 1970 Fall Joint Computer Conf.*, AFIPS Press, Montvale, N.J., 1970, pp. 407-414.

37 Greenberg, Stanley, *GPSS Primer*, John Wiley & Sons, Inc., New York, 1972.

38 Greenlaw, P. S., and M. P. Hottenstein, *PROSIM: A Production Management Simulation*, International Textbook Company—College Division, Scranton, Pa., 1969.

39 Herscovitch, H., and T. Schneider, GPSS III - an expanded general purpose simulator, *IBM Systems J.*, Vol. 4, No. 3, 1965, pp. 174-183.

40 Hills, P. R., *SIMON—A Computer Simulation Language in ALGOL*, in *Digital Simulation in Operations Research*, S. H. Hollingdale (Ed.), American Elsevier Publishing Co. Inc., New York, 1967, pp. 105-15.

41 IBM Corp., *General Purpose Simulation System—V, User's Manual* (Form SH 20-0851), White Plains, N.Y.

42 _____, *General Purpose Simulation System—V (OS), Operator's Manual* (Form SH 20-0867), White Plains, N.Y.

43 _____, *General Purpose Simulation System—V (DOS), Operator's Manual* (Form SH 20-0868), White Plains, N.Y.

44 _____, *SIMPL/I Program Reference Manual* (Form SH 19-5060), White Plains, N.Y.

45. Karr, H. W., Henry Kleine, and H. M. Markowitz, *SIMSCRIPT I.5*, California Analysis Center, Inc., Santa Monica, Calif., 1966.

46. Kiviat, P. J., R. Villanueva, and H. M. Markowitz, *The SIMSCRIPT II Programming Language*, Prentice-Hall, Inc., Englewood Cliffs, N.J., 1969.

47. ———, R. Villanueva, and H. M. Markowitz, *SIMSCRIPT II.5 Programming Language*, Consolidated Analysis Centers, Inc., Los Angeles, 1973.

48. Kleine, Henry, A survey of users' views of discrete simulation languages, *Simulation*, Vol. 14, No. 5, 1970, pp. 225-229.

49. Knuth, D. E., and J. L. McNeley, SOL: a symbolic language for general purpose system simulation, *IEEE Trans. Electron. Computers*, Vol. EC-13, No. 4, 1963.

50. MacDougall, M. H., and J. S. McAlpine, *Computer System Simulation with ASPOL*, Proc. SIGSIM/NBS Symposium Simulation Computer Syst., ACM, New York, 1973.

51. Markowitz, H. M., B. Hausner, and H. W. Karr, *SIMSCRIPT—A Simulation Language*, Prentice-Hall, Inc., Englewood Cliffs, N.J., 1963.

52. Palme, Jacob, A comparison between SIMULA and FORTRAN, *BIT*, Vol. 8, No. 3, 1968, pp. 203-209.

53. Parslow, R. D., *AS: An ALGOL Simulation Language*, in Simulation Programming Languages, North-Holland Publishing Company, Amsterdam, Holland, 1968, pp. 86-100.

54. Pritsker, A. A. B., and P. J. Kiviat, *Simulation with GASP II: A FORTRAN Based Simulation Language*, Prentice-Hall, Inc., Englewood Cliffs, N.J., 1969.

55. Pugh, Alexander, III, *DYNAMO II User's Manual*, The MIT Press, Cambridge, Mass., 1973.

56. Schriber, T. J., *Simulation Using GPSS*, John Wiley & Sons, Inc., New York, 1974.

57. Teichroew, Daniel, and J. F. Lubin, Computer simulation—discussion of the technique and comparison of languages, *Comm. ACM*, Vol. 9, No. 10, 1966, pp. 723-741.

58 ——, J. F. Lubin, and T. D. Truit, Discussion of computer simulation techniques and comparison of languages, *Simulation*, Vol. 9, 1967, pp. 181–190.

Applications

59 Amstutz, A. E., *Computer Simulation of Competitive Market Response*, The MIT Press, Cambridge, Mass., 1967.

60 Apter, M. J., *The Computer Simulation of Behavior*, Hutchinson Publishing Group Ltd., London, England, 1970.

61 Bartholomew, D. J., *Stochastic Models for Social Processes*, John Wiley & Sons, Inc., New York, 1967.

62 Bobrow, D. B., and J. L. Schwartz, *Computers and the Policy-Making Community*, Prentice-Hall, Inc., Englewood Cliffs, N.J., 1968.

63 Bonini, C. P., *Simulation of Information and Decision Systems in the Firm*, Markham Publishing Company, Chicago, 1967.

64 Burill, Claude, and Leon Quinto, *Computer Model of a Growth Company*, Gordon and Breach, Science Publishers, Inc., New York, 1972.

65 Carter, G., and E. Ignall, A simulation model of fire department operations, *IEEE-SSC Trans.*, Vol. 6, No. 4, 1970, pp. 282–92.

66 Conway, R. W., W. L. Maxwell, and L. W. Miller, *Theory of Scheduling*, Addison-Wesley Publishing Company, Inc., Reading, Mass., 1967.

67 Coplin, W. D., *Simulation in the Study of Politics*, Markham Publishing Company, Chicago, 1968.

68 Crecine, J. P., A computer simulation model of municipal budgeting, *Management Sci.*, Vol. 13, 1967, pp. 786–815.

69 Feller, R. B., and J. D. Thompson, The simulation of hospital systems, *Operations Res.*, Vol. 13, 1965, pp. 689–711.

70 Forrester, J. W., *Industrial Dynamics*, The MIT Press, Cambridge, Mass., 1961.

71 ——, *Urban Dynamics*. The MIT Press, Cambridge, Mass., 1969.

72 Fraser, Alex, and Donald Burnell, *Computer Models in Genetics*, McGraw-Hill Book Company, New York, 1970.

73 Fromm, Gary, and L. R. Klein, The Bookings-SSRC quarterly econometric model of the United States: model properties, *Amer. Econ. Rev.*, Vol. 55, 1965, pp. 348–361.

74 Glass, D. V. (Ed.), *Social Mobility in Britain*, Routledge & Kegan Paul Ltd., London, England, 1965.

75 Guetzkow, Harold (Ed.), *Simulation in the Social Sciences*, Prentice-Hall, Inc., Englewood Cliffs, N.J., 1962.

76 ———, A. F. Chadwick, R. A. Brody, R. C. Noel, and R. C. Snyder, *Simulation in International Relations: Developments for Research and Teaching*, Prentice-Hall, Inc., Englewood Cliffs, N.J., 1963.

77 ———, H. P. Kotler, and R. L. Schultz (Eds.), *Simulation in Social and Administrative Science*, Prentice-Hall, Inc., Englewood Cliffs, N.J., 1972.

78 Hamilton, H. R., S. E. Goldstone, J. W. Milliman, A. L. Pugh III, E. R. Roberts, and A. Zellner, *Systems Simulation for Regional Analysis*, The MIT Press, Cambridge, Mass., 1969.

79 Hannsmann, F. (Ed.), *Operations Research in the Design of Electronic Data Processing Systems*, Crane, Russak & Company, New York, 1973.

80 Harbaugh, J. W., and Graeme Bonham-Carter, *Computer Simulation in Geology*, John Wiley & Sons, Inc., New York, 1970.

81 Knight, D. E., H. W. Curtis, and L. J. Fogel (Eds.), *Cybernetics, Simulation, and Conflict Resolution*, Third Ann. Symp. Amer. Soc. Cybernetics, Spartan Books, New York, 1971.

82 Kochenburger, R. J., *Computer Simulation of Dynamic Systems*, Prentice-Hall, Inc., Englewood Cliffs, N.J., 1972.

83 Lowry, I. S., Seven models of urban development: a structural comparison, *J. Amer. Inst. Planners*, Vol. 31, No. 2, 1965.

84 MacDougall, M. H., Computer system simulation: an introduction, *Computing Surv.*, Vol. 2, No. 3, 1970, pp. 191–209.

85 Meier, R. C., W. T. Newell, and H. L. Pazer, *Simulation in Business and Economics*, Prentice-Hall, Inc., Englewood Cliffs, N.J., 1969.

86 Naylor, T. H., *Computer Simulation Experiments with Models of Economic Systems*, John Wiley & Sons, Inc., New York, 1971.

87 Orcutt, G. H., M. Greenberger, J. Korbel, and A. M. Rivlin, *Microanalysis of Socioeconomic Systems—A Simulation Study*, Harper & Row Publishers, New York, 1961.

88 Patten, B. C. (Ed.), *Systems Analysis and Simulation in Ecology*, Academic Press, Inc., New York, 1971.

89 Pool, I. S., R. Abelson, and S. Popkin, *Candidates, Issues, and Strategies: A Computer Simulation of the 1960 Presidential Campaign*, The MIT Press, Cambridge, Mass., 1965.

90 Prais, S. J., Measuring social mobility, *J. R. Statis. Soc.*, A118, 1955, pp. 56-66.

91 Schmidt, J. W., and R. E. Taylor, *Simulation and Analysis of Industrial Systems*, Richard D. Irwin, Inc., Homewood, Ill., 1970.

92 Seaman, P. H., and R. C. Soucy, Simulating operating systems, *IBM Systems J.*, Vol. 8, No. 4, 1969, pp. 264-279.

93 Taylor, J. G., and J. A. Navarro, Simulation of a court system for the processing of criminal cases, *Simulation*, Vol. 10, No. 5, 1968, pp. 235-240.

94 Tomkins, S. S. (Ed.), *Computer Simulation of Personality*, John Wiley & Sons, Inc., New York, 1963.

95 Weber, J. H., A simulation study of routing and control in communication networks, *Bell System Tech. J.*, Vol. 43, No. 6, 1964, pp. 2639-2676.

Statistical Considerations

96 Felder, H., The GPSS/360 random number generator, *Digest of Second Conf. Appl. Simulation*, Assoc. for Computing Machinery, New York, 1968.

97 Fishman, G. S., Problems in the statistical analysis of simulation experiments: the comparison of means and lengths of sample records, *Comm. ACM*, Vol. 10, No. 2, 1967, pp. 94-99.

98 ———, and P. J. Kiviat, The analysis of simulation-generated time series, *Management Sci.*, Vol. 13, No. 7, 1967, pp. 525-551.

99 ———, and P. J. Kiviat, The statistics of discrete-event simulation, *Simulation*, Vol. 10, No. 4, 1968, pp. 185-195.

100 ———, The allocation of computer time in comparing simulation experiments, *Operations Res.*, Vol. 16, No. 2, 1968, pp. 185-95.

101 ———, Estimating sample size in computer simulation experiments, *Management Sci.*, Vol. 18, No. 1, 1971, pp. 21-38.

102 Hunter, J. S., and T. H. Naylor, Experimental design for computer simulation experiments, *Management Sci.*, Vol. 6, No. 7, 1970, pp. 422-35.

103 Ignall, E. J., On experimental design for computer simulation experiments, *Management Sci.*, Vol. 18, No. 7, 1972, pp. 384-89.

104 Mihram, G. A., *Simulation: Statistical Foundations and Methodology*, Academic Press, Inc., New York, 1972.

105 Naylor, T. H. (Ed.), *The Design of Computer Simulation Experiments*, Duke University Press, Durham, N.C., 1969.

106 ———, Kenneth Wertz, and T. H. Wonnacott, Spectral analysis of data generated by simulation experiments with economic models, *Econometrica*, Vol. 36, 1969, pp. 333-53.

107 ———, Kenneth Wertz, and T. H. Wonnacott, Methods for analyzing data from computer simulation experiments, *Comm. ACM*, Vol. 10, No. 11, 1967, pp. 703-10.

INDEX

Absolute clock time, 41
ABS statement, 139, 347
  use with READ, 322
Action time, 31, 61, 63, 66, 187
Activities, 2
Addressing:
  indirect, 218
  relative, 338
  symbolic, 338
ADD statement, 323
ADVANCE block, 31, 66
Air conditioner sales model, 10
Allocation of storage space, 326
  standard size table, 327
ALTER block, 299
Analytic methods, 8
Arithmetic variables, 236
Arrival rate, 107
  measurement of, 163
  peak load, 227
ASSEMBLE block, 274
  changing scan order, 124
  restriction on redefinition, 348
Assembly format, 40
Assembly program, 37, 337
Assembly sets, 53, 267, 273, 293
  on jobtapes, 318
ASSIGN block, 200
Attributes, 2 (*see also* Standard numerical attributes)
Autocorrelation, 17
AUXILIARY statement, 44, 329
  use with macros, 343
  use with READ, 322

Auxiliary storage feature, 329
Availability feature, 98
Balking, 292
Block counts, 44, 74
Block definition statements, 35, 349
Block departure time, 26
Block diagrams, 29, 30
Block symbols, 349
Block types, 29, 349
Boolean variables, 256
  in UNLINK block, 285, 289
BUFFER block, 121
  example of, 122, 288
BUFFER option, 116
Chains, 25
  current events, 26, 368
  delay, 369
  future events, 26, 368
  GPSS, 368
  interrupt, 369
  match, 369
  transaction, 26, 368
  user, 282, 369
CHANGE block, 314
Change status flag, 371
CLEAR statement, 47
  effect on jobtapes, 318, 319
  relation to RMULT, 336
Clock time, 13, 20, 31
  absolute, 41
  relative, 41
Comments statement, 36, 57
Communication system example, 203

Concurrent events, 23, 34
Conditional operators, 251
Conjugate blocks, 270
Continuous numerical valued functions, 183
Continuous uniform distribution, 62, 334
Control program example, 272
Control statements, 358
COUNT block, 258
CREATE statement, 323
Cross-references, 40
Current events chain, 368
Data packing, 237
Delay chains, 369
Delay flag, 53, 254
DELETE statement, 323
DEPART block, 147
Differences between GPSS V and GPSS/360, 375
Discrete attribute valued functions, 229
Discrete numerical valued functions, 183
Disk unit simulation, 141
Distribution tables, 152
EJECT statement, 57
ENDABS statement, 139
  use with READ, 322, 347
ENDGRAPH statement, 60
ENDMACRO statement, 343
END statement, 41, 50, 51
  effect on jobtapes, 318, 319
  effect on save data sets, 321
ENDUPDATE statement, 323

ENTER block, 89
Entity, 2
  permanent, 31
  temporary, 30
Entity function, 204, 340
EQU statement, 204, 340
Errors, 51
  assembly, 51
  execution, 51
  warning messages, 51, 55
EXAMINE block, 297
EXECUTE block, 315
Exponential distribution, 176
  table for, 177
  test for, 177
Facilities, 31, 83
  availability of, 98
  comparison with storages, 97
  effect of RESET statement, 47
  output statistics, 103
Factory model 1, 86
Factory model 2, 89
Factory model 3, 91
Factory model 4, 93
FAVAIL block, 102
Flags:
  delay, 53
  interrupt on match chain, 140
  trace, 53
Floating-point numbers, 187
Floating-point variables, 240
FORMAT statement, 58
Free format coding, 338
  example of, 339
FUNAVAIL block, 99, 102
Function follower statement, 185
FUNCTION statement, 185
  continuous numeric, 183
  definition of, 182
  discrete attribute, 229
  discrete numeric, 183
  entity, 204, 340
  error conditions, 185, 229
  evaluation of, 186
  list attribute, 229
  list numeric, 183, 186
  use at GENERATE block, 186
  use to give uniformly distributed numbers, 187
Furniture factory example, 274
Future events chain, 26, 368
Gasoline filling station example, 259
GATE block, 246
  in a match mode, 278
  use for single or multiple releases, 252
GATHER block, 272
  changing scan order, 124
  restriction on redefinition, 348
GENERATE block, 30, 31, 63
  effect of blocking on mark time, 151
  effect of CLEAR statement, 49
  EXECUTE block exception, 315
  jobtape restriction, 318
  redefinition of, 348
Grade of service, 160
Graphic output, 56
GRAPH statement, 59
Groups, 294

HELP block, 324
  use with LOAD feature, 332
House sales model, 10
ICT statement, 347
INCLUDE statement, 57
INDEX block, 209
Indirect addressing, 218
Industrial dynamics, 6
INITIAL statement, 199, 245
Interarrival time, 18, 176
Interrupt chain, 369
JOB statement, 50, 51
  effect on jobtapes, 318, 319
  effect on save data sets, 321
Jobtapes, 318
JOBTAPE statement, 318
  use with READ, 322
JOIN block, 295
LEAVE block, 89
LINK block:
  with field C option, 290
  without field C option, 290
List attribute valued functions, 229
List numeric valued functions, 183, 185
List processing, 24
LIST statement, 348
Load-dependent service time, 228
Load feature, 331
  use with READ, 322
LOAD statement, 331
  use with macros, 343
Locations, 35, 38, 40, 51
Logical operators, 247
LOGIC block, 246
Logic switches, 32, 245
  effect of CLEAR statement, 49
  effect of RESET statement, 47
LOOP block, 209
Machine shop example, 13, 18, 26, 32, 37, 43, 48, 56
  in free format, 339
Macros, 343
MACRO statement, 343
Manpower allocation example, 300
MARK block, 150
Mark time, 53, 64
  effect of blocking at GENERATE block, 151
  effect of SPLIT block, 270
Mark time word, 150
MATCH block, 270
  changing scan order, 124
  restriction on redefinition, 348
Match chain, 271, 369
  preemption when on, 271
Matrix savevalues, 198
  effect of CLEAR statement, 49
  effect of RESET statement, 47
  range of values, 196
MATRIX statement, 199
Models, 4
  continuous, 4, 6
  discrete, 4
Modifier, 62, 63
MSAVEVALUE block, 202
Multiple definition of blocks, 347
Normal distribution, 178
  table for, 181
  test for, 179

NOXREF statement, 348
Occupancy of storages, 104
ORG statement, 347
ORIGIN statement, 59
Output editor, 56, 332
OUTPUT statement, 56
Parameters, 30, 196
  formats, 64
  listing of, 55
  as operands, 203
  range of values, 196
  SPLIT block effect, 270
Peak loads, 227
Permanent entities, 31, 83
PREEMPT block, 129
  interrupt mode, 130
  priority mode, 132
Preempt count, 55, 131
PRINT block, 312
  use with LOAD feature, 331
Priority, 64, 112, 118
  mode of PREEMPT block, 132
  SPLIT block effect, 270
  use for scan control, 124
PRIORITY block, 116
QTABLE statement, 154
QUEUE block, 147
Queuing discipline, 290
Queues, 147
  effect of RESET statement, 47
  limiting waiting time, 292
  statistics on, 148
Queuing discipline, 290
Random number generation, 333
  effect of CLEAR statement, 47
  effect of JOB statement, 50
  effect of RESET statement, 47
  in GPSS, 334
Random variables, 16, 20
  continuous, nonuniform, 171
  discrete, 171
  uniform, 187, 334
READ statement, 321
REALLOCATE statement, 44, 328
  use with macros, 343
  use with READ, 322
Reallocation of entities, 328
Redefinition of entities, 347
Relative addressing, 338
Relative clock time, 41
RELEASE block, 85
Remarks, 36
REMOVE block, 295
REPLACE statement, 323
REPORT statement, 56
Rescanning, 372
RESET statement, 46
  use in contiguous runs, 105
Response time, 160
RETURN block, 130
REWIND statement, 319
RMULT statement, 335
Run control, 66
Run length feature, 44
SAVAIL block, 103
SAVE statement, 320
  option with SIMULATE, 321
SAVEVALUE block, 201

Savevalues, 32, 198
  effect of CLEAR statement, 49
  effect of RESET statement, 47
  range of values, 196
Scan, GPSS, 371
SCAN block, 298
Scan indicator, 371
Scanning algorithm, 26
  GPSS, 368
Scheduling rule simulation, 285
SEIZE block, 85
SELECT block, 258
Selection factor, 67
Selection modes of TRANSFER block, 67
Service rate, 107
  load-dependent, 228
Shipping example, 248, 255
Shopping example, 188
SIMULATE statement, 38, 41, 50, 51
  SAVE option, 321
Simulation, 1, 13
  algorithm, 22, 26
  comparison with analytic method, 8
  continuous, 10
  digital, system, 7, 14, 18
  execution of, 22
  study, progress of, 14
  system, 7
  technique of, 7, 9, 13, 14
  validation of, 16, 74
  verifying, 17
Simulation languages, 27
  GPSS, 1, 27
Simultaneous events, 113, 370
  possible violations, 374
SNA (*see* Standard numerical attributes)
Snaps, 45, 56
  use with LOAD feature, 331
SPACE statement, 57
SPLIT block, 269
  changing scan order, 125
Spread, 62
Standard deviation, 152, 181
  of normal distribution, 181
Standard numerical attributes, 32, 77, 350
  blocks, 78
  chains, 307
  facilities, 106
  groups, 307
  savevalues, 210
  statistics, 166

  storages, 106
  symbolic references, 342
  system, 78
  transactions, 210
STARTMACRO statement, 343
START statement, 45, 46
Statement format, 35
  blocks, 35
  fixed, 35
  free form, 35, 36, 339
Statement numbers, 38, 40, 51
STATEMENT statement, 60
Statistical outputs, 24
Storages, 31, 87
  availability of, 98
  comparison with facilities, 97
  effect of RESET statement, 47
  output statistics, 103
STORAGE statement, 88
  redefinition restriction, 348
Suffix notation, 197
SUNAVAIL block, 103
Symbolic addressing, 338
Symbolic entities, 340
  exceptions, 37
Symbols, 37, 338
  for SNAs, 342
SYN statement, 340
System analysis, 9
System design, 9
System image, 19, 20
System postulation, 9
Systems, 2
  examples of, 3
Tables, 151
  effect of RESET statement, 47
  weighted tables, 153
TABLE statement, 153
TABULATE block, 151
  difference mode, 162
  interarrival mode, 162
  rate mode, 55, 163
  weighted mode, 152
Temporary entities, 30, 84
TERMINATE block, 30, 66
Termination counter, 45, 66
TEST block, 249
  possible violation of simultaneity rules, 374
  time-consuming conditions, 374
TEXT statement, 57
Time limit on waiting, 260, 292

TITLE statement, 57
TRACE block, 311
  use with LOAD feature, 331
Trace flag, 53
Traffic system example, 69
Transactions, 26, 30
  displacement by preemption, 133
  displacement when a function is unavailable, 101
  format, 53
  format on jobtape, 317
  interrupted, 130
  number, 53, 268, 311
  preempted when not at ADVANCE block, 140
  preempted when on match chain, 140
  saving of, 316
TRANSFER block, 67
  ALL mode, 55, 96
  BOTH mode, 55
  conditional mode, 91
  fractional mode, 68
  function mode, 191
  parameter mode, 207
  PICK mode, 96, 336
  simultaneous mode, 254
  subroutine mode, 208
Transit time, 150
Truncation, 63, 187
Unavailable feature, 98
Uniform distribution, 62, 334
UNLINK block, 284
  changing scan order, 124
UNLIST statement, 348
UNTRACE block, 311
Update feature, 323
UPDATE statement, 44, 323
  use with macros, 343
User chains, 282, 369
  effects of RESET statement, 47
Utilization, 48, 103
  as a design factor, 106
Variables (*see* Variable statements)
Variable statements, 236
Virtual environment, 328
Warning messages, 51, 55
Weighted tabulation, 153
WRITE block, 316
X statement, 59
Y statement, 59

SOUTHEASTERN MASSACHUSETTS UNIVERSITY
T57.62.G67
The application of GPSS V to discrete sy

3 2922 00108 481 0